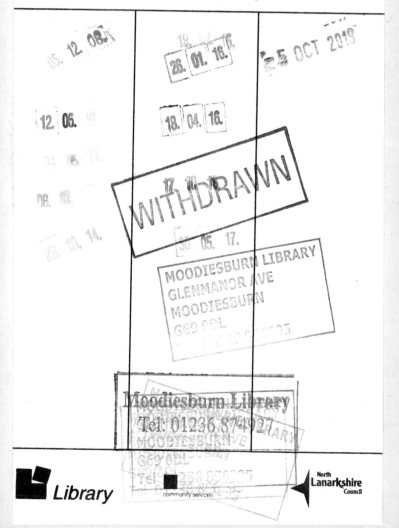

Also by Tony Geraghty:

Non-Fiction

Brixmis: The Untold Exploits of Britain's Most Daring Cold War
Spy Mission
March or Die: France and the Foreign Legion
The Bullet Catchers: Bodyguards and the World of Close Protections
The Irish War: The Military History of a Domestic Conflict
This Is the SAS: A Pictorial History of the Special Air Service Regiment
Who Dares Wins: The Special Air Service – 1950 to the Gulf War

Fiction

Freefall Factor
Passage to Paradise: The Voyage of U1081 and Other Stories

GUNS FOR HIRE

THE INSIDE STORY OF FREELANCE SOLDIERING

TONY GERAGHTY

PIATKUS

First published in Great Britain in 2007 by Portrait
This paperback edition published in 2008 by Piatkus Books

A CIP catalogue record for this book
is available from the British Library

ISBN 978-0-7499-2873-5

Edited by Andrew John
Text design by Paul Saunders

Typeset by Palimpsest Book Production Limited, Grangemouth, Stirlingshire
Printed and bound in the UK by CPI Mackays, Chatham ME5 8TD

Piatkus Books
An imprint of
Little, Brown Book Group
100 Victoria Embankment
London EC4Y ODY

An Hachette Livre UK Company
www.hachettelivre.co.uk

www.piatkus.co.uk

This book is dedicated to all those who practise honourably the much misunderstood profession of arms and those of whatever profession who choose to live one day as a lion, rather than spend a lifetime as a lamb. An increasingly conformist, obedient world needs them.

Acknowledgements

The author is indebted to the expert team at Piatkus which helped guide him through more than one minefield. He is grateful to those other writers – scholars and soldiers alike – whose knowledge and experience shaped his thoughts about what amounts to a revolution in military affairs. The final direction that will take is still guesswork. Personal friends such as the late Dare Newell ('Mr SAS') and others still alive, who must remain anonymous, have broken bread with me and have sometimes defied bureaucracy to give me uniquely valuable advice. They know who they are. Any errors are my own.

CONTENTS

INTRODUCTION

I t was once described as the second oldest profession. Now, thanks to the chaos of Iraq, Afghanistan and the global war on terror, it has acquired military chic. The freelance soldier, whether fighting for money or reputation, or for an adopted cause, has always been a fascinating but little-understood phenomenon – never more so than now. For those who would emulate his adventurous lifestyle, the 'mercenary' is heroic; for those who do not know bloodlust, or the euphoria of surviving the battle, he is horrific. One thing is certain: the freelance soldier, at his most committed, enjoys warfare as a terrier delights in ratting. It is what he does, existentially.

This book explores the phenomenon historically, politically and militarily, since all these forces interact ever faster in a shrinking world of instant communications and firepower often unregulated by law. I draw on extensive contacts in the field to portray the mercenary life, but in a context that demonstrates how it has evolved since 1945 in ways that directly reflect geopolitical, economic and cultural changes worldwide. It is not just soldiering that has changed: the apparent realities of the UN as the world's policeman and even the viability of the nation-state are now in question. Since 9 September 2001 – the event now known universally as 9/11 – the world has been taken over by a global war on terror, in which there are many armed players who wear no uniform.

Major themes linking campaigns apparently separated by time and distance are the privatisation of the means of making war, including arms manufacture; the loss of Britain's military independence; the pursuit of ever-scarcer natural resources, notably oil, and the freelance soldier's useful status as a deniable warrior.

Most British security companies, including those that provide armed security services outside the UK, reject the very word *mercenary*. To them, even to whisper the M-word is character assassination. The semantics matter. Dominick Donald, a former *Times* leader writer working as a senior analyst for the former Scots Guard Tim Spicer's Aegis organisation, defines a mercenary as 'an individual selling combat services to the highest bidder'.[1] Others distinguish between the mercenary warrior who overturns a government and the legitimate contractor who defends it. There are, however, freelance soldiers who risk their lives for a cause – often a lost cause – rather than money. They, too, are often categorised as mercenaries. The same armed force might contain both sorts of animal.

The key difference between what they represent and what mercenaries do, security companies argue, is that, although their freelance soldiers sometimes carry arms and might use lethal force, they do so only on behalf of legitimate entities (including governments, reconstruction workers, other private companies, war journalists and aid workers) in a defensive, protective role. Hundreds of these protectors died in Iraq alone between 2003 and 2006. Many more returned home with shattered bodies and disabled minds. Much of their work, in disciplines as various as mine-clearance, ransom negotiation, hostage rescue, emergency evacuation and threat analysis, is pro-life and does not require them to carry weapons. The firms also claim that they and their operators on the ground are accountable, though not necessarily legally so in all circumstances.

They prefer to be known as private security companies, or PSCs for short. Companies that do provide more direct military assistance, including military training, are described as 'private military companies', or PMCs. The British Foreign and Commonwealth Office lumps both groups together as 'PM/SCs'.

This book traces three separate traditions within the freelance military world. They have evolved from a common root but, as with the separation of Neanderthal from *Homo sapiens* and other primates, they are no longer the same creature. The three types are the *traditional mercenary*, familiar since the wild days of postcolonial Congo in the 1960s and subsequently; the *modern private security operator*; and the *plausibly deniable warrior*, who carries out covert missions for legitimate governments or their intelligence agencies. Often, the former mercenary, adapting to changing times, is to be found in one of the other two categories.

This history attempts to illustrate each of the three by reference to operations that proved to be historically significant. It is not a catalogue of every adventure. Many, such as Bob Denard's repeated occupations of the Comoros Islands or Mike Hoare's military farce in the Seychelles in 1981, made exciting reading but little political sense.

One of the changes wrought in the world by the attack on New York's Twin Towers is that the freelance military culture, functioning beyond the customary laws of war, has been adopted by the United States and Britain. Washington stridently opposes efforts by the International Criminal Court to contain the excesses of conflicts in which non-combatants are often the first to die. As Prime Minister Tony Blair put it after the 7/7 London bomb attacks during the summer of 2005, 'The rules of the game have changed' – even if constitutional lawyers disagreed.

For some that change was already obvious. Thousands of Iraqi civilians, many of them women and children, were killed during the Allied offensive of 2003 and many more after that. Another aspect of the change has been the official endorsement of freelance soldiers, such as the three American convoy escorts whose murder in April 2004 triggered another massive slaughter of Iraqis at Fallujah.

Who are these freelance soldiers? Most often originating in the ranks of, say, the French Foreign Legion, the Special Air Service and Parachute regiments, Royal Marine Commandos or the Gurkhas, they have traditionally functioned in a particularly chaotic culture outside the norms of human law and human behaviour. Washington's adoption of a policy of preemptive warfare has created just such a culture, a value-free world in which a conflict fought without rules and without regard to national sovereignty has become the norm. When such a world is created by democratic governments of the West, it is no coincidence that a new breed of freelance soldier has come into his own, maintaining traditional qualities of ruthlessness and deniability but employing a thoroughly modern modus operandi. Thanks to the innovations of such people as Alastair Morrison (a decorated SAS hero) and Tim Spicer (formerly a lieutenant colonel with the Scots Guards), the freelance soldier has also become part of a well-ordered corporate structure.

An estimated 30,000 freelances operated in Iraq soon after the 2003 invasion, some 4,000 more than the number of British ground troops deployed at the height of the formal war. After the US, the freelance sector was numerically the second power in the Coalition. 'Without them,' the UK's *Guardian* newspaper points out, 'the US and Britain would be under pressure to deploy more soldiers to Iraq.'[2] An estimated 14,000 were foreigners. So many Foreign Legion veterans joined private military companies in Occupied Iraq, that after the invasion, 40 or more '*anciens*' were able to form up in Baghdad for the annual Camerone commemoration (of the 1863 battle between the French Foreign Legion and the Mexican Army) and its attendant ritual parade.

The rest were locally hired Iraqis. The freelances were hired with government funds by more than eighty companies. The Pentagon spent at least £150 million on private security contracts during the first year of occupation, in the greatest bonanza of its kind since Sir John Hawkswood's White Company massacred for the pope in the fourteenth century, or the East India Company ran a private army of 257,000 men three centuries later.

It was also a bonanza, of a different sort, for a floating army of jihadist warriors, many of them battle-hardened veterans of Afghanistan and elsewhere. Approximately 3,000 non-Iraqi Muslim freelance fighters, including about 150 British volunteers, joined the insurrection in Iraq. Many signed up to Al-Qaeda's own foreign legion.

In June 2005 the UK Foreign and Commonwealth Office confirmed that it had contracts worth 'over £250,000' with Control Risks Group, guarding British embassy staff in Iraq (two contracts), and Amorgroup Services Ltd (two contracts plus a third to train Iraqi police). 'Our officials,' said the ministry, 'had also met the following security companies: Aegis (six meetings); Kroll; Hart; Global, Erinys Security, Group 4, Olive, Janusian, Blue Sky and Hart in respect of various tenders in recent years.'[3] On the other side of Whitehall, meanwhile, the Ministry of Defence was becoming distressed by the loss of regular soldiers to the private sector.

Yet another, largely American, category comprises individuals hired by the CIA's paramilitary wing, the Special Activities Division. The first American to die in the renewed Afghanistan combat, Johnny 'Mike' Spann, was one of these. He was killed on 25 November 2001 while interrogating an Al-Qaeda suspect as the prison erupted around him. Two others, Christopher Glenn Mueller and Bill Carlson, were killed in an ambush on 25 October 2003 while tracking insurgents, probably during a hunt for Osama bin Laden.

There are a number of reasons why the freelance soldier and his brethren are back in business with official blessing. The end of the Cold War in 1991 and the collapse of the Soviet Union left a power vacuum in those parts of the world – notably Africa – where client states and other armed bands had fought one another as surrogates of East or West. The continent was by then awash with infantry weapons, beyond the approximate control of a superpower to limit atrocities. From Afghanistan to Somalia, from Algeria to the Congo, the warlords seized control. Like other criminal syndicates, many became successful traders, dealing in such commodities as opium, heroin, cocaine, diamonds, coltan (a valuable metallic ore) and slaves. Anyone rash enough to challenge them – people such as the Congolese human-rights activist Pascal Kabungulu Kibembi – was courting assassination. Kibembi was murdered, probably by members of the country's armed forces, in August 2005.[4, 5]

Simultaneously, the major powers were cutting their standing regular armies drastically. Their combined military manpower dropped from 6,873,000 in 1990 to 3,283,000 in 1997 and the downward trend continues. The number of soldiers on UN peacekeeping duties also dropped from a peak of 76,000 in 1994 to around 15,000 by 1998. Marching in step with the trend, the US bankrolled almost 4,000 contracts with PMCs. As a result, hundreds of thousands of trained soldiers came onto a jobs market that was glad of their services.

Meanwhile, in an oil-thirsty world, such territories as Angola and Equatorial Guinea became natural targets for a form of piracy, led by African generals turned entrepreneurs (and a few wealthy Europeans). Sierra Leone, rich in diamonds, was racked by civil war. Long John Silver came into his own until, in 1993, Angola and Sierra Leone were rescued by a mercenary team known as Executive Outcomes (South Africa) and the PSC Sandline (Britain). They were welcomed as saviours by the survivors of the machete and by Peter Penfold, the UK High Commissioner in Sierra Leone, only to be repudiated by the British government when it pretended that the export of weapons to the duly elected government of Sierra Leone was against UN rules.

The British experience was conditioned by 30 years of terrorism and guerrilla warfare arising from the Irish Troubles. What had been, before 1969, a largely orthodox regular British army defending the notional Cold War front line from fixed positions in Germany mutated into a counter-insurgency force that often operated outside civilian law. Military undercover agents proliferated. A new form of covert Special Forces culture was created that came close, at times, to the mercenary soldier's approach to conflict. Its tactics included targeted assassinations.

By 2005, the Metropolitan Police were prepared to shoot on sight people they believed might be suicide bombers, even if they knew there was always a possibility that a suspect might be unarmed and innocent, as has happened on two occasions. Undercover soldiers took part in one of those operations, as trackers.

There was another specially British contribution to this change in military culture. This was the evolution of Special Forces to run guerrilla and terrorist campaigns against Nazi Germany and Japan from behind enemy lines during World War Two. Such soldiering encouraged a freedom to dare, and to think, in a way that was foreign to the ordered structure of traditional regular forces. It was represented by such exotic and varied organisations as the Chindits, Commandos, Special Operations Executive, Popski's Private Army, Force 136, the Special Air Service (SAS) and the Special Boat Service (SBS).

Some of them stayed in business after 1945. SAS veterans in particular exploited freelance soldiering from the 1960s onwards. One firm indiscriminately offered courses in silent killing, using SAS techniques. David Stirling's WatchGuard and Jim Johnson's KMS (now David Walker's Saladin) provided bodyguards for British diplomats and foreign VIPs and much else. It is a thriving trade, which earns political and diplomatic currency as well as money, though not all contracts are equally virtuous. In December 1998 the SAS veteran Ken Connor revealed:

> Saddam Hussein's bodyguards were trained by former SAS men ... Between 1988 and 1990, German, American and British military training teams, composed of former SAS men, visited Iraq. One, made up from ex-SAS NCOs, trained his bodyguards. The knowledge they passed on to the Iraqis would make an assassination attempt difficult, but not impossible.[6]

The story of KMS deserves a separate history. Founded by Lieutenant Colonel Jim Johnson, an SAS commander turned Lloyd's broker, it became the deniable hub of clandestine operations on behalf of the Secret Intelligence Service (MI6) in Yemen (where around eighty British and French mercenaries, assisted by the Israeli secret service Mossad, tied up an Egyptian army of 70,000 between 1962 and 1967) and elsewhere.

From time to time the British government found it expedient to release SAS soldiers from regular service to serve as deniable guerrillas in a war aimed at regime change. (It is no coincidence that one deniable mercenary group was called 'Expedient Force'.) Some worked secretly, and deniably, against the Russians in Afghanistan in 1982, before rejoining the regular army. In 2006, members of the same regiment were given leave of absence from regular army service to work in the private sector to 'load up' in Iraq, and return with no loss of seniority or pension rights. Others, from time to time, were detached to work with MI6.

In its regular but clandestine role in the seventies, the SAS reversed the tide of history to make the key Gulf territory of Oman safe for the West. A new entity – the Sultan's Special Force (SSF) – emerged, to be trained and led by former SAS regulars, now operating as freelances on contract. The SSF is still a key component of stability at the doorway to the Gulf and the world's richest oilfields.

The power vacuum of the postcolonial era is also represented by Mike Hoare's activities in the Congo. Modern disasters such as the Angolan affair in 1976 (run at arm's length by the CIA) and the implications of employing deniable forces around the world, notably in Latin America and Africa, were part of a Cold War fought with live bullets by surrogate armies. I was personally involved in the Angolan story, regrettably trapped between the moral ambiguities of this type of conflict and my role as a journalist, and was interrogated at Scotland Yard as a result. One highly successful SAS veteran, operating in Nicaragua in 1985, was described as 'Uncle Sam's British mercenary'.[7]

Not all these adventures ended ignominiously. Such successes as the SSF as well as the Yemen campaign involved an interesting cast of deniable phantoms, including Sir Peter de la Billière, Britain's field commander during the first Gulf war in 1991, as well as Jim Johnson and David Stirling's wartime comrade John Cooper. In the Yemen, Cooper and Johnson also worked alongside legendary French mercenaries including Roger Faulques and Bob Denard.

The dogs-of-war tradition did not die, unfortunately, with the firing squad that ended the squalid life of Costas Georgiou, a.k.a. 'Colonel Callan', in Angola. In 2004, Simon Mann, son of an England cricket captain and an SAS veteran, was sentenced by a Zimbabwean court for his part in a conspiracy to seize control of Equatorial Guinea. Mark Thatcher, son of the former prime minister, was also implicated in the proposed coup. The irony was, and is, that Mann and another of those imprisoned were founders of the highly successful, shiny and new model private army known as Executive Outcomes.

Their later operation ('the Wonga Coup'), laughable in its ineptitude, would have found no place in this history but for the impact it had on African opinion. It triggered a new wave of legislation to control thousands of South Africans, black and white, working around the world, including men serving in the British armed forces. It might also have undermined attempts by the newly created British Association of Private Security Companies to collaborate with Whitehall in generating a new code, complete with Ombudsman, to regulate the trade. It also left some difficult questions unanswered. There is good evidence that the Foreign and Commonwealth Office knew of the plot in advance but did not warn Equatorial Guinea, the target of the plot, while making contingency plans to evacuate British citizens from the country if the coup happened.[8] There is also the issue of Simon Mann's alleged confession to the police who arrested him in Zimbabwe which, he claims, resulted from blackmail.[9]

This book does not pretend to be a complete account of the evolution of freelance soldiers everywhere. It does not even scratch the surface of much mercenary activity in the modern world. One missing chapter, for example, is the impact of the Balkan wars of the mid-nineties on freelance soldiering, from which a whole generation of young war veterans spilled over into Africa. During the 1980s, British mercenaries turned up everywhere from Surinam to Croatia by way of Colombia. Former SAS men also trained, and sometimes led, warriors on both sides in Sri Lanka. Many thousands of demobilised Russian soldiers have joined the private sector in Eastern Europe, including Chechnya. An army of jihadists spread around the world like a pandemic after their victory over Russia in Afghanistan.

While the ancient and medieval worlds serve up some rich and colourful cases, it is hard to identify their relevance to contemporary reality. Rather, I would unfold a largely Anglo-American story, which starts with the Foreign Enlistment Act 1870 – the only British law still invoked to control freelance soldiers serving outside the UK – in order to identify some of the turning points of the modern story. Thereafter we follow a bloody thread that leads from Ireland to the United States and continental Europe, to Israel and to the evolution of British Special Forces and, thereafter, to the peculiarly British entry into private, corporate, armed security by way of close protection. Only thus can the current – extraordinary – situation be properly explored.

In the disordered world after 9/11, British and American governments adjusted to a world without a clearly identifiable enemy. In the old days the red star on the fur hat, if not snow on their boots, told us who the enemy might be. For diplomatic reasons, NATO soldiers on manoeuvres had fought against 'Orange Forces' rather than the Red Army, but even then the soldiers could identify their enemy in any given encounter much more easily than they do today.

The brave new post-Cold War world is more ambiguous, and is one in which humanitarian goals – such as the protection of refugees, aid workers and even journalists – may be linked to armed realpolitik. As the veteran foreign correspondent John Simpson has revealed,

> Now, if we go somewhere like Iraq or Afghanistan or Saudi Arabia, someone else has to come: a security adviser. In my case, it is usually a superb ex-Royal Marine called Craig Summers. He is not armed, though the BBC has taken the difficult decision to allow our security advisers to carry guns in Iraq. So far [September 2005] they have never had to use them.[10]

A dialogue has begun between relief agencies, civil servants and private security firms, on the neutral ground of the university campus: at Birmingham University's Centre for Studies in Security and Diplomacy in 2002 and Oxford University in 2005. In 2006 that august body the Royal United Institute for Defence and Strategic Studies hosted the first annual conference of the British Association of Private Security Companies (the BAPSC). Such meetings, following an earlier workshop at Tufts University, Boston, MA, brought together government officials, academics, aid agencies and private military companies. If, as yet, there was no formal government recognition of the private security sector, something was changing on the ground.

The rules governing geopolitics also changed with the end of the Cold War. International law prohibiting attacks on sovereign nation-states, which were defined as 'wars of aggression', had been the legal gold standard since 1945. In 1999 the gold standard was dumped by the West in its attack on Yugoslavia, in the name of humanitarianism. The UN Security Council was persuaded to sanction the invasion of Kosovo, to protect Muslims from Serbian ethnic cleansing. Kofi Annan, retiring as UN General Secretary in 2006, reflected on the horrors of Darfur and publicly expressed his conversion to the new legal doctrine.

He said, 'We must give real meaning to the principle of "responsibility to protect", which means, in essence, that respect for national sovereignty can no longer be used as an excuse for inaction in the face of crimes against humanity.'[11]

He could have mentioned the use of humanitarian aims to justify the invasion of Iraq in 2003. That campaign was soon followed by a consummation of interests linking the freelance soldier to public policy and government budgets. As one academic expert noted, even before the Iraq bonanza, 'From 1994 to 2002, the US Defense Department entered into more than 3,000 contracts with US-based firms estimated at a contract value of more than $300 billions.'[12] A key element of US participation in the Balkan wars of the nineties – in Croatia and Bosnia as well as Kosovo – depended upon logistics provided by a private contractor, Kellog Brown & Root Services. The role of another US company, MPRI, was probably crucial in the defeat of a robust Yugoslav army.

At the turn of the twenty-first century, even though the Iraqi bubble was less buoyant as the country melted down into civil war, the future of the freelance soldier never looked better. For the rest of the world, it had never been more bleak. Two factors combined to make confrontation more likely and pessimism necessary. First, there was the West's dependence on oil. The US, as President George W. Bush conceded, had become 'addicted to oil'. Second, the US was economically dependent on military spending as a means of balancing the books and thereby trapped in a sort of distorted Keynesianism. As a result, the US, now the world's only superpower, had become dangerously asymmetrical: it had the biggest guns combined with the greatest need of oil from the Gulf and other politically unstable areas and an international debt of around $8 trillion (that is, 8 followed by twelve noughts).[13]

Islamic Fundamentalism, meanwhile, emulated the IRA's mystical search for spirituality through violence. As one of republicanism's godfathers – Pádraig Pearse – put it, 'Bloodshed is a cleansing and sanctifying thing.' Al-Qaeda predicted, after the Madrid bombings of 2004, dissolution of the nation-state as a prelude to the creation of a worldwide caliphate under sharia law. The idea of nationhood had been the accepted model of sovereignty since the Treaty of Westphalia ended the Thirty Years War in 1648. But, in its statement claiming the Madrid atrocity, Al-Qaeda pronounced, 'The international system built up by the West since the Treaty of Westphalia will collapse, and a new international system will rise under the leadership of a mighty Islamic state.'

Pressure upon the nation-state came not just from Islamists. Britain learned the hard way from its closest ally that independent military action had not been a realistic option since the UK's aborted (and unlawful) Suez invasion in 1956. Subsequently, aside from internal counterinsurgency or postcolonial 'low-intensity' conflicts, war could be conducted only with the consent of the superpower. There were many reasons for this, including such technical embarrassments as the control of satellite intelligence for navigating missiles. The veteran British Labour politician Tony Benn recalls, 'As I learned when I was Energy Secretary, Britain is entirely dependent on the US for the supply of our Trident warheads and associated technology. They cannot even be targeted unless the US switches on its global satellite system.'[14] In addition, the weapons needed regular overhaul in American facilities.

According to the journalist and defence writer Max Hastings, within Europe military impotence has bitten deep into national morale and morality as well as the technical means of defence. In October 2005 he suggested,

> It should be a source of ... grave alarm, that all our partners in Europe save France have abandoned any pretension to a serious defence policy. Their politicians, their media, their publics appear to have reached the conclusion that there is absolutely no cause which they can imagine being worth fighting, sacrificing lives, even spending more money for ... This is an amazing development ... The world should be amazed ...
>
> A great country such as Germany, and such lesser ones as Spain, Belgium and Holland, have by their budgetary actions shown that they reject the principle accepted by every serious society for centuries, that it is impossible to have an effective foreign policy without a credible defence policy and plausible armed forces.[15]

If, as scholars such as Peter Singer contend, the litmus test of true nationhood is a monopoly over the use of force,[16] then Britain has not been a strategically independent nation for half a century. So where does British sovereignty now lie? The German Foreign Minister, Joschka Fischer, among others, argues that the Westphalian model of sovereignty has been obsolete since 1945. As he put it in a speech, 'The core of the concept of Europe after 1945 was and still is a rejection of the European balance-of-power principle and the hegemonic ambitions of individual states that had emerged following the Peace of Westphalia in 1648, a rejection which took the form of closer meshing of vital interests and the transfer of nation-state sovereign rights to supranational European institutions.'[17]

What emerged after 1945 was NATO, dominated by the United States. For half a century prior to the invasion of the Yugoslav province of Kosovo in 1999, NATO was a strictly defensive alliance in which a military attack on one member would be seen as an attack upon all. NATO was an excellent supranational entity, with a joint high command and the military capacity to intervene in a variety of scenarios, informally as well as formally.

The Kosovo operation, headed by the US and Britain, without UN approval, changed the doctrine to one of pre-emptive intervention for humanitarian purposes. In attacking Kosovo, NATO dumped its *raison d'être* by invading a country offering no threat to any of its members. France and Germany supported this operation at the time. As Peter Beinart, senior fellow at the US Council on Foreign Relations, points out, 'Blair made it the centrepiece of a new foreign policy creed, which he called the "doctrine of international community".'[18] Britain's European allies did not appreciate that it would become the template for the Iraq invasion, launched on a false premise (weapons of mass destruction) as well as humanitarianism (to save the Iraqi people from Saddam's regime). The role of freelance soldiers in both operations has been virtually ignored.

In fact, PMCs were key players in both wars as well as other Balkan conflicts in providing logistics, retraining security forces in territories occupied by the US and Britain, and acting as bodyguards, convoy escorts and intelligence analysts, though some would argue that there is a significant difference between freelance fighters and freelance advisers. In some cases, freelance soldiers, including British citizens, have become effectively embedded in regular US front-line armed forces in Iraq, fighting alongside them and enjoying legal immunity from any consequences, including, as one told me, 'a massacre of civilians'. Since many of the allied 'regulars' are, in fact, reservists, the freelances, retired from regular armies after a lifetime, are often the true professionals.

I know of at least one variant of this theme, a British reserve officer doubling as an intelligence analyst for a private security company in Iraq. His regular army corps regards that as a benefit, since he learns as much as a freelance on 'the Circuit' as during his periods of regular, uniformed duty in the same country.

There are also disturbing allegations that legal immunity has encouraged a minority of mercenaries to kill civilians at random, or for target practice, from the armed mobile convoys they run on public roads in Iraq. That process, in its turn, gave rise to a rare phenomenon: the soldier, whether freelance or regular, publicly expressing doubts about the morality of what he and others were doing in Iraq.

But the apolitical approach by most freelances to the business of armed conflict as a commodity chimes perfectly with the current American approach, effectively controlled by commercial interests, notably the oil lobby. Oil – its acquisition and protection – is one of the major themes of this history, whether it is the care of BP in such disparate areas as Colombia, Algeria, Georgia and Pakistan, Shell in Nigeria or American assets elsewhere.

In an age when US foreign policy reflects the philosophy of the nineteenth-century Prussian military thinker Carl Von Clausewitz ('Warfare is the continuation of political dialogue by other means') rather than submission to international law, freelance soldiers might be forgiven for believing that they serve a respectable moral and political cause, since that is the new orthodoxy of Bush's White House and was such in Blair's Downing Street (it remains to be seen what the new prime minister will bring to bear).

The Iraqi watershed, and the privatisation of international conflict, had one ironic outcome. A Special Forces veteran in the private sector could earn up to £14,000 a month. The SAS regular soldier, as a junior NCO, would expect no more than £2,000 a month. A haemorrhage of skilled manpower left the army to join the private sector. So severe was the problem that the regiment had to make discreet appeals to its old comrades to stop poaching.[19]

The SAS, it must be said, had an ambiguous attitude to the process. Its pre-release courses included advice about offshore taxation, implying a future on the Circuit, such as work as an international bodyguard, or convoy escort, or both, with payment into a foreign bank account. As an MoD spokesman explained, the army had a duty of care and would give any information it could 'to help guide a soldier's future career'.

In 2005, when appeals to loyalty did not do the trick, the Ministry of Defence circulated a classified memorandum to commanding officers of infantry regiments, advising them to stress to their men 'the perils of work in the PMC environment' and to 'highlight losses: fourteen killed in May this year in Iraq alone'.[20] According to the Iraq Coalition Casualty Count, an independent monitor, 28 of the 258 freelance soldiers then killed in Iraq were British. A Pentagon report covering the period between 1 May 2003 and 28 October 2004 concluded that the freelances had suffered 1,000 casualties, including 166 fatalities, of whom 64 were Americans. South Africa, another leading player, lost about 12 men.

The MoD advised its commanders to remind the soldiers that freelance contracts were generally short-term, while

> the PMCs make limited or no pension provision or life insurance cover for their 'operators' . . . Protection and equipment provided to PMC personnel are less than good. They have no armour and their weapons are of poor quality. Professional standards are, in general, not high.
>
> There is no moral commitment to company staff when things go wrong. On one occasion, two British PMC operators were killed outside the entrance of an army base and were left to rot for a whole day before being collected. Where possible, do not give access to [regular military] bases to PMC staff.[21]

The Ministry's own track record in caring for newly disabled soldiers was not above reproach, either. As a former member of a tank crew put it, 'Once you are discharged the MoD doesn't want anything to do with you. The attitude is, "Let's just get another number in to replace this one." . . . They blew me up but they don't want anything to do with me.'[22]

The MoD also claimed in August 2005 that, while the number of soldiers who had recently left the army to join PMCs – about 140 – was insignificant in terms of overall resignations, 'there are some hot spots where momentum has been established'. The greatest concern was about the loss of elite Special Forces soldiers to the private sector. This, however, was nothing new. Some 30 years earlier the adjutant of the reserve regiment known as 21 SAS had circulated a warning that service with the SAS was incompatible with work for such private firms as KMS.

He might have said, 'Except for the exceptions', for, when it suited Whitehall, SAS men were released from regular service to take part in deniable private operations or, in a few cases, because their activities in Northern Ireland had made them unusually controversial. For other reasons, probably, the MoD even had a special department to facilitate the secondment, and more, of officers to foreign armies.

The reality was that, since the end of World War Two, UK Special Forces veterans such as David Stirling, John Cooper, Alastair Morrison, Jim Johnson, David Walker, Mike Gooley, Arish Turle, Simon Adams-Dale and a host of others had pioneered the privatisation of soldiering, usually with the approval – and sometimes on behalf – of the Ministry of Defence and/or the Foreign Office. In a real sense, they anticipated the Thatcher revolution as well as the 'corporate warrior' concept marketed by Tim Spicer.

Most of the 'grunts' they employed who survive are not unhappy with their lot. One with long regular British army service, followed by a contract in Baghdad, told me, 'When the army kicks you out at a youthful forty or so, what else do you do? Finding a totally civilian job is very hard. All the experience you have, whilst transferable, is in a language and working environment that is totally alien to the majority of civilian managers. Gone are the days of the shared National Service experience, which the civilian manager could call on to understand what the ex-military potential employee is saying, or has done.

'The only exposure a civilian manager has to the military is what he/she reads in the paper or sees on TV. As someone who has sought work in the civilian sector I find it extremely hard to deal with recruiters. I speak a different language and have a career history that is meaningless to them. I would also argue that, in a world that is increasingly nervous or risk-averse, why would an employer take on what is in effect an unknown and unproven quantity?

'An ex-soldier still has to pay the bills. So the comfortable option is to stick with what we know, and, if that means working in Iraq or Afghanistan, so be it. Moreover, the money on offer is very good, enabling a financial cushion to be built up either to see you through the lean years or to retire early on. I know people who have worked the Circuit for ten to fifteen years after leaving the forces, following a full career, and have now retired to Spain, Crete or wherever and are now living off the proceeds, backed up by the military pension that kicks in at age fifty-five. One of the security managers in Baghdad commutes from Rio! Two ex-SAS ops managers used a year in Baghdad to buy a villa in Crete and to retire there with their wives.'

At a macro level, Margaret Thatcher, first elected in 1979 on a ticket that promised to cut waste out of the public sector, went on to privatise such strategic assets as North Sea oil and the Royal Ordnance Factories (ROF), suppliers of weapons and ammunition to the British army. When it was sold in 1987 for £180 million to British Aerospace, ROF had 16 factories and 19,000 workers. It was inevitable, thereafter, that, if the means of warfare were up for sale to all bidders, then the same would happen to the skills needed to implement warfare.

The MoD, an enthusiastic convert to market forces (until its own status quo was disturbed), ran a profitable sideline in training the armed forces of friendly foreign governments in such arcane skills as close protection and intelligence analysis. The Al Yamamah contract supplied the latest Tornado fighting aircraft to a fundamentalist Islamic regime in Saudi Arabia. Many senior military officers went through a revolving door after retirement, leading to lucrative jobs with arms companies contracted to supply the regular forces they had just left, on pension. The culture that mixed private profit and national defence in Britain, as in the US, pervaded the military world.

Other forces were tearing apart the old order. The IRA taught terrorists everywhere the advantages of 'Sinn Fein' – Ourselves Alone – in arms procurement and manufacture. The Internet provides online courses in bomb making. Since not every grievance can be resolved, it is inevitable that violent direct action to express grievances will increase. The stress that this process imposes on democratic, open government – limited by a proper awareness of human rights – will require vastly greater investment in internal security and, probably, greater reliance on deniable, covert operators.

As a result of the Irish war, MI5 in London has been supported for years by a Special Forces team known as 'the Increment'. Other Special Forces soldiers routinely join Scotland Yard's armed patrols in civilian dress. The distinction between police and military formations is crumbling and will continue to crumble. As the political scientist Mary Kaldor has noted, 'The ongoing war in Iraq is a new type of war . . . In new wars . . . forces are needed that combine soldiers, police and civilians with the capacity to undertake humanitarian and legal activities.'[23] Will a sufficient number of 'white knight' mercenaries be available? Some experts think there is reason for optimism.

The case for the freelance soldier was put shortly before the Iraq war by Doug Brooks, president of the International Peace Operations Association, in response to a re-examination of their role by the British Foreign Office. In this version the agenda is also changing from aggressive military interventionism to the defensive role of protector. Brooks claimed,

> PMCs offer the only military forces both willing and capable of providing rapid and effective military services in most Third World conflicts. Their operations have saved tens of thousands of lives but their potential is even greater. Working as 'force multipliers' – that is, training indigenous armies – PMCs can provide the competent military backbone to ensure the success of UN or regional multinational peacekeeping or peace enforcement operations . . .
>
> More critically, given an international mandate, PMCs can decisively intervene in instances of genocide, as in Rwanda. Executive Outcomes' offer to the UN of a rapid intervention force during the Rwanda genocide was declined at a time when member states were callously turning their backs to UN pleas for military support. [24]

Others support that view. The intelligence analyst and visiting fellow in war studies at King's College, London, Kevin A. O'Brien, asserts, 'The international community, as has been witnessed once again in Kosovo, has demonstrated time and again its unwillingness to become involved in regional conflicts where Western foreign policy concerns are not threatened directly: this gap will continue to be filled by the private military company.'[25]

Colonel Tim Collins, a former SAS soldier famous for his 'Before Agincourt' speech to the Royal Irish Rangers on the eve of the Iraq war, goes further. In a BBC discussion in 2005 he said, 'Sadly, the standard of nations' armed forces, the standard of leadership in those nations, is so uneven and in some cases so corrupt – and the United Nations in my view is so badly broken that it needs repair – that there may be a case to give private military companies and more nation-states an exact mission under UN auspices with a set of end-states required.

'For instance in Darfur [Sudan, the scene of many massacres] you say to a private military brigade, "You will come under UN auspices. You will vet everyone you have in that brigade and by, say, February we want the entire province secured and all routes open so that we can have access for humanitarian advisers. Once you have done that, we will replace it with either a UN standing army's troops or we will replace it with another private military company to provide that security." What we can't continue doing is [providing] the fourteen million [dollars] set aside by the UN to police Africa, for which we get precisely nothing while people are still starving and dying. That has to stop. The money is going into the pockets of dictators and it has to stop . . . Frankly, the UN deployments around the world, plenty in Africa, have become a racket . . . There is a cynical gravy train in many places where, if there is no imperative, nothing happens.'[26]

That is not the way Kofi Annan and other UN mandarins saw it. The UN's 1989 International Convention against the Recruitment, Use, Financing and Training of Mercenaries attracted only 12 signatories (three of whom then employed freelance military personnel). This did not influence Annan. He told a 1997 conference discussing the civil war in Sierra Leone, 'I don't know how one makes a distinction between respectable mercenaries and non-respectable mercenaries.'[27]

The debate continues at the UN and in Africa, but the facts of a changing world make such lofty isolation unrealistic. In a post-9/11 and post-7/7 culture, little distinction can now be made between the developing and developed worlds. We all live on a global battleground. Indeed, a learned research group at Oxford University now suggests that World War Three is up and running and that it has been kick-started by the availability of war-making machines.

Professor Neil Johnson, a physicist on the team using a system of statistical analysis known as *power-law statistics*, offers the chilling thought that we are looking at conflict through the wrong end of the telescope. He measures casualty statistics around the world caused by terrorism, plotted logarithmically against the number of such attacks. He argues that, while the conventional approach of political analysts is to seek micro-explanations such as the motivations of the warring groups, the causes and outcomes have much more to do with 'the mechanics of how people now do war . . . It is like looking at different markets. We now know that a lot of the fluctuations are universal, irrespective of whether you're looking at trading in New York or Shanghai.'[28]

Three elements recur throughout this modern history. They are the peculiar role and character of Special Forces, the evolution of privatisation of public assets since privatisation was pioneered by Margaret Thatcher, and the West's addiction to oil. It is a dark paradox that the Cold War years from 1946 to 1991, haunted as they were by the possibility of Mutual Assured Destruction, or MAD, now seem, by comparison, to be an age of stability. We increasingly live in a world of failed states, superstition and virtual anarchy.

What has changed is not just the degradation of international law and the way war is fought. Armed forces on both sides of the Cold War, and long before, were motivated largely by patriotism and self-sacrifice. During World War One, the image of Lord Kitchener and his proclamation, 'Your King & Country Need You!' were holy writ. They, however, were citizen armies, not professional military machines. The move towards exclusively professional armies in the UK and USA has divorced civilian communities from the forces defending them. In Britain, an official policy that prohibits senior officers from talking to trusted, knowledgeable correspondents without the inhibiting presence of a minder, complete with tape recorder, has isolated the armed forces even further. Soldiering in Britain has long been advertised by the Ministry of Defence not as a patriotic vocation, but as a good career move.

In the world of the multinational corporation, patriotism does not even rate as a fashion accessory, still less a complete uniform (to be swapped for a locally made civilian suit, made in Iran, if necessary). What the mercenary sometimes does – betraying his paymaster and deserting the battlefield – has made him a profoundly sinister figure to the French, who attach to him the virtually untranslatable phrase 'les Affreux' ('the Horrors'). The best hope must be that the mercenary will honour his contract and that the contract will compel some approximation to human values. Loyalty to your mates is an almost universal virtue among professional soldiers but that does not always translate into loyalty to the paymaster in the commercial world.

The unexpected, brief captivity of 15 Royal Navy and Royal Marines service people by Iranian commandos in the Gulf in 2007 demonstrated another new reality: loyalty to one's bank balance. With the enthusiastic backing of the Ministry of Defence, the 15 were encouraged to strike 'I was there' deals with newspapers and television outlets, putting them, officially, in the same 'exceptional' category as a winner of the Victoria Cross.

Patriotism, some argue, is asking too much. It might even be an impediment to good business practice. As an expert financial witness to an inquiry into a Bank of England scandal (the Bank Rate Tribunal, 1958) once put it, 'It might not be patriotic, but it makes sense to me.' As the occupation of Iraq entered its fourth year, allegations of financial malpractice among regular SAS soldiers (similar to the 'phantom *firqa*' scandal in Oman 30 years before), as well as among contractors in the private sector, were growing, reflecting the obsession with money that is the mercenaries' credo, as well as poor accounting.

In Iraq after 2003, fraud and corruption flourished like exotic weeds in a dark world of unaccountable funds. Billions of dollars, provided by Iraq's continuing oil revenues as well as US taxpayers, were siphoned away from reconstruction projects. An audit by the US government's Special Inspector General for Iraq Reconstruction found that in just one Iraqi town officers involved in reconstruction 'cannot properly account for or support $96.6 million in cash and receipts'.[29] It might not have been patriotic, but it made sense to someone.

There has been another pervasive cultural change that makes the professional warrior less popular than during the wars of national survival. As Professor Christopher Coker argues, we have become a risk-averse society. Anyone who deliberately lives dangerously is seen as a threat to the rights of others not to be confronted with the impending reality, for all of us, of death. ('In the past, risk-taking was illustrative of bravery. Today is has a measure of irresponsibility . . . We live at a time when death can be postponed . . .'[30])

Thus the committed warrior has to be seen as someone in actual, or potential, need of treatment for a psychological sickness. The lustre formerly attached to military heroism has grown thin. On that basis, the freelance, professional soldier may expect an even worse press than hitherto. There would be a political price to pay for that, of course. The jihadis, whatever their faults, believe sufficiently in their cause to die for it, willingly. The West, as they see it, has gone soft and is ripe for conversion.

As a result of all these changes in the way our world functions, the vast expansion of commercial, privatised – and corporate – warfare that followed the invasions of Afghanistan and Iraq, where the freelance soldier, alongside the GI, was handed an elaborately written licence to kill, Wild West style, needs to be examined carefully. Legal immunity covering the use of lethal force, introduced by the Coalition Provisional Authority and known as Order 17, was subsequently made part of the Iraqi government's code.

The indefinite, undefined war on terror after 9/11, 7/7 and the invasions of Iraq and Afghanistan, fought without rules or mechanisms of international control, challenged everyone's values, including those of the professional warrior. An increasing number of freelance soldiers, riding the boom in privatised, armed security, were not fit or trained for the job. The word on the Hereford SAS circuit was that genuine professionals walked away from one contract in Iraq rather than risk serving alongside four recently retired postmen. An Italian freelance soldier ritually executed in Iraq proved to be a recently retired baker. Hungry men from all over the world were queuing up to join the industry.

Meanwhile, the legal twilight within which the private operator kills his enemy, or is himself killed, is another reflection of an increasingly disordered world. It is one in which governments 'render' prisoners to be tortured by proxy, and civilians are bombed as a pre-emptive act of self-defence. If the freelance soldier is part of such a world, playing a largely defensive role, he is not, by a long way, the most immoral actor in it.

This was also a cheerfully cynical world in which yesterday's enemy became today's friend, with a libation of a few hundred dollars. The Iraq narrative took a surprising twist in 2007 and beyond as the British SAS General Graeme Lamb negotiated with enemy forces on behalf of the Baghdad government. Perhaps it was not a coincidence that Sunni militias were persuaded to change sides, firqa-style, to fight for the Coalition against former allies representing Al-Qaeda. The friendly militias, known as 'Concerned Local Citizens', numbered 67,000 by November 2007. About 37,000 were under contract to the US and were paid $300 a month. No-one uttered the word 'mercenary', but it seemed that the Coalition might have identified a survival strategy, as patented by the SAS in Dhofar, 1970–1976.

ORIGINS:

'The Business of America is Business'

When the French Foreign Legion formed up its first parachute unit – *le Premier Bataillon Etranger de Parachutistes* – at Haiphong in 1948, some of the Legion's greybeards raised an interesting objection: it was that, once these soldiers had jumped, they could land almost anywhere, free to desert if they chose. In practice, of course, men descending into an isolated battle zone, particularly hostile jungle, would be unwise to go anywhere other than the agreed rendezvous. But the story neatly illustrates the psychological difference between the regimented regular foot soldier and the freelance warrior. Faced with a problem for which there was no text-book answer, generations of young British paratroopers were expressly taught, 'Use your airborne initiative!' We were reminded that, once on the ground, we were on our own until we reached the RV. It is no surprise that so many parachutists, happy to take total responsibility for their own destinies as they jump into the void, turn to freelance soldiering when they are demobilised. Lions do not always need to be led by donkeys.

That common factor aside, the mutations described in this story – the mercenary, the deniable warrior and the modern private security operator – inherit several different traditions. Two of them now dominate the inter-national, private, armed security industry. They are the British 'Bulldog Drummond' culture, elitist and patriotic, and America's dedication to private capital unimpeded by – often in charge of – central government. The differences still show up sharply in practice.

Britain's experience was shaped by her confrontation with the white South Africa. The voortrekkers, like the pioneers of America's West, generated a culture of movement and self-determination in the mid-nineteenth century from which, in 1900, sprang the Boer Kommandos. The Kommandos practised hit-and-run guerrilla warfare on horseback, in which, as one of their leaders said, 'Each man was practically his own commander.'

It was only a short step from that experience to the beatification in Afrikaner tradition of the White Giant of the mercenary world, in which a few bold men could win against all odds. The tradition lives on, though a Black African government in Pretoria has now driven hundreds of South African mercenaries (many of them black) into exile, to Iraq, Afghanistan, Sudan and the Congo.

The Boers' British enemy, including Winston Churchill, learned from South Africa the effectiveness of lean-and-mean irregular warfare, through which a few hundred men could tie up tens of thousands of orthodox assets. Churchill, both a soldier and war correspondent in South Africa, and a later advocate of British Special Forces, was not alone. Colonel Dudley Clarke, co-founder of the wartime British Commandos, was born in the Transvaal. His father was one of the mercenaries who took part in the Jameson Raid in 1895–6, an event that triggered the second Boer war.

The British were fighting another, more protracted, guerrilla war before, during and long after the South African conflict. What the Boers did on horseback, the Irish did on foot and with more venom on the streets of Dublin. On 21 November 1920 Michael Collins's assassins – 'the Squad', the men in trenchcoats – stormed eight unguarded houses in the Irish capital occupied by the cream of Anglo-Irish military intelligence. Twelve intelligence officers were shot dead and others wounded.

A few months earlier, Assistant Commissioner Redmond, head of police intelligence, was shot in the back. A resident magistrate inquiring into Sinn Fein funds was travelling on a tram when his killers tapped him on the shoulder and ordered him out with the words 'Your time has come.'[1] So it went on. The rebels had penetrated British intelligence. Collins's programme of targeted assassination robbed the British of any coherent knowledge of their enemy. The result was military defeat and Irish independence.

These events were watched with passionate interest by two British officers who would play a key role in later years in the creation of guerrilla armies to oppose Hitler. Lieutenant Colonel Colin MacVean Gubbins, an army intelligence officer and Lieutenant Colonel John Charles (Joe) Holland, a Royal Engineer, served together in Ireland for three years and witnessed the success of Collins's murder squads. They became pivotal figures in the evolution of Britain's various irregular warfare units before and during World War Two, particularly the Special Operations Executive.

As M. R. D. Foot, the SOE's official historian, put it, 'The Irish [thanks to the example set by Collins and followed by the SOE] can thus claim that their resistance provided an originating impulse for resistance to tyrannies worse than any they had to endure themselves. And Irish resistance, as Collins led it, showed the rest of the world an economical way to fight wars, the only sane way they can be fought in the age of the nuclear bomb.'[2]

SOE was chosen, in Churchill's words, to 'Set Europe Ablaze'. The organisation's political chief was Hugh Dalton, who said it should be 'comparable to the Sinn Fein movement in Ireland'.

The third source that inspired the postwar evolution of freelance soldiering was the Special Air Service Regiment, formally created by David Stirling in the summer of 1942, together with other adventurous spirits, backed up by Ralph Bagnold's Long Range Desert Group. During the Cold War years, men who had served in both SOE and SAS – reinvented in 1950 by Brigadier Mike Calvert as the 'Malayan Scouts (SAS)' – were absorbed into Special Forces. Calvert, with the Irish experience in mind, once told me that he conceived the Malayan Scouts as a modern 'Black and Tans', a militia rather than a regular regiment, easily dissolved if political nausea resulted.

Back in Britain, the evolving postwar SAS became a haven for people still hungry for action. A typical case was Major Dare Newell, who saw service in Albania with SOE, in the Japanese-occupied Malayan jungle with Force 136 and, finally, with the postwar SAS as its regimental adjutant. He was affectionately known as 'Mr SAS'.

The focus for freelance activity was the Duke of York's Headquarters, King's Road, Chelsea, headquarters of SAS Group and home of 21 SAS (TA). In the loft above Group HQ, in a building known as Centre Block, Newell had a camp bed and a store of whisky. Equally influential was an exclusive establishment nearby, the Special Forces Club (of which I am a sponsored member). During the immediate postwar years, it was not only a centre for war veterans of SOE, MI9 (the escapers' agency) and other exotic groups disbanded after 1945, it was also a reservoir of talent should a 'stay-behind' force be required to resist a Soviet invasion.

On the walls of the club, portraits of a generation of young men and women of many nationalities who died young – at the hands of Gestapo torturers; in front of firing squads; victims of parachute accidents or ambushes – still commemorate their commitment to lost values. Later generations of Special Forces soldiers, reflecting the reckless impatience of their world to defeat the Nazis and liberate Europe, did not adjust easily to a politically correct culture outside the Special Forces time warp. Some of the next generation, in fact, were the sons of SOE fathers.

Another influential watering hole was White's Club in St James, its walls permeated by 250 years of elitist, testosterone-driven gambling. Stirling had used it since his days as an officer cadet. It was a haunt of the first commandos. It was the place where the Yemen plot was hatched in the 1960s. It was also an arena within which Stirling would talk loudly and indiscreetly about some of his military enterprises, just as participants in the ill-conceived Wonga operation did in Cape Town, regardless of operational security.

The first private military companies set up after the war – Keenie Meenie Services (KMS), controlled by Jim Johnson, a recent commander of 21 SAS, and David Walker, alongside David Sterling's firm, Watchguard International (created in 1965 in response to the Yemen campaign) – were part of this culture. After Control Risks (CR) came into being in 1975 to haggle with kidnappers and secure the liberty of high-flying businessmen, a few energetic characters worked simultaneously for more than one company. David Walker, for example, was with both CR and KMS for a time before running his own Saladin Security organisation.

Sir David Sterling accepted Walker's invitation to become president of Saladin shortly before he died in 1990. At the time, Sterling was discussing with Walker covert operations to be launched against Saddam Hussein and aid to Jonas Savimbi during the continuing Angolan war, undeterred by the CIA's failure there and the catastrophe of 'Colonel Callan's' blood-soaked operation.

The PS/PMC pioneers established an early link with influential insurance companies. As fears of executive kidnap, terrorism and political risk grew in the wake of aircraft hijacks, airport massacres and other perils in the 1970s, the multinationals were glad to find any organisation that could keep them safe. A spectacular rescue of German beauty queens from a hijacked Lufthansa airliner at Mogadishu in October 1977 was led by an SAS major, Alastair Morrison, with Sergeant Barry Davies. It was brilliant PR for the regiment and an operation that sent a message of hope to political hostages elsewhere. Morrison later created Defence Systems Ltd, one of the most successful new-wave PSCs, and became rich.

US security companies are not the result of sacrificing a military elite to savage gods, but hard-nosed capitalism: the driving individualism of such obsessive personalities as Andrew Carnegie, corporate America, and the need to dragoon the workforce into the boss's mould of best practice. The godfather of labour control, like Carnegie, was a Scot. Allan Pinkerton, born in Glasgow in 1819, migrated to the US in 1842. He opened a shop making and selling barrels near Chicago. The shop was also a safe house for escaped slaves. He became America's archetype detective by accident. Gathering wood in a forest, he came upon a gang of coiners who were making counterfeit money. He alerted the police, helped in the arrest and was appointed deputy sheriff of Kane County.

In 1850, a mere eight years after sailing down the Clyde, he set up his own Pinkerton National Detective Agency, providing detection services of every kind. In particular, he gathered evidence to capture train robbers and counterfeit artists. (In the twenty-first century, South African freelances were doing a similar job in the Congo to apprehend diamond smugglers.)

His big break came in 1861. Investigating a railway case, he exposed a plot to assassinate Abraham Lincoln in Baltimore, during a halt on Lincoln's journey to the inauguration ceremony. Lincoln changed his itinerary, passed stealthily through the city by night, and hired Pinkerton to set up his Secret Service to dig up military information in the enemy South during the Civil War. Pinkerton adopted the nom de guerre 'Major E. J. Allen' as he went on an espionage mission through Tennessee, Georgia and Mississippi. His agency, by now thriving, adopted an enlarged eye as its logo above the slogan 'We Never Sleep'. The 'private eye' was born.

In 1865, after the Civil War, Pinkerton – like so many of his successors – went to the private sector. He led the hunt for the James Brothers. His men pursued 'the Wild Bunch', including Butch Cassidy and the Sundance Kid. His agency also became an essential tool in breaking the power of trade unions. One of his agents, James McParlan, penetrated a terrorist Irish-American group known as the Molly Maguires. As a result, 20 of its members were executed.

Significantly the legal process was handled by the private sector. As a local judge later admitted, 'The Molly Maguire trials were a surrender of [Pennsylvania] state sovereignty. A private corporation initiated the investigation through a private detective agency. A private police force arrested the alleged defenders and private attorneys for the coal companies prosecuted them. The state provided only the courtroom and the gallows.'[3]

After Pinkerton died, his sons Robert and William took over. In 1892 the Amalgamated Iron and Steel Workers Union called out its members at the Homestead plant, Pennsylvania, owned by Carnegie and Henry Frick. Strike breakers, protected by 300 Pinkerton agents, were brought in on armed barges. A battle with the pickets left seven Pinkerton agents and nine workers dead.

In 1910, a rival company – the William J. Burns Detective Agency – was founded. In July 2003, Securitas AB acquired the US companies of Pinkerton and Burns to create Securitas Security Services USA Inc., one of the world's leading security companies.

One of Carnegie's early successes resulted from the Civil War, when iron was needed to feed the battlefield. This history was repeated when World War One gave the US arms industry its first taste of international success, from the safe haven of a continent separated from the killing fields of France by 3,000 miles of ocean. To meet the cost of the war, Britain sold off its substantial holdings in American railways, then began serious borrowing on Wall Street. More money was borrowed from the American government when the US joined the war in 1917. The loans were tied to purchases from American companies, launching the US economy on its way to superpower status.

The massive US industrial base was a war-winning asset, but, while American arms and motor companies profited, Britain, with a US war debt of $850 million, was bleeding financially as well as physically, along with vanquished Germany. Washington was unsympathetic. When the issue was raised with President Calvin Coolidge in 1925 he snapped, 'They hired the money, didn't they?' As he also observed, 'The business of America is business.'

Efforts to negotiate a realistic settlement involving all of America's European debtors ended without agreement in 1934. Every debtor except Finland defaulted. Theoretically, Britain still 'owes' the United States $4.4 billion for the war that ended in 1918, a war that – thanks to the unreasonable reparations bill heaped on Germany – carried the seeds of the next world war, from which America benefited even more.

The debt incurred by Britain for Lend-Lease military aid between 1939 and 1945 and a postwar loan of $375 billion effectively crippled the country's economy for generations. The 1945 loan, worth more than £50 billion in twenty-first-century money, was not cleared by the Treasury until 31 December 2006, when Whitehall sent its final cheques totalling £42.4 million – equivalent to about 95p for every adult – to Washington.[4]

The pragmatic approach of American capital to armed conflict was perhaps best illustrated by the activities of the Ford Motor Company in Germany and Vichy France during World War Two. The company's founder, Henry Ford – famous for his aphorism 'What is good for Ford is good for America' – might have added, 'And good for Nazi Germany.' By 1942 Ford in Germany had supplied one-third of the 350,000 trucks used to motorise the Wehrmacht and drive its blitzkrieg strategy, to the disgust of advancing US soldiers, who recognised a Ford when they saw one.[5]

The postwar years of the Cold War, notably the space/ballistics race, generated more work and profit for US arms, and the technicians to support them, notably in the aerospace industry. A crucial aspect of the Cold War was that it was a financial war of attrition, culminating in the Star Wars project for which, as one cynic observed, a spare planet was needed to test it. The Soviet Union tried, and failed, to match Uncle Sam's strategic poker play, and went bankrupt in the process. The result, after the fall of the Berlin Wall in 1989, was the biggest bargain sale of lethal weapons in history, as Warsaw Pact nations such as East Germany, as well as Russia, disposed of hundreds of thousands of tanks, military aircraft and small arms. Many of the assault rifles ended up in the hands of illiterate boy soldiers in Africa and fed the small wars that have plagued the world since 1990.

A year or so after the Cold War ended, the modern PSC – a solid, corporate entity, totally unlike the chaotic dogs-of-war culture – sprang into existence, fully formed, like Athena from the head of Zeus, ready for the next conflict. The leader was an American oil giant, Halliburton, accompanied by its little brother, KBR (Kellog, Brown, & Root). The company's expertise in building rigs in remote, harsh regions made it a natural candidate for a privatised logistics industry to fill the gap left by a US army reduced by one-third in pursuit of the peace dividend. Halliburton, swiftly followed by DynCorp and others, became the key to America's military and political power projection in the monolithic post-Cold War world. As some experts concur, 'Only military amateurs think first of combat.

Professionals think of logistics . . . Logistics is the lifeblood of war.' But with world power and can-do technology came the can-do hubris that marked the Bush presidency. As Iraq was to demonstrate, not everyone wanted a T-shirt proclaiming 'MADE IN THE USA'.

The essential support provided for the humanitarian intervention in Kosovo from 1999 is but one impressive example of Halliburton's muscle. Within three months, the company's engineering subsidiary had erected 192 barracks for 7,000 soldiers, 13 helicopter pads, two air maintenance workshops, 12 huge dining halls and much else. Equally impressive was Camp Bondsteel, a base for 5,000 men with its roads, sewerage, independent power – even a detention centre. Following the flight of thousands of Kosovar Albanian Muslims from Serb vengeance, it was KBR that responded to the need for shelter. International agencies were unable to cope.

Throughout their history, such companies benefited from links to influential politicians. The history of Dick Cheney as Halliburton's chief executive officer before and after his pivotal role as US Secretary of Defense is one example among many. As early as 1937, the logistics company Brown & Root (later a subsidiary of Halliburton) survived thanks to the influence of Lyndon Johnson, later President. Such is its power now that as the author P. W. Singer puts it, 'Wherever the US military goes, so goes Brown & Root . . . US military planners no longer even envisage the possibility of a large-scale intervention taking place without Brown & Root or one of its business competitors providing the logistics.'[6] (The same company took over the management of some British military resources, with mixed results.)

If the footprint of the big logistics companies was as clear as the tracks of a battle tank on a neighbour's lawn in the global village, the influence of privatised US military trainers was less evident but equally potent. Alongside the British KMS enterprise in Yemen, Sri Lanka and elsewhere, the American enterprise Vinnell was a pioneer in a business that mixed business with espionage and plausible deniability. Vinnell was another construction company, created in Los Angeles in 1931, that morphed by way of military construction into covert military activity and finally military training. A Pentagon official, in an interview with the *Village Voice* in March 1975, described the company's operation at the time as 'our own little mercenary army in Vietnam', which was used 'to do things we either didn't have the manpower to do ourselves or because of legal problems'.[7]

Further evidence of Vinnell's involvement in deniable, or 'black', operations was the cover it gave to Wilbur Crane Eveland, a CIA operator in
Africa and the Middle East in the 1960s.[8] During much of that time he was
working in collaboration with the UK's Secret Intelligence Service.[9]

In February 1975 it picked up a contract worth $77 million to train the
Saudi National Guard (SNG) as part of America's long love affair with
Saudi oil and its royal family, guarded by the SNG. The team's headquar-
ters was bombed by dissidents in 1995, killing five Americans and two
Indians. In May 2003 Al-Qaeda guerrillas hit a number of targets in
Riyadh, including the Vinnell compound, where 26 people including nine
Americans died.[10]

Another company prominent in the training of local defence forces
friendly towards the West is MPRI (Military Professional Resources Incorporated). Like Vinnell, it was in business as a PSC before the watershed of
9/11 or its successor in March 2003, the invasion of Iraq. MPRI is ubiqui-
tous. Pursuing its 'democracy transition' programme, it has offered to train
military personnel at every level in Bosnia, Nigeria, Taiwan, Ukraine,
Croatia and Macedonia. It is well dug into the Coalition's Phoenix
programme to train the Afghanistan National Army. Some of its job offers
in that theatre – such as Fire Support Mentor/Trainer: Commando
Training Program – suggest something close to personal participation in
military operations.

The case of DynCorp, a firm with operational experience in South
America long before the post-9/11 boom, characterises the easy relationship between US governments and carefully chosen clients in the private
security sector. DynCorp is in part at least a private military company. It
owes its existence to a decision by President Harry S. Truman in 1946 to
provide work for war veterans and to market surplus military hardware. Its
contracts with government departments, some of them secret, lead many
observers to believe that it is a plausibly deniable cut-out for special operations around the world. It has been in the front line of the drug wars in
Peru and Colombia.

An authoritative article in the *Nation* on 23 May 2001, citing a secret
contract between the company and the State Department, concluded,

From its main operating base at Patrick Air Force Base [Cape Canaveral]
Dyncorp oversees . . . a fleet of 46 helicopters and 23 fixed-wing aircraft
which can operate from 23 locations spread out over Colombia, Bolivia

and Peru. In some cases, DynCorp's operations are not limited to fumigation and search-and-rescue but, according to the contract, include maintenance and pilot training, aircraft ferrying . . . reconnaissance and flying local troops to destroy drug labs and cocoa or poppy fields.[11]

DynCorp's reputation was damaged by a series of scandals before and after the invasion of Iraq, where it had a contract to train the police. In 2000, two whistleblowers working for the firm were dismissed when they complained about the sex-trafficking of young women and girls in Bosnia. At least thirteen other DynCorp employees were removed from Bosnia and seven were dismissed.[12] Concerns were also expressed about the quality of aircraft maintenance by some of the team in South America. It was alleged that their previous experience had been as waitresses, cooks and cashiers.[13]

The company's useful work elsewhere, including close protection of US diplomats in Gaza (where three of the company's bodyguards were killed) and mine clearance in Afghanistan, is overshadowed by failures for which, usually, no one is held accountable. This apparent immunity has strengthened the belief that, so long as DynCorp loyally serves America in areas too dangerous for orthodox diplomacy, taking the flak, it is beyond the law.

In 2004, DynCorp cried foul when Tim Spicer's British firm Aegis unexpectedly won a major US contract worth £158 million to become the interface and intelligence co-ordinator between Coalition forces and the private security sector in Iraq. Part of the DynCorp complaint raised questions about Spicer's fitness for the job. The US company contended 'that Aegis lacked the requisite responsibility to perform this contract due, in part, to certain alleged activities of Aegis's principal director and largest shareholder'. The complaint was rejected by the US watchdog, the General Accountability Office.[14] The Aegis contract is a rare case, one in which the Pentagon trusted a non-American enterprise more than the claims of one of its own longstanding client companies.

The surge in private security after the Twin Towers attack of 2001 became a bonanza after the invasion of Iraq in 2003. But the shape of the industry – notably the different treatment accorded private security operators by the US and UK governments – was by then already established. It is now an international army in waiting, beyond the control of most governments, but influenced by market forces. For that reason, the main players in America and Britain favour self-regulation as the route to respectability.

PART I

.

MERCENARIES

1

AFRICA:

They do things differently there

Black Africa has for centuries provided a template for freelance military operations, conducted without regard for human rights by foreigners. In the eyes of too many Europeans, it is another country in the way the past is another country, a place where things are done differently. Joseph Conrad's *Heart of Darkness* is a commentary on the white man's relationship with the demon within himself, as well as the dark continent 'where the merry dance of death and trade goes on in a still and earthy atmosphere as of an overheated catacomb'.

From the slave trade to the present time, it is a story of enigmatic atrocities – enigmatic because of the pulsing sense of life, not death – that engages those who set foot on its red soil. The British Council driver turns to his passenger as they hit the dirt road at the end of the tarmac on the edge of Freetown (named for its history of sanctuary to former slaves), saying, 'Welcome to Africah, Mistah Tony!' He means that Africa is a place where a man can still walk silent and barefoot on the earth, and know he belongs. In Sierra Leone, the normal greeting is not 'Good morning!' (a shorthand way of thanking a European god for surviving things that go bump in the night), but 'How de body?' The reply, even among amputee victims of the country's latest violent binge, is 'De body fine !'

A mile or so along the coast from Lumley Beach there is a settlement that has been renamed 'Adonkia'. The name resonates with macabre humour. In its most recent war, a party of rebels were on their way downhill, through the forest, to attack the place. A hunter, going the other way, warned them, 'Don't go down deha, man. De enemy is waiting. Dey will massacah you.' The rebel leader, fired up for battle, replied, 'Ah don' care.' He and his men were promptly ambushed and buried on the spot. The locals commemorated the event by changing the name of their village to echo the dead rebel's last words, as a joke but also as a coded reminder of the dangers of hubris.

Africa is special and Whitehall – or parts of it – know that. They keep a discreet eye on some of those who go there and what they do while they are there. For example, thanks to a confidential document that somehow escaped from the Foreign and Commonwealth Office in 2002, we know that the Defence Ministry's Intelligence Secretariat has long kept an unofficial database detailing information about private military companies and their staffs operating in Africa, and only in Africa; certainly not in the US or some other 'friendly intelligence state'. There is another reason why Africa has a particular place in the history of British freelance military adventures. The Jameson Raid into the Transvaal in 1895–6 resulted in the only prosecution brought under the Foreign Enlistment Act 1870, which was still, in 2007, the only British law to control mercenary activity.

Africa is another place. They do things differently there. During the Rwandan genocide of 1994, in four months or so, using no weapon more sophisticated than the domestic machete, one ethnic group murdered around 800,000 of their neighbours. The incitement was by word of mouth, through a local radio station ('How many cockroaches have you killed today?') and on the street, by word of mouth, through what is known in Kigali as 'Radio Trottoir.'

In the Great African War (for control of the poisoned riches of the Congo) around 3.9 million people were killed between 1998 and 2006, giving Africa the dubious distinction of the greatest bloodletting since the end of World War Two. The acceptance of early mortality as well as the presence of rich pickings made it a natural target for predators from outside the country. That will not change. A new rush for Africa is under way as a result of oil. Both China and the US have already started competing for access to the world's last big reserves, outside the Middle East, in Angola, Chad and Nigeria (where, so far, British security guards have been notable for their role as hostages rather than protectors).

In the 1960s, decolonisation was a catalyst for freelance soldiering in the scramble for diamonds and copper in Katanga, where child labour is still employed, in medieval conditions, in opencast mines. Over the next three decades, the Cold War was fought on African soil by superpower surrogates, including British mercenaries.

In 1998, the intervention of Executive Outcomes and Tim Spicer's Sandline was decisive in ending the butchery of a civil war in Sierra Leone. As a result of the chagrin of Whitehall and the UN, it also marked a turning point in official thinking about the use of private military and security companies. But for the most part, foreign mercenaries in Africa, black and brown as well as white, have assumed a colonialist mentality, claiming a licence to overturn legitimate governments as well as to kill. Modern PMCs assert that they work *with* governments, not to bring them down, which is why they reject any comparisons with the Wild Geese, whether it be those who fled Ireland with Patrick Sarsfield in 1691 or the mercenaries serving in the Congo in 1961.

The Sierra Leone Affair triggered a series of parliamentary and other inquiries that changed perceptions hitherto clouded by the word *mercenary*. So far, the logic of the various reports – that there is a legitimate role for private companies in international security – has gone unheeded by the UK government and the UN. But, as Darfur should remind us, the problem of Africa will not go away. And, short of some form of regulation, 'les Affreux' – 'the Horrors', the psychos of Katanga, 1960–4, Angola, 1976, and Equatorial Guinea, 2004 – will continue to sink their teeth into the carcase of Africa.

Black Africa has not been a passive victim of this process. During the bush wars preceding the liberation of South Africa from apartheid, a Special Forces group known as 32 (Buffalo) Battalion, 'the Terrible Ones', was built from the survivors of the right-wing FNLA (the National Liberation Front for Angola) defeat in Angola. In 1976 these losers – having fought for the same cause as 'Colonel' Callan's British mercenaries – retreated to exile in South Africa, where they were reformed into a force that attacked behind enemy lines. They became a black SAS, serving a white master, led by whites from Britain, Rhodesia, the United States and South Africa.

When the African National Congress came to power in 1994, following a prolonged guerrilla war, the new regime was saddled with the remnants of 32 Battalion. The new government disbanded the unit in 1992 and dumped the survivors with their families in Pomfret, a remote, barren settlement built around an asbestos mine on the edge of the Kalahari

Desert. Yesterday's heroes, speaking Portuguese, were largely ignored by the DDRR (disarmament, demobilisation, reintegration, rehabilitation) programme to resettle other veterans. Left to their own devices, they became mercenaries, working for mining companies in the Congo and elsewhere.

In March 2004, the notorious 'Wonga' coup plot aimed at Equatorial Guinea ended ignominiously in Zimbabwe, when Simon Mann and 60 of his mercenaries were arrested, and in Equatorial Guinea, where the alleged coup leader Nick du Toit was also detained with at least fourteen other foreigners. Most of the rank-and-file in both groups were veterans of 32 Battalion, still living in the time warp of Pomfret.

The South African government already had a law – the Regulation of Foreign Military Assistance Act – passed in 1998 in response to the activities of Executive Outcomes (another concern in which Simon Mann was involved) in Angola and Sierra Leone. The impact of the Wonga Plot on the image of South Africa elsewhere in Black Africa was damaging. Pretoria tightened its anti-mercenary law even further, without any visible improvement. The South African government also began a process of draining Pomfret of basic resources such as medical facilities, in an effort to disperse the settlement's lost legion.

To some outsiders it seemed that these internal sanctions were an exercise in revenge. As the BBC's Southern Africa correspondent Barnaby Phillips remarked, having visited the place, 'The families in Pomfret will tell you that these alleged mercenaries are also victims of South Africa's ugly past.'[1]

A similarly vengeful spirit pursued Simon Mann personally. As he completed his sentence for illegal possession of arms in Zimbabwe, he was secretly deported to Equatorial Guinea in February 2008, accused of plotting to overthrow that country's President Teodoro Nguema. Mann still claimed that there was no plot, only a contract to guard a gold mine in the Democratic Republic of Congo. He claimed, 'If I go [to Equatorial Guinea] consider me dead.'

2

CONGO, 1960–1:

The unquiet spirit of Patrice Lumumba

Of the millions of victims of violence in Africa, one still has a face and a presence that refuse to be obliterated by the bullets, bayonets, the shallow grave and the subsequent acid bath that was meant to erase his existence. Patrice Emery Lumumba, the only democratically elected prime minister of the Congo, was murdered on 17 January 1961 by fellow Africans manipulated by the CIA, which feared his emerging links to Soviet Russia and the Belgian government, which wanted the country's diamonds, uranium, copper and cobalt. During the four years that followed, the country had four prime ministers, four civil wars and two constitutions. It has been a killing ground ever since, and a profitable playground for every sort of mercenary.

More than 40 years later, the Belgian government finally admitted, 'Certain members of the Belgian government and other Belgian participants were morally responsible for the circumstances leading to the death of Lumumba.'[1] In July 2002, a former staff director of the US House of Representatives subcommittee on Africa, Dr Stephen R. Weissman, published official documents to

show that the key Congolese leaders who brought about Lumumba's downfall were players in 'Project Wizard,' a CIA covert action program. Hundreds of thousands of dollars and military equipment were channeled to these officials, who informed their CIA paymasters three days in advance of their plan to send Lumumba into the clutches of his worst enemies . . . The plans and payments were approved by the highest levels of the Eisenhower administration . . .

Unlike Belgium, the United States has admitted no such moral responsibility . . . The full story remained hidden in US documents which, like those I have examined, are still classified despite the end of the Cold War, the end of the Mobutu regime and Belgium's confession.[2]

One American, however, did break ranks. John Stockwell, the son of an engineer working for a Presbyterian mission in the former Belgian Congo, spent his formative years in that country. He later became a CIA case officer, in charge of the Angola Task Force and subsequently confirmed the Agency's role in the assassination.[3]

Lumumba, like Gamel Abdel Nasser of Egypt and Mohammed Mossadeq of Iran, was a visionary not to the taste of the West. For want of something better, he turned to Soviet Russia for aid. In the eyes of the West he demonised himself further by writing verses that rehearsed the griefs of slavery and the wickedness of American plantations. At home, his political power lay in his rejection of tribalism in favour of a national, and anti-Western ideal. As one admirer put it, 'Lumumba was the only Congolese leader who rose above ethnic difficulties and tribal preoccupations that killed all the other parties.'[4] In that sense, he anticipated the statesmanship of Nelson Mandela.

Lumumba survived as Prime Minister just 67 days before he was dismissed by Washington's client President Kasavubu. Fleeing house arrest, he was captured and, on orders from Brussels, handed over to his enemies in the breakaway province of Katanga, an area rich in copper, then still effectively controlled by Belgian mining interests. The UN ignored his pleas for help, though he had invoked the UN in the first place. An Indian officer serving with the UN peacekeeping force in the Congo, Major General Indar Jit Rikye, was a witness to Lumumba's Calvary.[5]

'He was chained in the back of a truck. He was bleeding. His hair was dishevelled. He'd lost his glasses. We could not intervene . . .' – on orders from the Secretary-General, apparently. Once in Katanga, Lumumba was taken into the bush and shot dead. He was aged 36.

A CIA plot to murder Lumumba was overtaken by events but the Agency was close enough to the action for one of its officers to drive around the town of Lubumbashi, after curfew, with Lumumba's body in the boot of the car, 'trying', as Stockwell reveals, 'to decide what to do with it'. The man finally disposing of his body was a Belgian policeman. He later said, 'We did things an animal would not do. We were drunk. Stone drunk.'

The matrix of circumstances that brought about Lumumba's downfall – Cold War politics, neocolonial greed, tribalism – acted as a catalyst for the reintroduction into African life of white mercenaries. It was arranged by an African Machiavelli, Moise Tshombe. The pro-American, anti-communist son of a successful entrepreneur, Tshombe arranged for both Belgian and French military delegations to assist the secession of his province, Katanga, from the infant state of Congo. Two weeks after independence in 1960, while still in office, Lumumba had persuaded the UN to dispatch a peacekeeping force with the intention of bringing Tshombe to heel.

As the political situation went into meltdown with Lumumba's murder, regular Belgian and French forces were replaced by mercenaries, some of them members of the official delegations. The wily Tshombe, known as 'Mr Cashbox', privately promised full support to each group, without telling the other. Within a few years Tshombe would be betrayed in turn by his French allies, but not before his mercenaries, led by Roger Faulques, had killed 1,000 UN troops when they attempted to end his secession.

Faulques, Robert Denard, Jean Schramme and many other warriors who turned up in Africa and elsewhere were part of a lost generation. Faulques and his Foreign Legion comrades had been thrown into an unwinnable war in Indo-China. Some were former members of the defeated, disbanded Wehrmacht. After the agony of Dien Bien Phu, Faulques was one of those in the Foreign Legion who were promised, by Paris, a new beginning, in his case in Algeria. So he and his comrades fought another war in defence of the political lie that Algeria was an indissoluble part of mainland France. Betrayed by Charles de Gaulle's grant of independence to Algeria, much of the French army there, led by the 1st Regiment of Foreign Legion Parachutists, mutinied in April 1961, even as the Congo was disintegrating. *Le Premier Régiment Etranger des Parachutistes* (or '*Le Premier REP*') was disgraced and disbanded.

The survivors who made their way to Katanga were not in the business of war for money, but for reputation and, in an incoherent way, revenge. As one of them later said, 'When I arrived in Katanga on Sunday evening in the spring of 1962, I had 51 New Francs – less than the price of a whisky – in my pocket. A few months later when I left, I had 100 New Francs. The rest I gave to the families of my soldiers killed by the United Nations . . . Money, offered as the sole reason for signing up [for mercenary service], is a ridiculous attempt to defame and diminish us in the eyes of public opinion.'[6]

In January 1961 Tshombe wrote to Roger Trinquier, former commander of French special forces in Indo-China, selling the defence of Katanga as a crusade against communist domination of central Africa. He offered Trinquier command of his army. Trinquier reported the approach to the Army Minister, Pierre Messmer, himself a Foreign Legion veteran, as well as to Prime Minister Michel Debré and Jacques Foccart, the sinister Minister for Africa. All gave him covert clearance to go ahead. Like the British involvement in Yemen, this operation was never approved by the French government as a whole but by a junta within it. Trinquier went to Katanga and prepared plans for a new, modern army.

Things did not go to plan. A participant recalled that after the murder of Lumumba – who was given martyr status among the French intelligentsia – direct French intervention in Katanga became politically impossible. But, soon after, an anonymous, but senior member of the emerging mercenary group that would call itself 'Les Katangais', found himself in Trinquier's office in Rue Cambon, in central Paris, where, also, was Major Roger Faulques, freshly discharged from the Premier REP.

Trinquier, putting down the telephone, announced triumphantly, 'There it is. I have the agreement of Monsieur Messmer.'

A few days later, on 26 February, Trinquier, Faulques and two other para officers identified as 'Y de L' (a former intelligence officer with the Maquis – the resistance movement – in occupied Brittany) and 'LE' (parachuted into Occupied France by the Free French) travelled by train to Rome, from where they flew to Salisbury.

Meanwhile, Tshombe planted small advertisements in local newspapers from Brussels to Johannesburg, by way of Salisbury, inviting volunteers with military experience to sign up for interesting work in Africa. Between July 1960 and 13 September 1961, in ones and twos, the volunteers trickled into Katanga. The French veteran Tony de Saint-Paul – later to die in the Yemen civil war – was one of the first to arrive.

There were some courageous Belgians, the eyewitness recalled: 'Van de Wale, Crevecoeur, Jansens, Lamouline, Bocquillon, Jacques Dufrasne. The last two – what a paradox! – were veterans of the Belgian battalion with the UN in Korea. There were also a few Germans, Italians, South Africans and some Rhodesians.' And there were two airmen, one a former RAF pilot, strafing the UN from an old Fouga aircraft. Later, Jan Zmbach, a Polish veteran of the Battle of Britain, would run a Katangan Air Force of 10 Harvard T-6 bombers and two Vampire jets.

The war between Tshombe's forces and the United Nations began like a slow chess opening. In 1960, Tshombe had reluctantly allowed a small force to enter his province, so long as it did not intervene in local events, which explains how the UN soldiers became spectators of Lumumba's downfall. They were present to ensure the withdrawal of Belgian troops who had been sent to protect their fellow countrymen. But in August 1961, as the Congo disintegrated, 5,000 Blue Helmets attempted a round-up of all foreign mercenaries. The foreigners were, at that stage, far from being a destabilising influence to match the bloodthirsty image of 'les Affreux'. Some had imported their wives to live with them in comfortable villas in the capital, Elizabethville.

The head of the UN Mission, the Irish diplomat Conor Cruise O'Brien, announced that, during Operation Rumpunch, his men had lifted and deported 273 non-Congolese soldiers. Of these, 55 were Belgians, four British, one Pole, one Hungarian, one Dane, two Portuguese, one Swede, eight Italian, one South African, one New Zealander, four Dutch, 11 French and five 'others'. 'Katanga's secession is ended!' he proclaimed. Out in the bush, Faulques and around 30 other serious freelance soldiers were leading their own teams of Katangan gendarmes.

At 4 a.m. on 13 September, Indian and Gurkha troops under the command of General Rikhye attacked the post office in Elizabethville, held by a handful of Katangans and mercenaries. A French survivor of the operation alleged that 'the Indians and Gurkhas threw wounded men from the roof, a height of 60 feet'.[7]

There were also alleged atrocities in a similar assault on the central radio station. It was the beginning of a week-long urban battle in which the remaining mercenaries used guerrilla tactics against inexperienced Irish, Swedish, Malay and Danish soldiers who did not know the neighbourhood. As one mercenary put it, 'We knew the town like our own homes. The locals were on our side. To borrow a Marxist phrase, we were the fish swimming in a sea of Katangans ... crossing the gardens and villas with the complicity of the owners, to throw grenades or hit convoys with bazookas.'

Any UN soldier who wandered too far from his own was likely to be kidnapped and murdered by Katangans. An Indian major 'ended his career on the front bumper of a vehicle driven into stones'. At night, Katangan tom-toms sent messages of doom to the Blue Helmets.

About 100 miles from Elizabethville, 150 men of 'A' Company of the Irish army's 35th Battalion were sent to Jadotville, to protect Belgian nationals. It was a fatal misreading of the local situation. As most of the Irish troops attended Sunday mass, a superior force of Katangans, Belgians and mercenaries attacked their headquarters. The Irish commanding officer, Commandant Quinlan, had made sure that his perimeter was defended by World War One vintage Vickers machine guns dug into slit trenches.

In the four-day battle that followed, an estimated 300 Katangans were killed. In spite of their inexperience, no Irishmen were killed. UN efforts to lift the siege at Jadotville were blocked by strafing from the Katangan Fouga, flown by a former RAF, Belgian-born pilot, at a bridge. Next, the mercenaries cut the beleaguered garrison's water supply. A helicopter flew in some water, which proved to be contaminated. The men of 'A' Company had fought honourably but what registered on the public consciousness was the public surrender, negotiated by Quinlan as the alternative to an impending massacre as his men ran out of ammunition as well as water. Unfairly, the odour of surrender – accepted by the French mercenary Michel de Clary – clung to the Irish soldiers in their own homeland until 2005, when a commemorative plaque was unveiled at Custume Army Barracks, Athlone.

The public relations disaster of Jadotville was compounded a day or so later, on 18 September, when an aircraft carrying the UN Secretary-General, Dag Hammarskjoeld, crashed in Rhodesia. Hammarskjoeld, a Swede, was on his way to meet Tshombe to negotiate a ceasefire. The only survivor of the crash, an American security guard, said that Hammarskjoeld had changed his mind about landing at the last moment and ordered the pilot to alter course. There was an explosion on board the plane soon afterwards.

By now, a number of Western governments, including Britain's, were expressing unease about the UN offensive. Conor Cruise O'Brien and the UN military commander, fellow Irishman General Sean McKeowan, were recalled by Hammarskjoeld's successor, U Thant.

O'Brien was 'released' from UN service as he prepared to set off from New York for his next visit to Katanga on 1 December. He blamed the

British government. During the two months since he had launched the Elizabethville offensive, an uneasy truce had stuck together. It was not to last, if only because the stalemate that followed the failure of Operation Rumpunch was a political victory for Tshombe and the mercenaries.

From 5 to 19 December UN aircraft, including four Canberra bombers of the Indian Air Force, bombed and strafed Katanga's main centres, having first eliminated Tshombe's tiny air force at Kolwezi. In the battle for Elizabethville that followed, Faulques' men employed the same guerrilla tactics as had succeeded nine months earlier, but they were totally outgunned and outnumbered by an Indian army brigade. Faulques himself, dressed in casual civilian clothes and shiny city shoes, smoking a cigarette, and carrying no visible firearm, was photographed emerging from a hedge to hurl a grenade at the Irish headquarters. The surprise was that the mercenaries held out for so long. Denard, in particular, used mortars and mobility to inflict heavy casualties on the Indians.

The UN victory was apparently sealed when Tshombe agreed to the reintegration of his province into the vast Congo Republic, a country larger than Western Europe, inhabited by hundreds of tribes owing little to one another. It took another offensive, a year later, to make the agreement stick. By then, Denard was in command of the mercenaries. He and the remaining 30 or so diehards retreated to Angola, following Faulques's departure there. They were not finished with Africa yet. They had also created a legend, for good or ill, of 'les Affreux' and 'les Katangais'.

3

CONGO 1964–7:

The myth of the white giant

In 1964, just a year after he had surrendered to a UN force of 20,000, Tshombe was lured from exile in Europe with a poisoned gift: premiership of the whole of the Congo under the presidency of his rival Kasavubu. The reason was that the country had disintegrated. An unpaid army had mutinied. An alternative 'army' – teenage youths armed by China and persuaded that they were immune to incoming gunfire – had occupied most of the main towns. Drunk on alcohol, drugs and testosterone, they played out a theatre of sadism wherever they took control. Cannibalism solved the food problem for the young lions (the 'Simba') as well as stray dogs. The dogs wore their own skins. The Simba dressed in monkey skins and feathers. Edward Behr, a veteran war correspondent, summed up what was happening with the barbaric name for a book he entitled, *Anyone Here Been Raped and Speaks English?*.

Tshombe landed back in the Congo as the UN was pulling out. He had been chosen because the West could not think of an alternative. Certainly it was not the UN. As the Blue Helmets departed, 3,000 Europeans became hostages of the Simba. Tshombe, as it happened, had prepared secretly for a comeback. He was in touch with an Irish veteran of the British army, Major Mike Hoare, who now lived in South Africa, running a safari company.

Hoare and his deputy Alistair Wicks, an Old Harrovian living in Salisbury, advertised for 'fit young men' interested in six-month contracts for

£100 a month. Many of the volunteers who responded, in a long tradition of the mercenary world, were misfits and alcoholics. The best of a poor bunch were 38 Germans from Namibia, a former German colony. Some of these promptly dropped out when they discovered that they were going into action immediately.

Hoare's first operation, across a lake in motor boats whose engines failed, was an inauspicious beginning. Things improved at Kamina, a vast air base in Katanga, where he drilled and disciplined volunteers who had not been weeded out. He acquired some useful NCOs, notably John Peters, from Yorkshire, a former SAS soldier with a contempt for la-di-dah English officers.

Like many successful mercenaries, Peters was a natural guerrilla. Most of the men of Hoare's emerging 5 Commando did not care to move by night, or off the road, without their jeeps. They depended on speed and surprise in daylight attacks on rebel villages.

For one attack, however, a night manoeuvre was necessary if the Simba supply line from neighbouring Sudan was to be cut before an enemy column could dig in on the banks of the strategic Nzoro River. Hoare recalls, 'I sent for John Peters. I explained the tactical position and affirmed that I would never give the order for our columns to move at night . . . but if he could find volunteers it would be a valuable night's work.

'Without so much as a second thought he decided to take the whole of Force John-John [Peters's elite combat group of 100 men] at once . . . Twenty minutes later the whole sky was lit up with a gigantic fireworks display. Force John-John had met the enemy column in the act of trundling on to the bridge. A lucky shot from Peters's jeep hit an ammunition truck and blew it sky high.

'The battle lasted ten minutes at the end of which Force John-John had met the enemy column and captured eleven trucks and mountains of arms and ammunition.'[1]

Hoare's Commando was romanticised as 'the Wild Geese' in the Anglo-Saxon world because of its English culture, not only in its use of the language for operational purposes, but also its emphasis on discipline. Hoare was an idealist who sought a higher purpose in his work. Its 300 men were split into troops averaging 30, commanded by two officers. Each troop operated independently, sometimes over vast distances. The Commando was also used as the spearhead of a reformed Congolese National Army, 'advised' by Belgian regulars and mercenaries. And like some later enterprises such as Executive Outcomes and Sandline in Angola and Sierra Leone, it saved lives as well as taking them, filling a power vacuum beyond the reach of the UN or local governments.

The author Anthony Mockler, in his extensive work *The New Mercenaries*, noted,

> Five Commando was almost certainly more successful in the circumstances than a similar British regiment would have been; for regular armies are tied down by rules, traditions and handbooks, and the mercenaries were freer to experiment. One unit of Five Commando used a repentant Simba who would dress up as a woman and scout forward whenever they suspected an ambush, and certain part of the mercenaries' superiority was due to this sort of ability to improvise.[2]

In another surprise operation, in December 1964, 5 Commando was on its way to relieve a small missionary town named Poko, in Upper Congo. The Simba set an ambush on the only approach road. The mercenaries got wind of what was happening and hacked a route through the bush to enter the town from the rear. There, a surprise awaited them. The Simba turned, waved and shouted their ritual war cry, 'Mai Mulele!' ('Sacred Water of Mulele'). It appeared that the Simba believed that the white faces coming from the north must be Russian allies, the same who were supplying their weapons. As one contemporary report has it, 'The Simbas' disappointment was short-lived: the mercenaries gunned them down to a man.'[3]

The role played by 5 Commando and other mercenaries in rescuing hostages – particularly Europeans – from the Simba made headlines at home and made the mercenaries, for a short time, popular heroes. At Bafwasende, Hoare's men again attacked from the bush and shot a Simba captain carrying written orders to murder all the white prisoners. Those included eleven Italian nuns and three British female missionaries. Eight Dutch priests and six Britons were dead. So, too, was 16-year-old Heather Arton, who had come to Congo to join her British parents for the school holiday. A Simba chieftain used her as his slave. When her parents were forced to join a death march, the chieftain offered the girl his protection. Her answer was to break away from him and join her parents in their fatal trek.

The Simba war lasted around two years, through most of 1964–5. Hoare's soldiers arrived in the national capital, Leopoldville, in August 1964. In a surprise attack less than a month later, one of 5 Commando's subunits was the cutting edge of the liberation of Albertville, on the shores of Lake Tanganyika, a port and logistical treasure used by the Simba to import arms from their headquarters in Burundi. The offensive was given teeth by B-26 fighter bombers flown by anti-Castro Cubans, recruited by the CIA. They pulverised enemy strong points. Regular Congolese troops, led by white officers, hit the city from north and south, in two columns. The mercenary vanguard, faced with young warriors convinced that their leaders' magic rendered them fireproof, turned the streets into an abattoir. Then they attacked each shack in turn with machine-gun fire, followed by grenades, and then torched it. After eight hours, the Simba retreated, leaving 450 dead. Tshombe's stock rose. So did that of army General Sese Seke Mobutu.

After the battle, one eyewitness saw a German volunteer, dead drunk, wave bundles of banknotes beneath the nose of Mobutu, demanding that he should be able to open a bank account in the capital. Mobutu was unimpressed. 'These whites are a rabble,' he commented.

The odour of victory was contagious. A journalist representing a Paris magazine, who happened to be a reserve army officer in France, 'exchanged his Leica for an FAL (Belgian automatic rifle) with a degree of success. "This was carnage," he wrote.'[4]

More successes followed. 'The mercenaries', *Time* reported, 'were organised into small units and sent to shore up besieged garrisons and to lead – and often plan – attacks on strategic rebel towns.' A mechanised brigade of 2,000 men led by a Belgian colonel and 250 mercenaries advanced north, covering 250 miles in four days. By now, the no-longer-immortal Simba were retreating before a shot was fired.

Their stronghold was the town of Stanleyville (named after the explorer Henry Morton Stanley) in Orientale Province, bordering Sudan. There, 'rebel savages, hopped up by dope and voodoo spells, pillaged the city . . . From the surrounding countryside came tales of kangaroo courts that forced their victims to swallow gasoline, then sliced them open and ignited them.'

The Simba leader, Christophe Gbenye, held 60 American and 800 Belgian hostages. On 9 November he announced that harm would come to them if Tshombe continued to receive help from both countries. Washington and Brussels secretly prepared their riposte, involving dense military planning by Joint Chiefs of Staff. On 24 November, in Operation Red Dragon, a battalion of Belgian paras, flown from Europe by way of

Ascension Island by 14 American C-130s, dropped on the Stanleyville airfield and an adjoining golf course. The first wave – 320 men – cleared the runway of obstacles within 32 minutes.[5] The Belgian commander, Colonel C. Laurent, helped his men to push a heavy truck off the runway. A lance corporal in charge gave the order, 'The next time I count three, push.' The colonel pushed.

The Simbas meanwhile marched 250 European civilians into Avenue Sergent Kitele, adjoining Lumumba Square, and ordered them to sit. Then they massacred them, firing at point-blank range. Across the River Congo, another 28 hostages 'were hacked to pieces on the street . . . Four Spanish nuns and a number of Spanish and Dutch priests . . . The usual mutilations were carried out . . . and flesh was cut from the bodies to be eaten.'[6]

At the airport, while Belgian troops were occupying a guest house, a paratroop captain answered a ringing telephone. He heard a voice urging rebel leaders at the airfield to hurry to the Victoria Hotel in the centre of the town, where the hostages were being held. The paras immediately swept into the town, where they were halted briefly by machine-gun and small-arms fire. This skirmish ended when the arrival of Belgian armoured jeeps spread panic among the Simba.

A US army analysis reported, 'One block from the Victoria Hotel, the Belgian troops heard scattered shooting. As they came into view of the hotel, they saw 400 to 600 civilians huddled together in the square. A minute before, a rebel officer had ordered them gunned down . . . killing twenty-eight hostages including one American, Dr Carson.' Carson, a revered medical missionary, was the hostage the US most wanted to rescue, alive.

Of 2,000 whites in Stanleyville, all but 60 were saved. Four hours later, the mechanised brigade, led by Hoare's commando, drove into Stanleyville in good order. However, as *Time* noted,

> Some of these white soldiers lived up to the name by which they are universally known – mercenaries. They were not above searching bodies for cash or blowing a few safes in the Stanleyville banks. But a great many of them are fighting for Tshombe's government out of conviction.

Gbenye and his courtiers had already departed, carrying away 680 kilos (1,500 pounds) of gold from local mines, and $6 million from the Congo Bank. In the rebels' barracks, the mercenaries hunted down surviving Simba and killed them.

Stanleyville was not the only scene of such horrors. At Paulis, 225 miles north-east of Stanleyville two days later, the second parachute operation ('Dragon Noire') rescued another 355 people, but not before Simbas had tortured to death missionaries they had imprisoned for three weeks. Elsewhere, the combined force of Congolese army and Hoare's mercenaries saved 600. The Belgian paras lost two dead and 11 men wounded. All the survivors had horror stories to tell the world. Yet, too promptly, the Belgian para-commandos were withdrawn.

A declassified US army analysis explains why. 'The overall objective in public information would be to minimize visibility of the operation as much as possible and to limit the picture of the United States' role. Every effort would be made to avoid contacts between the participating US military personnel and the press.' In spite of that,

> the New York Times, in a story datelined 20 November at Brussels – announced the presence of US planes and Belgian paratroopers on Ascension and stated that they were so located in order to be readily available to go to the aid of white hostages being held by rebels in the Congo.
>
> Secretary General U Thant of the United Nations immediately announced that any movement of Belgian paratroopers to Ascension by US aircraft might be a cause for Security Council action . . . On 23 November the New York Times followed up with a story from Leopoldville announcing that an airdrop of Belgian forces into the Congo was believed to be near . . . On the following day another story from Leopoldville told about Belgian paratroopers having been ferried from Ascension to the Congo.

Such reports were useful early warning for both the Simba and the hostages' political enemies in the communist and 'non-aligned' bloc. There were other diplomatic complications. 'During the early afternoon of 22 November the task force was visited by Belgian military and civilian representatives' as part of a combined operation with the mechanised column spearheaded by mercenaries.

> Before leaving Belgium [said the US army document] Colonel Laurent [the paras' CO] had been told that the combined US/Belgian operation was to have no connection with the operations of the Congolese Army forces, but his later discussion with Colonel van de Walle [commanding the Congolese mechanized column] convinced him that mutual advantages could result

from a co-ordinated movement on Stanleyville. Obviously, Congolese Army assistance in the search operations to discover where the hostages were being held would be useful.

The document made no reference to Hoare, or the French-speaking 6 Commando also under Van der Walle's command. Yet there is little doubt that there was, in effect, some degree of collusion between the mercenaries and the joint US/Belgian task force. American planners had suggested a third Dragon operation – White Dragon – to rescue hostages at Bunia, a mining town 400 miles east of Stanleyville. 'Apparently the Belgian commander considered that only one additional operation was within the capabilities of his force,' the US army analysis reveals. So it was left to Hoare's team to save 76 survivors of atrocities whose victims were, as usual, male and female missionaries.

Gallant and effective though it was in the short-term, the intervention of the US/Belgian task force was no more than a short-term sticking plaster so long as the porous border between northern Congo and the Sudan remained open. In one direction it was the Simbas' supply route. In another, it was the Simbas' safe haven. In the spring of 1965, Hoare was still trying to plug the gap with 270 freshly recruited mercenaries from South Africa, Rhodesia and Britain, supported by 750 Congolese commandos.

In April, Simbas armed with modern automatic weapons counter-attacked Paulis, scene of Operation Black Dragon. A total of 28 fighter bombers flown by Cuban mercenaries was needed to bring rockets to bear to dislodge them. The endgame was near. Before the month was out, Hoare had taken Watsa, the last rebel stronghold. The enemy left their weapons and vanished into the rainforest. He had been expected to clear the area within nine weeks. The last offensive had taken just three.

Hoare resigned happily in December 1965, claiming with some justice that his men had saved nearly 1,800 European hostages, defeating the Simba rebellion and heading off a communist takeover of the Congo. They had also looted abandoned Belgian homes on an impressive scale. Hoare was succeeded by the Yorkshireman John Peters, but, with the end of the Simba War, there was little fighting left for fighting men.

Tshombe departed in circumstances less happy than Hoare's. The Congo President Kasavubu sacked him, announcing, 'The mission I conferred upon him in 1964 has been completed. Therefore, out of the habitual rules of democracy and since his government has not resigned on its own initiative' – following a recent election almost certainly won by

Tshombe – 'I have today put an end to its functions.' Once again, Tshombe was in polished exile, in Madrid.

Less than a month later General Mobutu, following Africa's habitual rules of democracy, mounted a successful *coup d'état* against Kasavubu, and was installed as the CIA's man in the Congo for many years to come. They were no less bloody than the years that had preceded his rule. Under Mobutu the new mercenary order was intended to exclude anyone with a lingering loyalty to Tshombe. Alongside Peters, Bob Denard, a Frenchman, took command of the Francophone 6 Commando but the plots against Mobutu, and hopes of restoring Tshombe to power, continued.

There was one other, more insidious inheritance of the Congo, handed down like a malevolent gene from one generation of mercenaries in Africa to the next. It was the myth, cultivated by the Simba in their more gloomy moments, of 'the White Giant'. They reasoned that, if their skins were not protected from bullets by the magic of *dawa*, their adversary must have come from another, equally occult dimension.

Many of the mercenaries came to share this believe in the myth of white supremacy, which went beyond the cultural assumptions of apartheid. It might almost be described as 'white-giant syndrome', as a result of which the mercenary knew that all that was required to win the battle was a show of force and a white face, or even the rumour that Europeans were coming. In Katanga, the message was sometimes relayed ahead of the advance, by telephone, to the opposition. The only permitted exceptions to the supremacy rule were black rulers such as the Brussels-educated Tshombe or the more uncouth Mobutu, who enjoyed the power of patronage, preferment and purse string. In Black Africa, the White Giant myth would be one of the most potent reasons for the failures to come, from Angola in 1976 to Equatorial Guinea in 2004.

Tshombe was not to live happily ever after. After he had retired to Europe for a second time, he was lured into a trap in 1967. A French intelligence agent named Francis Bodenan persuaded the African exile that he could profit hugely from a property-development deal in the Mediterranean. Bodenan had entered prison as a rough diamond, serving his term of a twelve-year sentence for his part in a case of murder. He emerged as a highly polished businessman with sufficient funds to hire a British executive jet. He was a credit to the French penal system. Once Tshombe was on board and out of Spanish airspace, Bodenan pulled a gun from his jacket and ordered the two British pilots to fly to Algiers. There, everyone on board was arrested. The pilots and Bodenan were released after a decent interval. Tshombe died in captivity, allegedly of natural causes, two years later.

His kidnap triggered a mutiny by 200 French-led mercenaries, ostensibly loyal to Mobutu, in eastern Congo. Within a few hours, another 200 mercenaries flew into the country from Angola. In the border city of Bukavu, the veteran Belgian mercenary Schramme led remnants of Tshombe's old Katanga gendarmerie in attacks on a local army garrison. After several days' fighting, a curfew on all Europeans and what one report described as 'grisly retaliations against the remaining whites by Mobutu's troops . . . a planeload of bruised and battered mercenaries landed in Rhodesia'.

Like much else surrounding Tshombe, from the deaths of Lumumba and Hammarskjoeld to his own end, mysteries remain that will be for ever, almost certainly, beyond solution. Had Tshombe met Denard a few months before he was hijacked? Was he planning a second return to Katanga? Was his return the key to the mercenaries' revolt against Mobutu?

Would the CIA want to counter such a move? Tshombe, one might suppose, was a natural ally of America, but he suffered from a fatal disability. He was too intelligent and sophisticated, a capitalist with a network of European connections. Mobutu, a natural assassin in the mould of Saddam Hussein (like Saddam, he occasionally hanged publicly political opponents, *pour encourager les autres*), was a more reliable ally in the Cold War and even, in the eyes of the International Monetary Fund, a better bet in spite of his kleptomaniac approach to state funds. When it suited the CIA to support Tshombe, it did so, but only so long as he was no threat to their nominee Mobutu.

There are good reasons not to attribute Tshombe's abduction to the CIA. First, Bodenan had no history of dealing with the Agency. Second, Algiers was not an ally of America.

So why would those who engineered the kidnap choose Algiers as a safe haven for one who was still, potentially, the most dangerous man in Africa? The most plausible explanation is that, faced with America's increasing grip on Central Africa, elements within Paris – possibly in the office of Foccart – wanted Tshombe on tap, a political asset-in-waiting, should the chance come to destabilise the Congo yet again. Mobutu expected the Algerians to extradite Tshombe to face a death sentence. The Algerians did nothing, possibly under French pressure, for two years until Tshombe achieved his own endgame, dying in his sleep.

4

ANGOLA 1974–2002:

A war for slow readers

In the spring of 1975 the CIA was licking its wounds following America's panic retreat from Vietnam. The Agency's native spies in Vietnam had been dumped and compromised by abandoned, unshredded files as their breathless, round-eyed case officers stampeded aboard the last aircraft out of the country. It was not the best time to plot another secret war, yet that is exactly what the CIA, pressured by Henry Kissinger, Secretary of State, and boss of the National Security Council, proposed. The chosen battleground was Angola, a country rich in slaves, oil, diamonds, gold, uranium and iron on which Portuguese colonisers had grown fat for 500 years. As the Portuguese pulled out after a 15-year war of independence fought by three tribal armies later rebranded as political factions, the CIA spotted a vacuum into which, just possibly, the Soviets might move.

Although some grown-up diplomats in the State Department believed that there was no need for more violence, the norms of the Cold War decreed that it was time for a pre-emptive strike (just as, in 2003, Iraq would have to be occupied by force before it was 'too late'). Since this was the Cold War, however, the US could not be seen to be publicly engaged. The Angolan conflict, like hundreds of others beyond the northern hemisphere, was to be fought by local surrogates or deniable operators – including mercenaries.

It was one of many. When the Church Committee (a Senate committee set up to study government intelligence-gathering operations) ran its enquiry into the CIA in 1975, it discovered that the Agency had run 900 major and 3,000 minor operations during the preceding 14 years, responsible for tens of thousands of deaths.

Angola was just another distant battleground, a faraway country of which Uncle Sam knew but little. So the CIA's geopolitical briefing was carefully crafted for slow readers. When Bill Colby, the CIA director, explained how things were to the National Security Council in the White House, he said, 'Gentlemen, this is a map of Africa and here is Angola. Now in Angola we have three factions. There's the MPLA. They're the bad guys. The FNLA, they're the good guys and there's UNITA and Jonas Savimbi we don't know too well.'[1]

Ostensibly the three factions were to have awaited formal independence on 11 November before running normal elections. But as John Stockwell, boss of the CIA Angola Task Force, later revealed,

> The United States scotched that absolutely. Our solution was that the CIA, without approval from the National Security Council, delivered $300,000 to Holden Roberto [the FNLA leader] and ordered him to send his people into Northern Angola ... His side was always the bloodiest, the most violent. They went down and promptly killed fifteen MPLA political activists [unarmed teenagers] and from that time on, the fate of Angola was cast, it was written in blood.[2]

The CIA's budget to stoke up a new war in Angola was used to support Jonas Savimbi, leader of UNITA, in the south of the country, as well as Holden Roberto in the north. Over the next few months it would grow to $31.7 million. However, since the Agency denied any direct involvement, deceiving Congress and the American public, this expenditure had to be siphoned away from limited contingency funds. Within a few months the Soviets would take up the challenge and throw $225 million, soon increased to $400 million, at the Angolan civil war.

The CIA, perversely, knew that so long as it could not go public in this conflict, it was unlikely to win. Stockwell, an old Africa hand, his childhood spent in the Congo, advised his masters to do the job properly or not at all. Instead, the Agency's chosen strategy was to 'deny the MPLA' – deemed to be a Soviet client – 'an easy victory'.[3]

From the beginning of this doomed enterprise, Washington's insiders had reason to doubt Roberto's claims to have an army of 30,000. Stockwell went to see for himself. He reported, 'I had trouble counting thirty badly armed, disorganised, rabble kind of troops. He was a cocktail party cowboy who'd spent his whole career politicking in Kinshasa [capital of Zaïre, now the Democratic Republic of the Congo, controlled by his brother-in-law Mobutu]. Roberto knew nothing of military operations or logistics or organisation.'

In Savimbi, 'I found a different kind of revolutionary. He'd spent twenty years inside Angola, leading the guerrilla fighting himself.'

At an early stage, the CIA secretly obtained military help in southern Angola from the white supremacist government of South Africa. South Africa, concerned about the postcolonial domino effect on its northern borders in Rhodesia, Mozambique and, potentially, Namibia, supplied regular troops backed up by modern weapons and armoured cars. They invaded Angola from the south. In response, as one of the MPLA leaders explained, 'We were alone, poorly equipped, poorly trained, poorly armed. We requested help from the Cubans to help us resist that aggression.' Castro's Cuba, ideologically opposed to colonialism, sent 400 military trainers to Angola.

Russia was not consulted. But, as Kissinger read the situation,

We thought with respect to Angola, that if the Soviet Union could intervene at such distances from areas that were far from the traditional Russian security concerns, and when Cuban forces could be introduced into distant trouble spots, and if the West could not find a counter to that, then the whole international system could be destabilized.[4]

This was a curiously naïve analysis, unless we were to believe that power projection was an American prerogative, ring-fenced as if it were a sacred text. The MPLA still held the capital, Luanda, when Angolan Independence Day approached, but a reinvigorated FNLA army backed by elite troops from Zaïre was advancing from the north without serious opposition. At CIA headquarters in Virginia, a celebration party was all set to roll, once confirmation came that Luanda had been 'liberated'. Stockwell's team decorated its office with crêpe paper. Wine and cheese were laid out. As he later wrote,

People came from all over the building, from the Portuguese Task Force, the French Desk and the Special Operations Group to drink to the program's continued success.

Then the Cubans' 122mm rockets ['Stalin Organs', with a 12-mile range which the opposition could not match] began to land in the Quifangondo valley, not like single claps of thunder but in salvos, twenty at a time. The first salvo went long, screaming over the heads of bewildered FNLA soldiers ... The next salvo was short and the little army was bracketed, exposed in an open valley without cover. Soldiers' hearts burst with a clutching terror as they dived to the ground or stood helplessly mesmerized, watching the next salvo land in their midst. And the next. And the next.[5]

As CIA field officers watched aghast from a nearby ridge, around 2,000 missiles rained like English arrows at Agincourt on Roberto's troops as 'they fled in panic, scattering across the valley ... abandoning weapons, vehicles and wounded comrades alike. Survivors would call it Nshila wa Lufu – Death Road.'

Back in Virginia, the CIA abandoned the canapés and went back to war. Cuban intervention was followed by overt Russian aid as Moscow shipped hundreds of tons of arms, tanks and missiles direct to Luanda. The CIA was able to cobble together a few boatloads of its own to supply Savimbi in southern Angola. Stockwell records that, by late November, 'the Soviets had sent seven shiploads to our one, a hundred planeloads to our nine. They had opened their wallets and put real money on the table.' The chosen solution was to employ up to 1,000 mercenaries, but at that point, no more secret funds were available.

Much of this money had simply disappeared into the bottomless vaults of African sponsors, including Mobutu, Zaïre's hard-up dictator, who received $2.75 million, ostensibly as a cutout to supply arms to FNLA and UNITA. Local CIA station chiefs were free to hand out the dollars, which were spent on such military essentials as an ice-making plant (to provide fresh fish for a ruling elite), a fishing boat (a snip at $150,000) and an 8-metre (26-foot) yacht, used for pleasure cruises for friends of the anti-communist crusade. Down to its last $7 million, the Agency went to market to recruit 20 French and 300 Portuguese freelances.

At the insistence of the Paris government, French mercenaries had to be supplied by Bob Denard, in a mirror image of his use as an agent for the British operation in Yemen. He drove a hard bargain, insisting on an advance payment of $350,000 into his offshore bank account before he had recruited a single volunteer. The bill rose rapidly to $500,000. When the soldiers arrived they were trained by the CIA to use SA-7 anti-aircraft missiles. In the event the missiles misfired and the French fled, before their contracts ended, to South Africa. Thirteen Portuguese mercenaries hired at a cost of $1.5 million got only as far as Kinshasa, in neighbouring Zaïre, before they returned to Europe, though an earlier group of white Portuguese Angolans stood their ground.

The FNLA army was now on its last legs but help, of the wrong sort, was at hand.

On 5 October 1975 a former British Parachute Regiment soldier named Nicholas Mervyn Hall, aged 23, recently released from a military prison, read an article about the Angola war in the *Sunday Times Magazine*, written by the paper's Africa correspondent, Martin Meredith. Hall, said his wife Lesley, was 'restless and wanted to become a mercenary soldier'.[6] Hall was a disturbed man. He left school with seven GCE O-level passes and one A level. In 1968, following a breakdown, he spent a month in a mental institution. He joined the army and was posted to Belfast in August, 1970. The city was then a place of Wild West gun fights and explosions. Hall, surprisingly, was integrated into the Intelligence Section of the First Parachute Battalion, an elite fighting unit responsible for the Bloody Sunday massacre at Derry in 1972.

By unexplained means, Hall acquired useful information about an impending 'Protestant backlash'. This was a possible pogrom of Catholics, leading to all-out civil war, following the breakdown of order in Northern Ireland in 1969. At Hall's court martial his counsel, Leslie Kirk QC, said, 'He was able, through people that he met in Belfast, to visit homes and get information which we haven't gone into for obvious reasons.' Towards the end of 1971 Hall 'was getting somewhat disillusioned and depressed. He then met a man who was said to be a weapons buyer for the Ulster Volunteer Force.' The UVF was the not-so-secret Protestant army, matching IRA terror with its own.

On 12 December, Hall stole six 7.62mm rifles and three sub-machine guns from the battalion armoury and sold them to the UVF for £600. 'The price should have been £1,000 but he was short-changed,' said Kirk. Hall then went on the run, frittered the money away and gave himself up on Christmas Eve. Perhaps he believed in Santa Claus.

Kirk said that a psychiatrist's report about Hall indicated that punishment 'would only reinforce Hall's antisocial nature'. Furthermore, the report indicated that, 'if the hearing had been before a civil court, Hall might have been ordered to be detained at Broadmoor', a hospital for psychopaths. Kirk's plea of mitigation was original. 'Ask yourself if these offences could have been committed by a man in his right mind. He thought he was doing something useful in arming people who were anti-IRA. It's a naïve story. The offences were committed in a naïve way, by a naïve person.' He was sentenced to two years in prison and dismissed from the army with disgrace.[7]

In 1975, Hall advertised his services as a freelance soldier in two London newspapers. According to Mrs Hall, those who responded, by an odd coincidence, included some of his old comrades from 1 Para. These were the London Cypriot Costas Georgiou, his cousin Charles Christodolou and Michael Wainhouse. Georgiou and Wainhouse were now ex-soldiers as a result of a robbery they carried out on a Belfast post office, using army weapons. Their haul was £93. They were sentenced to five years in prison. Now reunited, the four men picked up work as a team of builders while they looked for a war.[8] Having read Meredith's piece, Hall chose Angola. His naïve mind saw the conflict as an anticommunist crusade. Others could smell loot including abandoned banks and diamonds.

Meredith, author of the article that alerted Hall, was receiving treatment for bilharzia (a blood infection) at the London Hospital for Tropical Diseases on 9 October 1975 when

> two men walked into my ward to ask some questions about an article of mine which had been published in the *Sunday Times Magazine* on October 5. They were nervous and evasive, but in a roundabout way eventually disclosed that they were former British army paratroopers interested in going to Angola as mercenaries. They did not give their names and I did not ask for them.[9]

Meredith referred them to Denis Herbstein, a South African journalist working for the paper, who had followed the Angola story, 'but I warned them that Denis might not be willing to help'. He then telephoned Herbstein to warn him of the mercenaries' approach. In a statement made seven months later, Meredith said, 'My interest (and Denis's) was purely journalistic: it seemed worthwhile to keep track of the two men if their activities later proved to be of public concern.'

Mrs Hall, in her statement to the *Sunday Times* in May 1976, said that her husband and Georgiou asked Meredith for contacts with the FNLA 'and he told them how to contact its British representative. This would have been in or about October of 1975.' By whatever means, Hall and Georgiou assuredly were directed to the FNLA's representatives in Britain.

The mercenaries were given a loyalty test before being accepted by Holden Roberto. This was an act of war in Soho, London, against the premises of MPLA sympathisers. Hall, after his earlier taste of prison, declined the chance to indulge in arson in central London. But Georgiou accepted and on 6 November he burned out the offices of the Mozambique and Guinea Information Centre at 12 Little Newport Street. Five days later, Angola became an independent state.[10] The capital, Luanda, was controlled by Roberto's enemy, the MPLA.

Exactly how a connection was made between Roberto and Hall's emerging team of British and American fantasists, amateurs, bank robbers, psychopaths, plus a handful of idealists, remains a mystery. According to John Stockwell, commander of the CIA Angola Task Force, the Agency searched the world in the autumn of 1975 'for allies who could provide qualified advisers to put into the conflict, or better yet, regular army units to crush the MPLA . . . We canvassed moderate friends – Brazil, Morocco, South Korea, Belgium, Great Britain, France and even Portugal without success.'

When efforts to persuade the British government to provide regular soldiers failed – the UK was preoccupied with its own war in Ireland as well as commitments in NATO Europe and the Gulf – Uncle Sam tried again. 'Astonishingly, we found that nowhere in the CIA, not even the Special Operations Group, with all its experiences in Southeast Asia, was there a file, reference list or computer run of individuals who might be recruited as "foreign military advisors."' Couldn't London help find some British mercenaries? 'The British refused to help.'

This in itself is surprising, for several reasons. First, it is the only case in living memory where a UK government, including its secret services and its deniable outposts such as KMS, had refused to genuflect to Washington, particularly the CIA, when called upon to assist a military adventure, other than, perhaps, Vietnam. Indeed, some SAS/KMS graduates were already engaged in the dirty war of the Contras to destabilise the leftist government of El Salvador.

Stockwell suggests that Hall was acting as a recruiting sergeant for

Holden Roberto, the FNLA leader, as early as October 1975. By December, the gang of four were in Angola. According to Mrs Hall,

> between early December, 1975, and January, 1976, the four men travelled to Angola. They were offered various farming and mineral concessions in lieu of a fixed salary, concessions which depended on an FNLA victor. Within a week Mervyn was commissioned by Holden Roberto . . . to return to the UK to recruit mercenary soldiers. My husband promised Roberto that within ten days, twenty-five British volunteers would be provided.

Georgiou, enjoying a godlike power over anyone within shooting distance, renamed himself 'Colonel Callan', after a fictional secret agent then popular on British television, and stayed in the field. Hall, meanwhile, returned to Britain within days to find more mercenaries.

An investigation by Linda Melvern and Stephen Clackson published by the London *Evening Standard* on 29 July 1976, says,

> Hall now claims that when he returned to Britain to recruit a mercenary force, he was given a contact name at the American Embassy. He asked this contact for more money and was refused . . . Hall's claims are born out to a degree. He did go to the American Embassy on 3 January at 3 p.m. He spent more than an hour in the Political Section on the second floor.
>
> According to Embassy information, he presented a letter of accreditation in French signed by the FNLA 'President' Holden Roberto. Then, according to Embassy sources, he hinted at getting more money from them because now he was able to get at least twenty instead of ten specialists. He claimed the original money had come from the CIA, or so Roberto had said.
>
> The Embassy did not dismiss him out of hand. According to them, they were keenly interested in events in Angola and because of frequent references by Hall to CIA men in Kinshasa, felt the need to contact their Embassy there. They received a blistering reply by cable from Kinshasa to the effect of 'Have nothing to do with this man . . .' The Americans then tipped off their 'British counterparts'.

Hall's boast to the Americans was without foundation. He travelled initially to see a contact in Edinburgh. Lesley Hall went with him. It was fruitless. On the way back to London, 'Mervyn said to me that he had decided to make contact with Martin Meredith of the *Sunday Times*. He had only a short time within which to recruit his twenty-five volunteers and he was desperate.'

The soap opera gets personal

Until my uninvited visitor arrived, the only remarkable thing about Wednesday, 14 January 1976, was that it was the day after my 44th birthday and I was hunkered down at my desk in the *Sunday Times* newsroom nursing a hangover.

'Are you Tony Geraghty?'

He was a stocky little man in his twenties, with weasel eyes and wolverine teeth. His jug ears stood out from his head like radar aerials. The accent was unmistakeably Geordie. He was a rough diamond who had easily penetrated the newspaper's porous security. The news desk, equally careless, had obligingly pointed me out to him. I lived in another world. As my newspaper's chief reporter, I had been treading a careful path for some years between decent caution and paranoia from wars in Africa to the Middle East, by way of Northern Ireland. I had been locked up from time to time in all these areas. My reports from the Troubles across the water had made many enemies and had invited the usual death threats, arrests and interrogations. I had also written about the mercenary game. This, like Belfast, was another culture where unstable people found a natural playground.

I smiled and assumed a relaxed, avuncular air. 'Who are you then, sunshine?'

'Major Nick Hall, representing the government of President Holden Roberto of Angola.'

The documents he showed me seemed genuine and he flashed a formidable roll of new American $100 bills, the numbers on them running in sequence. But the man carrying all this paper, even by the standards of our former regiment, was not convincing officer material. It was not just his youth. He exuded barely controlled aggro. I thought my visitor might have stolen the real Hall's identity or even murdered the real major. I was wrong about that.

We could agree about one thing. Everyone knew Roberto was taking a hammering. As the *Daily Mail* informed us,

American-supported forces in the Angolan civil war may have collapsed . . . fleeing for their lives into neighbouring Zaïre. The 20,000-strong army of FNLA (Front for the Liberation of Angola) seems to have been routed by the better-trained and equipped Communist-backed troops under the command of Russian and Cuban officers . . . Serious concern at the deteriorating situation kept Foreign Secretary James Callaghan's African advisers working late in Whitehall.

In London, Hall admitted, 'The bulk of our army has deserted and we are left with about 300 loyal troops, some of them only twelve years old. We urgently need help from every country in the West.'

Callaghan and Roberto were not alone in worrying about Angola. Henry Kissinger was also expressing concern. On 16 January, two days after Hall's first approach to me, Kissinger telephoned his friend Frank Sinatra. Sinatra was then almost as famous for his links to the Mafia as for his fame as a singer. Thanks to Freedom of Information (US version), we now know that, as Congress attempted to bar further CIA intervention in Angola, Kissinger jokingly suggested that he needed some of Sinatra's 'enforcers' to straighten the situation out.[11] Who should be 'straightened' was not clear.

But why had Hall come to me? He claimed that he had read an article I had published some months earlier, about an unusual insurance offer. An obscure broker in rural Norfolk had underwritten the risk of mercenary operations in Africa to which about a hundred men had signed up, run by another failed ex-paratrooper – and bankrupt road haulier – named John Banks. Banks had been released after being told his services were no longer required.

It was clear to me that someone more intelligent than Hall had briefed him well. Like Meredith, I had a choice to make. Whatever decision I took would be deeply flawed, morally in one direction, professionally in another. The professional option won, but by assisting my sinister visitor I could be guilty of crossing the line that separates the war reporter from the participant.

Yet to play it safe, refusing to get involved, would have been to abdicate of my duty to learn what was happening. This affair, clearly, was an issue of serious public interest. I chose the first course, making it clear that, if I assisted Hall, I would be an 'embedded' reporter with his team. In time that decision would land me in trouble with Detective Chief Superintendent Harry Mooney, in charge of Scotland Yard's murder squad, for allegedly having blood on my hands, as well as generating an assassination contract on me, arranged by the man now seeking my help. I did not know that I was also becoming involved in one of the CIA's dirtier-than-usual operations.

A telephone call to the broker was all it took to arrange a meeting that evening with the broker's contacts. The broker had the list of Banks's volunteers (who were to have taken take part in a proposed attack on Rhodesia) locked in his safe. Hall was not congenial company. He could not recall the plate number of his hired car or on what level of the multi-level car park he had left it. We spent hours looking for it. His temper was also on a very short fuse. We arrived at the broker's cottage at Holt in Norfolk at about midnight and were shown into the kitchen. We were met by the broker and a man I later knew as Les Aspin. Aspin, a former RAF corporal, claimed to have worked as an assassin and SIS double agent during the Irish war. Hall and Aspin joined other people I did not see in another room. I remained in the kitchen with one of Aspin's heavies acting as a watchdog.

After about two hours, Hall emerged from the conference and we drove back to London. On the way back I warned him not to get involved with Banks. Hall dismissed the idea. The people he had met, he said, were merely 'an enthusiastic bunch of amateurs'. But back at the Piccadilly Hotel at 5.30 a.m. he told his wife that the group he had met, through me, was well organised, adding, 'We don't have anything to worry about now. It will all be taken care of.'

I had arranged to interview Hall at 4.30 p.m. that day. He lay naked on his bed, staring at the ceiling, saying nothing. His wife seemed unsurprised. Next day, he tried to elude me by checking out of the Piccadilly Hotel at 7 a.m. I traced him with the help of the black cab he used to move to the Tower Hotel, near Tower Bridge. I also obtained details of telephone calls he made from the hotel. Some were to Hereford, home of the SAS. One was made to Peter McAleese, an ex-SAS mercenary who had his own network of friends prepared to go to war anywhere, any time.

Things moved quickly during the rest of the week. As well as John Banks and his piratical gang of ex-Paras, and a separate group of SAS veterans headed by McAleese, the team also included Dave Tomkins, a safe-blower, his buddy Chris Dempster, a former Gunner, and Aspin. Within two days after that, Hall had the first 25 of his 150 men ready to move and fight for £150 per week.

The day before the group was due to leave, Aspin, under the nom de guerre 'Mr Allen', contacted me to suggest a meeting near the Tower Hotel, where he occupied room 615. I left a hurried, handwritten note for the news desk: 'If I'm not back by 3 p.m. can someone start making enquiries at the Tower Hotel?'

Aspin tried to warn me off joining the expedition. I questioned his motives, telling him, 'I know I'm straight but I'm not too sure about you.' He did not like that. Dempster and Tomkins, in their account of the story,[12] said,

> The only thing that seemed likely to go wrong was news of the mercenary recruitment breaking in the press the next [Sunday] morning – perhaps provoking the government to intervene and terminate the mission. With this in mind, Les Aspin phoned *Sunday Times* reporter Tony Geraghty to see what he was up to. Geraghty admitted that he knew Hall and the others had taken refuge in a hotel 'not a thousand miles from the Tower of London with a name that begins with "T"'. He suggested a meeting to talk things over and Aspin, in true cloak-and-dagger fashion, agreed to a clandestine rendezvous at a sandwich bar stall close to Tower Bridge.
>
> When Aspin returned from the meeting he reported that Geraghty was willing to keep the story under wraps for the time being but only on condition that he was allowed to accompany the mercs to Angola as an accredited war correspondent, thereby stealing a march on rival journalists.

Aspin, Hall, Banks and Tomkins

> held a meeting of their own to discuss Geraghty's proposal. Hall, for one, didn't want Geraghty any more involved than he already was. He was afraid that news coverage of any kind would jeopardise plans for further recruitment. Someone suggested that the best solution to the problem would be to have Geraghty 'rubbed out'. The suggestion appealed to Hall who offered $6,000 to anyone prepared to remove Geraghty from the scene. For some reason everyone turned and looked expectantly at Dave Tomkins.

Tomkins, safe-blower and Cockney hard man, had no military experience. He found the money tempting, but not tempting enough to blind him to the obvious drawbacks. He pointed out that Geraghty would undoubtedly have told his editor at the *Sunday Times* what he was working on and if he suddenly disappeared, it wouldn't take the police long to make the right connection.

After further discussion it was agreed to have Geraghty disposed of once they were in Africa. He would be allowed to accompany the men to Kinshasa but his coverage of the war would end at the first convenient ditch in Zaïre or Angola. It would obviously be much easier to explain away the death or disappearance of a war correspondent in a combat zone than that of a reporter in the heart of London. Geraghty's future having been decided, John Banks and Dave Tomkins drove back to Camberley for their last night with their families.

The casual attitude of the group to murder was to become the hallmark of operations on the ground in Angola. It would provoke an unnecessary fratricidal massacre and, finally, the execution by firing squad of some of the leaders in keeping with the CIA's unnecessary secret war in Angola. To complicate matters further, it was becoming clear that there was no honour among plotters, who were – that same night – plotting against one another. Hall had told Aspin that he wanted to elbow Banks aside. Banks in his turn had planned to replace Hall once they reached Kinshasa.

Sunday morning came and with it a characteristic stroke in dealing with an inconvenient reporter, short of assassination. A version of the Angolan recruitment story appeared in the *People* newspaper under the name of Trevor Aspinall, complete with political gloss:

An ex-soldier who was jailed for gun-running has recruited a squad of British mercenaries for Angola. Their task: to help fight the Communist takeover of the former Portuguese colony on the side of the FNLA. The 25 men have been recruited by a young Briton who has become one of FNLA President Holden Roberto's top military advisers.

Hall was quoted as saying, 'I just can't understand how nations can stand by and watch this brutal communist takeover.'

This was a classic 'spoiler' story of a type sometimes used by Whitehall to blunt the impact of a dangerous exclusive. The byline on it was that of the ghostwriter who had helped produce Aspin's colourful memoir, *I Kovacs*. Aspin, on his own admission, had been a double agent for SIS working against Irish republicans but, like others involved, he did not always live in the real world.

Most of the recruits, including a youth aged 17 with no military experience, had no passports. Instead, the authorities at Heathrow and Belgium were prepared to accept documents issued by Banks' firm, Security Advisory Services. It was one sign of official complicity in what was happening, confirmed by Banks himself in a sworn affidavit on 15 March 1976. He claimed that, by the time the first party left for Angola, 'I had had a close relationship with the Special Branch for about three years and had told them about the recruitment . . . That was why there was no hindrance at the airport.'[13]

We boarded the coach to Heathrow at 7 p.m. on Sunday, 18 January, surrounded by press photographers. As Dempster and Tomkins later wrote

The only journalist who had been allowed to join the mercs on the coach was *Sunday Times* reporter, Tony Geraghty. Wearing an anorak and carrying a bulging backpack, Geraghty looked well equipped for his African safari. However, since Hall's recruiting activities had already been exposed by the *Sunday People*, Geraghty was no longer considered a serious threat to plans for future recruitment. At the airport, Hall told Geraghty that his invitation to accompany the mercs to Angola as a war correspondent was cancelled.

I was not surprised or disheartened by Hall's treachery. I was confident that my newspaper would make it possible for me to stay with the story and travel to Africa as an independent correspondent. To my astonishment, the *Sunday Times* decided the cost was not worth the story. One of the world's greatest newspapers could not afford an air ticket to send its chief reporter to Zaïre (the Congo) on an assignment that was already commanding world attention.

Not for the first time I discovered that some news editors do not have the imagination to believe in a story that is outside their experience. I had come close to dismissal in 1969, at the start of the Irish Troubles, when Whitehall denied my suggestion that the IRA was back in business in Belfast. Later – when it became apparent that I had got it right – a Conservative government minister had asked a *Sunday Times* executive, 'How much longer will you employ an IRA reporter?'

In spite of the paper's refusal to assign me to the story in Africa, however, I still had two excellent sources within the mercenary force who promised to keep me informed of what happened. The fees they sought were modest. What mattered more to them was that someone they could trust was watching their backs and keeping in touch, if necessary, with their next of kin.

It is not plausible, even given assistance from the insurance company in Norfolk that had underwritten the life cover for John Banks' aborted assault on Rhodesia, that Hall could have assembled this number of men so swiftly without some other, invisible hand to guide him. Whose hand? Was it the same influential agency that could square things away with the Home Office so as to arrange for the departure of the mercenaries from London to Kinshasa, via Brussels, without passports? For Hall to approach a journalist in such circumstances was unwise and unnecessary, jeopardising his operational security, unless it was part of a carefully crafted process of building a cover story for the real source of Hall's recruitment drive. These were not matters that commanded the attention of the inquiry run by Lord Diplock when the murder of British citizens, by their ostensible comrades, was over.

Going Ape in Africa

From the outset, once they set foot in Africa Callan (a.k.a. Costas Georgiou), his fellow assassin Sammy Copeland and their inner ring of ex-para psychopaths – the mercenary advance guard – killed people as a mundane, daily process. Copeland, a former Parachute Regiment sergeant, had been court-martialled in 1971 for illegal possession of firearms and thrown out of the army. It is unclear whether he served a sentence in the same prison as Callan, Wainhouse and Hall.

The FNLA's problem was that the victims of Callan's aggression were not, in general, the enemy but Angolan civilians or black FNLA soldiers on his own side. Some were shot dead at point-blank range for no better reason than to test the firepower of a newly acquired gun. Others, such as a man delivering bread to his unit, died when Callan's unpredictable rage seized him. Within 48 hours of their arrival, the first group of British mercenaries, reduced to 19 as a result of desertions, witnessed a massacre of black allies, who were disarmed, stripped naked and humiliated by Callan before he cut them down with automatic fire. During the campaign around 170 others, singled out for individual treatment, were taken to a favoured bridge at Quiende and shot through the head before being fed to the crocodiles.

An early white casualty was one of Callan's own, who shot himself, accidentally, through the thumb. The explosives expert, Tomkins, was evacuated temporarily, when one of his own booby traps blew a hole in his buttocks. Others were killed or injured driving over their own mines. Their puny anti-tank rockets bounced like harmless pebbles off the armour of the enemy's Russian-made T-54 tanks. The initials 'AP' on their grenades were taken to mean 'armour-piercing' rather than 'anti-personnel'.

Wainhouse later claimed,

We all did crazy things and not just for the money. Men literally threw themselves at tanks although we had no real equipment to knock them out. The only way was to get on the turret, open the hatch and drop a grenade inside. Unfortunately, the T54 hatch locks from the inside. We did try to soak a stretch of road in petrol in the hopes of igniting it under a tank and forcing the crew out, but of course we found we did not have enough petrol. We managed to knock out a few tanks by firing American 66mm rockets in pairs at the tracks.[14]

As three of the mercenaries made a third failed attempt to penetrate the Russian armour, 'the tank blew them to bits with the heavy machine gun . . . Those men really had guts.'

Callan's infantry skills were as lethal to his own side as to the enemy. When someone could induce his usually broken-down vehicles to move, he favoured frontal assaults on well dug-in positions. His men, when they went into action, were repeatedly ambushed. Of 96 recruits who arrived from Britain on 29 January in a second wave, a dozen or so were hospitalised as casualties. Meanwhile the main recruiters – Hall and Banks – kept their distance from the front line and lived to profit another day. A year after the Angolan debacle, Banks appeared as the star prosecution witness against John Higgins, Provisional Sinn Fein's Luton representative, who was accused of trying to buy arms from Banks for the IRA. Banks, acting on behalf of Special Branch, was an unconvincing witness, but Higgins was sent to prison for 10 years. Banks was given police protection.

By then it had become apparent that the effect of the British, Portuguese and six American mercenaries on the advance of a regular, co-ordinated modern Cuban army was no more than a tactical pinprick. Its main impact was on public opinion as the horror stories made headlines around the world. In particular the slaughter of 11 of the second wave of mercenaries, a day after their arrival, by Callan and his men caused revulsion. On 1 February the victims, many of whom had no military experience, had been left at a rear headquarters in the town of Maquela. They were warned to watch out for advancing Cubans. Some of them believed they had signed up for non-combat duties and – a deadly error – had refused to become Callan's guerrillas.

In the early hours of the following day, when some of the original mercenary advance guard drove into the place to collect a spare vehicle, the incomers panicked and opened fire, shooting up their allies before fleeing north towards the border with Zaïre. They were quickly intercepted, taken back to Maquela and ordered to strip. Callan asked who had fired the first rocket, wrecking the mercenaries' vehicle, but, surprisingly, leaving its four occupants unhurt. The culprit was Phil Davies, aged 22, a former soldier from Birmingham.

He stepped forward, smiling awkwardly. 'Me, sir,' he said. Callan put a pistol to his head and shot him three times, grunting, 'This is the only law here.'

The others were driven to a gently sloping valley some miles away and told to start running. As they did so, Copeland and Tony Boddy picked them off like fleeing rabbits. Most of the execution party, acting under duress, aimed off but Boddy, according to Dempster, excitedly exclaimed, 'I *got* one!' Another of those ordered by Callan to kill their fellow mercenaries was Andy McKenzie. From his death cell in Luanda, McKenzie wrote that acting under duress, he fired two shots, adding: 'If I had not done it, I would have been killed like the others.' Copeland, he said, 'did most of the killing, like a madman.'

It was unclear how many were slaughtered during the turkey shoot. Scotland Yard identified 14 in all, eight of whom were former regular soldiers who rapidly concluded they wanted no part of Callan's army or its random murder of local civilians. Other authorities believe that 11 bodies were left to rot that day and that men killed in other ways had been included in the massacre list in error.

Shortly afterwards, Copeland was sentenced to death by Hall at a field court martial. Hall's only previous experience of such tribunals was his own. Another of the mercenaries then administered the *coup de grâce* with brisk pistol shots to the back of Copeland's head, and the relaxed postscript, 'That's him finished, then.'

The last mercenaries retreated across the border into Zaïre on 17 February. They were led by McAleese, one of the few mercenaries to have maintained military discipline throughout the campaign. Almost four months later, on 11 June, the MPLA staged a show trial in Luanda of 13 captured mercenaries, including Callan, McKenzie, who had lost a leg, and three Americans: Gustavo Grillo, Daniel Gearhart and Gary Akers. A fourth American, George Bacon II, 'a highly respected former CIA paramilitary officer', died in a Cuban ambush on 15 February. The other prisoners were little more than ciphers.

The Americans had barely set their boots on Angolan soil when they were made prisoners by the advancing Cubans, who had now conquered the whole of north Angola. Some of them were taken prisoner because they thought that the capsule that came with their French army rations labelled '*boisson instantanée*' was 'instant poison' ('poison *instantané*') rather than 'instant drink', a flavouring of absinthe to add to their brackish water bottles.

The mercenaries' trial was very much to the taste of Black Africa and the communist world and a decided reverse for the CIA. A revolutionary tribunal sentenced Callan, Andy McKenzie, 'Brummie' Barker and the American Gearhart to death by firing squad for war crimes. The rest were given prison sentences ranging from 16 to 30 years. The sentences had been agreed in secret three months before the trial began. One of the men, sentenced to 24 years, later described his first reaction to the decision: 'I wanted to kiss the judges. I expected to be shot.' He served eight years.

Angola's President Neto ignored pleas for clemency from the British and American heads of state and the four men were shot dead on 10 July 1976. The executions were a shambolic affair as a result of which Gearhart – killed for the crime of representing America – and Barker died only after initial attempts to kill them failed. Of 143 mercenaries in this campaign, another 18 died in the field. The total number of dead mercenaries was thought to be about 60.

After the campaign, senior Scotland Yard officers, led by Detective Chief Superintendent Harry Mooney, ran a murder investigation into the 14 deaths at Maquela. I was one of those interviewed by him. A decision to let the whole matter drop was taken by Prime Minister Harold Wilson. On 12 February, the Director of Public Prosecutions, Sir Norman Skelhorn, announced that no action would be taken against several of those allegedly involved in the massacre.

For the prisoners in Luanda, however, the affair was far from over, while in the south, UNITA would continue its own guerrilla war, backed by South Africa, for years to come. Gary Akers, aged 21, a former corporal with the US Marine Corps, was one of six idealists who had paid for their own flights from America to join the campaign at the eleventh hour. Wounded in one of the last ambushes, he was sentenced to 30 years by the Luanda tribunal. He served seven before being freed under a complex international exchange of prisoners of war. His story of imprisonment is one of boredom punctuated by beatings, interrogations and normal treatment.[15]

For long periods, 'my daily routine was exercising and reading the Bible . . . Everyone just sat on their beds and read or slept.' Boredom led to fights among the prisoners.

On 27 May 1977, MPLA dissidents in Luanda ran a short, unsuccessful *coup d'état* and overran the prison. The guards fled. The dissidents lined up the mercenaries for another round of executions.

> We waited and waited . . . and we patiently watched a confrontation between the leader of the assault and the commanders. The leader, a pregnant woman, wanted to kill us immediately. She had driven the lead BDRM [armoured car] that rammed the gates. Her officers finally convinced her to lock us up and kill us later.

Within hours, the coup had failed and the prison was full of people involved in the affair. They were taken off by the truckload and executed on an industrial scale. In spite of that, the prison population grew from 100 to 1,000. 'People were tortured day and night. Screams filled the dark halls.'

The merest sign of resentment by the white prisoners to their conditions prompted reprisals. Akers and the British mercenary John Lawlor spent a year inside a one-man cell with space for only one bed, 'so we took it in turns to lie down. We got food through the little window in the door. There were no lights.'

Later, after surviving his first attack of malaria, Akers was allowed to work in the garden. He cultivated 19 papaya trees and 23 peppers. He moved on to work as the prison's car mechanic. It was an open regime. 'There was a little girl and her sister who . . . came and talked to me. My clothes were ragged and one day the little girl came with thread and needles to sew them.'

When Akers talked to the child about *his* America, rather than the demonised local version, the visits ceased. He reflected,

> I never considered myself a mercenary. I was a professional soldier . . . A mercenary has no scruples. He'll kill anybody. He robs, rapes, has no sides, no loyalties. He'll even shoot his own men if it suits his purpose. A professional soldier has political allegiances. He doesn't kill innocent civilians . . . He's there to fight the enemy.

There were other examples of moral courage among those tainted with Callan's dogs-of-war image. One remarkable case was John X, then aged 21. He had already served with a Territorial Army battalion of the Parachute Regiment and wanted to take up arms against communist expansion, as he saw it, so as to make the world a better place. He was one of the last volunteers to arrive and was driven into an ambush in an overcrowded Land Rover commanded by Callan's cousin, Shotgun Charlie. His right leg was shredded by heavy machine-gun fire. He was one of two prisoners to appear for trial in a wheelchair. He was sentenced to 16 years and served eight, much of that time in solitary confinement.

On his return to Britain, though one leg was permanently damaged, he says he was recruited by the SAS as an adviser specialising in combat survival, before returning to work in Africa. Asked to identify the secret of survival in the extreme circumstances of the Luanda prison, his answer is surprising. 'There is no such thing as solitary confinement if you believe in God. Given that belief, you are never alone.'

The Cold War effectively ended with the break-up of the Soviet Union on 25 December 1991. The Angolan civil war outlasted it by more than a decade. Long after the superpowers had tired of the last CIA battleground in Africa, the war between Jonas Savimbi's UNITA and the MPLA government continued in the south of the country. In 1988, Cuban and South African forces clashed at Cuito Cuanavale in the biggest ground battle fought in Africa since World War Two. It ended in stalemate. Although the MPLA and its allies took more casualties, it led to independence for Namibia and foreshadowed the end of the South African apartheid regime.

The Angolan peace accord did not last. Savimbi was killed in an ambush during his last guerrilla campaign on 22 February 2002. Six weeks later, the two sides agreed a ceasefire. By that time, white mercenaries had returned to Angola, this time with the blessing of the MPLA government, to protect its oil assets. The company concerned was the South African firm Executive Outcomes (EO). In 1992, a few months after the end of the Cold War, EO was contracted to recapture from UNITA an important oil refinery at Soyo. This it did with surprise, speed and audacity. The refinery was retaken intact.

Luanda – now ditching the anti-mercenary rhetoric of the show trial – hired 500 South African and British military technicians to train its army, to plan and lead offensive operations. By August 1994, UNITA's control of the country had shrunk by 20 per cent.

The short-lived peace accords followed. A year later, the beleaguered government of Sierra Leone also called on the mercenaries to prop it up. So, out of the bloody soil of West Africa, a new form of freelance soldiering – that of the corporate warrior, representing the power of the multinational rather than the nation-state, or the rugged individual – was born. The cost to Angola, by the time the war ended there, was 500,000 lives, most of them civilian.

PART II

•

PLAUSIBLY DENIABLE

5

YEMEN 1965–8:

'Do you fancy going into Yemen and burning the Migs?'

In the autumn of 1962, one man bestrode the Middle East like a colossus. Gamal Abdel Nasser, President of Egypt, the soldier son of a postal worker, had overturned a corrupt monarchy and defied British attempts to secure the Suez Canal. Backed by Soviet Russia, he had started building the Aswan High Dam as much as a monument to national pride as a step to economic self-sufficiency. At the age of 17, he had written the script for his own greatness: 'Where is dignity? Where is nationalism? ... Egyptians sleep like men in a cave. Who can awaken these miserable creatures who do not even know who they are?'[1] By the fetid banks of the Sweet Water Canal, where flies swarmed over the faces of sleeping babies, hope of a life free from poverty and disease stirred, if faintly, under Nasser's rule.

Not all of Nasser's pan-Arabist schemes – including a grandiose United Arab Republic linking Syria to Egypt – withstood the impact of what a contemporary British leader, Harold Macmillan, described as, 'events, dear boy, events'. An essentially secular nationalist, Nasser had also confronted the fundamentalist Muslim Brotherhood, the source of later jihads, without achieving a clear-cut victory. Like the Brothers, Egypt's communists got their comeuppance in prison or on the gallows in spite of Moscow's influence.

By 1962, Nasser's power no longer depended upon specific losses or gains. His charisma, his melismatic voice and the oratory he was prepared to project onto the streets of Cairo through an antique loudspeaker, even when British bombs destroyed Cairo Radio in 1956, embodied a state of mind that pervaded and seduced the Arab zeitgeist. It was the spirit of optimism, the odour of victory in the morning. The message, and the example of his 1956 victory over the French, British and Israelis (with a little help from the United States), was clear to the fellaheen listening each night to the Voice of the Arabs (as Cairo Radio was often called during the Nasser regime). They could defeat their enemies, however powerful.

Six years after the Anglo-French debacle at Suez, a group of republican officers serving a traditional monarch in Yemen mounted a *coup d'état*. Some of the plotters had been trained in Egypt. Others had been groomed by Egyptian advisers in their own capital, Sana'a. They were led by a politically illiterate commander, Field Marshal Abdullah Sallal. They all believed in Nasser and the invincibility of his policies, as well as his destiny (and, by extension, theirs also).

Sallal's timing seemed right. The ruling Imam, Mohammed Al-Badr, had been enthroned for only eight days, since the death of his father. Aided by 150 Egyptian paras, the capital was taken and opposition scattered in the jebel, without any hope of recovery. Rumours that the Imam was dead were just that, however. He had eluded capture by dressing as a woman and, out on the jebel, the tribes were rallying to him.

Egypt recognised the new regime within 48 hours. It was the beginning of a story of attrition and grief, including the loss of 10,000 Egyptian soldiers, which Nasser would describe to a friend as 'my Vietnam'. More than any other episode except, perhaps, Israel's pre-emptive demolition of the Egyptian Air Force at the beginning of the 1967 Six Day War, the Yemen misadventure called Nasser's judgement and his *baraka*, his ability to survive any crisis, into question. The role of a handful of British freelances and French mercenaries, deniable in London and Paris, was decisive in prolonging the campaign far beyond anything Nasser expected at a time when Israel was preparing its next war on the Arabs. What has not been established for certain, until now, is the role Israel and Iran played in these machinations.

To be fair to Nasser, he quickly recognised that to commit thousands of his soldiers to a war for nothing much except a principle – the principle being 'to drive the British from all Arab territory', including, this time, the Aden Protectorate, neighbouring Yemen – might be a mistake. Sallal's demands for support had started with a request for a symbolic flight over

Sana'a by a single Egyptian Mig. But, as both Saudi Arabia's royals and the Hashemite King Hussein in Jordan backed the Imam with funds and air support for a Royalist guerrilla army, the situation worsened. Thousands of Egyptian soldiers joined the fight, and started taking casualties from an enemy they often never saw, in ambushes they could not prevent.

In the stand-off that followed, Egypt (emulating the British in Waziristan and Iraq in the 1930s) used air power and punitive columns on the few roads in the area to contain ungovernable mountains. The Royalist forces, secretly supplied by camel train from Aden in the south and less secretly by Saudi Arabia to the north, lived a troglodyte existence in caves by day and emerged only cautiously by night to set up their pinprick ambushes and the occasional, pointless frontal assault on a republican-held town.

The view in London was that this war of attrition would undermine the adjoining British colony of Aden, where UK forces were already on the back foot, fighting a classic guerrilla/terrorist war. Indeed, Aden terrorists were rapidly supported by Sallal, who claimed the city and its more primitive Federation sheikhdoms as part of a Greater Yemen.

In Washington, there were fears for the security of Saudi oil. Like Cairo, President Kennedy's administration in Washington had also given prompt recognition to Sallal's military government. But within two months, after his own Arabists in Riyadh had pointed out that a prolonged war in the region involving Saudi Arabia might damage US interests, Kennedy offered mediation to end it. He was rebuffed by the Saudis, as were the UN and even Nasser himself. Within three months of the Yemeni coup, Nasser offered to withdraw his forces if only Saudi Arabia and Jordan would cease helping the Imam's tribesmen. The Saudis declined, since this would leave Sallal's junta in control of Sana'a.

At an early stage, in the autumn of 1962, various Western intelligence agencies, including Mossad, wanted to push events in another direction. The key players were colourful veterans of British wartime special forces, military intelligence officers and clandestine SIS (MI6) operations during the Cold War. The core group comprised wealthy Scots with an undiminished appetite for adventure. The links that connected the principals in this unusual operation deserve an organogram. They reflect the intensely intimate, longstanding relationships that exist among the cognoscenti of the freelance military world. Here is an outline of this peculiar matrix of familial, regimental and political loyalties.

Billy McLean, Conservative MP for Inverness, served in Special Operations Executive in Albania during World War Two with Julian Amery, Air Minister in the Conservative government of the day under Prime Minister Harold Macmillan. He was also, conveniently, Macmillan's son-in-law. McLean and Amery were former schoolmates. McLean had married Amery's sister. At a critical point during the Albanian adventure they depended upon the British Resident Minister at the Allied military headquarters in Italy. The Resident Minister at the time was Harold Macmillan.

Another significant player was David Smiley, a cavalry officer who had also served with SOE in Albania and whose freelance sword, after 1945, was first at the service of the Ruler of Oman and, later, the Ruler's Saudi enemy.

Then there was George Kennedy Young, a former officer of the Lowland King's Own Scottish Borderers who joined SIS during the war. During the Cold War, Young rose to be deputy director of 'the Firm', as SIS is also known, until his extreme patriotism made him too hot to handle, at which point he resigned, became a merchant banker and military entrepreneur. His successor, Tim Milne, was an acquaintance of Jim Johnson, a former Welsh Guards officer who had commanded 21 SAS (Volunteer Reserve) Regiment based in Chelsea.

Johnson was a friend of Paul Paulson, then running the Middle East and Africa desk of SIS and, like Milne and the Soviet spy Kim Philby, a former pupil of Westminster School (though Johnson belonged to a later generation than Milne and Paulson, who were contemporaries). As the operation gathered momentum, Paulson was instructed to work alongside Amery as part of an SIS team that included John da Silva, formerly head of station in Bahrain.

When the Yemen operation was being hatched, Johnson was a Lloyd's broker before combining with others to create the remarkable private military company sometimes known as KMS. It had other names, including Rally Films, and was constructed at a meeting attended by Frank Steele, an SIS Middle East specialist, and such SAS luminaries as Major Dare Newell, the regiment's liaison officer with the Firm (and a former SOE warrior), Colonel David ('Dinkie') Sutherland, another wartime SAS soldier now representing MI5, and Brigadier Mike Wingate-Grey, a former SAS director. A faceless representative of the Treasury was also present.

Johnson, unsurprisingly, was a friend of the SAS founder, Colonel David Stirling. Stirling's television company, Television International

Enterprises, hosted KMS in its basement at Sloane Street, Chelsea, when the latter set up shop in 1963. Observing the success of KMS, Stirling created his own private military company, WatchGuard International, in 1967, helped by Colonel John Woodhouse, father of the postwar SAS.

Stirling also proposed that Johnson should recruit his niece, Fiona Fraser, daughter of the wartime commando leader Lord Lovat, as 'a really loyal, PV-d girl' to run the KMS office. She was then aged 18 and a quick learner. As one of those involved put it, 'You could say she rapidly became a major gunrunner.'

Both Stirling and Johnson were acquainted with the Foreign Secretary of the day, the Earl of Home (later Sir Alec Douglas Home, another Scottish laird) as well as Dick White, director of SIS and, like other holders of that office, known on the street as 'C'. The first leader of the privatised ground troops in Yemen was John Cooper, Stirling's wartime driver and, later, an SAS major before working for the Sultan of Oman.

The political anchor of this web, with the personal approval of the Prime Minister, was Julian Amery. His public appointment was as Aviation Minister. From his private office in the ministry, however, Julian Amery would wear another hat: 'Minister for Yemen'. Against the protests of a cautious Dick White and the Foreign Office under Home, Amery's robust agenda was, 'By giving Nasser a bloody nose, we get the Russians.'

But, according to George Kennedy Young, the Yemen operation was the brainchild of Israeli intelligence. He described the episode in a hyperbolic account of his life written in the third person.[2]

Young had already left MI6 for merchant banking [Kleinwort Benson] when Mossad approached him to find an Englishman acceptable to the Saudis to run a guerrilla war against the left-wing Yemeni regime and its Egyptian backers. 'I can find you a Scotsman,' replied Young, and over a lunch in the City he introduced Colonel Neil ('Billy') McLean MP, to Brigadier Dan Hiram, the Israeli Defence Attaché. The Israelis promised to supply weapons, funds and instructors who could pass themselves off as Arabs, and the Saudis eagerly grasped the idea.

The notion of an alliance between the Houses of Saud and David, preposterous though it would have seemed in the 1960s, was to prove to be the case. In the aftermath of the 1956 Suez disaster, loyalties were shifting. The

British Establishment was split between those who wanted revenge (the Suez Group, later the Aden Group) and those prepared to swallow the pill of defeat and move on. As a result, Cabinet discussions were dominated by the issue of recognition of the new regime in Sana'a. To support the Royalists openly would have been to risk another split with the US and that – as Suez had demonstrated – could be deadly for the British economy. But recognition of Sallal would be to surrender to blackmail. Egyptian aircraft were already flying missions in support of rebels in northern Aden and the RAF, in response, had mounted reconnaissance missions over Yemen.

Like his fellow Scot George Kennedy Young, McLean belonged to a generation of restless veterans of special operations during World War Two. He had been parachuted into occupied Albania to organise partisan resistance against the Nazis. When the Yemen coup occurred, he was the Member of Parliament for Inverness and was visiting Saudi Arabia. He went on to Yemen.

On 19 December 1962 McLean, newly returned from his reconnaissance, called on his old friend, Prime Minister Macmillan, to deliver his report, suggesting that the Egyptians could be defeated. The die was cast. On 1 January 1963, a Cabinet committee received an unsourced intelligence analysis – in practice, the McLean report – suggesting that to recognise the republicans in Sana'a would be to hand control of the Gulf to the Americans, who made little secret of their wish to supplant the British in the region. Any military operation would have to be deniable and run at arm's length. In the spring of 1963, this infant – if illegitimate – operation received a sort of paternal recognition by elements within the British government.

Tom Bower's biography of the SIS chief Sir Dick White records,

> In a secret decision, Macmillan appointed Amery as 'minister for Yemen' to mastermind British support of the Royalists. Faced with a divided cabinet obstructing any chance of an agreed government policy, and anxious to be personally distant from any involvement, the prime minister allowed Amery to supervise a 'private war' against Nasser. There was no public announcement nor any mention in the official cabinet minutes. 'It was a private war, totally obscured from public view and remarkably successful,' declares Amery.[3]

One close observer of subsequent events later recalled, 'David Stirling, Brian Franks [then colonel commandant of the SAS], Julian Amery and Alec Douglas Home [Foreign Secretary] met in London one evening at the request of Billy McLean.' The meeting seems to have taken place at White's Club in mid-April, 1963. By then, British positions in the Aden Federation had come under attack from Yemen (as well as from within) and McLean had made three arduous journeys into the country. A Royalist delegation had visited Israel and unmarked Israeli and Iranian planes were flying arms into areas controlled by the Imam.

McLean told the gathering, 'Whatever the Egyptians are telling Washington, the coup is not a success. Resistance continues. We have to get some sort of operation going.' As one participant later reported, 'Alec [Home] said, 'I will talk to SIS but they say they have no agents in Yemen and it will take six months to set something up.' As the Aden Group read the situation, both Home and the head of MI6, Dick White, were reluctant to fish in these troubled waters.

There was another inhibition. During World War Two, Special Operations Executive had become expert in running disruptive operations in occupied territory. After the war, although that role was to have been accepted by SIS, the intelligence service turned up its nose at anything so vulgar. It preferred the role of John le Carré's George Smiley, weaving a web of information and spookery.

Stirling's response to SIS hesitancy was, 'Rubbish. I can produce a guy in London who has just given up command of 21 SAS [the volunteer reserve regiment then based at Duke of York's Headquarters in Chelsea]. He could put something together.'

The new player Stirling had in mind was Jim Johnson, a debonair Welsh Guards officer now turned Lloyd's broker, still seeking adventure. Franks telephoned Johnson. Over a drink, in an apparently casual aside, Franks asked, 'Do you fancy going into Yemen and burning the Migs which are upsetting the tribes and bombing them? The tribes have no defence against them.'

There was a further meeting in London involving Johnson, McLean and the Imam's Foreign Minister, Ahmed Al Shami. Johnson asked what funds were available. Al Shami promptly signed a cheque for £5,000. It was negotiated through the Hyde Park Hotel account, a process made easier by the fact that Colonel Franks, one of the architects of the postwar SAS, was also chairman of the hotel board.

Johnson promptly took leave of absence from Lloyd's and set up an operational headquarters in the basement of Stirling's office at 21a Sloane Street, a short walk away from the headquarters of 21 SAS on King's Road, Chelsea. His problem was 'that very few people in the regiment spoke Arabic at that time. We found three serving [SAS] corporals. Two of them later became majors. They were aged about nineteen at the time.'

Colonel John Woodhouse, commanding the regular 22 SAS Regiment, 'produced some "unattributable" Swedish sub-machine guns from the armoury at Hereford'. An armoury of exotic and deniable weapons has long been one of the regiment's most useful assets in running clandestine operations. For this job, the weapons were brought to London and stored in Johnson's house at 13 Sloane Avenue. Soon afterwards, as part of the clandestine operation, Woodhouse was posted to Aden to join the British military staff there.

With Stirling's help, Johnson also recruited Stirling's wartime comrade-in-arms, John Cooper. Cooper was now a contract officer with the Sultan's Armed Forces in Oman. In May 1963 he was upcountry when he received a telegram from the Omani capital, Muscat, delivered by Land Rover after a journey of two days. Stirling's cryptic summons said, 'Meet me soonest in Speedbird Hotel Bahrain.'[4] At Bahrain he was briefed by the Medical Officer of 21 SAS, Captain Philip Horniblow. Horniblow told Cooper that he was to lead an Anglo-French reconnaissance in a Middle Eastern country. Like Johnson, Cooper also got leave of absence.

Johnson, meanwhile, was talent hunting in Paris with David Stirling, helped by a colonel who had served with the British-trained French SAS during World War Two. Johnson and Stirling discovered that the French intelligence service was also uneasy about what was happening in Yemen. If the British were worried about Aden, the French were equally concerned that their strategically useful outpost in Djibouti (a Foreign Legion base) might be destabilised. The French Intelligence Directorate, DGSE, brought in two mercenaries who had already become famous as a result of their recent exploits in the Congo and, before that, Algeria.

The senior of the two was Colonel Roger Faulques, a former intelligence captain of the 1st Foreign Legion Paras in Algeria, a right-wing opponent of De Gaulle and a scarred survivor of a Vietnamese prison camp. With him was the burly soldier of fortune from the backwoods of Les Landes, Robert Denard. According to John Cooper, the two elements of the new team – French and British – came together on 6 June, the anniversary of D Day (and Cooper's birthday) at a mansion in Paris.

The meeting, which became convivial, continued into the early hours. One of those present recalls, 'We were entertained royally. The French side said they had a lot of ex-Foreign Legion Paras who had served in Algeria and spoke Arabic. It was the wrong Arabic, Maghrib Arabic. They were unintelligible to everyone but themselves.' The gathering included senior government officials from London and Paris. Unlike McLean, Franks and Stirling, they were not minded to commit themselves to a serious campaign without some ground truth. What emerged was not a decision to take part in the war, or even to train the Royalist guerrillas, but to send a reconnaissance team to Yemen under Saudi auspices. It was to be a modest affair, to begin with, comprising four French and four British freelance deniables led by Cooper. Even this low-level operation was almost stillborn for reasons better suited to an unwritten comic opera by Offenbach.

The gestation period of the operation was a bad time for Her Majesty's Government. In March 1963, Margaret Argyll, the only child of a self-made Scottish millionaire, was a society beauty exposed to toxic publicity as a result of her husband's divorce petition. Her husband, the Duke of Argyll, claimed that Margaret had had sex with 88 men, including two Cabinet ministers and three members of the royal family. The affair was given a further sensational twist by efforts to identify one of her lovers, whom she was fellating, from a Polaroid photograph. The photograph showed most parts of the body except the lover's head. It was widely rumoured – and, in time, confirmed – that the man in question was Duncan Sandys, then Commonwealth and Colonies Secretary, and the minister directly responsible for Aden. It was also unfortunate that the only Polaroid camera in the country at that time was in the possession of the Ministry of Defence.

Margaret Argyll never revealed the Headless Man's identity. But her denials were not convincing. One of those involved in planning the Yemen operation reveals, 'Everything was ready when the scandal of the headless photograph blew up. Sandys rang Stirling and said the operation had to stop because of the scandal.' The link might not be obvious, but if – and when, as it turned out – Cooper's presence in Yemen was compromised then it could convey to some uncharitable beings, such as politicians and journalists, a sense that all was not well with the body politic under the premiership of Harold Macmillan.

The government's gloom deepened that spring as a result of the

Profumo affair. John ('Jack') Profumo was a popular Minister for War, married to Valerie Hobson, a famous actress. He had a brief affair with a showgirl named Christine Keeler. They met at a party at the Astors' stately Berkshire home, Cliveden. For months, without a word being published, the affair was hot gossip among the London cognoscenti. The political angle that invested it with some element of public interest was the fact that Keeler, like Argyll, had other lovers, one of whom was the Soviet naval attaché in London, Yevgeny Ivanov. Could pillow talk compromise British secrets?

The matter became public when Labour MPs Barbara Castle and George Wigg raised it under protection of parliamentary privilege during a debate on Army Estimates. Profumo, in March 1963, made a personal statement to the Commons in which he claimed there was 'no impropriety whatever' in his relationship with Keeler. In June, however, he decided – bravely, by the standards of later generations – to admit the truth. He confessed that he had misled the House.

He resigned on 5 June, the day before the deniables met in Paris. According to John Cooper, the affair broke as the team was packing its kit. Cooper later revealed, 'Colonel David was informed by the Foreign Office that our trip would have to be cancelled as the government could not handle any more political embarrassment.'[5]

Whether the government's nerve cracked because of the Argyll or the Profumo affair, or the impact of both, it was certainly the case that the FO ordered Stirling to stand down the operation. Johnson, anticipating events, arranged for the deniables' advance party to be picked up after dark from remote corners of Herefordshire. Cooper took a car hired by Johnson, and returned with the others the next morning to Johnson's Chelsea home. The men were three regular SAS soldiers released from normal duties ostensibly to take special leave. They were Sergeant Geordie Dorman, a mortar expert; Corporal Chigley, a medical orderly and Trooper Richardson, an all-round firearms expert.

They were joined the same day at Johnson's home by two French volunteers, driven from Paris in an official staff car by a uniformed military driver, a manoeuvre made necessary by an industrial dispute that had grounded Air France. One of these was Tony de Saint-Paul, alias Roger de Saint Preux, a 'mercenaire affreux' of the Katanga campaign. A fluent Arabist, he was a man of theatrically sinister appearance: tall, thin, with a shaven head, a goatee beard, brooding, sunken eyes and abnormally large ears. In battle, he wore a traditional curved dagger in his ammunition belt. He would be dead before the year was out.[6]

That night Johnson decided to put the team on a flight out of London, bound for Libya, en route to Nairobi and Aden, without delay. He reasoned that the SIS duty officer would not act to put the brakes on the operation before the day shift took over at 9 a.m. Working against the clock the night before, he telephoned a number of airlines, seeking flights out of Britain for his team. The Italian firm Alitalia had spare capacity on its departure to Libya in the early hours.

Johnson promptly booked seats for three of the men. He found a place on another flight, to Tripoli via Rome, for Cooper. The Frenchmen were sent direct to Aden from London on the twice-weekly Comet flight. Cooper and the other British deniables would join the same flight during a refuelling stop at Tripoli. They did not all think of themselves as 'mercenaries', though some seem not to have resented the description, properly applied, as professional freelance soldiers. But one, who would take command of the force later, suggests, 'Branding us as mercenaries will . . . send out a quite inaccurate image of the spirit and ethos of the Yemen operation. Mercenaries are defined as soldiers of fortune who fight only for money and for the highest bidder. The first people who went in dined with the Foreign Secretary no less [Lord Home] the night before they departed.

'The need to be released from the British Army was to make the operation unattributable. A few years earlier, politics would have allowed the operation to be carried out overtly and in uniform. Some did rejoin 22 SAS and most of us discussed the possibility. I was also offered a military training job with MI6 [SIS] with whom we worked very closely throughout.'

So much for the background. Johnson drove the first team to Heathrow, and, with a sigh of relief, saw the men and their heavy equipment safely out of the country. He would have been less relieved had he known what was to happen at Tripoli. As Cooper later reported in his book, 'We had just collected our baggage from our various incoming flights when one of the cases broke open, spilling out rolls and rolls of plastic explosive. Some of the Libyan security guards actually helped us repack the stuff.' Cooper explained away the distinctive odour of the explosive by telling the Libyans that he was supplying marzipan to various Arab heads of state.

The alarm bells rang in Whitehall at the start of the working day. The Commonwealth Office, headed by Duncan Sandys (Secretary of State for the Colonies), called Stirling, who was able to deny knowledge of any movement of freelance soldiers out of Britain. Stirling then called Johnson to tell him that the operation had to stop. Johnson replied, 'It is too late. They have left. They are halfway across already.'

Johnson, not for the first time, was living dangerously. One of his contacts in SIS had counselled him, 'Jim, whatever you do, don't organise this. If we got an extreme left-wing government and people like Wedgwood Benn [in charge] we might need you to do things we would not be allowed to do.' By a droll coincidence, Benn, while at Westminster School, had been a contemporary of Johnson.

As well as the former SAS commander John Woodhouse, the British military staff in Aden at that time had just acquired a promising young officer from the same regiment. This was Peter de la Billière, a future general commanding Britain's forces in the first Gulf War, but at that time a junior officer aged 28. De la Billière's official job was to correlate intelligence reports from battalions of the British-controlled, indigenous Federal Regular Army in the bandit country of the north, near the Yemen border. Early in 1963, as he records in his autobiography, he became a secret agent, lubricating the movement of the team by way of Aden, up country to the border province of Beihan, whose local ruler, the Sharif, was a British ally.[7]

The team's first liaison officer was not de la Billière but Tony Boyle, an RAF officer who was the High Commissioner's aide-de-camp and private secretary. Boyle set up VIP hospitality for distinguished visitors. Early in 1963, one of them was David Stirling. Stirling persuaded Boyle to help the deniables. Boyle, de la Billière recalls, 'evolved an efficient system whereby a Dakota would be parked on the airstrip close to the spot where the twice-weekly Comet from London came to a halt, and passengers and their heavy freight would transfer straight to it without passing through customs'.

As Boyle became more closely involved with air support for the operation elsewhere, having left the RAF, de la Billière took over.

Often I would meet someone off the London Comet, make what arrangements I could to ease his passage through customs and – to avoid being seen in contact – pass him a typewritten note asking him to book in at a certain hotel, where I would meet him for lunch next day.

Then I would send him up to Beihan, either by a Dakota of Aden Air, or by Land Rover, and he would slip through the Yemeni frontier at night.

Beihan, near the border, had a new airfield built to assist the growing number of RAF operations against Yemen in what was becoming an undeclared war between London and Sana'a. Cooper's advance party hit the ground running. As the Comet touched down at Aden, an Aden Airways Dakota taxied alongside. The deniables ran from one aircraft to another.

From the Beihan airstrip the team were driven to Nakoub, 15 miles from the border, to the Sharif's safe house. Next morning, dressed as Arabs, the party and its two guides – eight in all – loaded their camels and joined a long supply train of around 150 camels, carrying materiel to the Royalist fighters. The caravan moved by night and hid out by day to avoid Egyptian air attack. The march to the Khowlan mountains surrounding the capital, Sana'a, took almost three weeks. It was a tortuous journey, part of it in single file through minefields, along a route that avoided the Egyptian garrison at Sirwah. The journey ended in a mountain village called Gara, which was the forward headquarters of the Imam's relative, Prince Abdullah bin Hassan.

Cooper despatched a series of reconnaissance patrols, each accompanied by two freelances. Within hours, the first Egyptian air raid came in. Russian Ilyushin bombers struck first from high altitude with iron bombs and 20mm rockets. They were followed by manoeuvrable, slow-flying Yak fighters, able to pick off ground targets with rockets and machine guns. In a supersonic age it was a return to Biggles and the pioneering days of air-to-ground warfare.

To show he meant business, Cooper followed up a promising recce with a triangulated ambush overlooking a wadi, which the Egyptians had to climb to launch an assault on Royalist positions. Each firing point was camouflaged and defended by rocks, with a rock shelter behind it as an air-raid shelter. Specific rock cairns were placed as markers to ensure a co-ordinated onslaught. Soon, an enemy parachute battalion clambered up the hill on foot, hauling machine guns on wheels. It was followed by a line of T-34 tanks and artillery. Cooper, in his book, wrote,

As the enemy reached our markers, our men opened up with devastating effect, knocking down the closely packed infantry like ninepins. Panic broke out in the ranks behind and then the tanks started firing, not into our positions but among their own men. Then the light artillery opened up, causing further carnage.

At dusk, the Egyptians withdrew, leaving 85 dead. Cooper's force collected the weapons, which were also abandoned. They left the bodies unburied. Cooper and the three SAS regulars followed this with a mortar attack on an Egyptian hill fort, 'a beautiful soft target', which dropped bombs on the garrison as it woke up at first light. Having seen enough to establish that the Republic's side of the campaign was under the control of the Egyptians, Cooper and the other British soldiers prepared to return home. The French mercenaries opted to stay a little longer. During the long march back, Cooper's party ran out of water during a sandstorm that blew for several days. As the storm cleared, they discovered that they were less than a mile away from a Federation frontier post. Their ordeal was over, in the field if not back home.

Cooper was intensively debriefed by SIS officers, by Jim Johnson and David Stirling, and by Billy McLean MP. Each had a different agenda. SIS wanted ground truth, from which they concluded that Nasser's strategic objective was control of Saudi oil as well as expulsion of the British from Aden. Johnson and Stirling wanted to know what direction the freelance operation should now take. McLean wanted Cooper to obtain photographic evidence that the Egyptians were using napalm and poison gas in their aerial attacks on Yemeni villages. McLean's agenda was political and journalistic. He was writing articles aimed at swinging public opinion to support of the Imam.

The number of deniable warriors was growing now that Cooper's reconnaissance had demonstrated that the potential impact of trained guerrillas and modern weapons on the war could be a body blow to Egyptian ambitions. KMS had around 80 men on its books, drawn from veterans of the three SAS regiments, the French Foreign Legion and even the wartime Greek Sacred Squadron. Faulques controlled the French and Belgian volunteers, including Denard and Captain Guy Moreaux, and Johnson, the British.

By September 1963 their ranks included Major Rupert France, a wartime SAS veteran who had been on Smiley's staff in Oman. The party would soon be augmented by two officers from 21 SAS (Territorial Army), Mark Milburn and Bill McSweeney. They were joined later by Major Bernard Mills, a former Special Forces officer and an anonymous SAS signaller.

The indefatigable McLean had also recruited Colonel David Smiley, who operated in parallel with Cooper, while keeping a respectful distance.

Smiley, like McLean, had stirred up partisan attacks on the Wehrmacht in occupied Albania. From 1958 to 1961, Smiley had served the Ruler of Oman, the repressive Sultan bin Taimur. During that time he led a brief campaign at Jebel Akhdar, in northern Oman, against a dissident sheikh backed by the Saudis. Now, in 1963 – having declined the honour of commanding the three SAS regiments – he was, as he put it, a mercenary 'in the service of my former enemies, the Saudis.'

He wrote later,

> Although mercenary excesses in the Congo brought discredit on our calling, I maintain that it can still be an honourable one, with the important proviso that the mercenary's own conduct is honourable and that what he is doing is in the interests of his own country, or in defence of his own ideals ... I was – and am – certain that what we were trying to do in the Yemen was in the interests of Britain.[8]

He was not the only one to wear the 'mercenary' badge without embarrassment. As a member of Stirling's Watchguard team, John Woodhouse reported from Yemen to Stirling in 1965 that while 'the mercenary organisation in Yemen played a decisive part in defeating the Egyptian occupation because it sustained Royalist morale', in the field, 'the mercenaries did as they pleased.'[9]

From June 1963 to March 1965, Smiley's role seems largely to have been as an analyst in the field, surveying likely airstrips and drop zones during arduous journeys, and as an adviser to the Saudis – who largely bankrolled the operation – rather than as a combatant. Some of his friends believe that his true purpose was to act as an observer for SIS. He also worked as a correspondent for the *Daily Telegraph*, which was happy to give him journalistic cover without, apparently, considering the impact of that on bona fide journalists in the country. By the time Smiley took over command in 1965, 'at the height of the mercenary effort ... when I was commanding them, [they] never numbered more than forty-eight, of whom thirty were French or Belgian and eighteen British'. This apparent underestimate probably results from the fact that around half of the 80 freelances were operational at any one time, while the rest were on leave.

What is clear is that in 1963 Cooper soon returned to bin Hassan's mountain headquarters with a consignment of gold sovereigns, to pay the Royalist forces, before setting up an efficient radio, assisted by the French party, which, at the time, was down to two men. The operation had now moved decisively from simple reconnaissance to offensive guerrilla warfare, in spite of second thoughts by the British government following Macmillan's resignation in October 1963 and his replacement by Lord Home, who now surrendered his peerage.

Home lost the 1964 general election and was succeeded by the Labour leader, Harold Wilson. Home was not the steadiest of hands. His most memorable comment was, 'There are two problems in my life. The political ones are insoluble and the economic ones are incomprehensible.'

Soon, Egyptian signals intelligence identified the source of the foreign advisers' signals and hit the place from the air with 'silvery cylinders' according to Cooper, that burst open to throw a cloud of white matter that filled the wadi below the radio station. Cooper, racing to the scene, saw 'dozens of tribesmen staggering out holding their eyes and yelling for help'. Another victim of this poison-gas attack was 'Peter', the French companion of Tony de Saint-Paul. Totally blind, he survived a two-week camel ride to the Aden border before being taken home to France.

Saint-Paul was less fortunate. On 12 December 1963, he wrote to a friend describing ambushes, mines, booby traps and attacks on Sana'a. He hoped to return to France by early February, spend his money and perhaps get back to Yemen. 'The Egyptians' price on my head has now grown from $500 to $10,000,' he added. 'I hope they increase it even more.'

His luck ran out at Christmas, when a 37mm Egyptian shell caught him in the open. His body, in two parts, was placed in a trunk for repatriation. It was still there two months later, in February 1964, when the next wave of volunteers, including a French party, arrived. A girlfriend spent the money he bequeathed to her on a lover and a new sports car.

The reinforced francophone team included 'René', a one-armed survivor of the Korean war; the 'Admiral', a former sergeant major who dressed like a Yemeni; bazooka experts 'Freddy S' and 'Phillipe', both Belgian veterans of the Congo; 'Marcel', driving an old Chevy truck loaded with hand grenades between the rear headquarters and front-line positions; and the Englishman 'Bernard', a six-footer who was a liaison officer between the Saudis and bin Hassan's forward headquarters. They were paid $100 a month for their trouble.[10]

In general they did not operate in Cooper's sector. He was, according to his own account, left to operate alone for nine months, during which – using Royalist tribesmen – he built up a complete picture of the Egyptian forces' order of battle: how many, what units, what weapons, who commanded them. He lived on unleavened bread and syrup, and contracted tuberculosis.

This did not deter him from paying a bonus, in gold, to tribesmen who successfully blew the tracks off Egyptian tanks using mines he supplied. At last, his reinforcements – just two men – arrived. One was a national service officer from the Royal Sussex Regiment, Lieutenant David Bailey, who had volunteered his services to the Imam's Foreign Minister, Ahmed Al Shami. Some in KMS resisted the appointment of Bailey, a man with no Special Forces experience. But Colonel John Woodhouse, the architect of the postwar SAS, who spent five months inside Yemen for KMS and Stirling's Watchguard organisation, running the Howlan area east of Sana'a with Bailey as his only European companion, gave the younger man his seal of approval: 'A good shot and entertaining company.' Bailey was unique in other ways. One of the architects of the campaign described him as 'the only "walk-in" volunteer we took'.

The other man sent to join Cooper was Sergeant Cyril Weavers, an SAS reservist and Morse signaller. As the operation built up, the freelances created an elaborate Royalist signals network that was at least as important in halting the Egyptian advance as the mines, mortars and machine guns the foreigners brought with them.

The operation now became a loose-knit, multilayered affair and continued over the next four years or so. Cooper's people initially worked through Aden with the complicity of the High Commission. He answered to Prince Abdullah bin Hassan in Gara, while Smiley, visiting Prince Al-Hasan Hamid al-Din in a cave nine miles north of Sana'a, had a separate channel of influence. Smiley's paymaster was a Yemeni minister, Amir Mohammed Hussein, who gave him a £250 bonus, 'enough for half a swimming pool in Spain'. In London, a Cabinet decision to give clandestine support to the deniables and Royalists in Yemen was not formalised until the summer of 1964, when Dick White, converted to the hawks' agenda, advised that Britain's occupation of Aden was near collapse. So, as it turned out, was the Tory government, for it lost power a few months later.

It would appear, however, that the left hand of government was unaware of what the right hand was up to. In May that year, Duncan Sandys, the Headless Man in the Argyll photograph, in his capacity as Colonial Secretary, visited Aden and reconvened a constitutional conference that had been stalled the preceding December by a grenade attack on the High Commissioner. The conference that took place in London in June concluded that the Aden Federation (linking the backward sheikhdoms to Aden City) should be made independent by 1968, but that a British base should remain to protect UK interests and the sheikhs.

As the late military historian Robin Neillands noted later, 'The British hoped that this announcement of departure would end the uncertainty and concentrate local minds in a bid to find and support a constitutional solution. The actual effect was to produce chaos.'[11]

In 1964 there were 36 terrorist attacks in Aden and the same number of casualties, including two British dead. As the SAS veteran and mercenary Pete McAleese points out, 'Figures (for terrorist attacks) rose through 1965 to 286 incidents, 239 casualties with six servicemen killed and eighty-three wounded.'[12] Many were grenade attacks and the targets were sometimes British children.

The Secret Intelligence Service team headed by Da Silva now began its own carefully limited cross-border campaign, similar to the 'Claret' operations – ultra-secret, deniable operations in which regular soldiers (usually Special Forces) crossed international borders to launch offensives – in Borneo, using the RAF to drop rifles to Royalist tribesmen and identifying Egyptian targets, including political personalities, for assassination. The RAF also bombed the Yemeni fort and town of Harib, provoking international outrage.

On the Aden Federation side of the border, a parallel war was being fought in the scorching mountains of Radfan. In April 1964, regular SAS soldiers from A Squadron were surrounded at an isolated hill position in the jebel. Two men – Captain Robin Edwards and Trooper Nick Warburton – were killed. The families of the SAS casualties had been told that their men were on exercise on Salisbury Plain. In fact, the bodies were decapitated and their heads displayed on stakes in the Yemeni city of Taiz, possibly in reprisal for the mutilation of Egyptian soldiers by Royalist guerrillas in Yemen.

If press reports were to be believed, things were going somewhat better in Yemen. On 4 August 1964 the *New York Herald Tribune*'s special correspondent Sanche de Gramont reported, 'The Royalists have recruited thirty to fifty European mercenaries to form combat groups. These veterans of other wars have probably made all the difference between a total collapse by Royalist forces and a situation in which they control parts of the country from positions of strength.'

In fact it was touch and go for the Royalists that spring and summer. In an uncharacteristically aggressive ground offensive, the Egyptians had fought and manoeuvred for several months to outflank, and perhaps capture, the Royalist leader Imam al-Badr. An increasingly cautious British government declined to help him or his freelance advisers.

The French mercenaries increasingly went their own way, shuttling much of their material through Djibouti, but they were happy to show Smiley the results of their work. Smiley's guide was Denard, the flamboyant mercenary whose career, and trail of destruction, led from the Congo to the Seychelles by way of Biafra and Angola. Smiley described the aftermath of a typical Denard operation.

> The sight was indeed impressive. The Royalists had set their ambush in a valley between sand dunes and basalt rocks that looked like small volcanoes on the surface of the moon, and the grim relics of the battle littered the sand on either side of the track. There was a wrecked Russian T34 tank and the burnt-out shells of several armoured personnel carriers, and I counted – with my handkerchief to my nose – more than fifty decomposing bodies, half-buried by sand and half-eaten by jackals. I saw, also, six decapitated corpses: executed Republicans, they told me.[13]

The tribesmen were also being taught to think laterally by their Western instructors. They learned that a guerrilla armed with a broom and sufficient daring could halt a tank by stuffing the broom up the tank's exhaust pipe. In time, the tank crew would be forced to emerge, to a waiting execution party.

Both French and British teams depended on the Saudis for finance and, from 1964 onwards, on Israel for resupply by parachute. The reason for that, according to one of the organisers, was that the longstanding habit of hill tribes on both sides of the Yemen–Aden border of holding caravan trains to ransom, or pillaging them, endangered the Royalist guerrilla effort so badly as to make air drops an imperative. As one of the organisers put it, 'The tribes got so avaricious they stopped the convoys.'

Johnson discussed the problem with the Yemen Foreign Minister, Ahmed Al Ashami. Ashami obtained permission from King Hussein of Jordan to use Amman airport as the base for resupply. However, when Crown Prince Feisal, the Saudi ruler, learned that rival Arab royals were to play a critical role in the war, and take the credit, he said, 'Forget the

Hashemites. Get someone else.' Johnson made it clear that the only competent alternative would be Israel. The Saudi response, apparently, was, 'Don't tell me. Do it.'

One player said later, 'Some Arab heads of state, still regarded as heroes among their own people, were up to their necks in dealing with the Jews through me. At the Dorchester, I introduced the head of Mossad to someone we called "Uncle", who ran the Saudi intelligence service. Even at times of tension, we would agree that the diplomats could have their quarrels in public, while we maintained our links.'

Johnson, and his aviation expert Tony Boyle, now out of the RAF, found no difficulty in setting up clandestine parachute drops from an unmarked Stratocruiser, converted to enable supplies to move smoothly over rollers out of the tail. The Israelis, as serious professionals, wanted to be certain that they were dealing with people – including the ground party, receiving the supplies – who were as competent as they were themselves.

Cooper's CV in such matters was impressive. He had run 'reception committees' for air drops to the Resistance in occupied France in 1944 as well as similar operations during the Malayan campaign in the fifties. To demonstrate their faith in the team, Johnson and Boyle flew with the Stratocruisers. Their role was to be hostages and guarantors of operational security. It was a gruelling eight-hour, 2,000-mile round trip at 250 miles an hour, much of it at low level, by way of either French Djibouti or British Kenya.

Mossad was characteristically thorough. An emergency extraction plan included aviation-fuel dumps in various parts of the Yemeni wilderness to replenish rescue helicopters. The British observers were strip-searched before entering the preflight briefing room in Israel. Once cleared, they were issued with gold sovereigns to assist escape and with false passports. Johnson became a Canadian as well as an Israeli citizen known as 'Mr Cohen'. Serial numbers on the weapons sent from Israel had been erased. Wood shavings in which they were packed had been imported from Cyprus. The parachutes came from Italy.

The first supply drop, codenamed 'Mango', in February 1964, was to supply the Royalist Fifth Army. For a week beforehand, Cooper's team had been in routine contact with the Israelis to check the communications. The DZ, a mere 365 metres (400 yards) long, was illuminated by a pair of ancient car headlights powered by batteries and burning petrol in drums. Flying low over the Red Sea, under Egyptian radar, the Stratocruiser climbed to 3,000 metres (10,000 feet) before breaking radio silence, to confirm that all was well.

Cooper's men lit the flare path. The aircrew confirmed that they could see it and made a first pass over the DZ before turning back for the delivery from 76 metres (250 feet). Sixty parachutes rolled out of the Stratocruiser. The canopies, on static lines, snapped open. It was, Cooper wrote later 'a beautifully executed, professional drop'. Security around the drops was stringent, for they were 'in fact being operated by a "friendly" air force. If this had become known, the political repercussions would have defied description.'

On another of these flights, a KMS representative watched 14 tons of materiel flow out of the Stratocruiser in a single pass. It seemed perfect, until an Israeli dispatcher, responsible for the release, seemed about to follow his cargo as his parachute opened by accident. He was, however, tethered to the aircraft and lived to fly another day. On the ground that night Tony Boyle was in charge of the drop zone, watching the aircraft approach below radar ceiling, and below the 3,000-metre (10,000-foot) plateau where he waited for it. 'It went perfectly,' said one of the participants. 'The aircraft climbed to 200 feet above the DZ and discharged its load. The parachutes hardly developed but the stuff was intact.'

The Israelis' navigation, in a largely unmapped area, at night, was very, very good. What followed was not to Boyle's liking. A Yemeni praised Allah for the safe delivery of the cargo, adding, 'Now not only do we defeat the Egyptians in our country. We can go on to defeat the British in Aden!'

The cover on the KMS operation was blown by an odd coalition that included Egyptian intelligence, the *Sunday Times* and, subsequently, the Adjutant of 21 SAS, Captain Richard Pirie. By some means, the Egyptians had been able to intercept letters sent to Cooper from England in November 1963. Almost certainly, tribesmen had intercepted a courier and sold the letters on to the Egyptians. One was from Lady Birdwood, a political ally of George Kennedy Young. She detested blacks, Jews and all foreigners. Apparently unaware of Mossad's role, Lady Birdwood became part of the organisation resupplying the Yemeni Royalist forces from Aden. On one occasion, with Tony Boyle, she broke into a store containing medical supplies destined for Cooper's people, which the RAF had impounded. Having liberated the most useful material, she and Boyle sent it on across the border by camel.

Her letter offered condolences to Cooper on his hard time in Yemen. Another note, introducing Bailey and Weavers, was written by Boyle. The Egyptian intelligence services passed them out to the Cairo newspaper *Al Ahram* whose editor, Mohammed Hassanein Heikal, was a friend of Nasser. Heikal was also on friendly terms with a key member of the *Sunday Times* editorial team. First *Al Ahram*, then – in July 1964 – the *Sunday Times*, ran stories about the Yemen operation, using extracts from five letters to Cooper, which he never received.

The British government denied knowledge of the operation but the Americans were disturbed and said so. In spite of that, on Julian Amery's orders, RAF aircraft would later fly 50,000 Lee Enfield .303 rifles from Wiltshire to supply the Royalists by way of Jordan, while former RAF pilots, employed by Airwork, flew operational missions against Egyptian and Republican targets on the Yemeni border.

Subsequently, Pirie told the *People* newspaper that his office at 21 SAS had been used as a clearing house for mercenaries in the Yemen and elsewhere. Pirie had passed names and military records to a secret address. Potential volunteers 'usually heard something in a week or two'.[14]

Pirie's credibility was challenged when he went on to assert that the men's wages of £250 per month were paid through the Foreign Office and Ministry of Defence, a claim that Whitehall denied, probably correctly, since the operation was funded by the Saudis, while KMS was registered offshore. It was, and is, normal practice for freelance soldiers (along with oil-rig workers and many others) to be paid via overseas banks.

The rest of Pirie's account is correct. One of his successors as adjutant of 21 SAS recalls querying the absence 'on long leave' of a number of soldiers on the nominal roll. The regiment's chief clerk said he did not know. The adjutant then asked the RSM about the missing men, only to be told, 'I wouldn't go there if I were you, sir.'

None of the leaks deterred Johnson's people or MI6, or the Saudis, who declined invitations from an increasingly embarrassed Nasser to talk peace. By the spring of 1964, the only road for Egyptian supplies into Sana'a from the Red Sea port of Hodeida was no longer safe. As Nasser's English biographer Anthony Nutting put it,

Of all the reverses Nasser was to suffer during the eighteen years he presided over Egypt's destinies, by far the most humiliating was the disaster which overtook his intervention in Yemen, with all the shaming evidence that it revealed of the ineptitude and ineffectiveness of tens of thousands of Egyptian troops against a relatively small number of guerrilla tribesmen.

Well might he call his Yemeni venture, 'my Vietnam'. For with his failure to persuade the Saudis to pull out and agree to a negotiated settlement, he now had no alternative but to pile in yet more troops to prop up the gimcrack structure of Sallal's republican regime.[15]

Nasser had also lost his most valuable diplomatic asset in the West. President John F. Kennedy did not like monarchies, particularly Arab ones. The day before he was assassinated in November 1963 he had telephoned the British Prime Minister, Lord Home, to ask him to pull the freelances out of the Yemen. Home replied that he knew nothing of the matter. Kennedy was succeeded by Lyndon Johnson, a pro-Zionist.

The guerrilla/terrorist campaign against the British in Aden, supported by Cairo, as well as Egyptian-backed cross-border raids into the Aden Federation from occupied Yemen, had further diminished any hope Nasser might have had of finding support for his appeals to the Saudis to end the Yemen conflict. But Britain's credibility, equally, was overshadowed by the public commitment in July 1964 by a Tory government to withdraw from Aden by 1968, while retaining a military base there. Nasser was delighted.

The election of Harold Wilson's Labour government in October 1964 would result in an even more radical policy: withdrawal of all British armed forces from East of Suez. In February 1966, London let it be known it would not, after all, need a military base in Aden. Nasser did not believe this. A £150 million arms deal (Operation Magic Carpet) shortly before, through which the UK would supply the Saudis with a modern air force flown by British and Commonwealth mercenaries, convinced the Egyptian president that – as at Suez in 1956 – Perfidious Albion was up to its tricks and that the promise of withdrawal was worthless. One of those involved in the operation believed that 1,200 people were involved, many in Yemen.

As Nutting observes, 'There could be one answer to such machinations: to drive the British out of Aden with the utmost possible speed.'

In the light of the aviation deal, Nasser also decided to keep his troops active in Yemen, where a brief truce unravelled and fighting was renewed. Initially, among the tight-knit Aden group supporting the deniables in Yemen, it was business as usual regardless of what official UK government policy might be, even though the war was becoming a static affair in which two armies, exhausted by attrition, stared out at one another from their respective bunkers.

There was one significant exception to this situation. In the spring of 1965 the Saudis as well as the British freelances were unhappy about the increasing inertia of their war-weary clients. An ultimatum from both supporters prodded the Yemeni Prince Mohammed bin al-Hussein into action: either make a convincing attempt to cut the Egyptian main supply route between the capital Sana'a and the strategically important outpost of Marib, near the Saudi border, or kiss goodbye to further Saudi aid. After months of procrastination, Mohammed's First Army prepared for action. Bernard Mills had done the First Army's homework with his own reconnaissance for an attack on a pinch point at a place called Wadi Humaidat.

In a densely researched history of the Yemen war, Professor Clive Jones describes how 300 camels were needed to supply heavy weaponry, including 81mm mortars to firing points overlooking the road. An equally heavy burden of bribes was required to buy the temporary loyalty of a local tribe. Jones writes,

> In what was perhaps the most efficient battle fought by the Royalists, 362 soldiers of the First Army, backed by 1,290 tribesmen . . . directed by two British and three French mercenaries, cut this main supply route and, despite several days of determined Egyptian counter-attacks, held on to their positions.[16]

But the Saudis' customary strategy of bleeding Nasser slowly, without driving the conflict towards a clear conclusion, disillusioned many of the freelances. A French participant described the failure of the Royalists' last major push on Sana'a in 1966, led by Roger Bruni, a survivor of Dien Bien Phu. Three lorries carrying mercenaries led the way before dawn and set up mortars. At 9.30 a.m. the barrage began. The Republican garrison hit back with repeated salvoes from multiple rocket launchers known as 'Stalin Organs' and 155mm artillery. A French description of the action described how

> for eight hours, the plain around the city shuddered under the impact of bombs. Some 250 shells were fired by the mercenaries onto the town, the airport and the embassy quarter. 'Victory is assured,' the mercenaries

thought. 'Sana'a is going to fall.' But the [Royalist] infantry did not attack. Their commander, the Prince, did not wish to give the order ...

The embittered mercenaries said nothing. Their Yemeni allies congratulated them. The mercenaries, now thinking of another, better war, confessed, ironically, that they heard the call of giant toads on the banks of the Niger, where another conflict – the Biafran war – was beginning.

Some of the key British organisers were also becoming disillusioned. On 1 October 1966, in a private memorandum entitled 'Report on the Yemen War', Jim Johnson wrote

In view of the apparent lack of interest by HMG in the problem [of Yemen] and the stated indifference to our activities by MI6, coupled with the absolute disinterest and lack of us at the moment by HRH Sultan [Prince Sultan] we appear to have three courses open to us:

To withdraw as soon as possible from the Yemen before disaster overtakes us.

Convert ourselves into a purely intelligence gathering organisation and hope we will be used sensibly again.

Hang on in our present role and organisation and hope we will be used sensibly again.

All common sense points to our adopting the first course. We have discovered, trained and helped arm tens of thousands of tribesmen in previously unknown areas of Yemen ... All this without official Government encouragement whatsoever, far from it, in fact, on many early occasions we were actively frustrated and discouraged, and as this attitude has never really changed there is every pointer and reason why we should stop. There is no indication that HMG wants us to continue now.

Given the policy of both Tory and Labour governments to withdraw from the region, Johnson's pessimism was reasonable. He was also peeved with his Saudi paymasters. Matters came to a head soon after Johnson's memorandum of October 1966. He confronted a senior member of the Saudi royal family and asked, 'Do you want to win this war or not? The British have announced the date to leave Aden. If I go before they leave it will be a shambles.'

When it seemed clear to him that the Saudi strategy was to prolong a war of attrition without any clear outcome, so as to pin down an Egyptian army that might otherwise have invaded Saudi Arabia, Johnson convened a 'radio conference' of his team. Those who wished to stay could do so but the most significant players, including Boyle and Faulques, as well as Johnson, agreed that it was time to pull out.

Johnson had a final interview with a senior emir, in his office. Waiting for the next audience was Julian Amery, now no longer a minister. Amery offered some advice: 'Jim, behave properly.'

Johnson's resignation was received with Anglo-Saxon sangfroid by the emir, who said, 'Thank you, Colonel. We will remember you.'

Johnson had not finished. He had two requests: an orderly disposal of the weapons, particularly heavy mortars, under KMS control; and an enhanced month's pay for his men. He sought nothing for himself but, he pointedly explained, 'the French have a habit of blowing up aircraft of national airlines if they don't get paid properly'. The Saudi paymaster got the point. A month later, at the Hyde Park Hotel, 30 of the KMS team celebrated their payoff, and their return, with a champagne party. There was a survivors' reunion, probably the last, in England in 2007, which some veterans attended in wheelchairs.

The KMS team was replaced by David Stirling's newly created Watch-Guard International. WatchGuard had been active in Kenya and as a television company (TIE) in Hong Kong. (Stirling's other innovative marketing ideas included a scheme to sell submarines to the Saudis. It provoked some ribald jokes among the deniables: 'Up periscope!' 'Sorry, sir, periscope blocked by sand.')

Stirling arrived in the Saudi capital Riyadh on 12 December 1966, just over two months after the Johnson memorandum, seeking an audience of Faisal, now no longer Crown Prince, but King. The British ambassador, Morgan Mann, warned Stirling that the King was still incensed by 'Colonel Johnson's rude ultimatum'. In spite of that, Stirling was allowed to meet the Saudi Defence Minister, Emir Sultan, who guaranteed funds for what was still described as 'the Johnson Force', sufficient for two more months. Stirling also learned the latest reason for the Saudis' lack of appetite for a bigger war. They were vulnerable to air attack until a deal could be done with Britain for the supply of fighters.

In February 1967 Stirling's attempt to take control of the force was rejected by the Saudis, who confirmed that Gooley, his own man, was to be

'Commander of the Advisory Group attached to the Royalist Yemeni Army'. Gooley had joined the team in July 1965, when the British/SAS involvement 'was tiny'. His group was also known as 'Gooley Force' or 'Expedient'. Gooley's patron was Prince Zaid Sudairi, a member of the royal family. Later in his career, Gooley became a millionaire in the travel business and a charity donor.

In parallel, David Smiley continued his long and often painful perambulations around the country on foot, camel, donkey and wheels, checking drop zones and airstrips. But, as the war dragged on, the freelances suffered an increasing number of casualties. So did civilians. On 5 January 1967 nine Egyptian aircraft dropped 27 phosgene gas bombs on Kitaf, near the border with Saudi Arabia, killing 200 people.

In June 1967, the strategic picture changed with Israel's demolition of the Egyptian Air Force on the ground and its lightning occupation of Sinai in the momentous Six Day War. Nasser rapidly recalled his army of 50,000 still in Yemen, now an army of hostages to the new geopolitics. The Egyptian retreat was not complete – Egyptian air attacks continued – when, late in the afternoon of 24 August 1967, three members of Gooley Force, all former SAS soldiers, were on a routine journey from Amara to Quddum in northern Yemen. Two of the men were to relieve an unnamed comrade who had been manning an observation post in a cave for several days who was now showing signs of stress. The 50-mile route by Land Rover, through an area thought to be safe, should have taken around six hours.

Terry Falcon-Wilson was driving the vehicle on a crude mountain track as it descended into a wadi. With him were Allan Havelock-Stevens, aged 27, a former troop commander with D Squadron, Anthony ('Knocker') Parsons and a 14-year-old 'tea boy'/translator named Ali bin Abdurahman. Stevens, new to this theatre, was familiarising himself with the terrain. What happened next was still unclear some 40 years later.

A report compiled for the men's next of kin asserts,

They arrived at Al Abu Jubara at approximately 3.30 p.m. This is the first place where the mountain road comes down to a wadi between Amara and Quddum, about one hour from the last Royalist outpost outside Amara.

The Land Rover had reached the wadi bottom when they saw three men: one above the wadi on the left and two above the wadi on the right.

The wadi here is very narrow. One of the men from the right came down to the wadi bottom and signalled and told them to stop, in Arabic and English. The other two covered them with their rifles.

The Yemeni on the Land Rover (Ali bin Abdurahman) told Terry Falcon-Wilson to drive on but Terry said, 'He is OK. He speaks English.' The man spoke strongly to them in English but Ali did not understand what he was saying. The English got down from the Land Rover to talk but the Yemeni [Ali] remained in the back of the vehicle. The two men on either side called to him not to leave the car or he would be shot. After about twenty-five minutes the English, who were very angry, gave the man their money.

At that point, according to Ali, the only survivor, one of the three watchers

climbed up the hill to the right saying he would go to Sheikh Mohd bin Athlar [a local ruler] to get permission for the Englishmen to go on. (This was said in Arabic.) When he reached the others, the men above opened fire on the English. The Englishmen ran behind the cover of the vehicle. The enemy then fired several more shots at the English and at Ali. The English were struck by several shots and killed instantly.

Ali, who had only been wounded, went on firing at the enemy who shouted that they must now kill the Yemeni. The battle went on for an hour until the daughter of Sheikh Mohd Bin Athlar arrived and said they must not kill a Yemeni. After five minutes the girl came and took Ali's rifle and escorted him to the village (about five minutes away). The men ran off into the hills.

After about ten minutes Sheikh Abdullah bin Khamis al Awgari and four soldiers arrived by car on their way from Najran [a Royalist forward operating base in Saudi Arabia] to Quddum. Sheikh Abdullah, a strong Royalist, talked for about one and a half hours, then left for Quddum with Ali and the bodies. Because of a breakdown and air raids at Quddum they did not arrive till the afternoon of 25 August.

The report named the three killers and noted, 'They are from the nearby village and were known Republicans.' Their victims 'were buried in the French camp outside Najran, Saudi Arabia, at 9.50 p.m. on 26 August 1967'.

This version of events, provided by Ali, the only survivor, does not entirely match David Smiley's account in his memoir, *Arabian Assignment*. Smiley was on a reconnaissance in the area at the time. He met Ali the day after the murders. Smiley suggests that, since the three Englishmen antici-pated no trouble in a safe area, they had only one rifle among them, though Ali carried his own weapon. While two of the tribesmen covered the vehicle at a roadblock, the third questioned them in English for 20 minutes.

> Finally he asked for money to let them through, which they gave him, and then he demanded their rifles. Ali whispered, 'Do not give him your gun,' and held on firmly to his own. But the Englishmen innocently handed over their rifles [*sic*] whereupon the tribesmen opened fire, killing one of them instantly and wounding the others.

Ali, hit in the leg, had taken refuge behind a rock. The two surviving British soldiers stayed with the vehicle, 'where a grenade finished them off'. Ali exchanged shots with the killers until the 14-year-old daughter of the local sheikh appeared, shouting, 'Are you not ashamed? You have killed three faranghi (Europeans). Why would you stain your hands with the blood of this boy, who is one of our people?' The girl 'had then walked calmly over to Ali, taken his rifle and led him by the hand to her village'.

Smiley noted that one of the dead men – Tony Parsons – had been a good friend who had served in the SAS under his command in Oman. All the casualties were married with young children. Like most of the British mercenaries, 'he had come here to risk his life, not so much for the money, as for the adventure, and in the hope that he might be helping his own country as well; it was a tragic waste that he should lose it through trickery and murder'.

Trickery and murder, in this environment, were punished in the usual way. A team of Royalist commandos, trained by the British, carried out a revenge attack in the area where the Expedient team were ambushed. An intelligence analysis said that the commandos 'are reported to have destroyed half the village buildings as a reprisal and have brought back nine hostages against the production of the three killers'.

Such reprisals were a British tradition in the Middle East. During my mili-tary service with 16 Parachute Brigade in the Suez Canal Zone, most of an Egyptian village was erased in Operation Flatten. In 1964, two SAS soldiers (one of them Peter McAleese, who became a mercenary in Angola and Colombia) used petrol and high explosive to implode a house at Ataq, on the border between Adem and Yemen. One of them said later, 'It was a punish-ment ordered by the Political Officer for some infringement or other.'

Grieving relatives of the three dead deniables, seeking the truth decades later, were told by some of the men's former comrades, 'They all always carried rifles and a pistol. They were ambushed; stopped by one man while the other two, hidden in the rocks above, opened fire when they left the Land Rover.' A British soldier who identified the bodies believed that Havelock-Stevens was killed by two gunshot wounds to the chest. Another source believes that hand grenades were thrown, as Smiley suggests. Possibly they were, and were intended as a coup de grâce, without causing further damage to the bodies.

There was an eerie postscript to this episode. Shortly before his death Havelock-Stevens wrote a short story about an English desert lover, pining for Arabia. 'The call of Arabia was strong . . . I did not know why I must return but I did know that all I would bring back from that sunburnt country was weariness . . .' The Englishman conducts two British archaeol-ogists to a desert site. Their local guide is a teenage Arab boy, with whom the central figure of the story has an instinctive affinity.

The group are ambushed by tribesmen and tied up. After a night of captivity, the archaeologists and their protector wake to discover they are no longer bound, no longer prisoners. But the Arab boy is dead, his throat cut.

Havelock-Stevens had also made a will requesting that his body be repatriated. His remains were recovered early in 1968 by Gooley, as he oversaw the final disbandment of the Yemen operation. It was a bleak postscript to the adventure. Gooley had shared SAS service with Havelock-Stevens in Borneo. The dead man's relatives received ashes rather than an identifiable body. Smiley did not approve. He noted in his diary that, after breakfast on 28 February 1968, he 'visited the graves of the 3 British murdered last August'.

Last week Mike Gooley came out to remove one of the bodies to take it back to UK. A great pity, as the French [mercenaries] had buried them in a very nice graveyard, walled in and cemented. They had to smash the cement, dig up the body which was only half decomposed so they had to burn it. I cannot understand why people like bodies to be taken home. Once dead, the soul is not there and human flesh reverts to dust.[17]

During a bumpy flight from the Yemeni border to Jeddah soon after the deaths, Smiley found himself sitting alongside 'a very nice ex-paratrooper and SAS man, now a mercenary. He tells me the Saudis are paying £10,000 compensation to each of the widows of the three British killed. Very fair really as they all get high pay in view of the somewhat dangerous nature of their job.' It is unclear whether such compensation was actually available.

The remains of Parsons and Falcon-Wilson lie in Saudi Arabia, though a requiem mass was celebrated at Brompton Oratory church, Kensington, for Falcon-Wilson, a Roman Catholic. The deaths were not formally registered in Britain, nor did any inquests take place.

As the men's immediate commander, Mike Gooley had sent the men on their fatal mission, though this could not have been anticipated. Gooley's Yemen service was as a freelance, but he was not motivated by money. He told a friend: 'We were all *invited* to take part. The persuasion always highlighted [the fact that] our services were for and in the interests of the nation. We had to be released from regular service to make the operation unattributable.'

Gooley and two other SAS veterans created Trailfinders, a successful travel company, in November 1971. In 2006, he appeared as No. 227 in the *Sunday Times* Rich List (worth an estimated £260 million). The newspaper noted, 'The Mike Gooley Trailfinders Charity distributed more than £1.5 million last year ... including £400,000 to the Alzheimer's Society.' A Royal Society of Arts profile reported, 'A well-known philanthropist, he set up the Mike Gooley Trailfinders' Charity in 1995. Over the past ten years [1996–2006] it has donated almost £13 million to a variety of charitable causes, including Cancer Research UK and the Alzheimer's Society.'

The link between old SAS comrades within Trailfinders was still intact. One of Gooley's fellow directors was Viscount John Slim OBE. Lord Slim, like Gooley (and the long-dead Havelock-Stevens), was a veteran of the undeclared jungle war against Indonesia in Borneo, 1963–6.

One of the next of kin still has nagging doubts about the Yemen operation. She wonders whether the deaths of Falcon-Wilson, Havelock-Stevens and Parsons was random banditry or whether it is true that the Egyptians offered a £20,000 a bounty for the death of a foreign soldier in Yemen. But, after Egypt's stunning defeat at the hands of Israel shortly before, it is less likely that such bounties – witness the case of the French mercenary Tony de Saint-Paul – were still available. Egypt had had enough of Yemen and was now, suddenly, very hard up.

Exactly how many serving and former SAS soldiers died in Yemen is not clear. The KMS payroll – an official secret – still exists, but many of the names on it are noms de guerre. Members of the regiment killed in action are commemorated on the pillar of the parade ground clock at its Hereford base. (To stay alive, in SAS parlance, is to 'beat the clock'.) The plaques make no mention of Yemen, though six names are linked to South Arabia, from 1964 to 1967. These were casualties of Aden and the war in the Federation, upcountry.

Ken Connor, the regiment's longest-serving soldier, asserts that the Yemen operation

> became a litmus test for the future and, because of the number of people killed in action, it was not repeated. Other ways were found to use SAS men in support of covert operations, usually by giving them a permanent discharge from the army. They would then be rehired by a suitably deniable third party.[18]

Some of those involved in the Yemen adventure question Connor's assessment of a high body count. One of the organisers told me, 'I guarantee that these three – Parsons, Havelock-Stevens and Falcon-Wilson – were the only fatal casualties of the entire operation. No one [else] sustained any injuries of a lasting nature throughout.'

However, it appears that these three deaths, combined with the British withdrawal from Aden, at the fag end of the Yemen war, may have been the last straw for some of the foreign military advisers. Three SAS veterans remained, alongside a mixed crew of French, Belgian, Polish, German and Italians, some of whom concentrated their efforts on building a swimming pool far from likely trouble.

Smiley doggedly continued on his journeys, sometimes accompanied by an Iranian officer, since Iran was now involved in air drops as well as Israel. But, by 1968, even British diplomats were keeping Smiley at arm's length. One 'refused to keep two wireless sets for me in the Embassy'.

There is no evidence that any freelances remained active on the ground following Britain's retreat from Aden on 30 November 1967 after 128 years of colonial rule, a process initiated by another private army, the East India Company. The last Egyptian soldier left Yemen a month before the last British soldier left Aden.

In August of that year, the British Expedient team (Gooley Force) comprised 26 men plus six on UK leave. The French had 23 men in Arabia and six on leave. A total of five teams were operating in Yemen and others were training Royalist commandos. But the air war continued, with British freelance pilots flying Lightning fighters, and F86F Sabres for the Royal Saudi Air Force repeatedly struck at Yemeni positions on the border with Saudi Arabia between August and December 1969.

At the same time, following an Arab summit at Khartoum in August 1967, Nasser's army of 70,000 was withdrawing from Yemen, encouraged by a bribe of £135 million a year from Kuwait and Saudi Arabia as 'war-damage funds': compensation for lands lost to Israel in the Six Day War two months earlier. By a sad irony, the Khartoum settlement came within days of the deaths in Yemen of Gooley's men.

The Yemen stalemate was finally acknowledged as a political fact by both sponsors of the war – Egypt and Saudi Arabia – in 1970. It led to the creation of a national coalition in the new state of North Yemen. The Royalist leader, Imam al Badr, retired to suburban exile in Bromley. By then his opponent, Sallal, had been overthrown by fellow Republicans in a bloodless coup while Sallal was being fêted in Cairo.

The main beneficiaries of this conflict were Israel, Saudi Arabia and the United States. Communist expansion in Arabia had been contained and Uncle Sam's stake in Saudi oil was secure, at least until Saddam Hussein's invasion of Kuwait in 1990. Israel had benefited crucially from Yemen's role as Nasser's Vietnam as the Zionist air force destroyed its Egyptian counterpart on the ground, while Israel seized swathes of territory from Egypt, Jordan and Syria, including Gaza and the Golan Heights.

It could be argued that the clandestine, collusive alliance of France, Britain and Israel in opposing Egypt in Yemen was, in an ironic turn of history, a more successful replay of Suez 1956. The London warriors of the Suez group could be said to have had the last word, even if they were unheeded by those who wrote the history of Suez.

But the British, having surrendered first the Suez Canal Zone, then Aden, to Nasserist and Soviet communist forces as part of the great game to control the Gulf and its oil, now felt the pressure of subversion and guerrilla warfare on their last Arab satellite, Oman.

In Oman in 1970, as the Yemen conflict formally ended, so a communist-inspired revolution came within a hair's breadth of toppling Britain's client ruler, the repressive Sultan Sai'd bin Taimur. The communist-led attempt to drive him and his British allies into the sea marked the beginning of a new six-year war in which British Special Forces, SIS and British freelances would again work together to play a pivotal role. But the Yemen campaign, more vividly than any other 'private' war, was a role model for future deniable operations, reflecting the SAS way of going to war: small numbers of men punching above their strategic weight to create, in a favourite Zionist phrase, 'New facts'.

6

OMAN 1970–95:

How the Sandhurst Brotherhood saved a nation

Britain owes a debt of thanks and perhaps much else to a little-known freelance soldier for the UK's continued influence in Oman, the only gateway to the Arabian Gulf and the road (other than the still insecure route through Iraq) to a major slice of the world's oil reserves. The officer concerned was the key player in a colourful coup d'état engineered by the Secret Intelligence Service (MI6).

In July 1970, Timothy Landon, then a cavalry captain, was serving on secondment with the army of the country's ruler. Oman was in a bad way. For centuries, Britain had struck deals with Gulf rulers to protect its merchant fleet from local pirates, in exchange for security guarantees. An essential part of the arrangement was that when it came to internal politics, the ruler was left free by London to run his own territory as he wished.

In Oman, however, the British had a problem. Sultan Sa'id bin Taimur, the 13th hereditary monarch, was a despot of such monstrous character that his rule was trembling on the brink of collapse. The hands shaking his tree were those of the Baathist Iraqi regime of Ahmed Hassan Bakr (controlled from behind the scenes by Saddam Hussein) to the north and the communist South Yemen (People's Democratic Republic) in what had been the UK's Aden, to the south. More dangerous still, bin Taimur's abuse of his own people had created an ulcer within the Omani body politic.

Britain's concern grew following the discovery of oil in Oman. It sent John Townsend, an economist, to try to persuade the Sultan to take a tentative step out of the medieval world, towards the late twentieth century. He wrote later,

> My first meeting with the Sultan had a dreamlike unreality. I met a strange, small old man with a splendid set of Father Christmas whiskers, tended and guarded by burly young men of African origin who were known as 'slaves'. In excellent English he gave me careful instructions as to whom I should meet and what I might say. All the people with whom I was to work were expatriate. I was not to meet any Omanis . . . He said, 'Our people are not yet ready for development.'
>
> There was great poverty and disease. Nothing was done because the Sultan would not permit it. No man could leave his village and seek work without the permission of the Sultan. No man could repair his house without the permission of the Sultan. This remote old man, who never left his palace in Salalah [on the coast of the Gulf of Oman] and ruled by radio-telephone through expatriates had instilled such fear in his people that very few dared defy him.[1]

Taimur's regime anticipated the harsh rule of the Taliban in Afghanistan. There was no music or dancing. Western clothes, including sunglasses, were forbidden. Flogging and imprisonment were light sentences for disobedience. Collective punishments included the cementing over of water wells, spelling doom for entire communities. Other repressive devices, confirmed by the current Omani government, included curfews that were brutally enforced.

> Anyone found outside the city walls after the retort of the cannons would be shot unless he carried a lantern. Radios were banned as they were considered the work of the devil. Healthcare was virtually non-existent . . . A total national collapse was imminent.

On the high jebel of Dhofar, overlooking Salalah on the coast, the tribes were more than restive. They were in revolt, led by agents trained in Iraq. By 1966, not only did the Ruler's writ not run in these wild mountains. Some of his own bodyguard, on parade before Taimur, presented arms by way of a salute, then pointed their rifles at him and opened fire. Remarkably, they missed the Sultan though they did wing the palace guard commander, a Pakistani. The Sultan was driven away to the protection of his British-led force. There he said, 'We seem to be having a little trouble down at the palace. I wonder if you would be so good as to come down?'

By 1970, Taimur's rule extended only along a narrow coastal strip. Even the British Embassy, in Muscat 1,000 miles north, had a helipad and a convenient escape route overlooking the harbour. Encouraged by the Labour Defence Minister Denis Healey – a fighting officer during World War Two – SIS worked on a strategy to remove the problem. If a coup was the solution, then who had the credibility to succeed Taimur? The obvious choice was his son Qaboos. Qaboos was no radical, by Western standards. He was a benevolent, but absolute, monarch in waiting. He was also a graduate of the UK's Royal Military Academy, Sandhurst, who had served with a Scottish regiment in Germany, where he had acquired a taste for the heavy rhythms of martial music.

The initial obstacle was that there was no easy access to Qaboos. Like other key figures, the Prince was watched by palace spies working for his father. He was not free to talk to British agents. There was one exception, however. This was Tim Landon. He and Qaboos had shared a room and become friends at Sandhurst, where the young Omani cadet was sometimes as isolated as he would be, later, in his father's palace.

As one close observer of the events that followed put it, 'Landon had access to Qaboos. He suggested that Qaboos should take over from his father in the event of a coup. Qaboos agreed. With that essential piece of the jigsaw in place, the plot could now go ahead.'

Back in London, the Labour government of which Healey was part was replaced by a Conservative administration led by Edward Heath. Though Heath did not recall any personal involvement in the events in Oman on 23 July 1970, the action – brief, dramatic and clinically efficient – occurred less than a month into his watch.

SIS had warned Landon to have no further part in the plot. International opinion, as well as local sentiment, would demand a clean internal affair with no visible involvement of the British. On standby at Hereford, however, was an SAS bodyguard – most of them members of G (for 'Guards') Squadron – ready to move to ensure Qaboos's security if the plot succeeded.

The man who took the greatest risk was Sheik Braik bin Hamud bin Hamid al-Ghafari, an Omani aristocrat, Governor of Dhofar Province and a friend of Qaboos. Braik's people had become Taimur's victims. Early in the morning, Sheik Braik drove to the palace to demand that Taimur abdicate. He was accompanied by a group of armed slaves loyal to Qaboos. Taimur was not caught unawares. His spy network had alerted him. He knew also that he could no longer depend on his British officers. He armed himself with a Sterling sub-machine gun.

As the ultimatum party entered the main palace hallway the 'small old man with a splendid set of Father Christmas whiskers' roared – or, rather, squeaked – defiance at the intruders and fired a burst of 9mm at the nearest man, killing him. Another shot wounded Braik. Then, as he tried to retreat up the stairs, Taimur dropped the weapon and accidentally shot himself through the foot. The coup was over. It had taken, at most, ten minutes.

In a slick public-relations exercise, Qaboos released a proclamation that said in part

> My first act will be the immediate abolition of all the unnecessary restrictions on your lives and activities . . . Continue living as usual. I will be arriving in Muscat in the coming days and then I will let you know of my future plans . . . My people, my brothers, yesterday it was complete darkness and, with the help of God, tomorrow will be a new dawn on Muscat, Oman and its people.[2]

A British army medical team arrived on cue, and gave first aid to bin Taimur and Sheik Braik. Both were carted away on stretchers to a waiting RAF transport plane. They arrived in London the same day. After hospital treatment, the deposed Ruler was accommodated in a special suite at a luxury hotel until his death two years later. He was buried in Britain. The funeral was attended by just three people: two witnesses from the Foreign Office and one from the Omani Embassy. He was unmourned by any of his kin.

In Oman, meanwhile, the British specialists guarding Qaboos as he received petitions did so invisibly, from the cover of a two-way mirror. One petitioner's overemphatic hand movements were followed by the muzzles of SAS weapons, just in case.

With the aid of Tim Landon (as security adviser, on his resignation from the British army) and other British expatriate and armed-forces aides – some of whom continued to serve Qaboos as contract officers when they left the British army – the new Ruler set about recovering the loyalty of the jebel. The war that followed lasted six years, fought out of sight of the media. It was a blend of Kipling's North West Frontier, involving personal duels between adversaries who learned to respect one another, and the heavy weaponry of all-out, modern war. British Army, RAF and Royal Navy officers were seconded to upgrade the Sultan's Armed Forces and draw up long-term plans to put down the insurrection.

One novel posting was that of the British manager of the Bank of the Middle East. For a time, he took charge as the country's financial adviser. One of his friends said later, 'Everyone consented to this. He was a great success.'

For years, the Sultan's army had been content to leave the Dhofar mountains during three monsoon months – a hellish environment in which, according to a Persian legend, 'the sinner has a foretaste of what awaits him in Hades' – to the rebels. Occasionally the British-led force would blaze away with machine guns mounted on armoured cars at an invisible enemy high above them. As a change, the air force – six ageing Strikemasters flown by British pilots – would launch random attacks sometimes chosen casually in the European officers' mess the night before.

One SAS veteran recalled, 'We watched one of the ground assaults. I asked a contract officer what he thought he was doing. "Containing them," he said. "Keeping them in their place up there." "Yes," I said. "And they are keeping you in your place down here." As he raised his rifle, an incoming round hit the tip of the barrel at a range of several hundred yards. I said, "These guys are good."'

Soldiers from the regular 22 SAS Regiment, based in Hereford, expanded to squadron strength in Dhofar, slowly began intelligence-gathering incursions into the jebel. It was a slow start because of formidable political limitations imposed on the soldiers by the British government. 'Some of our enemy were little more than boys of about four-teen,' said the same veteran, 'but they were good shots and they could run like rabbits, zigzagging as they went. They were hard targets. One of them climbed to the top of a ridge facing us, stood up and waved. We did the same. It was a sort of recognition by both sides, a sign of respect.'

Later, as the SAS presence increased and many limitations were lifted, of necessity, the regiment became involved in a growing number of minor and major operations. Alongside offensive operations, bribes were used instead of collective punishment to persuade the *adoo* (enemy) to change sides. They did so in family-sized groups. Community aid such as veter-inary care for livestock went with medical care for humans. The practitioners were British RAMC (medical corps), RAVC (veterinary corps) and SAS bush doctors. One of these was Nick Downie, who walked away from his medical finals in London to join the regiment. He treated camels and humans alike. When a frail tribal elder died of a heart attack, he was blamed. Another team treated a young woman who was presented with chronic indigestion. When pregnancy was diagnosed, the girl's family were also outraged.

The greatest gamble of all was to equip the former *adoo* with modern Western firearms including the 7.62mm Belgian FN rifle to replace the mixture of AK-47s, Simonovs and – still a favourite – the .303 Lee Enfield. The .303 was the British army's standard-issue rifle during World War Two and long after, adapted as a sniper weapon. The teams of jebeli warriors who had been turned were known as *firqa*. Their most frequent greeting then, and for years to come, was not only '*Salam, `Aleikum*' ('Hello, peace be on you') but also '*Ooreed . . .*' ('I want'). The new alliance, in their eyes, was a cornucopia, a welfare state from which no dream was excluded. To celebrate the end of the Ramadan fast, one *firqa* fired 5,000 rounds of ammunition – the unit's entire stock – into the sky in a single *feu de joie*. In parallel with the *ooreed* factor went the hospitality of shared meals and comradeship – sometimes.

'One of our difficulties,' a former SAS officer recalled, 'was that we never knew whether the *firqa* would fight or not. It depended on whom they were fighting against. We would agree a battle plan, in which, say, we held the exposed flanks while the *firqa* advanced down some wadi to engage the *adoo*. After some time the *firqa* scouts would return and say they could not fight today. Why not? "Because my brother's family are on the other side." By then it was too late and the shooting had started. Our front markers would come on the communications net and ask, "Where the fuck's the *firqa*?"'

One British veteran recalls, 'The Dhofaris often referred to the insurrection as "The War of the Families". *Adoo* from the same tribe would frequently fight each other. Our main difficulty arose when members of the same family were on opposite sides.'

The *firqa* usually had one or two SAS soldiers embedded with them as 'advisers' to provide communications and liaison with either SAS support weapons teams (such as mortars) or the Sultan's Armed Forces including his air force. It was dangerous work if the latest demand for more (of anything they could think of) was refused. One officer, alone on the mountain with a team of well-armed and disgruntled allies, called down a demonstrative air strike by Strikemasters; it was just a show, but served to remind the dissidents that they, and their village, were vulnerable if they mutinied.

Some of those who bonded with their new allies went native. One former SAS soldier, now a freelance, led his team across the international border with South Yemen to blow up a fort as a reprisal for an assault by regular South Yemeni soldiers. In another extraordinary encounter, the same man greeted a grizzled, bearded figure squatting beneath an isolated tree. Naturally, he used Arabic to ask a few questions about troop movements in the area. The bearded one made eye contact and said, in Sandhurst English, 'I suppose you are going to offer me some beads, are you?'

As the war progressed, out of sight of the public at home, the entire SAS regiment was involved in it at some time. The 'team job' – officially, a British Army Training Team, or BATT – came into being. Such units comprised a handful of individuals to train Omani soldiers and *firqa* in handling heavy weapons, communications and mine clearance. It was one of these 10-man teams, at the seaside town of Mirbat, that fought an epic battle on 19 July 1972 against hundreds of well-armed *adoo* who swarmed down from their mountain base. They came close to overrunning the villa held by the team. One of the survivors, a Fijian, was still in business as a freelance soldier in Iraq more than 30 years later.

The Dhofar war ended in victory for Sultan Qaboos in the spring of 1976. By that time, South Yemen had used 130mm artillery to strike at Omani forces in a final effort to stave off defeat. With peace, however, came a classic dilemma. What was Qaboos to do about the hundreds of jebel warriors, friend and foe, well armed, with nothing much to fill their minds and time but mischief? The French solution, when France had faced a similar situation in 1830, had been to invent the Foreign Legion and export its dangerous skills to colonies in Africa and Asia. The Omani solution was to invent a new military formation with the aid of SAS veterans who had fought in the Dhofar war and who had now left the British army to become freelance soldiers.

Qaboos and his British advisers invented Firqa Force, a militia that spent some of its time in military training and meeting in their Firqa Centres (on the lines of British Territorial Army drill halls) to reminisce or discuss current problems on the jebel. This arrangement was an admirable solution to the dilemma of men who were not quite demobilised. The former enemy were able to retain their military pride and their self-image. They were paid enough and joined together in settling problems in their local areas.

Firqa Force was to have a profound and useful effect in shaping the new Oman. As one of those who helped plan it says, 'It unified the Dhofar tribes. In other circumstances they could have started a round of blood feuds. Had that happened the war would start all over again.' But in a world of international terrorism, much of it in the Arab world, something more was needed than a playground for old soldiers. Qaboos wanted his own, native SAS, independent of 'the Gaish' (the regular Omani army). It was to be a Praetorian Guard that owed him its special loyalty.

From this proposal the Sultan's Special Force, drawn entirely from the Dhofar war zone, but trained and led by British soldiers for the first 20 years of its life, was to be created. The private military sector, run by SAS veterans, was a crucial part of the operation.

'Our problem was that we had to avoid giving the impression that Qaboos's victory was a cover for British neocolonialism,' one of the planners reveals. 'Sultan Qaboos, probably advised by the Foreign Office, went to the private sector to get the people he needed.' The private sector, in this case, meant KMS, already a well-established private military company run by Jim Johnson, a former SAS colonel, and David Walker, an ex-SAS regular officer who had a reputation for taking on high-risk, clandestine missions and enjoying them. Johnson and David Stirling, the regiment's founding father, were well known to each other. Stirling also had the trust of SIS.

'The waymarks in setting up the SSF,' a source explained, 'led to Jim Johnson, who was linked to Stirling, who had Foreign Office (and SIS) connections. There was no way that Oman would be able to create a Special Forces unit with British help without the backing of the Foreign Office, advice from SIS and intervention by its executive arm, the SAS. The Arabian Gulf Desk in the FO played a major part in laying down the ground rules for British involvement in Oman with SIS on the fringes, after the coup of 1970. Officially, of course, Her Majesty's Government had no part in this.'

KMS – the name is shorthand for 'Keenie Meenie Services', SAS argot for undercover work – was the cut-out element, through which the emerging Sultan's Special Force could be deniable in Whitehall in the event of inconvenient questions from politicians or journalists. The company was not only able to supply a handful of former SAS officers and senior NCOs who could be persuaded to resign from the British army, but could also arrange for weapons and other equipment to be supplied at a reasonable cost. Financial integrity mattered in this as in all privatised military operations. During the Dhofar war there had been at least one scandal resulting from the creation, by a British officer, of 'the phantom *firqa*', a unit that existed only as a means of milking the Omani defence budget.

Ultimately, the SSF would emerge as a potent gendarmerie comprising motorised troops, maritime troops, and a special anti-terrorist team trained to storm hijacked aircraft and rescue hostages SAS-style. This unit would exercise with live ammunition in its own close-quarters-battle 'killing house' on the Hereford model.

At the beginning, there were birth pangs rather than growing pains. The first commanding officer laid the essential foundations of the force, but pressured by the demands laid on him – the '*ooreed*' syndrome – he moved on after 18 months. Three others tried, with limited success, to get the new unit on the road. They were succeeded in 1981 by Lieutenant Colonel (Julian) Tony Ball, one of the hardest and boldest characters to emerge from the postwar SAS.

Ball's army life had started in the ranks of the Parachute Regiment, where the legend was, 'His idea of a good time was to wrap himself in barbed wire and run about a minefield in the pouring rain.' He was commissioned into the King's Own Scottish Borderers, a Lowland infantry regiment. Running that regiment's reconnaissance platoon in 1972, he set up the army's first covert observation post in republican Belfast. Two years later he was in command of a secret surveillance team in the Province, which became known as 14 Intelligence Company.

Working in plain clothes, Special Forces men detached to 14 Company – 'the Dets' – learned to burgle terrorist weapons hides, photograph them and attach tracing devices to them. It was the most risky job in the secret Irish war. Ball personally led some high-risk, clandestine missions, some into the territory of the Irish Republic. He was also suspected (probably wrongly) of assassinating the IRA warlord John Francis Green in the Republic in 1975. He was awarded the Military Cross and made a Member of the Order of the British Empire (MBE).

Ball joined 22 SAS in 1975 but within three years he had been persuaded by the regiment's tribal elders to resign his commission and take command of the SSF. Soon after he arrived, he died with his friend Andrew Nightingale, an intelligence specialist, in a high-speed road accident on the desert road between Salalah and the inland air base of Thumrait. No other vehicle was involved. The probable cause was a blown-out tyre. One of those who were serving with SSF at the time recalled, 'Ball's death left the whole of the regiment – the Dhofaris – shocked. He had been there only a few months and was just getting into the whole thing.

'Nightingale, too, had some really good ideas, such as bringing the families [of contract soldiers] out from Britain so that instead of boozing in the bar at Thumrait you'd get conversation down in Salalah. The job was six months on and one month off. Essential continuity was at least provided by such people as the Quartermaster, Bill Bayliss (ex-SAS) and a former Regular Indian Army officer, Major S. B. Nair, employed as the unit's administrative officer to run a heavy support staff – clerks, drivers, mechanics, and so on – drawn from the Indian Army. In time they were replaced by Omanis.'

One man more than others stabilised the emerging SSF. This was Lieutenant Colonel 'Harrow' (not his real name), a former para and veteran of most of the significant SAS operations throughout the sixties and seventies. An apparently laid-back individual, Harrow combined tenacity and political sensitivity with a love of Arab culture that was worth hundreds of fighting men. He had experienced front-line combat in the Dhofar war and proved his credentials in the eyes of the men he commanded. By the standards of Britain, to be sure, he was an anachronism. On the jebel, this was no fiction but daily reality. Harrow was an asset. He stayed in command of the SSF for almost nine years.

His successor was a colourful, flamboyant veteran of the French Foreign Legion, part of the 1st Parachute Regiment ('les Paras Perdus'), which was the spearhead of the Algerian mutiny against President de Gaulle. The ex-Legionnaire went on to be commissioned in the British army – airborne Gunners and Gurkhas – before becoming an SAS colonel commanding the Intelligence and Security Group in Northern Ireland. The same soldier occupied a key position in the Coalition Provisional Authority – the de facto government of Paul Bremer in Iraq after the 2003 invasion. The last British commander of SSF was a former CO of 22 SAS.

All these men were nominated by General Johnny Watts, one of the architects of the postwar SAS, who was later to be appointed commander of the Omani Armed Forces. Some of these distinguished 'volunteers' seem to have been pressured by the British army's own career advisers into taking this foreign command. A device used by the Adjutant General's office was to offer the chosen candidate an unpalatable future as a desk warrior. For long-serving Special Forces soldiers of any rank, anything, even service in a foreign army, or in a private military company, was better than incarceration in an office calculating, say, the rounds used on a gunnery range, tank track mileage or the logistics of paperclip supplies.

In a few cases, SAS men who had been involved in high-profile shootings in Northern Ireland were offered, and accepted, freelance service in Oman as a means of avoiding further controversy. As one organiser put it, 'We buried such cases in Oman.'

The extraordinary survival of Oman's stability for decades after the Dhofar war had much to do with the integrity of men who were no longer bound by an oath of allegiance to their own government. They were like the best of the Foreign Legion, tied by nothing more or less than their given word, their contract and their commitment to a cause. That dedication was helped by the judicious use by Qaboos of Oman's oil wealth to create a model welfare state. Only one other country – Norway – seems to have used its oil revenues as wisely.

The spirit of Oman's British freelance soldiers was embodied by a man in a wheelchair. Tony Fleming's evolution from an overcrowded Liverpool slum, where he was one of many children, to Arabist scholar is the stuff of myth. Like many underprivileged boys, he found a release from poverty of all kinds in the army. From the paras he went to the Army Physical Training Corps to become a sergeant major. He represented the army and Joint Services as a middleweight boxer. He then volunteered for the SAS and in so doing, accepted reduction in his rank to that of trooper. So far, this was just another tale of physical courage and an appetite for adventure. During the final months of the Dhofar war he came under heavy fire during a contact near the Yemen border. A bullet destroyed his spine. His comrades dragged him out of danger and he was bumped away from the action in an armoured vehicle. 'I'm going,' Fleming said. 'Tony, hold on. You'll live!' one of his companions said. Fleming replied, 'Not that, you idiot. I'm going to fall off this fucking vehicle if you don't pull me back in.'

Fleming survived but he knew that the rest of his life would be without the use of his legs. He used the gratuity he received as compensation for his injury to study Arabic language and culture at Exeter University, followed by a postgraduate course at Cairo University. As his body shrank, his mind and moral authority grew. The SSF decided to sign him up as an intelligence officer. The then British commanding officer, say his friends, discussed the matter personally with the Sultan. Learning of Fleming's past, Qaboos observed, 'We must help him. His blood is in our soil.' Unconsciously, the Sultan was expressing a poet's view of the Foreign Legionnaire: that such a man is 'French not by the blood he inherits, but by the blood he sheds'.

The CO had to explain that Fleming did not want a 'pension'. The man in the wheelchair would want to work for his money. Fleming arrived by air soon afterwards. His wheelchair was carted from the aircraft to the arrivals hall on a forklift truck, with Fleming still in the seat. Some time later he reached the SSF's mountain headquarters at a camp known as 'the Goat Farm' in Dhofar. A steep ramp led up to the veranda. One of Fleming's friends offered to push him. Fleming said he would propel himself.

'If you don't make it,' said the friend, 'you'll lose a lot of face.' 'If you push me I lose even more,' was the reply. Slowly, painfully, Fleming forced the wheels to carry him to the top, inch by inch. On the veranda, no one moved. The reception party sensed that this was a trial, a moment of ritual. As Fleming reached the veranda, a senior Omani minister stepped forward and kissed him three times on the cheek. 'One kiss is routine for a distinguished visitor,' an eyewitness said later. 'Two kisses are a sign of respect. Three kisses say, "You are my brother."'

For several years after that, Tony Fleming was a key member of a team that learned to read the tribal politics of Oman as well as military matters. Some younger Dhofaris who joined the SSF were unsure about this 'legless' Englishman until they were set to rights by their elder brethren who had fought the Dhofar war: 'But for people like him you would not be here today.'

Fleming's body gradually wasted, though the eyes remained bright and the voice clear. Mourners at his funeral service in Hereford more than filled the crematorium chapel. Those who could not find room inside were content to listen from the gardens outside. Surprisingly, the SAS declined to allow Fleming's name to appear on its famous memorial clock tower.

During the years that followed the Dhofar war, the SSF was equipped for desert operations with specialist Land Rovers based on the 22 SAS design and advice from within the regiment. Dhofaris were quick learners. Within a few years, men who had gone to war barefoot learned to handle the complexities of desert and mountain driving and navigation. In the image of their SAS counterparts and conscious of the growing threat of worldwide terrorism, especially the hijack of aircraft and hostage taking, SSF's early priority was to develop a credible counterterrorist team.

Under specialist, freelance SAS instructors, the Dhofaris enthusiastically formed a sophisticated group capable of meeting any threat. Later, as the force expanded, a 'boat' element was introduced, again in the image of SAS/SBS amphibious Special Forces. Dhofaris of African descent, many of them fishermen descended from earlier generations of pearl divers, readily took to this role.

In its later years, the SSF took part, for the first time, in joint military operations with the Omani army, navy, air force and police to pursue organised gangs of smugglers. The smugglers trafficked drugs from Asia, across the hazardous Empty Quarter of Arabia to Red Sea ports en route to Europe. The British-trained desert drivers of SSF now had a focus for their skills beyond the basic business of securing the country's borders.

Once the SSF was firmly established in Dhofar, the Sultan decided to create a parallel SSF involving the peoples of Northern Oman with a view to overriding cultural and tribal differences. As it was, the regular Omani army was a cultural kaleidoscope including Baluchi mercenaries, Pakistani experts, British contract officers and a variety of regiments. All were progressively Omanised as the country positioned itself somewhere between the extremes now polarising the Arab world. Within an SSF formation, outside the regular order of battle, those in charge needed a finely tuned sense of local politics that had little to do with military affairs.

The British instructors had to accept that an expansion of the SSF to include all Omanis was very much a political requirement even if, to the SAS purist, it was too much, too soon. But it worked in the longer term, militarily as well as politically.

Disciplining these unconventional soldiers was a particularly sophisticated matter. If an individual Omani had to be disciplined then the SSF commander and his British officers had to weigh up the implications of tribal connections and sensitivities at a particular time. It was a delicate balancing act, leavened by a common sense of adventure, humour and simple buffoonery.

A Hunter aircraft of the Sultan's air force, flown by a British freelance pilot, made a low pass over the SSF headquarters at the Goat Farm as a 'wake-up' call, and hit the unit's aerial mast. The aircraft lost its nose cone and the pilot his dignity, but nothing worse. The SSF's Dhofari soldiers thought this very funny. The pilot got his nose cone back, in exchange for a party with the British SAS personnel. More serious was the failure of several members of an SSF rapid response team to answer a call to arms. It happened just once and the call was part of an exercise, not an official alert. As one former commander put it, 'It did not happen again. The Dhofaris proved quick learners.'

The influence of Britain's freelance soldiers in Oman was sometimes hard-earned. Living with the Dhofaris, joining their celebrations – to celebrate a sheikh's wedding or a camel fair – meant joining the feast. This was goat or camel meat, chopped up on the ground and crudely boiled before one of many chefs, as a gesture of hospitality, chewed it to tenderise it before spitting it out onto the guest's plates. The result, by European standards, was stomach-churning.

The success of the SSF can be measured by the fact that since its foundation, Oman has not had to fight a territorial war in spite of upheavals in surrounding territories. Alongside military preparedness the enlightened paternalism of Sultan Qaboos has transformed his country for the better. In the mid-1990s the last British commander handed over to an Omani officer. The process was done quietly, without public ceremony.

The SAS could say that they had given birth to a 'younger brother', for that was how those involved perceived their Omani counterparts. 'It was', said one, 'a close kinship of great benefit to those involved on both sides, as well as to their respective governments.'

There have been few cases where stealthy diplomacy has worked so well, at such little cost. For Landon, the friend Sultan Qaboos made at Sandhurst, the story ended like a happy fairy tale. 'He married a Hungarian countess and became very rich,' said one of his friends. By the time he died of lung cancer aged 64, in 2007, Brigadier Landon had amassed a fortune estimated at £500 million on the back of rising oil prices. He owned thousands of English acres including a hamlet in Hampshire. His fortune resulted from his long association with Qaboos, including oil transactions and deals to rearm Oman with modern weapons. His personal taste was for the traditional shotgun. As *The Sunday Times* Rich List noted in 2004, he had acquired '50,000 acres of grouse moor in the north of England to indulge his passion for shooting'.

7

AFGHANISTAN 1979–89:

'The British will probably be most forthcoming'

The first British private military company in Afghanistan was annihilated in 1842 by Pashtun tribesmen as it floundered through the Khyber snow towards the sanctuary of India. Just one man, a Scottish military doctor, reached safety out of a column of 16,000 men, women and children. The lost column was part of the East India Company's army, thrust into Afghanistan as part of a strategic chess match – 'the Great Game' – to defend British India from a notional occupation by Tsarist Russia. India was 'the Jewel in the Crown' of the British Empire. Today the Great Game continues, though the riches are expected to flow 1,040 miles in the other direction, through a 106-centimetre (42-inch) pipeline from the bountiful gas and oil fields of Central Asia to the Pakistani port of Gwadar, and onward to an oil-addicted America.

The current cycle of warfare in Afghanistan began as part of the Cold War on 3 July 1979, when President Jimmy Carter, still trying to recover his reputation after the disaster of Iran's seizure of US diplomats in Tehran, ordered the CIA to start covert operations to undermine the Marxist government in Kabul. The country was already in turmoil as the Kabul government imposed the sorts of repressive land reforms that had failed in Stalin's Russia and Mao's China. The strategic objective, Carter's National Security Adviser, Zbigniew Brzezinski later revealed in an interview with *Le Nouvel Observateur*, was to 'draw the Soviets into the Afghan trap . . . Their own Vietnam War.'[1] The surprise was that the

Soviets took the bait. It made sense in Moscow, if only to stabilise Russia's southern border.

On 27 December, almost six months after warriors began their guerrilla and terrorist campaign against Moscow's client government, the Russians' 40th Army – 80,000 men, 1,800 main battle tanks and 2,000 other armoured vehicles – raced through the Salang Tunnel, beneath the Hindukush, in a blitzkrieg attack. It was the start of a campaign in which they would lose 15,000 dead and more than half a million injured. Well over a million Afghan civilians also died. Many of the wounded were treated in Warsaw Pact hospitals outside the USSR, to contain the damage to public morale. (In East Germany, British military spies foraged through the dustbins behind the hospitals to collect used dressings for analysis by forensic intelligence. The MoD was interested in the type of ordnance – and traces of poison gas – reflected by this waste.)

As part of their strategic chess game, the Americans carefully weighed up the likely response of Western Europe to anything the US might do. Within a week of the Soviet invasion, the CIA secretly advised Carter:

> How the Europeans interpret the events in Afghanistan will strongly influence their response to the measures the US takes against the Soviet Union . . . The British will probably be most forthcoming. The government of Prime Minister Thatcher, which is uniquely sensitive to Soviet abuses of power . . . has already shown a willingness to undertake firm defense policy measures at considerable cost . . .[2]

The continental countries were 'highly dependent on continuing oil supplies from the Middle East and would find the prospect of growing Soviet influence on those supplies profoundly alarming'. (Britain was not. Her North Sea oilfields had just come on stream, only to be privatised.)

Implicit in the CIA document, which Carter seems to have accepted, was a need for indirect, deniable, proxy opposition to the Soviets in Afghanistan rather than confrontation or – even more drastic – nuclear brinkmanship. As it rapidly turned out, Thatcher was more than ready to do what was necessary. She had been in office only a few months but already had in mind a better-funded SIS. (During her years in office, the secret agencies' budgets doubled.) She promptly authorised SIS to run a campaign of 'disruptive action' as well as intelligence gathering. Some insiders saw in this a rerun of Edward Heath's snap decision, in his first week in office in 1970, to sanction an SIS-engineered coup d'état in Oman.

In 1998 Brzezinski was happy that the nine-year Russian war against the Taliban and other mujahedeen had 'brought about the demoralisation and finally the break-up of the Soviet empire'. He was entirely unconcerned about a resurgent Islam's emerging from the chaos. As he put it, dogmatically, 'There isn't a global Islam.' Nor, he implied, would there be a global jihad, or a global war on terror.

This blinkered understanding of Muslim culture was shared by many, including Congressman Charlie Wilson, who marched with the mujahedeen and returned to persuade Congress to increase the CIA war chest for Afghanistan to $120 million, a sum matched by the Saudis to repel the infidel Russians and spread fundamentalism. Some devout men volunteered to fight alongside the Afghan guerrillas. They included a wealthy young Saudi named Osama bin Laden.

It does not seem to have struck the governments of Carter (soon succeeded by the Republican Ronald Reagan) that well-armed jihadists might turn against their benefactors, who were, in fundamentalist eyes, just another group of heretic crusaders. Margaret Thatcher was eager to join the fight but, apparently better advised, agreed that British operators dabbling in the new Afghan war would support a warlord London regarded as a moderate, nationalist leader, Ahmed Shah Masood, later assassinated by fundamentalists in September 2001.

But that was all in the future when Thatcher made a high-profile visit to the border between Pakistan and Afghanistan in 1981, reaching her hand across the frontier to shake the hand of a bewildered Afghan border guard. She later told refugees in Peshawar, 'You left your country because you refused to live under a godless Communist system which is trying to destroy your religion and your independence.'[3] Her espousal of jihadism was a political and strategic error of epic proportions.

From the beginning, following the Soviet army's inept invasion of Afghanistan, the CIA, with considerable help from the British SIS and its executive arm, the SAS, fought a covert, deniable, proxy war similar to its campaigns in Africa and Latin America. One of the first recruits was an unlikely choice: an SAS reject named Philip Sessarego, who later claimed, falsely, to have been a 'badged' – fully qualified – Special Forces operator in a book describing how he trained warriors in Afghanistan.[4] His book, under the pseudonym 'Tom Carew', was a runaway success, although the BBC's *Newsnight* exposed his unfounded claim about SAS service.[5]

What got overlooked as a result of his exposure was that he had indeed been recruited by an American intelligence agency in 1981 to collect information about Soviet weapons – particularly the titanium armour on Hind helicopters – being used against the Afghan resistance at that time. Soviet helicopters were the weapons most feared by the Afghan fighters. They were an impervious aerial weapons platform from which bullets rebounded innocuously. The secret was Russian metallurgy, the one science in which the Soviets still had a clear lead over the West, whether in arming helicopters or building deep-diving submarines.

The agency that recruited Sessarego was not the CIA but its military counterpart, the Defense Intelligence Agency (DIA). Sessarego's knowledge of SAS techniques resulted from his real service in one of the regiment's support arms. He put this to some use when, with a team of three or four others, he travelled to Afghanistan and tried to cut fragments from the armoured hull of a crashed Hind, using a machine gun on automatic fire, loaded with a full magazine, as a cutting tool. The bullets ricocheted back at him. Perhaps not surprisingly, the colourful adventures in Afghanistan of 'Tom Carew' circle around the twin themes of recovering Soviet helicopter armour and service for the DIA.

Sessarego returned home to Hereford, bought a more effective instrument (a chainsaw) and went back for a second time. He also repaired some of the guerrillas' heavy weapons.

Had he known that the US would have paid $1 million for the instrument panel from a Hind he might not have sold his story to a newspaper, but his approach to operational security, like that of many mercenaries, was not up to SAS standards. Between his two trips, he visited the office of the *Sunday Times* to sell his story to me. Not only were the photographs and incidents he described convincing. A *Sunday Times* colleague encountered Sessarego in Peshawar, after Sessarego's most recent foray into the Afghan war zone. That colleague (Ian Jack, later editor of *Granta*), trying for an interview, was told, 'Speak to Tony Geraghty about this. He already has the story.' This was true. The article was indeed written, but not to be published until the second mission was over, to avoid compromising Sessarego and his colleagues. Within the *Sunday Times* a rumour mill was working overtime. Nevertheless, I was surprised to be faced with an internal complaint that I, not an arm of US intelligence, was running a mercenary team in Afghanistan.

The SIS did little better, to begin with, than the DIA. In a rerun of the Iran/Contra operation, the CIA was looking for plausible deniability in the form of a 'UK asset'. It approached SIS. For some reason – perhaps because of the traditional influence of the Royal Navy within MI6, whose first director was Captain Mansfield Cumming RN – SIS nominated a team of Royal Marine commando veterans led by a former SBS officer. Afghanistan is a landlocked country. In 1982 the deniables' mule train was ambushed. The British advisers were lucky to reach the sanctuary of Pakistan.[6]

It was at this point that the SIS turned to some of its old friends in the private sector. The firm's 'Proposal for Training Assistance in Afghanistan' observed:

> The existing system for training in Pakistan has a number of disadvantages, not least the requirement to train over 50 per cent (in practice a much higher percentage) Pakistan students on courses. The system does not allow instructors to get close to their Afghani students, to get a good feel for the operational conditions and requirements and to build that close relationship which is so important . . . Security under present conditions must be next to impossible to maintain.
>
> Training should if possible be conducted inside Afghanistan. This imposes difficult living conditions and poor logistic support on the instructors, but pays dividends many times over in the quality of training passed on. A small group of three or four instructors would be a sensible first deployment. They will be able to train relatively low numbers of students to a very high standard . . . Small groups of very well-trained men can achieve disproportionate success in a relatively short time. This demonstrates progress and raises morale.

The company's wish to train somewhere far away from Pakistan may also have reflected the oppressive control imposed on virtually all anti-Soviet operations by Islamabad's Interservices Intelligence Directorate, the ISI.

> The instructors will have a broad base of experience in unconventional warfare skills, but will expect to teach two main skills to start with: (a) Demolitions and sabotage; (b). Paramedical side.

The company, it continued, had a great deal of experience in procuring 'specialist items' of equipment. Normally, the firm would recommend a reconnaissance visit by the team leader ahead of the rest of the team but – revealing the pressure on the deniables to produce rapid results – the document added,

> Given the remote location of the likely base in this case, a reconnaissance visit would impost significant delay. It would be better to send the team together and accept that it may take a little time to settle in and collect together students and stores.

Instructors would receive three return air fares to the UK each year. 'It is proposed that they serve three tours of three months per annum in location . . . Company management will conduct liaison visits to the instructors in location.'

The cost of a three-man team for one year would be £160,000, including management fees, salaries, insurance, management visits, air fares to Pakistan and some equipment. The cost did not include local transport, accommodation or living costs. Payment terms were 50 per cent on signature of contracts and 50 per cent six months into the contract. The proposal concluded with a recommendation that a team of three or four instructors be deployed to 'lay the foundation for larger scale training by local instructors, expatriate instructors or a mixture of both'.

As it turned out, following the precedent set in the Yemen, Nicaragua and elsewhere, an initial two-man team of former noncommissioned officers was extracted from the Circuit to run a feasibility study for the 'moderate' leader backed by the Foreign and Commonwealth Office: Ahmed Shah Masood, warlord of the Panshir Valley, near the Soviet border. The American authority John K. Cooley discovered that Masood was 'one of the very few holy warriors who understood and often warned that the anti-Communist zealots of the war period would turn into anti-Western zealots after it ended'.

In 1982, two former SAS NCOs ran a short training operation (an SAS technique in which military lessons are promptly applied to real warfare) to improve the mujahedeens' battlefield co-ordination and communications. It did the trick. Soviet casualties rose rapidly. Then the winter snows brought the campaigning season to an end.

The training continued in Oman and Britain. About 20 of Masood's field commanders were given live-fire lessons using wire-guided missiles, mortars and heavy machine guns. SIS then took them to the grounds of a country house in the Home Counties. The SAS provided luxury accommodation that winter: camp beds inside a large tent, contained within a barn. Ken Connor, a soldier with a unique record of longevity with the regiment, later described how the Afghans 'were found to be suffering from some sort of vitamin deficiency and, in some cases, malnutrition'.

When they were fit enough, they were taken to remote training areas in Scotland and the north of England to learn how to use modern explosives in attacks on Soviet aircraft on the ground. The basic strategy recreated David Stirling's hit-and-run offensive against the Luftwaffe in the Western Desert. One of the training areas was on the impressive estate of a titled Englishman whose brother was a former commanding officer of 22 SAS. Another, on an inhospitable part of the west coast of Scotland, accessible only by landing craft, was a favourite SIS testing ground.

The training programme involved more SAS soldiers, some of them – like the deniables in Yemen and elsewhere – released temporarily from the regular army to work alongside the guerrillas with Masood's increasingly powerful Northern Alliance. Their liaison officer with SIS was a serving SAS lieutenant colonel. Twenty-five years later, he admitted in a conversation with me that Afghanistan was still too sensitive to be discussed on any terms. Why? 'Because of the people involved and the fact that Afghanistan is still an operational zone' – and possibly because the links to the mujahedeen (even Masood's men) had become an embarrassment, a reminder of Margaret Thatcher's support for jihadism.

In London, meanwhile, in 1982, Connor and one of his comrades were summoned by the SIS to a meeting with CIA agents who wanted a battle plan for a major attack on a Soviet airfield. The operation, to avoid visible US involvement, had to be carried out by non-Americans.

Planning and leading it should have been tailor-made for America's own SAS, known as Delta Force. Delta's founder, Colonel Tom Beckwith, had served on attachment with the SAS in Malaya. However, the debacle of Operation Eagle Claw, Delta's doomed attempt to rescue Washington's captive diplomats from Tehran two years before, had left its mark. There was also the clear need for plausible deniability. Not so much as a hint of Americana, even in the planning of this assault, would be tolerated.

Connor and his companion studied the air photographs: a line of 24 neatly parked Mig-21 fighters. They devised an entry strategy, force requirements, choice of non-commercial plastic explosive, weight to carry, time to target, withdrawal plan and much else. A month later, Connor recalls, the CIA summoned him back to London to look at the latest air photographs. 'There was one slight difference. There were still twenty-four Mig-21 fighters parked in a neat row along the perimeter track, but twenty-three of them had had their tail sections blown off.'

Covert action – defined by one American expert as 'an alternative to a failed or unplanned foreign policy' – increased after that. The DIA sent a second British team into Afghanistan to set up listening devices near Russian bases in the country. This one was equipped with a satellite dish, a transmitter, a keyboard and transponders to track the movements of Soviet aircraft and tanks.

At that time Western military missions led by the UK's Brixmis team (in theory, a diplomatic liaison mission whose real purpose was espionage) were already running similar spying operations against the Soviet armed forces in East Germany within Red Army training areas and on the very perimeters of Soviet air bases. It was risky work. An American regular army officer trying to emulate the British was shot dead when he was detected. What distinguished the kit carried by the freelances in Afghanistan in 1983 was that it was of a type controlled by the US electronic spy organisation known as the National Security Agency.

This became a problem only when a team of five British deniables was compromised in July of that year, three months after infiltrating Afghanistan from Peshawar, where the SIS station co-ordinated the operation. One agent was shot dead. Five others were captured.[7] Who were they? The Foreign and Commonwealth Office, of course, did not know. The FCO never knows, officially, about the activities of 'the Friends', as it describes SIS personnel.

The men concerned used false identities and bogus passports. They were named by Radio Kabul, then under communist control, as Stuart Bodman, aged 30 (shot dead); Roderick Macginnis; Stephen Elwick; as well as 'Tim', 'Chris' and 'Phil'. Their fate is still unknown. One of those familiar with the SAS operations in Afghanistan at that time told me that poor operational security among some of these elite troops provoked a temporary loss of confidence by SIS in the regiment. 'For example, one of the guys went into the country carrying a copy of his local newspaper, the Hereford Times. And not all of them were using bogus passports. SAS soldiers were rubbing shoulders with SIS operators and socialising with them in Scotland and elsewhere. They got the idea – wrongly – that Afghanistan was a doddle.'

In fact, the SAS were merely part of a larger espionage effort, run by SIS and the CIA in Peshawar and Kabul itself. A year after the British team was compromised, Richard Vandiver, third secretary at the US Embassy in the Afghan capital, was expelled for alleged 'actions against the interests of the Democratic Republic of Afghanistan, inconsistent with his diplomatic status'. Washington, as might be expected, dismissed the allegation, but one official, wisely remaining anonymous, told journalists that the expulsion of US diplomats from Afghanistan was 'something they do on a fairly regular basis. Two [US] diplomats were expelled last May and one in September.'[8]

It was all part of the routine rough-and-tumble of the Cold War. Anti-aircraft missiles were another matter. Thanks to SAS training and the vulnerability of Afghan airfields, the Islamic guerrillas' use of captured SAM-7 missiles sent shudders through the Soviet Air Force and civil Afghan airlines. On 28 October 1984 the guerrillas shot down a heavy Antonov-22 transport as it took off from Kabul. In September 1984 an Afghan Airline DC-10 carrying 300 passengers was hit but landed safely. An internal Bakhtar Airlines Antonov-26 carrying 47 passengers and five crew was shot down 11 miles from Kandahar. Everyone on board was killed.

As the war dragged on into 1986, agents from the CIA's Afghan Task Force based in Langley, Virginia, did become more directly involved in supplying some of the many factions and their warlords with modern war material. One of the first of these was a consignment of Blowpipe anti-aircraft missiles made by Short Brothers in the UK, tried, tested and much criticised during the Falklands war. Having tried Blowpipe, the CIA substituted their own shoulder-fired Stingers. One batch was delivered to a serving SAS major at Heathrow Airport, then transferred by way of Egypt and Oman to Pakistan. This was bread and butter to the Thatcher generation of SAS officers. In 1981, Major (later Lieutenant Colonel) Ian Crooke, with two NCOs, flew on an Air France flight with an undeclared cargo of guns, ammunition and explosives to stage a countercoup in the Gambia. That operation was not so much deniable as unauthorised, but endorsed after the event, when it was a success.

In Washington, the Reagan administration had assumed that the Afghanistan cargoes would not become public knowledge and that the missiles would not get into the hands of 'terrorist organisations bent on downing a commercial airliner'. By April of 1986, as some of the Stingers were being sent aboard military aircraft, members of Congress were told what was happening. Worse, as one Senate Republican aide pointed out, some of the recipients were 'a lot closer . . . to Khomeini [the Iranian ayatollah] than they are to us. There is concern that one of these guys could show up in Rome aiming a Stinger at a jumbo jet.'[9]

The SAS – and the deniables it sent to Afghanistan – had good reason to know what Stinger could do. During the Falklands war in 1982 it had received a special consignment of these weapons to replace Blowpipe, which was heavier and had a shorter range. The only instructor trained to use Stinger – Sergeant Paddy O'Connor – died in a helicopter crash off the Falklands before he could pass on his knowledge. The training manuals were lost with him. Undeterred, the SAS adopted its usual trial-and-error approach. On West Falkland, one of their men destroyed an Argentine Pucara with his first shot. It proved to be a lucky hit, since the next five missiles fell short, even though, theoretically, Stinger had a maximum effective range of 5.5 kilometres (3.4 miles).[10]

In spite of that, Stinger had a brutal impact on the anti-Soviet campaign. On the ground, the two armies – one Russian, the other loyalist Afghan – were ambushed if they moved on Afghanistan's narrow mountain roads. They depended increasingly on air cover. Stinger denied this so completely that medical evacuation, resupply, aerial fire power and attacks on columns bringing supplies from Pakistan became impossible. Even the last Soviet diplomat and his family, departing Kabul, had to take cover in the airport lounge after the aircraft sent to extract them was blown up as it landed.

In London and Washington, the effect of this not-so-covert action was seen as entirely beneficial. As the French scholar Olivier Roy put it in his paper 'The Lessons of the Soviet/Afghan Conflict', 'A staff of around 100 CIA officers; no American citizens killed or imprisoned; no retaliation against US interests and the nominal expense of $2bn over ten years: these were relatively low costs for one of the most important post-World War II conflicts.'[11]

The problem that had yet to emerge was that not all these missiles threatened the Russians. When the war ended with a Soviet withdrawal in February 1989, the CIA realised that some of them were still in the hands of an increasingly hostile guerrilla army. The potential sting that this threat represented had another, newly fashionable name. It was 'blowback', the damage caused by the law of unforeseen consequences when high-tech military hardware gets into the wrong hands.

As a burgeoning 'Stinger mythology' haunted Western intelligence agencies, a *Sunday Times* enquiry concluded that a Greek Cypriot agent, Andreas Antoniades 'took part in a covert CIA operation to disarm Afghan guerrillas by buying back missiles from them after the fall of the Taliban in

March 2002', but 'Antoniades had to leave Afghanistan after an ex-British soldier, Colin Berry, working with him, shot two Afghans in self-defence in a Kabul hotel room in February 2003'.[12]

Had the Northern Alliance, covertly backed by Britain, won the renewed Afghan war, then all might have ended well, with a reconstruction programme that stabilised the country. It was not to be. The Pakistani intelligence service, ISI, had a direct say in which factions would receive much of the war material flowing into the country across its border and the ISI favoured some of the most extreme fundamentalist elements in a country that disintegrated soon after the Soviet withdrawal in 1989. Masood was assassinated by Islamic extremists posing as journalists two days before the attack on New York on 11 September 2001, a fact that led some observers to speculate that the killing was ordered by Osama bin Laden.

The US and Pakistan, however, favoured the fundamentalist who emerged as victor from the rubble of his country. This was Gulbuddin Hekmatyar, organiser of guerrilla training camps around the Arab world and a member of the Muslim Brotherhood. He supported Saddam Hussein's invasion of Kuwait. In 1987, some of his men murdered Andy Skrzypkowiak, a British SAS reservist doubling as a television journalist, because, according to one report, Skrzypkowiak 'was bringing war footage of Masood's military victories to the West. They dropped a large rock on his head while he was asleep by the wall of a house.'[13] Hekmatyar had received millions of CIA and Saudi dollars.

Three years after the Soviets left, Afghanistan was again at war with itself. Masood's Tajiks were joined by a powerful Uzbek militia in the Northern Alliance, which seized Kabul. Hekmatyar's Pashtun army bombarded the capital with rockets and artillery. In 1994 alone, 25,000 civilians were killed and one-third of the city was rubble. In the south, near the Pakistan border, local warlords took over and stripped humanitarian agencies of vehicles and offices. The movement that emerged to restore order was the Taliban ('student') organisation. With support from Pakistan, the Taliban steadily took control. Osama bin Laden's army of foreign Muslim volunteers became one of its allies.

By 1998 most of Afghanistan was under sharia law and bin Laden's training camps 60 miles south of Kabul were notorious. In the same year, bombing teams trained and inspired by bin Laden attacked three US embassies in East Africa, killing 257 people and causing 4,000 other casualties. Soon afterwards, on the orders of President Bill Clinton, cruise missiles smashed the camps but not the emerging Al-Qaeda network.

The fundamentalists' attacks on the US, following a bombing at the World Trade Center in New York in 1993, were protests against the continued, highly visible presence of US forces in Saudi Arabia after the first Gulf War in 1990–1. That, in its turn, had had its origins in the invasion of Kuwait by Saddam Hussein. Ironically, Saddam was not a religious fundamentalist but a secular dictator. And, as noted elsewhere, freelance American military trainers from Vinnel had been working in Saudi Arabia for years before, training the royal family's bodyguard.

8

NICARAGUA AND ELSEWHERE, 1984–2006:

Spreading democracy – America's first War on Terror

Within a three-day period in March 1985, when all right-thinking Brits were cursing IRA terrorists, bombs exploded in two streets 6,000 miles apart. One of these attacks missed its intended target but wiped out, randomly, 80 civilians and wounded another 256. The worst casualties, including 40 dead, were girls leaving a Beirut mosque after Friday prayers. The second explosion was a bomber's spectacular – torching a military ordnance dump alongside a hospital in Managua, capital of socialist Nicaragua. Providentially, no one was killed.

These attacks were not the work of 'terrorists' in the normal sense of that word. They were directed by British freelances who had served their time in the SAS and were now acting for a clandestine wing of the US intelligence service, the National Security Council. It is possible that the same British team orchestrated both events. That the two attacks were politically connected there is no doubt. They were part of a complex helix of plots and double-dealing known as the Iran/Contra Affair. It was the gravest military/political scandal to hit Washington for years, surpassed only by President Richard Nixon's great banana skin, Watergate.

The Iran/Contra Affair happened on President Ronald Reagan's watch. Reagan, a B-movie Hollywood actor, was a darling of the Republican right, who had proved his reliability by helping the FBI to identify liberals in his profession during the era of the McCarthy witch hunts. At that time he was head of the Screen Actors' Guild. In the early eighties, as President, he was preoccupied with two crusades: a global struggle against communism, fought with special venom in Latin America; and the Iranian problem, particularly the plight of American hostages chained to walls somewhere in Beirut.

Reagan's readiness to license the wilder spirits in his retinue, overriding the US Constitution, would lead to a bizarre arrangement through which America would arrange for Iran to receive thousands of wire-guided TOW missiles (wire-guided anti-tank missiles) for use in its ongoing war with Iraq, in exchange for the release of American hostages remotely controlled by Iran, but held by Hezbollah in Lebanon. One of the hostages was the CIA station chief in Beirut, William Buckley, who did not benefit from this arrangement. He was tortured to death. It is said that a tape recording of his dying screams traumatised his colleagues in Virginia.

Iran could afford to pay cash for the missiles and it did so, over the odds. Much of the untraceable money was then used to bankroll a clandestine war in Nicaragua, intended to destabilise the socialist government there as part of Reagan's global crusade. Recycling funds in this way, said Marine colonel, Oliver North, struck him as 'a neat idea'. Washington had much experience of destabilisation. Its troubles with Iran arose from its success, 30 years earlier, in bringing down the democratically elected Tehran government of Premier Mohammed Mossadeq, an operation it shared with Britain's Secret Intelligence Service.

Mossadeq unwisely claimed Iranian oil for the Iranians and seized the assets of the Anglo-Iranian Oil Company. The British response was to send 16 Parachute Brigade (including the author) to Cyprus, as the first step in a coup-de-main response: a parachute drop on Abadan. At the last moment, the operation was stood down. The agencies achieved with dollars what the Red Berets might have done using brute force. Mossadeq was duly replaced by Washington's client, the Shah, whose rule in its turn was punctured in 1979 by the fundamentalist revolution of Ayatollah Khomeini.

Khomeini's men, including a future Iranian prime minister, seized the entire US embassy staff and made them hostages. A badly planned helicopter assault by Special Forces (Operation Eagle Claw), intended to free the captive diplomats, ended in self-destructive panic and chaos.

By now, Iranian attacks were inflicting mortal political hurt on Washington. The Democrat President Carter was part of the collateral damage.

He was discredited by the failure of Eagle Claw and was succeeded in 1981 by Reagan, a man easily persuaded that there were reds under America's bed in Nicaragua. Matters got worse in 1983 when a suicide bomber drove a truck bomb into a US Marines barracks in Beirut, slaughtering 241 American servicemen and women. The culprit was Hezbollah, backed by Iran.

By running covert wars against communism in Nicaragua and Islamic fundamentalism in Beirut, the Reagan administration became enmeshed in more than two conflicts. It was also at odds with the US Constitution. To address that small embarrassment, it required warriors who enjoyed, in Oliver North's phrase, 'plausible deniability'. A team of British Special Forces veterans filled the bill nicely. The arrangement might almost be said to be hallowed by tradition, since the original demolition of Mossadeq's government had been a joint venture with SIS.

For the first years of the Nicaraguan war, in which a Marxist government was opposed by CIA-backed 'Contra' (for Counter-Revolutionary) rebels, Congress was happy to vote funds for limited action. But the Contras were ineffective. They failed to penetrate far enough into the country to hold ground, declare a provisional government and win some political credibility in Washington.

The CIA had a timetable and the Contras were not meeting it. So in 1984, to speed things up, the Agency bought a mother ship from which its operators launched attacks to mine Nicaraguan harbours. One casualty was a Japanese freighter. Congress had not been informed of these actions. The result was the Boland Amendment, prohibiting funds and military aid 'for the purpose of overthrowing the government of Nicaragua'. Reagan's team took the view that the President's prerogative in conducting foreign policy entitled him to sideline Congress and raise funds from private sources, or even foreign governments. In this patriotic spirit, the National Security Council (NSC) – the President's principal forum for considering national security matters with senior advisers – went shopping for free-lance soldiers.

The NSC was headed by Vice Admiral John Poindexter, a brilliant physicist who would later command a civilian team known as Policy Analysis Market (PAM), trading internationally in such events as coups, assassinations and terrorist attacks. PAM was a gambling saloon where the chips were human lives.[1] Poindexter's deputy was Oliver North. It was never established how much Reagan – recovering from colon cancer and later to be a victim of Alzheimer's – knew about their private wars, still less the secret dalliance with the Iranian enemy, and – North's 'neat idea' – the use of Iranian money to fund the Contras. North called it, with unconscious irony, 'Project Democracy'.

The title was actually invented by Reagan during a visit to the British Parliament in 1982. His vision, as he put it, was 'to determine how the US can best contribute – as a nation – to the global campaign for democracy now gathering force'.[2] It was a blueprint of a sort we would see decades later for the export of Western-style governments around the globe, by force if necessary.

British involvement in these machinations, according to one investigation, started in December 1984 when David Walker, a former Royal Engineer and SAS major, was introduced to North by US Navy Secretary John Lehman.[3] Years earlier, Walker and Lehman had been fellow undergraduates at Cambridge. A memorandum drafted by North said that Walker 'suggested he would be interested in establishing an arrangement with the FDN [one of the Contra forces] for certain special operations'.

Peter Kornbluh, a respected American analyst specialising in Latin America, asserts, 'North, to have plausible deniability, turned to foreigners like David Walker . . . He was a "unilaterally controlled British asset": that is, a foreign intermediary hired to conduct specific tasks who, if caught, could still plausibly deny that the United States government was involved.'[4] By that time, Walker had left the SAS to join Jim Johnson's KMS team in Kensington, a group already held in high esteem by SIS and others in Whitehall. They could be said to be reliable deniables.

The Ministry of Defence, according to one source, promoted the firm's services in a brochure that offered 'Training in counter-insurgency skills, quick reaction forces, all aspects of Special Forces techniques, air, land and sea infiltration, small boat work, parachuting, communications, and demolitions.' There was more. Thanks to the political influence that accompanied KMS close-protection teams, Walker also had goodwill among senior members of the Saudi royal family, including Prince Bandar, the Saudi ambassador to Washington. Bandar was later to provide millions of dollars for Contra operations.

North was particularly concerned about the impact of Soviet-supplied helicopters on the Contras. According to Kornbluh, 'Walker thought it was possible to actually conduct a sabotage mission inside Nicaragua to blow up these helicopters on the tarmac. If killing the helicopters proved a mission impossible, Walker offered a backup plan. That was to equip the

Contras with surface-to-air missiles, preferably in his mind the British-made Blowpipe missiles, which are very well suited to the terrain, are relatively simple to use and to be trained to use.'

The suggestion appealed to North. In the sort of battleground where deniable wars are fought, two weapons are decisive: the helicopter gunship and its counter, the surface-to-air missile. This truism would hold good in Afghanistan, where another combination of British and American deniables supplied Stinger to the Taliban. In the case of Nicaragua, there was one obstacle. Prime Minister Margaret Thatcher was not willing to allow weapons supplied directly and publicly from Britain to be used in a toxic Latin American war. Another way had to be found. In April 1986, Alan D. Fiers Jr, chief of the CIA Central America Task Force, suggested to North 'a source for missiles and a price'.[5] Soon afterwards, North's diary records his efforts to acquire 100 Blowpipes from Chile.

This was another less-than-neat idea. True, Thatcher and Reagan had a shared friend in Chile's President Pinochet, a customer for British arms, including Blowpipe. End User Certificates were falsified[6] and with Reagan's knowledge, over the next year or so, North approached Chile in response to what one investigator described as 'the Contras' never-ending search for antiaircraft missiles'. But, as rich American backers signed cheques to arm the Contras at special White House receptions (ostensibly to benefit a tax-exempt charity, the National Endowment for the Preservation of Liberty), no one seems to have mentioned to North or the Contras that, just four years earlier, Blowpipe had failed hopelessly in Britain's Falklands war and had now been junked by the MoD. It was just as well, perhaps, that the deal did not proceed.

Undeterred, David Walker offered to provide pilots to run clandestine airdrops into Nicaragua. This scheme worked rather better, for a few months. Led by a former Royal Navy Harrier pilot, the KMS aircrew, as one of the firm's bosses later recalled, 'sometimes returned with foliage attached to their wings'. As Kornbluh points out, 'The NSC and CIA for that matter wanted foreigners to be the people who would actually be going to fly over Nicaragua precisely because, if they were going to be shot down, they didn't want Americans to be on board. They wanted foreigners because that gave extra plausible denial of US involvement.'

This cunning plan also unravelled when North agreed to replace the British pilots with American veterans of CIA missions into Vietnam, where they flew under the label 'Air America'. One source suggests that the change was in response to the Brits' fondness for noisy, indiscreet parties. Whatever the reason, it was a fatal decision. The team had operated from a safe house in El Salvador under the control of a former CIA pilot named William Cooper. Cooper and two of his former buddies, Buzz Sawyer and Eugene Hasenfus, were also, perhaps, overconfident of their natural superiority over the Nicaraguans. They carried documents that could compromise the operation if the worst happened. Only one of the three – Hasenfus, against orders – wore a parachute. A former Marine, Hasenfus, aged 45, was the 'kicker', responsible for discharging the cargo over the drop zone.

On 5 October 1986, as Cooper's team flew low over a break in the jungle canopy, a young Nicaraguan conscript aimed his Soviet SAM-7 at the sky and fired. It worked better than Blowpipe. The weapon's heat seeker tracked the slow-flying C-123 Provider cargo plane and hit it. As the aircraft dived out of control, Hasenfus managed to throw open a cargo door and dive out. His parachute worked and he landed unhurt in the jungle. He was the only survivor.[7]

Sandinista soldiers found him and put him on trial. He made some interesting admissions. According to the *New York Times*,

> he said the chief American military adviser in El Salvador visited a rebel safe house in San Salvador to tell operatives working there to stop raising hell in nightly outings around the town . . . He painted a picture of a covert operation that had the trappings of professionalism, but in fact was poorly run.[8]

Four of his fellow crew members had worked with him for Air America. Sentenced to 25 years in prison, he served less than two months.

While KMS was paid at least $110,000 for the services of the British pilots, the effect of Cooper's all-American own goal dented the credibility of claims where it mattered most – in Washington – on behalf of the Contras, that they were gallantly winning a war for democracy, without external help. As Kornbluh recalls, 'In the spring of 1985, the Reagan administration was gearing up for its first attempt to restore aid to the Contras, that is to say, to get Congress to reverse itself and re-enact legislation that would let the CIA fund the Contras.

'Walker was needed to conduct what was in the parlance of the Pentagon known as a "perception management" programme, that is to say, create a perception of the Contras' being able to operate freely inside the perimeter of [the Nicaraguan capital] Managua, so that lobbyists like North, the President, Casey [CIA Director] and Secretary of State [George Shultz] could go to Congressmen and say, "You see? The Contras are inside Managua. They can operate at will. They are blowing up munitions dumps. We can't cut them off now. They've finally marched into the centre of the city." [9]

In fact, the Contras remained a long way from the capital throughout their war for the simple reason that, as inheritors of a fascist tradition, they did not enjoy popular support. But, on 5 March 1985, it seemed as if they were indeed a force to be reckoned with. That night, a series of explosions in the city centre tore apart a barracks, an army headquarters and a munitions dump. One eyewitness said, 'The whole hillside was engulfed in flames . . . Huge blocks of concrete starting falling all around me. One hit the street next to me leaving a huge gash in the pavement. It seemed like the end of the world.'

The complex that was so precisely blown to pieces included a hospital used by civilians as well as soldiers. Some of the medical staff were injured by flying glass. Others evacuated 150 patients who had been sheltered, providentially, by a stone wall.

Who was responsible for this expert operation? In 1988 the television current affairs programme *World in Action* pointed the finger at David Walker. The *Observer* repeated it on 23 November 1994. Mr Walker denies the accusation. His friends note that he did not take legal action at the time in accordance with a Special Forces tradition of silence in public about all secret operations, a policy, as one put it, of 'Never Confirm, Never Deny'. Nevertheless, there is clear evidence that he was running some clandestine military operations at that time on behalf of Oliver North. For six days in July 1987, North gave evidence to a congressional enquiry into the Iran/Contra Affair. [10] He was initially reluctant to talk publicly about his links with David Walker, 'an international specialist in insurgency and military matters', because there were 'equities that belong to other governments that are at stake here'. Under pressure, North confirmed that he had authorised Walker to perform military actions in Nicaragua in support of the Nicaraguan resistance (that is, the Contras) in Managua and elsewhere, 'to improve the perception that the resistance could operate anywhere it so desired'.

Senators were not overjoyed that a foreigner was acting as a surrogate for a covert American military programme. Senator William Cohen questioned 'whether it is appropriate to use private entrepreneurs to carry out covert objectives without specific and very rigid guidelines to make sure that profit motives don't contradict or corrode the public purpose . . . Whether it is a tolerable practice to authorise a covert solicitation of foreign countries to pay for programmes either not authorised by Congress or rejected by Congress.'

He had in mind Brunei among others. He might have included Saudi Arabia. Outside the Senate Caucus Room, Foley commented, 'I think [Walker] was more involved than we shall ever know. But I can't tell you today the extent to which he was involved. The idea . . . that American officials in the intelligence community, the National Security Council, should use the services, however expert and able, of an international military specialist such as Major Walker strikes me as extraordinary.'

At a closed, 'executive' session of the committee, North faced tougher questions. He was asked about his role in 'arranging' for the Managua explosion and replied, 'I personally had no role in it whatsoever. It is my understanding that foreign operatives were engaged in that activity and assisted.'

'Was it David Walker?' – 'It is my understanding that Mr Walker provided two technicians involved in that.'[11]

Walker declined an invitation to give evidence to the committee. Some of his contemporaries on the SAS circuit suggest that, at the time, he was within Washington's jurisdiction, playing golf with North. When this invitation elicited no response, a Congressional investigator 'explained to him that we were willing to meet with him in private in any place of his choosing in virtually any part of the world'. He sent Walker a list of questions, including the extent to which arms and explosives had been used in Nicaragua. He received no reply.

Back in London, the Labour MP George Foulkes, later Baron Foulkes, put down 'question after question' for Prime Minister Thatcher's attention, about the man who was becoming known as 'Uncle Sam's British Mercenary'. Not only did Thatcher maintain the same monumental silence as Walker, according to Foulkes, '. . . she was so embarrassed, so oppressed by the questions that eventually she used parliamentary procedure to stop me asking further questions.'

October 2006 was a time when political ghosts returned to haunt Washington and Managua. Nicaragua's former Marxist President, Daniel Ortega, was running for office again, presenting himself as a born-again democrat and moderate capitalist. North, serving the latest Republican in the White House, went on the campaign trail in Managua. This time the dark force he opposed was no longer an extinct Soviet dragon, but a group of Latin American states led by Venezuela's Hugo Chávez, asserting an oil-rich independence from Washington's orbit. North's intervention was as counterproductive as his earlier operations with David Walker. Ortega was re-elected as President of Nicaragua after years in the political wilderness.

His vice-president is Jaime Morales, a former Contra leader who has joined Ortega under a banner of reconciliation. During the campaign Morales said that the 2006 Bush administration and some Congressmen were 'stuck in the past, refighting the war. They have not evolved and think the same factors exist here, those of thirty years ago. They are . . . pretty backward, held by ultra-conservatives that are still in very high positions in US power structures.'[12]

The civil war which Ortega and Morales finally ended cost 30,000 lives. And as *Time* magazine acidly noted, while 'the new Ortega may still prove to be the old caudillo . . . his victory is a reminder of the price the US so often pays for prematurely declaring its mission accomplished.'[13]

Back in 1985 North, when he was not crusading on behalf of the Contras, was also pursuing President Reagan's war on terror in the Middle East. It was to prove another doomed enterprise. Reagan had ridden into town on a wave of patriotism accompanying the release of 52 US Embassy hostages from Tehran after 444 days' captivity. He declared, 'Let terrorists beware that when the rules of international behaviour are violated, our policy will be one of swift and effective retribution.'[14] He would later follow that up, in April 1984, with a presidential finding (National Security Decision Directive 138) noting that, in the preceding year, 250 US citizens had been killed in terrorist attacks, the largest number recorded:

> Terrorism has become a frightening challenge to the tranquillity and political stability of our friends and allies. During the past decade alone, there have been almost 6,500 terrorist incidents. Over 3,500 people have been killed . . . and more than 7,600 wounded. American citizens have been the victims of more than 2,500 terrorist incidents.[15]

These figures were probably an underestimate. In October 1983 a suicide bomber detonated a truck full of explosives at a US Marine barracks near Beirut International Airport, killing 241 Americans. Six months earlier, in a similar operation, 63 people including 17 Americans (eight of whom were senior CIA men) were slaughtered. There were also numerous hijacks, kidnaps and assassinations. The US peacekeeping force was withdrawn from Lebanon as it became apparent that, by being there, the GIs were a lure for terrorists – 'tethered goats', in Special Forces jargon – rather than a deterrent. Reagan's new policy was given strident expression in October 1984 by Secretary of State George P. Shultz, in an address to the Park Avenue Synagogue, New York, entitled 'Terrorism and the modern world'.[16]

It was a scary document that began by recalling that in Brighton two weeks earlier 'one of the oldest and greatest nations of the Western world almost lost its prime minister, Margaret Thatcher, to the modern barbarism that we call terrorism'. It went on to argue, in a clear reference to covert, unconventional operations, that 'our nation has forces prepared for action, from small teams able to operate virtually undetected to the full weight of our conventional military might'. But public understanding would be needed in advance of the use of such power. 'The public must understand before the fact that there is potential for loss of life of some of our fighting men and the loss of life of some innocent people . . . that occasions will come when their government must act before each and every fact is known' to ensure 'public support for US military actions to stop terrorists before they commit some hideous act or in retaliation for an attack on our people'.

If America was to 'respond or pre-empt effectively . . . there will not be time for a renewed national debate . . . We never have the kind of evidence that can stand up in an American court of law. But we cannot allow ourselves to become the Hamlet of nations . . . Fighting terrorism will not be a clean or a pleasant contest but we have no choice but to play it.'

Here, plainly laid out, was an agenda for covert, pre-emptive use of lethal force, or for retaliation, without pause for thought or argument, or adequate proof, combined with an acceptance that innocent lives would be lost.

It was Israel's intelligence service, Mossad, that identified for the NSC team, Robert (Bud) McFarlane and Oliver North, the people responsible for the Marine barracks attack. Within a few days, according to the Mossad veteran Victor Ostrovsky, 'the Israelis passed along to the CIA the names of 13 people who they said were connected . . . including Syrian intelligence, Iranians in Damascus and Shi'ite Mohammed Hussein Fadlallah'.[17] Sheikh Sayyed Mohammed Hussein Fadlallah, born in 1935 in the Iraqi city of Najaf, is a Muslim scholar and a source of spiritual inspiration for

Hezbollah. Living in Beirut, he was the most accessible of the targets identified by Mossad.

On the afternoon of Friday, 8 March 1985, the sun shone on the crowd leaving the Imam Rida Mosque on the main street of Bir el-Abed, a Beirut suburb. No one took much notice of the Datsun pick-up truck loaded with vegetables parked outside an unfinished shopping mall. In fact, the vegetables concealed around 340 kilos (750 pounds) of explosive. Fadlallah, his prayers ended, was about to walk onto the street 'had it not been for a lady who insisted on talking to me. I was tired at the end of the day and did my best to get rid of her, but she insisted and pleaded. As she was speaking to me, the explosion thundered. We discovered afterwards it was near my house.'

The *Washington Post* correspondent Nora Boustany – still reporting from the Middle East more than 20 years later – wrote,

> About 250 girls and women in flowing black chadors, pouring out of Friday prayers ... took the brunt of the blast. At least forty of them were killed and many more were maimed. In all the bomb killed eighty persons and wounded 256 ... The bomb devastated the main street ... brought down the façades of four buildings, damaged twenty others 200 yds away and destroyed dozens of cars.
>
> It burned babies in their beds. It killed a bride buying her trousseau ... It blew away three children as they walked home and it left a nine-year-old girl permanently disabled with a chunk of shrapnel in her brain that cannot be removed.[18]

Fadlallah's immediate response was both cool and chilling: 'The message has arrived and we have understood it well.' A year later, Hezbollah released a 68-page report announcing the execution of 11 people linked to the bombing. It also provided information about an alleged network operating with Lebanese army intelligence, the Christian Phalange Party, the CIA and Mossad.

The distinguished journalist Bob Woodward – co-author of *All the President's Men* – identified other players in his CIA history, *Veil.* He asserted that a senior Saudi conspired with the CIA director Bill Casey to eliminate Fadlallah.[19] As Woodward puts it, they believed that

> Fadlallah had been connected to all three bombings of American facilities in Beirut. He had to go ... The Saudis came up with an Englishman

who had served in the British Special Air Service . . . This man travelled extensively around the Middle East and went in and out of Lebanon from another Arab state. He would be an ideal leader of a sophisticated operation.

To help matters along, Woodward suggests, the Saudis provided a slush fund of $3 million. The Saudi royal family 'categorically' denied it.[20] But, Woodward insisted, 'The Englishman established operational compartments to carry out separate parts of the assassination plan; none had any communication with any other except through him.' One cell obtained explosives; another, the vehicle; a third ran a stable of spies to monitor Fadlallah's movements. Yet another group 'was hired to design an after-action deception, so that the Saudis and the CIA would not be connected'.

Significantly, this was not a suicide bomber, so someone had to be found to take on the risky assignment of driving the bomb to its destination, relying on the integrity of the bomb maker to fit a timer that would not detonate the device prematurely. Woodward says, 'The Lebanese intelligence service hired the men to carry out the operation.'

The closest thing to an admission that the usual Washington suspects were the puppet masters of this operation, as in Managua, came from McFarlane, President Regan's security adviser and North's boss in the NSC. In a carefully polished statement to the US Public Service Broadcasting network 'McFarlane . . . says that the operatives who carried out the attack on Fadlallah may have been trained by the US, but the individuals who carried it out were rogue operatives and the CIA in no way sanctioned or supported the attack.'[21]

A similar analysis was offered by the veteran Associated Press diplomatic affairs expert, R. Gregory Nokes. An unidentified 'senior US official' had told him that the CIA had been working with the Lebanese government to train a counterterrorist unit and that 'the tragic attack could easily have occurred as *The Washington Post* [i.e. Woodward] described, although this official couldn't himself confirm it'.[22]

However, Nokes identifies a political logic that obstinately points back to Washington. He suggested some 10 days after the attack, 'While the facts are in dispute, the circumstances of the attack against Fadlallah fit a policy strategy laid out by Secretary of State George P. Schultz last year' (at the Park Avenue Synagogue). Some in the Reagan administration had opposed Schultz's anti-terrorism strategy. As a result, it was modified.

Nokes quoted an expert on terrorism, Robert Kupperman of George-town University, to the effect that 'the administration decided to work with foreign intelligence services, rather than use Americans in carrying out counterterrorist actions. But that raised the worry, expressed by one senior official this week, that the foreign services would act in their own interests and engage in unauthorized attacks that would embarrass the United States. My guess is that these guys [in the Fadlallah operation] went off on their own.'

Nokes concluded, 'While the facts of the Beirut bombing may never be known for certain, it has been widely reported that soon after the attack, President Reagan terminated the CIA co-operation with Lebanese intelli-gence.'[23]

Astonishingly, North continued to bargain with the Iranian authorities, who were behind the attacks on America that had provoked the terrorism crisis in the first place. The arms-for-hostages trade continued until November 1986, when the Lebanese newspaper *Al-Shiraa* revealed what was going on. By then, Iran had received more than 1,500 missiles. Three US hostages had been released only to be replaced by three new prisoners in what Shultz described as 'a hostage bazaar'.

The *Shiraa* article provoked uproar. Reagan, on television, vehemently denied that such an operation ever happened. Not for the first time, jour-nalists were accused of fabricating a story . . . until, a week later, the President retracted, while still insisting that the weapon sales had not been part of any hostage deal. It was a tawdry performance by a mediocre actor. Later, the public learned that, of $30 million paid by the Iranians, only $12 million had reached the US government. The rest had been used to fund the Contra war in Nicaragua. Admiral Poindexter, McFarlane's successor at the NSC, resigned and North was dismissed. Fourteen people were charged with crimes of various sorts, but, in the end, North's conviction was overturned on a technicality. Vice-President George Bush pardoned six other people, including McFarlane, who had survived a suicide attempt.

McFarlane's suicide note to the congressional inquiry was revealing. In it, he admitted negotiating a multimillion-dollar contribution to the Contras' war chest from his old friend, the Saudi Prince Bandar.[24] Suicides do not usually lie. The letter was further convincing evidence of the links between the Saudis, the McFarlane/North team and the Contras, if not David Walker (who has told friends he does not know who engineered the attack) or people close to him.

North, after his marathon grilling by Congress in front of television cameras, became a folk hero in his country, a man standing tall enough to defy the laws of lesser men, shredding hundreds of files, just excluding the US Constitution (which was not formally shredded) in pursuit of some higher patriotic ideal. Reagan recovered his popularity, if not his wits, by the time he left office. The enigmatic Major David Walker quietly got on with his business, now named Saladin, in the private-security sector. In 2007 he was a respected member of that community.

Meanwhile, the world had to wait many years for further, convincing confirmation from two key sources that British expertise engineered the attempted assassination of Sheikh Fadlallah. In 2004, Fadlallah himself told Paul Cochrane, a British editor working for a body called World-press.org, that the Saudi Arabian ambassador to the US paid William J Casey, chief of the CIA, $3 million 'to assign agents, British MI6 agents and Lebanese, to plan the assassination. They failed.'

In 2007, the ambassador concerned, Prince Bandar bin Sultan, told his amanuensis William Simpson that he had learned from Saudi intelligence that a group organised by a former British Special Air Service man and CIA agent were involved in 'a rogue operation.' He claimed that the operation was never financed by Saudi Arabia. Indeed, Simpson asserts, 'immediately after the attempt on Fadlallah's life, Bandar approached the Muslim cleric [Fadlallah] on behalf of King Fahd, who was anxious that the religious leader did not believe the accusations of Saudi involvement. The sheikh assured Bandar that he held the US and not Saudi Arabia responsible and the two shook hands as friends. Later, Bandar offered to pay Fadlallah $2 million in food, university scholarships and other aid in exchange for an agreement not to attack US targets in Lebanon.'

9

SIERRA LEONE 1997–8:

A less than ethical foreign policy

To misquote Jane Austen, it is a truth universally acknowledged that a government in possession of a serious political embarrassment must be in want of a scapegoat.[1] Thus it was with Dr David Kelly and the case of the dodgy dossiers used to justify the invasion of Iraq in 2003, and thus it was with Peter Penfold, Her Majesty's High Commissioner for Sierra Leone, in 1997–8, to say nothing of Lieutenant Colonel (Retd) Tim Spicer OBE, freelance soldier. When oceans of justification flowing from White-hall through various sonorous reports are distilled, the story of the Sandline Affair is one of missing documents, muddled thinking and ambiguous language in a UN Security Council resolution, and the misuse of that ambiguity by senior Foreign Office officials and government ministers to say one thing while doing another.

Whitehall cynicism is not a novelty. What makes the story of Sierra Leone unique is that scapegoats were not needed in this case to explain away a military failure. This was not another Bay of Pigs, or an Operation Eagle Claw (whose US commander memorably said after the abortive entry into Iran, 'You can't make chicken chow mein out of chicken shit'). The restoration of democracy to Freetown, after months of bloody anarchy on the streets of that capital, was a military, political and cultural success. Subsequently, the British government snatched defeat from the jaws of victory. 'Project Python' (as it was known to the freelances) was the ultimately deniable operation, still in some respects mysterious, and –

despite evidence to the contrary – denied vehemently by the British Establishment after it had served stated British foreign policy.

The need for scapegoats arose from an addiction to political correctness on the part of a Foreign Secretary (in the guise of Robin Cook) pursuing his Holy Grail – 'an ethical foreign policy', emulating South Africa's version – and panic by officials who had been told plainly that the exiled president they were there to help was employing mercenaries in the absence of any other source of reliable, skilled soldiers. FCO officials, to a man (and woman), then sat on their hands and apparently said nothing to their ministers. The ministers, whose failure to know what was going on, even when it was published in British newspapers, or sent in two intelligence reports to the office of the Prime Minister, demonstrated an equally awesome ability to be unaware of the facts of life.

The Sandline Affair – named after Spicer's company – resonates still. It spawned a long-running war-crimes tribunal, a series of government and parliamentary inquiries, accompanied by much ruthless news management and an unexpected by-product: a Foreign Office Green Paper that accepted, in principle, the utility of private military companies.[2] The White Paper that was to have followed, like much earlier action, remained under Tony Blair's blotter.

The backstory to this Whitehall farce is a tale of conflict on two fronts. The ground war in Sierra Leone, bankrolled by blood diamonds, was one in which mercenaries recruited by the South African enterprise Executive Outcomes and, later, Sandline had engaged for years before the Battle of Whitehall began in 1998. Most of the soldiers were South Africans but they included some colourful British SAS veterans such as the Fijian Fred Marafono and Will Scully (working for a company called 'Cape International'), who fought a day-long battle to defend a thousand terrified refugees holed up inside the Mammy Yoko Hotel, situated near the sweeping, two-mile golden beach of Lumley Bay. Scully was later awarded a Queen's Gallantry Medal – normally given to members of the regular armed forces – 'for saving lives during a coup'.[3] The citation failed to mention where, or when, the coup had occurred.

This particular coup – the latest in a series after Sierra Leone was granted independence in 1961 – occurred on 25 May 1997. Major Lincoln Jopp MC, the leader of a British team training the Sierra Leone army, later described how 'I was there to train the government forces. Obviously I wasn't much good. The week that the young officers were due to give talks on "The Roles of the Military in a Democracy", they had another idea. They staged a coup instead!'[4] The junta's other idea, under their leader Captain Johnny Koroma, was an instant pay rise derived from looting. They called it 'Operation Pay Yourself'.

For the British government, and in particular its High Commissioner Peter Penfold, this was not going to become just another domino in the collapsing structure of the Western model in postcolonial Africa. A total of £2 million of UK taxpayers' money had been invested in the electoral process in Sierra Leone a year earlier, which had brought President Ahmad Tejan Kabbah to power. Penfold, as he said later, was determined that, this time, democracy would prevail.[5] The problem, as so often in Africa, was that while the international community passed pious resolutions, the situation on the ground was a case for bullets as well as words. No external agency was capable, or willing, to do what was necessary.

During the turbulent, drunken days that followed the coup, a rebellious army made common cause with illiterate young dissidents armed by neighbouring Liberia under a flag of convenience known as the Revolutionary United Front (RUF). Liberia was paid for its aid in blood diamonds, illegally exported from Sierra Leone. As the mob looted Freetown, Kabbah fled to sanctuary in neighbouring Guinea. His government-in-exile was recognised by the UK as the official government of Sierra Leone. Following the logic of its own policy, Britain said it backed the restoration of Kabbah's government, but by peaceful means. Blair and his Foreign Secretary, Cook, had not learned from Jopp's experience.

During the 10 days that followed the coup of 25 May 1997, as thousands of Europeans and Lebanese traders were airlifted to safety by the US navy, the mob moved against the foreigners' sanctuary, the Mammy Yoko Hotel. It was a convenient backdoor route out of the country for helicopters and small boats, ostensibly defended by Nigerian soldiers who dominated a West African peacekeeping force known as 'Ecomog'. On 2 June, when the hotel came under heavy fire from mortars, rocket-propelled grenades (RPGs), heavy machine guns and (mysteriously) a Russian-made helicopter armed with missiles, the only people who stood their ground were Scully, the ex-SAS freelance, and Jopp, the clean-cut regular British officer.

Throughout a day that resembled the SAS Battle of Mirbat (see Chapter 6), Scully, armed with a general-purpose machine gun, moved from one side of the hotel roof to another to blast away at the rabble surrounding the building. At the start, Jopp acted as Scully's target spotter, from an exposed perch at the top of the hotel water tower. Later he was injured by the back-blast from an RPG fired by an incompetent Ecomog soldier, then wounded again by shrapnel. He was later awarded a Military Cross. Penfold, observing the action from the roof of the High Commission on high ground about two miles away, was active in negotiating an evacuation by US forces. He had learned the hard way that he could not depend on his masters in London. The day the coup began was a bank holiday in Britain and there was no one available to advise him at the FCO in London.

As the day wore on, the Nigerians – with 12 men wounded – melted away. Scully, in an incredible one-man battle in which his only movement had to be on his stomach, kept the rebels at bay. After dark, more than 1,000 refugees crept away through a back entrance, to a beach rendezvous where, next morning, US navy helicopters lifted them to safety. The total number saved by the carrier *Kearsage* was 2,516. Of these, 1,261 were evacuated in four hours, while the rebels kept busy ransacking what was left in the Mammy Yoko.

It was providential that Scully was on the scene, but it is also worth examining what had brought him to Sierra Leone just 11 days before the coup. He had signed up, through contacts on the Circuit, to train Mende tribesmen to fight RUF rebels still crossing into Sierra Leone from Liberia. The tribesmen were Kamajors, aboriginal hunters who had not entirely given up cannibalism. In earlier conflicts, mercenaries working for the South African enterprise Executive Outcomes in Angola and Sierra Leone had run successful counterinsurgency operations for both governments. One of them was Fred Marafono, who – according to Scully – had brought to bear his SAS experience of training former enemies in Dhofar in units known as '*firqa*'.[6]

The idea appealed to Sierra Leone's Defence Minister, Chief (and ex-Captain) Sam Hinga Norman, as well as President Kabbah. They knew their government faced a potential threat from their own regular army as well as the RUF. At times, there was nothing to distinguish one group from another. As a result, a new word was coined in Sierra Leone: *sobel*, meaning 'soldier-rebel'. The Kamajors, trained and equipped by the world's leading counterinsurgency experts, would emerge as a third force in the politics of the country.

Because of the controversial nature of the Kamajors – not the regular Sierra Leone army's favourite people – Marafono and Scully were ostensibly committed to guarding a gold mine about 150 miles upcountry, but as Scully later confirmed, in his candid memoir *Once a Pilgrim*, the ex-RAF

Harrier pilot who hired him admitted, 'It's a cover for the real job.' To have gone public at that stage, however, might have precipitated the coup even sooner, even though it was not a question of whether, but when.

There were other strange fish in this exotic sea. Around 350 mercenaries working for Executive Outcomes, ostensibly, had pulled out of the country as part of an earlier peace deal. The secret Kamajor training programme was meant to replace them. In practice, many of the foreign mercenaries remained in remote parts of the country to protect diamond mines in a 'stay-behind' role. Others signed new contracts with Spicer's Sandline company, or its associated security firm, Lifeguard. They included Marafono, acting as gunner aboard a helicopter flown by two South Africans, Juba Joubert and Neil Ellis. Their commander was a former US Green Beret colonel, Bernie McCabe, who – as Spicer confirmed – 'spent a lot of time with the Kamajors "behind enemy lines".'[7] Not surprisingly, there was a widespread belief in Sierra Leone after the coup that Executive Outcomes never went away.

Handsome concessions in some of the mines appear to have been granted by Kabbah to Branch Energy, a subsidiary of a DiamondWorks, listed on the Toronto Stock Exchange. A government inquiry conducted by Sir Thomas Legg later concluded that Sandline 'has working and personal links with other companies operating in the fields of military and security services, and mineral extraction. In the former category, these include Executive Outcomes and Lifeguard and, in the latter, DiamondWorks and Branch Energy.'[8] Throughout the Legg and Commons inquiries, the same exclusive coterie of names and companies repeatedly emerges to make common cause in seeking contracts and persuading the government to support their activities, which, in a half-hearted way, it did, by adopting a policy of deliberate ambiguity, exemplified by public statements that the UN arms embargo on Sierra Leone applied only to the rebels, when it knew this to be untrue.

From the outset Branch Energy and its network of former intelligence officers and Special Forces veterans seemed to wield great political influence in London as well as Africa. Shortly before Peter Penfold, the High Commissioner, took up his appointment in Sierra Leone in March 1997, two months before the coup, 'he went on the FCO's advice to . . . visit Branch Energy, as one of the leading British companies in Sierra Leone'.[9] There he met another influential figure, Tony Buckingham, a former Special Boat Service Marine turned North Sea diver who had morphed into 'an international businessman with a major shareholding in DiamondWorks'. Buckingham, according to Tim Spicer, 'acted as patron to Sandline, although he had no involvement with its ownership or operation'.

Such was the background to Kabbah's strategy, in December 1997, for a return to power in Freetown, from his exile in a Conakry hotel, near his neighbour and confidant, Peter Penfold. Penfold had not been provided with a secure radio link to London. It put him, yet again, in a position where he was obliged to devise tactics on the hoof, so long as that accorded with his own government's strategy of restoring Kabbah. Sierra Leone, although controlled by a rag-tag army, was far from isolated. Scully, among others, was running a clandestine service by boat in and out of the country. One mission was to take an American agent back to the US Embassy in Freetown to destroy confidential documents.

Sandline, with at least 15 operators in the country, shared a base at Lungi, 10 minutes away across a creek from the capital by helicopter. Sandline's helicopter provided Sam Hinga Norman and others with the flexibility to co-ordinate a guerrilla war inland, using Kamajor foot soldiers, when Norman had no other direct means of contacting his men.

For months during junta rule, the Sandline helicopter team also rescued 'a large number of people' from remote areas upcountry. As Spicer points out,

> There was no one else to do it . . . While we were happy to do it, we did so at our own risk and at considerable cost, and none of the sums laid out in this work were ever repaid by the employers of the expatriates we rescued . . . We were simply British citizens helping other British citizens, doing work the British government should have been doing.

This work, he points out, was not covert. It was known to the US State Department and the FCO, via Penfold and John Everard, the deputy head of Africa Department (Equatorial), known as AD(E).

Back in London, there was also a buzz of diplomatic activity involving Kabbah, Foreign Office ministers and officials, aimed at isolating the rebel regime by imposing sanctions on supplies of fuel and weaponry. In view of Liberia's ready support of the rebels, it was always a losers' strategy. Kabbah, meanwhile, had also been approached by Spicer, with an offer to 'study military means' as a route to restoration. As early as 4 June, the day after the beach evacuation orchestrated by Penfold and Scully, Spicer telephoned John Everard, Deputy Head of AD(E), to tell him that he would consult the Nigerian dictator General Abacha about 'the possibility of Executive Outcomes' involvement in military restoration of President Kabbah. Asked if HMG would object,' says the Legg Report, 'Everard "refused to be drawn".' If this was not a green light, it was not a red one, either.

The following month Rakesh Saxena, an Indian-born Thai banker, based in Canada and travelling on a Yugoslav passport that was not his, contacted Sandline, offering money for a countercoup in return for diamond concessions. Saxena was later arrested in Vancouver on a charge of embezzling $2 million from a Bangkok bank. Spicer had known for months about the allegations surrounding Saxena, but, as he later commented, 'You meet a lot of strange people in this business. Saxena was not a proven villain and as yet the Canadian government had not deported him.'

Regular contacts now began between Spicer, Bowen and Buckingham on one side, and with Kabbah and Penfold on the other. There was one hiccup on 1 August, when the *Toronto Globe & Mail* inconveniently reported that Sandline was involved in a plan to overthrow the junta. The report was copied to London by the High Commissioner in Ottawa. The FCO in London responded with a press line, saying, 'We deplore the recruitment of mercenaries. If any evidence came to light that British citizens recruited as mercenaries were themselves engaged in illegal activities, that evidence would be referred to the prosecuting authorities.'

The copied report and the press line were then filed by AD(E) and apparently forgotten. The story should have identified at an early stage the question that was to dog Penfold and Spicer months later. This was, 'What, if anything, was illegal in assisting the restoration by force of a democratically elected government in Sierra Leone?' What was or was not legal would be defined by two contradictory documents, both concerned with sanctions.

The West African governments' economic group, known as 'Ecowas', imposed sanctions on 29 August with a resolution that specifically included, if necessary, the use of force to restore democracy. The UN adopted a separate resolution, crafted by the British, ambiguously expressing strong support for Ecowas.

For the next eventful six months, it occurred to no one that sanctions on arms supplies could be interpreted so as to apply equally to the rebels and Kabbah's legitimate government, but that, finally, was the political dishonesty upon which Cook and others depended to preserve their virginity in this matter. In all its public statements, the British government's propaganda machine publicly insisted that the resolution imposed 'sanctions *on the military junta* in Sierra Leone' [my emphasis]. Later, Robin Cook would tell the Legg inquiry that while he and his Minister of State, Tony Lloyd, 'approved the goal of drying up arms supplies to *all* parties in Sierra Leone . . . this aspect of the policy was not published abroad . . . partly because of sensitivities about the possible role of Ecowas, which, unlike HMG had explicitly contemplated the use of force . . .'.

This astonishing admission of a policy of disinformation by Cook was cynically compounded months later in the Commons, when he told MPs, 'Much of the *presentation* [my emphasis] was indeed that the UN resolution was aimed at the military junta. In that the statements were *entirely* [my emphasis] correct – the embargo applied to the junta. It did not apply only to the junta, however . . . In defence of the news department and my officials, I should say that someone in the outside world who took a news line as an authoritative statement of the legal position would be very odd.'[10]

The implication of this was that his department's propaganda was to be taken with a large pinch of salt. Further confirmation of Cook's pragmatic approach to the 'entire' truth was his comment, reported by the Commons Foreign Affairs Committee, that he was 'relaxed about his officials' 'kite flying and brainstorming' about alternatives to the announced policy.'[11]

The disinformation strategy took a more sinister turn in October, when UN Resolution 1132 was incorporated into British law. A UN embargo is implemented in Britain (with a seven-year prison sentence for disobedience) by a process that evades parliamentary scrutiny. The conjuring trick is an Order in Council, approved in secret by the Privy Council. In this case, the wording of the Order in Council differed significantly from the woolly phraseology of the UN resolution and moved decisively against a commonsense interpretation of it.

As rewritten by Foreign Office legal experts, the Order in Council applied equally to both sides in the conflict, even though Kabbah, the lawful president, and the UN's own legal experts would later challenge that interpretation. Much worse, FCO officials did their best to ensure that word of this interpretation was not circulated among those most directly involved, including High Commissioner Penfold. As the MPs' Foreign Affairs Committee noted, the FCO did not give the Order full publicity, but 'instead, it was treated in a disgracefully casual manner'. The department most concerned, Africa Department (Equatorial) was not consulted when it was drafted, and the goalposts moved. Nor was Penfold. There was no public announcement of the Order, 'and no attempt was made to notify the principal officials concerned'.

The deadly Order in Council took effect on 1 November 1997. Meanwhile, Penfold and Spicer, as well as many others, continued to contemplate the public use of force oblivious of the fact that, in secret, the government had decreed that any step in that direction, if it included the supply of arms, could result in a seven-year prison sentence. Kabbah, in exile in Conakry, asked Penfold's opinion about a deal with Spicer. According to Spicer, the emerging deal involved a command-and-control group of military advisers to work with the Kamajors and Ecomog, helicopter support and a shipment of arms for the Kamajors, to be supplied via Ecomog and a Special Forces unit at a total cost of $10 million. 'Kabbah', wrote Spicer, 'had discussed our involvement in Sierra Leone with [Penfold] before agreeing to the deal.'

The Legg report asserts that Penfold assumed, as did President Kabbah, that the arms embargo was targeted on the junta. 'He did not doubt that the contract was legal, nor did he believe that it was contrary to HMG's policy, the goal of which was to restore President Kabbah.'

In fact, there was a quite specific deal on arms, signed off as an end-user certificate by Kabbah on 15 January 1998, 'ordered by the Government of Sierra Leone and solely for its own use within Sierra Leone'. The shopping list comprised 2,500 assault rifles, 180 rocket launchers, 50 machine guns and quantities of ammunition and spare magazines. Back in London two Joint Intelligence Committee reports (on Sierra Leone) sent to the Prime Minister's office on 28 January and 25 February 1998 contained references to Executive Outcomes and Sandline, but neither mentioned arms supplies.

For months after the Spicer/Kabbah contract, senior Foreign Office officials would deny all knowledge of what was going on. They should have known. Not only did Penfold try to keep his bosses informed, but the Ministry of Defence was also knocking on the FCO's door. The MoD had sent a liaison officer, Major Peter Hicks, to Conakry on 14 February 1998. The day he arrived 'he was introduced to Mr Rupert Bowen' (the former SIS officer now working for Branch energy) 'who spoke to him for about twenty minutes'. Next day, Hicks – who, unlike Penfold, had been equipped with a secure communications link to London – reported that Bowen had told him that 'they were expecting a shipment of small arms in the next few days, which was for onward delivery to the Kamajors'.

On 28 February, Hicks reported that the arms consignment, a total of 35 tonnes, had arrived. Hicks's report was immediately passed to the FCO Communications Centre and copied to the resident clerk for action. That official telephoned a member of AD(E), describing the contents of the message. The Commons Foreign Affairs Committee inquiry found that 'the AD(E) member's advice . . . was that no urgent action needed to be taken and that the report need not be retained. The Clerk accordingly put the report in the disposal tray where it was later destroyed.' A backup copy was also ordered to be destroyed.

Hicks sent a second report two days later, relating a conversation with Brigadier Bert Sachse, a South African working for Sandline's allied company, Lifeguard. Hicks had been told that

> the 37 tonnes of weapons and ammunition brought in by EO [Executive Outcomes] in the last week are under the control of the Nigerian troops at Lungi [across the bay from Freetown]. General Maxwell Khobe, the Nigerian Task Force Commander of Ecomog, has issued . . . 250 rifles, 10 machine guns and 100,000 rounds of ammunition to Hinga Norman for use by the Kamajors.

The MoD faxed this report to the resident clerk at the FCO early on 2 March 'but the Resident Clerk does not recall receiving it and no record of the matter now exists'. If the FCO had become a black hole for sensitive information, this was not the case at MoD, whose Defence Intelligence Staff desk officer for the region 'told us that he received all Major Hicks's reports and was in daily communication with him by telephone and was aware that the import of arms into Sierra Leone by Sandline would have been a breach of the embargo'.

On 30 December, Penfold wrote to the head of AD(E), Ann Grant, telling her that Kabbah had signed the arms contract 'for the civil defence militia' (code for Kamajors). The arms would start to flow in January. He added, 'As you know, it has always been my view that only a serious threat of force will persuade the junta to stand down, therefore I welcome this development.' The letter could not be traced within the FCO.

On 28 January 1998, Penfold received from Spicer a copy of the military plan codenamed Project Python, which implied the supply of arms to Kabbah. Next day, at the FCO in London, he gave a colleague a copy of the plan. By this time, the Foreign Office was being stalked by a big beast of the political jungle, Lord Avebury. As Eric Lubbock, he joined the Liberal Party in 1960 and achieved a stunning by-election victory at Orpington. Within three years he was his party's chief whip. A Buddhist and human-rights campaigner, Avebury used his political nose to detect a cover-up within the FCO when he read, on the Internet, the *Toronto Globe & Mail* article.

As the Legg report puts it,

> Lord Avebury had long taken a special interest in Sierra Leone. His consequent flow of letters and Parliamentary Questions to Ministers, and his telephone conversations with Africa Department (Equatorial) staff, generated a fair amount of work for the Department. As a result, Ms Grant had earlier invited Lord Avebury to a meeting with her on 23 January, so that she could fully explain the Government's policy on Sierra Leone.[12]

Penfold still regards Avebury's intervention as 'unhelpful'. Avebury believed that it was possible to negotiate a peaceful settlement with the rebels. In her reply, Grant told Avebury, 'Our commitment . . . is to fight for the reinstatement of the elected government.' He asked whether this meant that the AFRC (Armed Forces Revolutionary Council, the title used by rebel soldiers) 'were meant to lay down their arms and put themselves at the mercy of Kabbah'. Grant said this had to be 'worked out by Ecowas'. She 'did not think the Nigerians would go for a military solution because that would mean they would be pilloried by Ecowas and the international community'.

It was a deeply flawed analysis. On 5 February the countercoup began in Sierra Leone. The Kamajors rose in revolt in various parts of the country, while Ecomog troops advanced on Freetown. After heavy fighting, the Nigerian-led force secured the capital five days later. On 9 February, a telegram from the British Embassy in Washington included a State Department report that 'the Kamajors are much more effective since concluding their contract with Sandline'.

Sandline had effectively created a military Third Force, the Kamajors, but it was now clear that its arms shipment was irrelevant to the outcome.

In the Foreign Office, meanwhile, the political focus had shifted as a result of Avebury's interventions. The day that the countercoup exploded, Avebury wrote again to Ann Grant to ask, 'Is it an offence for a British firm to bring weapons into Sierra Leone and if so, what action can be taken against Sandline, or against Mr Spicer himself?'[13]

Spicer's view of the way things turned out was that 'the politicians were trying to have it both ways: using Sandline to help Kabbah when it suited them, then using us as a chance to parade their moral superiority when it all became public knowledge'.[14]

By now, a sense of unease was infecting some of the FCO team, notably the new deputy head of AD(E), Craig Murray. Murray was one of those prepared to criticise the High Commissioner for his 'freelance tendencies'. He recommended Penfold's recall. (Murray, in his turn, was to achieve fame as a maverick diplomat. As ambassador to Uzbekistan, from August 2002 to October 2004, he was asked to resign from the Foreign Office after openly condemning the torture of dissidents. His personal life in chaos, he had a breakdown and was treated for depression. He resigned from the service in 2005).[15]

Grant did not alert ministers to the implications of Avebury's campaign, but on 8 March the *Observer* alleged that Penfold had held secret talks with Sandline 'at a time when they were allegedly plotting to overthrow the military junta'. Minister of State Tony Lloyd expressed concern at what was happening. He was not told that a Customs investigation into Sandline had been triggered a month earlier by Grant. On 3 April Customs officers raided the offices of Sandline and the FCO itself. Ministers apparently remained in the dark.

The immediate scapegoat for the government's policy of ambiguity and disinformation was Penfold. The High Commissioner had saved the lives of around 5,000 people, including around 800 in the Mammy Yoko, when he threatened the rebels with a bombardment by the US navy if they did not back off. Yet in the Commons on 27 July 1998, Tam Dalyell referred to 'a career-ruining letter of rebuke' sent by the FCO to Penfold. Dalyell pointed out, 'On 11 May, the Prime Minister was widely reported as going out of his way to praise the High Commissioner, who was accused of co-operating with a mercenary operation mounted by Sandline International. According to the Prime Minister, Mr Penfold had done "a superb job" . . . What differed between May and July?'

Cook replied that the Prime Minister 'indeed said that Peter Penfold behaved as a hero during the original coup. In fairness to myself, I repeated that point when I said that Mr Penfold showed great courage and commitment during that original coup and that he had since won high standing for Britain in Sierra Leone. He is entirely entitled to have that good record taken into account against the explicit findings on the Legg report on his contacts with Sandline . . . that is why I do not intend to institute any formal proceedings against him.'

Cook's ethical policy did not apply to his own staff. The customary distribution of medals and awards followed after the crisis, but Penfold was ignored. After the uproar, he applied for 15 posts within the FCO. He was more than qualified for all of them. He was rejected in every case and retired on pension in 2002. In Sierra Leone he was honoured as a Paramount Chief.[16]

The story did not end happily for Chief Sam Hinga Norman, chief of the Kamajors, graduate of Mons Officer Cadet School in Aldershot, and ultimately Kabbah's Minister of the Interior. During the 1997 coup, he had survived, with some help from Penfold, by hiding for four days at the top of a lift shaft. He was regarded by many, including Penfold, as a hero.

Surprisingly, to those who had fought for Kabbah, Norman, with two others, was indicted by the Sierra Leone Special Court in 2003. The indictment alleged the use of child soldiers aged less than 15. In addition,

civilians, including women and children, who . . . simply failed to actively resist the combined RUF/AFRC forces were termed 'Collaborators' and specifically targeted by the Kamajors . . . Victims were often shot, hacked to death, or burnt to death. Other practices included human sacrifices and cannibalism.

The trial was run by an ad hoc international court backed by the UN, with Kabbah's agreement. It began work on 3 June 2004, funded by the US. It is controlled by a distinguished panel of lawyers from around the world. The prosecution case against Norman and two others was concluded on 14 July 2005 after 75 witnesses, many protected by pseudonyms, gave evidence. Some of the evidence was heard at closed sessions. The trial was not expected to end until some time in 2007. (Norman died while receiving 'routine' medical treatment at a military hospital in Senegal on 22 February 2007. He was the second prisoner indicted by the

Sierra Leone Special Court to die in custody. In July 2003 Foday Sankoh, former leader of the rebel Revolutionary United Front, also died while receiving medical treatment.) Little mention seems to have been made of private military companies. The view of one court official, in an email to me, was that, 'I am aware of Sandline International. I am not convinced they did much.'

Others did not share this view. Tim Spicer's ex-Green Beret colleague Bernie McCabe 'spent a lot of time with the Kamajors "behind enemy lines"'. The Legg report says,

> Mr Michael Thomas, the [US] State Department's desk officer for Sierra Leone, mentioned to Mr Philip Parham [a UK diplomat in Washington] on 9 February 1998, as the counter-coup began in earnest, that the Kamajors seemed to have become a lot more effective since concluding their contract with Sandline.

On the ground, the rebels increasingly complained about the new weapons and tactics adopted by the Kamajors during the second half of 1997 and linked those to the intervention of mercenaries. Not only were modern firearms in Kamajor hands. More crucial was their unexpected night-fighting capability combined with better intelligence and targeting of CDF bases, as well as the impact of the Sandline helicopter.

There was also the testimony of some trial witnesses. On 10 February 2005 prosecution Witness TF2-006, Bobor Tucker, leader of a Kamajor 'death squad', described how, after the junta's coup, he accompanied one of Norman's co-accused 'to acquire ammunition from Executive Outcomes, a private military company that had been hired by the government'. Several weeks later, 'a helicopter landed at Talia Yawbecko carrying . . . Norman himself, among others, along with a supply of fuel, food, guns and ammunition'. He denied lying and 'agreed that the Kamajors fought in order to restore the legitimate government to power'.[17]

On 2 June 2005, Witness TF2-187, aged 28, a married woman, alleged that Kamajors captured three pregnant women and sacrificed them by slitting open their stomachs and decapitating their foetuses. The heads of the foetuses were placed 'like flags' on sticks, in preparation for the arrival of Sam Hinga Norman. He had delivered guns and ammunition by helicopter. After he arrived, she alleged, the Kamajors smeared blood from the sacrificed women on themselves and sang a song in Mende, which, roughly translated, suggested that they received medicine and strength through pregnant women. Norman, she alleged, was accompanied by two uniformed police officers.[18]

Defence counsel, not surprisingly, challenged the witness's credibility. But in view of repeated references to the role of helicopters in the concealed jungle war that raged through much of Sierra Leone in 1997 and 1998, as well as the degree to which some witnesses were polarised in favour or against the accused, it would have been useful, perhaps, to have objective testimony from the military advisers involved in the campaign. One expert prosecution witness, who might have been expected to allude to the advisers, was Colonel Richard Iron, sent by the MoD in London to analyse the Kamajor (deodorised by the title 'Civil Defence Force') command structure. He believed that Norman – who described himself as a 'national co-ordinator' rather than a military combatant – was indeed the CDF commander, surrounded by staff officers.[19]

He described how, as their tribal structure broke down, the Kamajors mutated into a new form that controlled, centrally, a large number of fighters. By the end of 1997, he said, the CDF 'could launch limited counter-attacks against junta forces to prepare for the Ecomog intervention in February of 1998'. There were between 5,000 and 10,000 fighters at the Talia base and thousands among dispersed forces elsewhere. The offensive force took part in major attacks on two towns in late 1997 and early 1998. Their morale was boosted by initiation rituals as a result of which the fighters believed they were immune to bullets.

Colonel Iron also concluded 'that CDF commanders [Kamajors] resisted Ecomog efforts to bring the CDF under Ecomog control'. This issue of command responsibility was central not only to the trial of Norman and his colleagues, but also to the case presented in London to defend the actions of Penfold, Spicer and others who believed they had acted on behalf of the lawful government of Kabbah. Ecomog was the anointed instrument of that strategy.

Colonel Iron seems not to have discussed the role of foreign military advisers in all this. They did not appear as witnesses. Their role, even in the abstract, was not up for discussion. Only once, and then obliquely, did it seem possible that the subject might be raised. Arrow J. Bockarie, one of the defence counsel, put it to Iron, 'Colonel, you came to know that the government – did you at any time know that they were instrumental in providing logistics like arms and ammunition?' Before the witness could reply, however, Bockarie apparently had second thoughts, and added, 'I'll abandon that one and that will be all for this witness.'

Norman's defence was that, while in exile in Conakry, Kabbah asked him to co-ordinate all CDF activities in the country with those of Ecomog, based in Liberia at that point, in order to extend their presence into Sierra Leone and effectively to reinstate the democratically elected government. Ecomog was to provide logistical support to the hunters, who would in turn facilitate Ecomog's movement due to their knowledge of the terrain as well as their familiarity with civil populations. He, also, did not mention the foreign advisers.

Sierra Leone's agony did not end with Kabbah's restoration to power in March 1998. By January 1999, RUF rebels had again seized parts of Freetown. By the time they were driven off, weeks later, 5,000 more people had been killed and the city was gutted. In May 2000, several hundred UN troops were abducted and 1,000 British paras were sent on Operation Palliser to rescue UK hostages. Some of them were at risk when the safety catches on their SA80 rifles jammed as RUF rebels attacked two forward trenches held by the paras near Lungi airport. Tim Butcher, the *Daily Telegraph* defence correspondent, reported,

It was before dawn on 17 May when the rebels crawled to within forty yards of the trenches. With numerous paramilitary groups fighting on the side of the British-backed government, the [Para] Pathfinders were under orders to shoot only if they were certain that their targets were RUF rebels.

A Nigerian peacekeeper stood up at the last minute to challenge the rebels. They opened fire and it was then that the [British] soldiers found they were unable to defend themselves. They had to rely on support from other Pathfinders equipped with older and more reliable General Purpose machine-guns.[20][134]

Muddles of that sort, of course, are more commonly associated with badly armed and organised private military companies. In Sierra Leone, however, the mercenaries took care not to carry guns that might not fire. The Ministry of Defence did its best to suppress news of the debacle, to avoid damaging the morale of soldiers still equipped with the defective rifle.

The Sierra Leone civil war was not over officially until January 2002.

Between March 1998 and September 2000, the British government spent another £65 million – in addition to the original £2 million spent on the 1996 elections – in a programme to stabilise the country. Some critics, including Penfold, believe that the government's obsession with the Sandline contract meant that it had its eye off the ball when the rebels returned in January 1999. They perceive the Sandline row as an irrelevance akin to arguments among medieval theologians about the number of angels that might dance on the head of a pin. Nevertheless (at the time of writing) the trial of Norman could yet throw some light on the role played by Executive Outcomes, Sandline and its allies in assisting the Kamajors.

Questions also remain about the true agenda pursued by the British government after the 1997 coup. There was clearly a twin-track approach, one sanctioning force, the other not. Both strategies were accompanied by a consistent programme of public disinformation. Did the Secret Intelligence Service, perhaps, have an agenda to promote – deniably, of course – the desired outcome, only to be overtaken by Ecomog's shock offensive of February 1998?

The Commons Foreign Affairs Committee, denied access to secret intelligence concerning Kabbah's restoration, concluded,

> We greatly regret that we were not given access to intelligence material and that we were refused the opportunity to take evidence from the Director of the SIS ... From the point of view of the Government, we are not able to say that, in the Sandline affair, the SIS has a clean bill of health. We can neither condemn nor exonerate it ...

These comments did not go unnoticed by another committee of MPs, but one appointed by the Executive, not Parliament. It reports to the Prime Minister, not Parliament, and is part of Whitehall's magic circle. It is the Commons Intelligence and Security Committee. Its membership in 2007, for example, included Baroness Ramsay of Cartvale, a former spy.[21] In April 1999 the committee revealed,

> We were advised by the Chief of SIS that the Service had had two incidental contacts with Executive Outcomes and Sandline International in the latter half of 1997, but that there were no active dealings with these companies. He also informed us ... [censored]
>
> We were told that SIS's policy is – as far as possible and sensible – to

keep its distance from such companies [as Sandline] which, by their nature, attract former employees of the Service and others who may have had contacts with the Service in the past, and which may be pursuing their own separate agendas in countries in which the [intelligence] Agencies themselves are interested. Contacts are kept as infrequent as possible and are not initiated by SIS.

We established that SIS is aware that companies operating in these fields sometimes seek to use informal contacts, and their employment of ex-members of the Service, to give a false impression that their actions carry SIS or British Government endorsement . . . We were given categorical assurances by the Chief of SIS that the Service was not involved in any way with the counter-coup in Sierra Leone, or with the activities of the private military company Sandline International in that country.[22]

So, SIS denied everything. There was no 'black' operation in Sierra Leone. But, given the agency's vocation, one in which deception is one of the tools of its trade, it would deny everything, wouldn't it?

There was an ironic postscript to the Sandline Affair. This British company – commended by an American authority for its 'robust' efforts in Sierra Leone – was replaced by two US firms, funded in part by the British taxpayer. International Charter Incorporated of Oregon ('Anytime, Anywhere') provides helicopter services, including 'surveillance to facilitate the monitoring of any movement of armed rebels'. Another of its tasks, it claims, is to provide 'support to higher level British military personnel'. In the autumn of 2002, ICI helicopters were contracted to support US Special Forces soldiers training five infantry battalions for emergency service in Sierra Leone. By September 1998 (before the last RUF rebellion) another American firm, Pacific Architects & Engineers, was recovering and repairing vehicles and equipment in Sierra Leone for Ecomog. A later $10 million State Department contract helped it retrain the Sierra Leone army and provide both transport and military supplies in Liberia and elsewhere in the region.

Both firms were still influential in West Africa in 2006. By then, PAE had trained 681 soldiers from six Ecowas-contributing countries including – as well as Sierra Leone – Chad, Niger, Mali, Mauritania and Guinea. As Sierra Leone's Chief of Defence Staff, Major General Sam Mboma, said in July that year, 'The Republic of Sierra Leone Armed Forces and the Pacific Architectural Engineers enjoy a very good relationship.' No one mentioned Sandline.

10

CROATIA 1995:

America's junkyard dogs

As he paced up and down in his cell at the Hague in December 2006, Ante Gotovina, the ex-Foreign Legion caporal-chef, the former mercenary soldier who became a general, a liberator and a hero in his Croatian homeland, must have reflected on the irony of his fate. One of his allies said that he was 'the kind of shady swashbuckler that the world of NGOs, diplomats and international lawyers just loves to hate'.

Within earshot, outside the prison, supporters who had travelled across Europe to demand his instant release chanted his name. Yet he knew he would be incarcerated for many more months before facing trial at a UN-sponsored entity known as the International Criminal Tribunal for the Former Yugoslavia, the ICTFY.[1] He had been inside for a year, ever since Spanish police – guided, some believed, by the British Secret Intelligence Service – pounced on him in a Tenerife restaurant, as part of an elaborate dance around the issue of which nations qualified for EEC membership and which did not.

The greater irony, however, was that Gotovina had saved America's face, and more, at a critical juncture in the Balkan wars that followed the dismemberment of communist Yugoslavia. In a lightning 72-hour offensive, he had destroyed the myth that the Serbian army was invincible. But, once he had served his purpose, Washington disowned him as completely as the British government dumped key players in the liberation of Sierra Leone.

Like Chief Sam Hinga Norman – his legitimate government's field commander in Sierra Leone – General Gotovina became the disposable captive of another ad hoc war crimes tribunal, once victory was secured. Washington even offered a reward of up to $5 million for his capture. As in Sierra Leone, it was victor's justice in reverse and a reminder of the perils of being too successful, against the odds and contrary to the predictions of Western experts.

Gotovina's allies, in a submission to the tenacious Hague prosecutor, Carla del Ponte, argue that if he was a war criminal then so were his accomplices, 'namely . . . but not limited to' US officials starting with one William Jefferson Clinton.[2] The exact identity of all of Croatia's closest American military advisers remains unknown but in 1995 the Virginia-based Military Professional Resources Inc (MPRI) was running two separate contracts to train the Croat military. One was a long-term management programme. The second was a Democracy Transition Assistance programme, a classroom operation to retrain Croat officers away from Soviet methods, to Nato norms. Neither contract is asserted by MPRI to involve any other type of military training. This limited role was not how the American diplomat Robert Frasure saw the relationship between his government and the Croat army. He told his fellow diplomat Richard Holbrooke: 'We "hired" these guys [the Croats] to be our junkyard dogs because we were desperate. We need to "control" them. But this is no time to get squeamish about things. This is the first time the Serb wave has been reversed. That is essential for us to get stability, so we can get out.'[3]

Frasure's use of quotation marks raises some interesting questions, which he will never address, for he died in a road accident two days after he wrote those words on his place card at lunch with the Croatian President Franjo Tudjman. Someone, certainly, was 'hired': notably the MPRI team as well as, by extension, the Croatian army. But did 'control', in Frasure's quotation marks, mean what quotation marks sometimes do: a semblance, a mere exercise, of smoke and mirrors? Did that have anything to do with subsequent allegations of war crimes by the Croats? As Frasure admitted, it was not a time to be squeamish.

Holbrooke, the recipient of Frasure's note, wrote a 400-page, critically acclaimed book about his role in the Balkan conflicts without mentioning either MPRI or General Gotovina. In Holbrooke's book, the Croat victory is usefully analysed from various angles, none of which implies the existence of expert American military advice.

Gotovina's offensive began on 4 August 1995, at a moment when President Clinton was trapped by the rhetoric of his election campaign three years earlier, to the effect that 'ethnic cleansing cannot stand'.[4] By 1995, as he faced a re-election campaign, things were hideously worse in the Balkans. During the preceding four years almost 300,000 people had met violent deaths. The countryside was scarred by trails of exhausted, fearful refugees, homes on fire and mass graves. The Serbs, encouraged by their leader Slobodan Milosevic, had overrun the UN 'safe haven' of Srbrenica, massacring more than 7,000 Bosnian men and boys in a four-day bloodbath. As the US Speaker Newt Gingrich commented, it was the worst humiliation for the Western democracies since the 1930s. So the Serbs had to be taught a lesson. On the Adriatic coast of the former Yugoslavia, meanwhile, American freelances were already training a new generation of Croat fighters.

Croatia never fitted comfortably into the six republics cobbled together in 1946 after the Soviet army liberated Belgrade. The Serbs, like their Russian brethren, belong to the Eastern Orthodox branch of Christianity, which they somehow accommodated with communism. Under Nazi rule, Croatia was granted independence. Militant Roman Catholics, the Croats had sent many thousands of soldiers to fight for Nazi Germany against the Red Army on the Eastern Front, in every part of Hitler's war machine including the SS, blessed by Franciscan priests.

In 1990, as the Soviet empire broke apart, Belgrade's grip weakened. The Croats elected Tudjman, an anti-fascist partisan, to lead them to full independence. In the mountains to the east of the country, the minority Serb community created its own mini-state of Serbian Krajina, backed by the formidable, Serb-dominated Yugoslav National Army (JNA). After Croatia declared independence on 25 June 1991, the JNA launched a military offensive combined with the war's first exercise in ethnic cleansing. Krajina was secured as a Serbian enclave within breakaway Croatia.

Within a year of Croatia's independence the American Defense Intelligence Agency was in the country, in search of interesting military truffles (as in Afghanistan 10 years earlier and in East Germany throughout the Cold War). The DIA sent Colonel Richard Herrick and an American Croat, Sergeant Ivan Sarac, to see what deals might be struck. Herrick was fluent in Serbo-Croat. He was an old Balkans hand who had been stationed in Yugoslavia in the eighties.

Herrick and Sarac represented two strands of American intelligence-gathering that are overlooked by non-Americans. The first is that the best

American soldiers are great linguists and among the most intelligent soldiers around. Grunts they are not. The second – vide Sarac – is that the USA is a polyglot culture. Germans, Italians, Poles, Irish, Russians and many others in Homeland USA do not lose their original roots, including their former languages, when they, and their descendants, swear allegiance to Uncle Sam. A by-product of this process is that American Special Forces and intelligence agencies have home-grown sources of military and political intelligence beyond the reach of other, more conservative nations.

Colourful rumours were to float around the Croatian capital, Zagreb, concerning the souvenirs Herrick and Sarac sent back to the US aboard nocturnal C130 flights. These, according to local sources, included Russian 500-kilogram (1,100-pound) sea mines, the latest Russian torpedo and samples of toxins allegedly sold to Saddam Hussein.[5] In return, the National Security Agency, the world's most sophisticated eavesdropping team, provided the Croats with some useful intercept equipment aimed at the Serbs and invaluable for the coming offensive.[6]

Beyond the conjecture about what the DIA might or might not have acquired from the Croats there were some hard realities. MPRI was intimately involved in the Croatian army before and after it whipped the Serbs, though it denies assisting Gotovina's offensive. Clinton himself has admitted that assistance to Bosnians and Croats came as a package, and – in another curious echo of Sierra Leone – precipitated a breach of a UN arms embargo through which the Croatians and Bosnians were able to acquire weapons needed in their wars against Serbia. He also confirmed that the US government authorised a private company to use retired US military personnel to improve and train the Croatian army.

The assault on Krajina was a hugely complex work of military orchestration, reflecting US battle plans for the World War Three in Europe. Few private military companies would have been up to the job, but the chorus of retired generals with MPRI at the time included one who boasted in 1997: 'We offer expertise from the greatest fighting force on earth, the US military,' while another emphasised the German idea of massive, concentrated force, or 'schwerpunkt', focussed 'like a flashlight on the battlefield.'

One of MPRI's principals, however, claims that MPRI was more concerned with ethics than tactics. He said: 'The Croatians came to us [in March 1994] because they wanted to change their army from being an Eastern-style communist army into one based on democratic principles.[7] Furthermore, the international arms embargo on the former Yugoslavia prevented their dealing in 'military goods and services' (though, as noted above, Clinton admitted that the embargo was not enforced by Washington).

There is evidence of deeper, more direct US involvement in the Croatian offensive, codenamed Operation Storm. An enquiry by the independent, London-based journalist-training organisation Institute For War & Peace Reporting claimed that it had uncovered photographs of Gotovina at the US army's Fort Irwin training centre.[8] Fort Irwin, in the remote vastness of the Mojave Desert, California, has long been a tank-training area for large-scale military manoeuvres. The story did not die. Four years later, in January 2006, the German periodical Der Spiegel asserted, 'In preparing for the [Operation Storm] offensive, Croatian soldiers were allegedly trained at Fort Irwin in California . . .'[9]

Before the offensive began, American soldiers ostensibly attached to UN peacekeeping forces in Zagreb took part in that necessary preliminary, the Deception Plan. (As Saint explained in a paper for the US Military Review four years earlier, 'Deception must be part of the scheme of maneuver . . . Deception must be a synchronized effort.') American Blue Berets briefed journalists that the Croats' main line of attack would be on the north of Serb-held Krajina. 'The assault on Knin, the Krajina Serb "capital" and heart of their defences, would take much longer. "We were really suckered," recalls Eric Akerman of ABC Radio News [quoted by Robert Fox]. "In fact they managed to get into Knin within thirty-six hours."'

The offensive was also assisted by US airpower. In another preliminary, in line with the LandAir doctrine, two US military aircraft wiped out two Serb air-defence radar sites near Knin and Udhina, ostensibly in self-defence after the radars had locked onto the aircraft.

The attacking Croatian ground force numbered 200,000. They were opposed by 40,000 Serbs, dug in on the high ground. According to military theory, the Croats needed a superiority of at least three to one against the defenders. The Croats used two main axes of advance, north and south of Krajina, using armour and artillery to slice open corridors for infantry to advance in armoured personnel carriers. Heavily defended positions were bypassed and high ground ignored where practicable. As Saint himself had written, 'I want divisions to be able to move in a short period of time on multiple routes, with command and control systems that will allow them to move faster than the enemy.'

The blitzkrieg strategy worked brilliantly. As Professor Mark Danner, an American journalist, put it, 'Within hours, Croat commanders knew their code name [Operation Storm] had been well chosen, for everywhere Serb soldiers – 40,000 of them, with 400 tanks – retreated, melting away in the rising August sun.' There were comparatively few battlefield casualties. For the Croats and their American allies, the problem was that the Croats had also chosen to shell villages and towns 'in order (as a Croatian colonel serving as an information officer helpfully explained) "specifically to create a disorganised, mass panic and exodus of Serbs".' Then, Danner continued, 'waves of assault troops surged into town and looted stores and houses, followed quickly by militiamen come to pick the carcase clean.'[10]

Around 150,000 Serbs, mostly civilians, fled, clogging the roads and paralysing what military resistance remained. For days afterwards, some Croat fighters went on a killing spree that replicated the behaviour of some Serbs when they drove Croats out of Krajina in 1991. To coin a phrase, many of the Croats behaved in victory like junkyard dogs. Approximately 150 Serbs were murdered. The victims were shot, stabbed or burned alive.

In 2000, a new Croatian president, Stjepan Mesic, ordered Gotovina and six other generals into early retirement after they refused to co-operate with an investigation into war crimes. A year later, Gotovina was indicted by the Hague and disappeared. Secrets from his past started seeping into the public domain. According to the BBC, 'he spent much of the 1980s in Latin America, notably Guatemala, where he trained paramilitaries fighting that country's vicious civil war. Service in Paraguay, Colombia Argentina and Brazil followed and he eventually won French citizenship . . . A French court convicted him of robbery and extortion and there were reports of a growing involvement in right-wing politics'.[11]

Carla del Ponte, chief prosecutor of the ICTFY, accused Gotovina of complicity in seven crimes against the Croatian Serbs, ranging from the slaughter of livestock and 'spoiling' of wells, to the systematic torching of cities, towns and villages, and 150 murders. Gotovina was allegedly responsible as the commander, on his own account and by proxy, for the actions of subordinates under his control. Interestingly, the indictment did not address the military strategy of Operation Storm – including shelling towns and villages – or the methods used to express it. It focused instead upon the localised, personal, close-quarters activities of Gotovina's soldiers, a process that occurred after the Serbian retreat.

There was another singular aspect to the indictment. Much of it depended on Gotovina's activities as part of 'a joint criminal enterprise' with three named Croats, including the former President Tudjman, and others who were not named. None of those identified was an American, a point to which Gotovina's advocates would return.

Meanwhile, Gotovina went on the run, pursued by the British Secret Intelligence Service, apparently acting on behalf of Carla del Ponte. A team of British agents based in Zagreb, the Croatian capital, worked hard on what they called 'Operation Cash'. Why 'Cash'? Some wiseacres speculated that the name of the quarry in this manhunt, translated into English, was 'Cash'. 'Ante' was 'Tony'. Ante Gotovina was Tony Cash. The joke was good. The opsec – operational security – was not. Operation Cash began in 2003, when Croatia applied for EU membership. For a year, with the agreement of the Zagreb government, a team of British spies allegedly controlled by Anthony Monkton, a diplomat based in Belgrade, used a fleet of Bedford trucks containing powerful electronic hacking and telephone interception equipment to eavesdrop on calls to friends and relatives of Gotovina. In one enigmatic episode, one of the vans was damaged by fire.[12]

Gotovina still had powerful friends in the Croatian security apparatus. Some of them were identified in a document apparently emanating from SIS entitled 'Proposals for Improved Intelligence Co-operation', sent to Croatian intelligence with the suggestion that those named be arrested and prosecuted for assisting a fugitive. The document was promptly leaked to an extreme nationalist local newspaper, *Nacional*. A despairing British diplomat wailed, 'A lot of our people have been working very hard in Croatia for years and everything we try to do quickly spills into the papers. It's not just the odd rogue element or nutter. It's systematic.'

SIS had its own reasons, beyond the usual diplomatic ones, to wish to nail Gotovina's supposed friends. Some of them were suspected of supplying weapons to the Real IRA. A *Guardian* investigation by Ian Traynor in Zagreb claimed

An investigation by Scotland Yard's anti-terrorist branch, the Irish Garda and the Croatian police established that the missile used in the Real IRA rocket attack on MI6's headquarters at Vauxhall in London in 2000 was of

Croatian provenance. The same year the armoury found at a Real IRA arms depot in County Meath in the Irish Republic was sourced to Croatia.[13]

When the identities of a series of agents working for the US and the ICTFY prosecutor, del Ponte, as well as SIS were leaked, putting their lives at risk, virtually every Croatian police officer linked to Operation Cash was dismissed or moved on. Del Ponte, among others, was convinced that Gotovina was hiding somewhere in Croatia. In practice, his passports – French and Croatian – would later show that he had been anywhere but Croatia during the manhunt. The pursuers might have had better luck had they tried Tahiti, Argentina, Chile, Russia, the Czech Republic, Mauritania or Mauritius. Gotovina was finally arrested, leading the good life, in Tenerife.

While the manhunt continued, some formidable investigations beyond the control of the international court or SIS had established some promising lines of defence. *Newsweek*, on 21 August 2001, ran a long article by Roy Gutman – an LSE graduate with long experience of the Balkans – which suggested that the CIA as well as MPRI had assisted Operation Storm. It alleged that Americans in military uniform, operating from a secluded base on the Adriatic coast, had flown unpiloted drone reconnaissance missions 'to photograph Serb troops positions and weapons emplacements', and continued,

The images were transmitted back to base, analyzed and then passed on to the Pentagon. According to top Croat intelligence officials, copies were also sent to the headquarters of the Croatian general in command of Operation Storm. The classified reconnaissance missions continued for months, until long after Croat forces had pushed the Serbs into neighboring Bosnia. And the information proved vital to the success of Operation Storm, according to the Croats. Late in the 72-hour campaign, Croat officials say, the drone photos showed Serb forces massing for a counterthrust. The Croatian commander of the operation, General Ante Gotovina, massed his own troops at the point of the Serb breakthrough and shattered the assault.[14]

Gutman's claims were confirmed by Mate Grunic, Foreign Minister of Croatia at the time, in an interview with the Zagreb television station HRTV1. 'Of course I know [of American co-operation],' he said. 'They co-operated well. These aircraft were also used. During the Kosovo operation Croatia also co-operated successfully as a partner of NATO and the USA.'[15]

If the US was involved in the planning and execution of Operation Storm, however, its spokesmen disclaim responsibility for the aftermath. Pierre-Richard Prosper, Washington's roving ambassador for war crimes issues, admitted to *Newsweek* that the Clinton government knew of a military operation being planned in Croatia but 'we did not know about planning for criminal activity'. Peter Galbraith, US ambassador to Croatia in 1995, even questioned whether the Serbian exodus from Krajina was a war crime. He said, 'The fact is, the population left before the Croatian army got there. You can't deport people who have already left.'

Not everyone in the Clinton administration was complicit in Operation Storm. Ambassador Holbrooke describes the attack as 'a dramatic gamble' by the Croatian leader, Tudjman, taken against the advice of US diplomats. If that were the case, it would not be the first time that diplomatists, soldiers, spies and deniable agents, ostensibly on the same side, did not agree. It was a situation tailor-made for some well-connected freelance soldiers even if, in this case, their deniability was less than usually plausible.

Those who cried 'back' in this debate (and they included some senior US officers) did so because they feared that the Serbian leader in Belgrade, Slobodan Milosevic, would unleash the full power of the regular Yugoslav army against Croatia in revenge. That did not happen. The gamble worked. As Holbrooke admits, 'Zagreb's almost uncontested victory began to change the balance of power in the region.'[16] To paraphrase Winston Churchill after Alamein, Operation Storm might not have been the beginning of the end, but it was the end of the beginning. President Clinton later made it clear where he stood. He was rooting for the Croatians.

There would be more bombing, more brutality during the following weeks, in which NATO entered the war against the Serbs. At 2 a.m. on 30 August, Operation Deliberate Force included an attack by more than 60 aircraft on Bosnian Serb positions overlooking Sarajevo, the Serbs' killing ground, from which shells and mortar bombs had rained upon Bosnian Muslim civilians. Up to that point, Holbrooke says, 'it was the largest military action in NATO history'.

Three months after Operation Storm, on a remote USAF base at Dayton, Ohio – a locale that included a museum dedicated to American airpower, in a not-so-subtle hint to the Serbs – Milosevic, Tudjman and the

Bosnian President Alija Izetbegovic initialled a peace agreement. All three, in due course, were to be investigated by the ICTFY.

The status of Kosovo, previously an integral part of Serbia, was not addressed by the Dayton agreement. A home-grown Albanian guerrilla army, the KLA, embarked on a campaign of resistance to Serb domination, attacking civilians and employing the politics of provocation. The Serbs responded with great brutality. In the spring of 1999, NATO conducted a 78-day bombing campaign to force a Serbian withdrawal from Kosovo. An international mission headed by the OSCE took over the province. As a result of the massacres and other atrocities committed against the ethnic Albanians in Serbia, Milosevic was tried as a war criminal before the ICTFY. After five years as a prisoner of the tribunal, he died of a heart attack, in enigmatic circumstances, on 11 March 2006.

The Croat General Gotovina, meanwhile, had been detained only three months earlier. The arguments about his guilt, or lack of it, or the degree to which American soldiers, freelance military advisers, secret agents, politicians and diplomats should share the blame, were just beginning. The Gotovina lobby attracted some influential allies. One of them was Dr Robin Harris, an Oxford PhD, specialising in Croatian affairs, a former member of Margaret Thatcher's policy unit and, as she put it, 'My indispensable sherpa', in writing her memoirs.

In a commentary written for the *American Spectator* in March 2006, Harris argues that Operation Storm

> was an act not of aggression but of self-defense. The [ICTFY] indictment mentions 160 Serb civilians as having died. These deaths were caused by Croat civilians bent on revenge while Croatian police did nothing to help. That was, indeed, shameful. But it happened after the conclusion of the military campaign, not during it. Responsibility for maintaining order had been formally transferred by the Croatian government from the military to the civil authorities. Gotovina himself was no longer even in the area. He had joined Muslim and Croat forces in the continuing campaign within Bosnia.[17]

Harris is not alone in pointing out that the indictment refers to 'a joint criminal enterprise, the common purpose of which was the forcible and permanent removal of the Serb population from the Krajina region'. He was also not alone in asking, 'If "Storm" was indeed a "criminal enterprise" were high officials of the United States not also morally and even criminally, culpable?'

What of the Serb exodus from Croatia? It was 'ordered by the Serb leadership itself, for its own reasons. The text of the order . . . was published some weeks later in the Belgrade journal *Politika* . . .' The flight of 150,000 Serbs made complete sense in Balkan terms. 'It was to advance Belgrade's policies of ethnic cleansing and resettlement of Serbs in eastern Bosnia and Kosovo, parts of a planned Greater Serbia.' Alongside Gotovina, the main loser in this increasingly political trial, Harris suggests, would be the US, whose intelligence methods and sources would be embarrassingly revealed.

Croat nationalists spotted an even more intriguing potential witness for the defence. This was Florence Hartmann, a correspondent for *Le Monde* at the time of Operation Storm and, subsequently, official spokeswoman for the prosecutor who accused Gotovina. As the author of a biography of Milosevic, she argues that the Serbian civilian evacuation was indeed ordered by the Serbian leadership, a manoeuvre partly aimed at covering the retreat of the army.[18] Like Harris, she believes that the order was published by the Belgrade daily *Politika* on 23 August 1995, allegedly having been signed on 4 August, the day Operation Storm was launched. My own research in Belgrade in 2007 confirms that.[19]

The Gotovina trial promised to be an international political spectacular as well as a legal *cause célèbre*. By 2007 the tribunal had acquired a mixed reputation, partly due to its habit of serving subpoenas on journalists to give evidence of war crimes, or even arranging for their arrest if they disclosed court-confidential details such as the identities of witnesses. Would there be a subpoena bearing Clinton's name? Would he be asked whether 'rooting for the Croats' – as if this were a ball game – involved front-line participation by US agents in Operation Storm? It seems unlikely. In May 2003, according to the New York-based Human Rights Watch, 'the government of Croatia decided not to enter an agreement, requested a year earlier by the United States, exempting US citizens from Croatia to the International Criminal Court'.[20] The US has never recognised that arm of international law, to protect its citizens from the risk of a political show trial although – witness the reward it offered for Gotovina's capture – it has a more accommodating attitude to the ICTFY.

If Croatia's American advisers were summoned, would MPRI's trainers still maintain that they provided Gotovina's Ironsides with nothing more lethal than lessons in military ethics? If that is so, then the company has discovered a formula for strategic success that its rivals must envy. As one MPRI employee, quoted by PW Singer and others, noted: 'We made something of a difference, if only in the confidence we helped to instil.'

PART III

.

LICENSED TO KILL

11

IRAQ 2003-PRESENT:

A licence to kill – in some circumstances

The Iraq wars – that is, the invasion of 2003 ending in an optimistic presidential declaration 'Mission accomplished!' followed by a predictable guerrilla/terrorist campaign – marked a tectonic shift in international relations as they had been conducted since the end of World War Two. The old rules, from international laws of war to human rights, from the repudiation of torture to the defence of habeas corpus, were brutally rewritten so as to impose a new form of Western democracy everywhere, anywhere, any time, and to do it in Iraq with breathtaking inefficiency.

One of the changes was a revolution in the status of freelance soldiers. In 2002, the US army's Central Command had a cunning plan for invading Iraq, which envisaged a need for only 5,000 of its soldiers to be in the country by December 2006.[1] As things turned out, even the commitment of 140,000 American and 9,000 British regular soldiers was insufficient to hold down a country that was supposed to rejoice in liberation (vide France, 1944) but, ungratefully, behaved like a resentful, occupied land (vide France, 1940). Reconstruction could not proceed without armed protection and that, in keeping with the neocon philosophy that underpinned the invasion, had to come from the private sector though initially, even that was resisted by Paul Bremer, in charge of the Coalition Provisional Authority. When Eric Westropp of the British PSC Control Risks Group (CRG) suggested that his firm was in Iraq to assist investment, Bremer apparently replied, 'Investment in Iraq is illegal.' At an early meeting of the Iraqi Governing Council Bremer also famously said: 'I am the Iraqi government.'[2]

Yet Bremer himself needed the protective muscle of the private sector. Shortly before he departed, in order to cross Baghdad from that cultural capsule known as the Green Zone, he needed a convoy of 17 armoured Humvees, three helicopters provided by the Blackwater company, themselves escorted by two Apaches with an F-16 fighter to provide top cover.

In Iraq the freelance function was not – as in the Congo, Angola, Sierra Leone, Yemen and elsewhere – to wage war against other professional soldiers or to seize ground. It was essentially defensive, protective and reactive and was similar, in many respects, to the containment of mayhem by the British army in Northern Ireland.

What made it different was that this privatised military action was on a scale not seen for 250 years, before the evolution of the modern nation-state. It was also very, very public, unlike the concealed, deniable operations of early decades. For that reason alone, the new freelance teams preferred to be known as private *security* companies rather than private *military* companies. For some even 'private security' was too sensitive a phrase. South Africans, in particular, wished to avoid the embarrassment of falling foul of anti-mercenary laws at home and so preferred to be known simply as 'consultants'.

Their work was primarily personal protection for aid workers and journalists, as well as that of reconstruction specialists and convoy escorts, and the protection of oil facilities and other sensitive sites. But some of them were embedded operationally in US forces to a degree that made it impossible to distinguish between the freelance and regular soldier, between passive defender and proactive warrior.

At home in Britain and the US, meanwhile, some PSCs invented a whole new market, training journalists, aid workers and others in battlefield survival skills. As the writer David Isenberg notes, 'PMC operations [in Iraq] tread the difficult line in providing protection in a manner that meets the intricate demands of corporate, military and government ethics and come at a significant cost.'[3] He had in mind the PSC body count that, after two years of occupation, totalled more than 200.

Most of these freelance soldiers were American but many were British, Nepalese Gurkhas, South African, Canadian, French, Finnish, German, Dutch, Danish, Russian, Italian, Romanian, Turkish, Bulgarian, Croat, Macedonian, Polish, Egyptian, Lebanese, Jordanian, Indonesian, Fijian,

Filipino, South Korean and Colombian. Such a spread of nationalities exceeded that to be found in the average UN peacekeeping force. This limited more than conversational chitchat. In such mixed company, not everyone immediately understood orders in English such as 'Cease fire!'

It also demonstrated that the world market included a trade in soldiers as well as arms. In May 2005 an American entrepreneur recruiting free-lance soldiers from Ecuador as well as Colombia, boasted, 'We currently have over 1,000 well trained and combat experienced Colombian ex-military soldiers and police available. These forces have been fighting terrorists the last forty-one years and are experts in their fields . . . trained by the US Navy Seals and the US Drugs Enforcement Agency to conduct counter-drug/counter-terrorist operations in the jungles and rivers of Colombia.'[4]

Within the Green Zone there were around 1,000 Peruvians, the 'third rung' of security working for Triple Canopy, behind regular Iraqi and Georgian soldiers. They replaced Gurkhas for a third of the pay, $3,000, their Nepalese predecessors received.

However, those who got lucky in Iraq and stayed alive – the majority – went home in profit, though they then faced the additional challenge of reducing their tax liabilities. For those who died, however, the casualty rate was (as a macabre joke has it) 100 per cent. If Iraqi operators were included, the number of casualties would probably be well into four figures. The PSC Erinys, securing oil pipelines, lost about 20 dead and about 25 wounded during the first 18 months or so of operations. As many as 7,000 other contractors of all kinds, including non-combatants, suffered serious wounds.

The Iraq Coalition Casualty Count, a non-governmental body, listed 389 dead contractors between 10 April 2003 and 23 January 2007 while admitting that its list might be incomplete.[5] Most of them were not free-lance soldiers. The list included translators, drivers, engineers, intelligence analysts, cooks and gofers. Many were unidentified. A total of 157 (almost half) were American and 40 were British, under a third of the regular British army body count. Nineteen came from Nepal, of whom 12 were executed together on 31 August 2004. The means by which the contractors were slain varied from beheading to roadside bomb. A Pentagon analysis of the body count between 1 May 2003 and 28 October 2004 identified 166 fatalities among freelance soldiers (64 American) and 834 non-fatals.

Companies suffering significant losses included Blackwater (27 dead in

Iraq as of March 2007) and DynCorp (26 as at 20 January 2006), while the logistics firm KBR had lost 28 men as of 24 January 2007. Set against the level of their activity in the field, the companies would argue that such losses were a small percentage of the people notionally at risk. Nevertheless, the contractors' body count, while substantially lower than the number of deaths suffered by regular, uniformed soldiers, was assuredly the biggest in the history of freelance soldiering in modern times, reflecting a spectacular growth in the business. During the first Gulf war in 1991, the ratio of freelance soldiers to regulars was, at best, 1:50. During the 2003 invasion it was 1:10. The number increased after that. The total rose during 2004 to around 30,000, of whom 14,000 were Iraqi armed guards. By 2007 some sources suggested that the size of this private army, the second biggest force after the regular US contingent, was approaching 100,000, though it should be said that finding verifiable figures in this environment proved almost impossible.

Foreigners lured by pay of $500 a day or more quit their own armies to join the Iraqi gold rush. As one Welsh volunteer told his wife, before he was killed after 22 days' service, 'This is my chance to clear the mortgage.'

Some events could not be anticipated or insured against. To paraphrase Donald Rumsfeld, then Secretary of Defense, there were things that the companies knew, and things they did not know. They could not have anticipated the impact of misjudged policies on the part of the American occupation force on their own, primarily commercial concerns.

At the end of March 2004, a year into the occupation, miscalculations by the Bremer administration and the US military command succeeded briefly and disastrously in generating a violent opposition that united Sunni and Shia resistance groups. This unity was broken by a virtual civil war in which the two communities turned upon each other after the Iraq general election of December 2005. The elements that came together in a renewed war of resistance throughout much of Iraq in the spring of 2004 were diverse and complex, but they produced a simmering resentment that needed only a small spark to detonate an explosion.

At the centre of Sunni resistance was Fallujah, a staunchly Baathist, pro-Saddam city, which, nevertheless, remained quiescent during the invasion of March 2003. The subsequent occupation of an empty Baath Party headquarters and a school building by American paratroops was resented by some local people. What followed was familiar to anyone who witnessed the politics of provocation in Northern Ireland in the early seventies. Local people joined a protest march. Expressing a local insult, a boy hurled a sandal at a US jeep. An eyewitness, Chris Hughes of the *Daily Mirror*, reported, 'I watched in horror as American troops opened fire on a crowd of 1,000 unarmed people here yesterday. Many, including children, were cut down by a twenty-second burst of automatic gunfire during a demonstration against the killing of thirteen protesters at the Al-Kaahd school [four days earlier]. They had been whipped into a frenzy by religious leaders.'[6] In a scene reminiscent of Bloody Sunday in Derry in 1972, the same number of demonstrators – 15 – were killed.

Over the following year, Fallujah became a virtual no-go area for Coalition forces. The garrison that remained was hunkered down. It was supplied by a US catering company, which depended on Blackwater, a PSC in a hurry to prove that it could do a better job than its British predecessor, some of whose experts were wary about blundering into the town at a delicate time. On 31 March 2004 the company sent two two-man security teams into Fallujah without the usual tail gunner to watch their backs. They were ambushed at a bridge now known as Blackwater Bridge, dragged from their vehicles, lynched (again, in scenes reminiscent of Belfast), mutilated and set on fire.[7] The torsos of two of the men, Scott Helvenston, aged 38, a former navy commando, and Jerry Sovko, were strung from the bridge as a crowd of locals danced, and Iraqi police watched impassively.

The incident triggered the bloodiest month for US troops and civilians in Iraq since the invasion. As a report in the *Guardian* put it, 'The US response was to lock down the entire city of 300,000 and mount a protracted military campaign against it.'[8] During the siege of Fallujah (known to the American forces as Operation Vigilant Resolve) the firepower employed by F-15E and F-16 bombers, F-14 and F18 fighter bombers, Super Cobra helicopters, AC-130 gunships and British Tornado aircraft included three dozen 225 kilogram (500-pound) laser-guided bombs in the space of 48 hours, a hail of deadly fire from airborne howitzers and snipers on the ground. The *Sunday Times* noted that what had been launched as an action 'to hunt down the leaders of the lynch mob that killed and mutilated four US security contractors . . . has turned into a widescale military assault'.[9]

One expert estimate suggests that around 800 people, including around 600 civilians (300 women and children) were killed. The political impact was felt, but muffled, in Washington and London until a Downing Street memorandum, later leaked to the press, revealed 'deep misgivings within the British government over America's "heavy handed" tactics at Fallujah'.[10] More publicly, Nigel Aylwin-Foster, a British brigadier who had served with the Americans in Baghdad, said that the murder of the contractors was 'clearly an attempt to provoke soldiers' and the soldiers 'took the bait'. He added that the Americans' 'strong sense of moral authority' led them to assume, wrongly, that Iraqis would understand 'even if civilians were killed by mistake'.[11]

America's overreaction was watched, sifted, analysed by her enemies, who could not be blamed for concluding that freelance security teams were high-value targets. Soon, more were to die. The year 2004 proved to be a peak, with at least 154 freelances killed compared with 98 in 2005 and 76 in 2006.

Within the same week, on 28 March 2004, Bremer's team also succeeded in alienating a large percentage of the Shia community by closing down *Al Hawza*, a newspaper run by Moqtada al-Sadr, a charismatic 30-year-old cleric whose visceral opposition to US occupation matched his father's opposition to the secular Saddam Hussein.[12] Sadr, still a potent force in Iraqi politics in 2007, offered Iraqis an intoxicating cocktail of nationalistic politics and Islamic mysticism. The very name of his 'Mahdi' army was a reference to the messianic entity known to Shiites as the 'Hidden Imam', who had never died.

The Coalition Provisional Authority (CPA) accused *Al Hawza* of publishing 'many articles' containing false information and seeking to 'disturb public order and incite violence.' Another version, published by the British National Union of Journalists, suggests, 'The editor had printed a front page lead story that a "suicide bomb" in a bus queue was, according to eyewitnesses, a missile fired from a helicopter. The newspaper was closed down by the US Army the next day.'[13]

Al Hawza offices were raided around the country as angry protesters at the newspaper's offices in Baghdad warned the CPA to expect attacks from the Mahdi army. It was an ironic counterpoint to the West's boast that it had introduced a free, vigorous press into post-Saddam Iraq. At the beginning of the crisis, *Al Hawza* had a derisory readership of barely 5,000. Its closure won over the sympathy of previously uncommitted Shiites. At least half a dozen cities erupted in anti-Coalition violence at a time when the CPA had around 100 days left before it was to hand over to an Iraqi administration.

Dan Murphy of the *Christian Science Monitor* reported,

> With casualties heavy for both Sunnis and Shiites, many undoubtedly
> civilian, the violence forged an unlikely alliance. Both Sunni insurgents
> and Shiite militants expressed their mutual admiration. In Sadr City [in
> Baghdad] where Sadr's Mahdi Army holds sway, Shiite mosques have led
> blood drives for the citizens of Fallujah; in central Baghdad's Adhamiua
> neighborhood Shiite militias and Sunnis joined up in at least one
> attack.[14]

Al-Sadr was living, and continued to live, a charmed life that enhanced his
mystique. In August 2003 Bremer had wanted him arrested. But, as the
columnist Simon Jenkins noted,

> An Iraqi judge and court readily agreed. The military refused. The
> marines, eager to go home, point blank refused to enter Najaf for fear of
> casualties. The British were nervous. The CIA was 'near-hysterical' over
> the consequences and persuaded Rumsfeld to overrule Bremer, with the
> president's support. Moqtada and his Mahdi army went free and every
> insurgent in Iraq got the message.[15]

Between 28 March 2004, when the order to close *Al Hawza* was released,
and the end of July, 86 contractors were murdered. Two of the first victims
were Andy Bradsell, a former Royal Marine settled in Canada, and Christopher McDonald, working for the British company Olive. McDonald was
still a serving regular soldier, a colour sergeant of the Royal Irish Regiment,
on resettlement leave. On 28 March, according to an eyewitness, they were
in the rear vehicle of a convoy escorting a client to a power plant. 'Three
vehicles with armed men came alongside. Bradsell and McDonald sped
forward to put themselves between the gunmen and the client. While they
took the fire, the other vehicle sped ahead and managed to pull away safely.
Bradsell and McDonald were killed.'[16]

The impact of closing *Al Hawza* was also dramatically felt, and
recorded, by two British diplomats – Rory Stewart in Nasiryah and Mark
Etherington in Kut – and their Control Risks bodyguards. Both were
besieged. Both were lucky to survive. Kut had been bad news for Western
soldiers since the agonising five-month siege of British forces by Turks
there in 1915. The 12,000 survivors were 'herded like animals across the

desert, flogged, kicked, raped, tortured and murdered'.[17] The second siege of Kut, on 5–6 April, was on a smaller scale but the political stakes were almost as high.

The freelances were protecting a CPA base under the command of the Coalition governor, Mark Etherington. Etherington, a former paratrooper, had just completed a master's degree in international relations at Cambridge University in 2003 when the Foreign Office asked him to become the CPA governor of Wasit province, adjoining Iran.

As locally employed Iraqi guards deserted their posts, around 400 Mahdi army guerrillas hit the base with mortars, machine guns and missiles. Ukrainian Coalition troops in a nearby compound cowered behind their barbed wire before trying to run away. At one point, Etherington had to order his bodyguard to block the exit with their armoured vehicles to stop them, but most of them managed to desert later, as did the police and others who had taken Uncle Sam's dollar. Even an official US army counterintelligence team declined to take up firing positions.

As Mahdi guerrillas occupied buildings overlooking the rear of the villa, the CPA's final redoubt, rocket-propelled grenades (RPGs), rained on the building. The freelances returned fire from the roof of a hotel in the CPA base. An American version of the battle suggests that it was a US team from Triple Canopy that was in the forefront of the battle, though Etherington himself is clear that, after desertions by locally employed guards, 'Triple Canopy now consisted of only the three-strong international core that had first arrived.'

Etherington's efforts to summon further aid were effectively thwarted by the lack of communication in Baghdad among the various agencies (the CPA, the US military, the Special Forces network) who should have reacted – except, of course, that much of Iraq, other than the Kurdish north, was now erupting. At dusk on 5 April, a pair of Apache helicopters made a token appearance over the compound. Enemy fire paused, but resumed once the choppers had left. Early on 6 May, Etherington reluctantly joined an escape convoy led by a residue of Ukrainians. It was, he admits, a choice of that or 'a mutiny on our hands'.[18]

The British team parted from its 'allies' in the sanctuary of a US base a mere two and a half miles away, then – still guarded by the Control Risks team – made a dash for Baghdad in two armoured vehicles. The team was ambushed within 30 minutes, apparently trapped in the labyrinthine backstreets of a market town. The operators in the rearmost car, like true

Chikurubi Prison, Harare, 10 September 2004: The former SAS officer Simon Mann with fellow prisoners following the failed plot to seize control of Equatorial Guinea. Mann denied complicity.

Malabo, Equatorial Guinea, 16 November 2004: Nick du Toit, a South African arms dealer and suspect in the local coup attempt, enters court in handcuffs. He was sentenced to 34 years.

Leopoldville, Congo, January 1961: Patrice Lumumba, Congo's first democratically-elected Prime Minister, pinioned by soldiers as a preliminary to his murder. His legend lived on.

Katanga, Congo, December 1961: European mercenaries known as 'Les Katangais' (including a tough-looking blonde woman) confront photo-journalists during the withdrawal of Tshombe's private army before advancing UN troops.

Stanleyville, Congo, November 1964: Mike Hoare, former British officer and leader of 5 Commando, accompanied by a Belgian Para, evacuates white survivors from the Simba massacre.

Congo, 1964: A mixed force of Europeans and Congolese regulars take cover from rebel fire on the road to besieged Stanleyville.

Angola, October 1974: Boy soldiers of the US-backed UNITA guerrilla army of Jonas Savimbi at ease. UNITA was on the back foot at the time.

Angola, 1975: Portuguese freelance adviser with UNITA officer at a training camp during the civil war that followed Portugal's withdrawal from its former colony.

Afghanistan: Local children pose on the turret of a Russian armoured vehicle, one of thousands destroyed by Mujahedeen fighters in their war of resistance from 1979 to 1988, aided by British Special Forces including freelances.

Afghanistan: Mujahedeen guerrilla fighter under training by a western instructor with US Stinger anti-aircraft missile. After the war the CIA tried to buy back thousands of the deadly weapons it had earlier given away.

Nicaragua, 7 October 1986: Sandinista government soldiers flush out Eugene Hasenfus, a CIA-hired freelance, from the jungle. Hasenfus had parachuted to safety after his clandestine transport aircraft was shot down.

Washington, July 1987: Marine Colonel Oliver North takes the oath before a Congressional enquiry into the Iran-Contra arms operation.

Aden, 23 August 1967: Regular British soldiers at ease in Aden, shortly before the British withdrawal. Over the horizon to the north, British freelances were fighting a venomous guerrilla war against an Egyptian expeditionary force.

Oman, 1970: SAS soldiers offer medical care to former enemy and their families at the start of a six-year military and hearts-and-minds campaign. After regular service many British soldiers remained as freelance contract operators in Oman. (IWM)

Sierra Leone, 2000: Corporal Anthony Hyde, Prince of Wales' Regiment – part of the British Army Training Team – rebuilds the undisciplined local army following repeated coups. The turning point was achieved with help from Colonel Tim Spicer's team of freelances.

Sierra Leone, c. 2000: Chief Sam Hinga Norman (centre), leader of the tribal Kamajor militia and a key player, with British freelances, in restoring the legitimate government of Sierra Leone. In spite of that he was tried as a war criminal. He died in captivity in February 2007, awaiting a verdict.

Croatia, August 1995: Serb-Croat refugees trek into exile under the impact of the Croatian Operation Storm. President Clinton was 'rooting for the Croats'.

Madrid, 8 December 2005: Croatian General (and former French Foreign Legion NCO) Ante Gotovina arrives at Torrejón military air base in a police van following his arrest. He later faced controversial allegations of war crimes arising from Operation Storm.

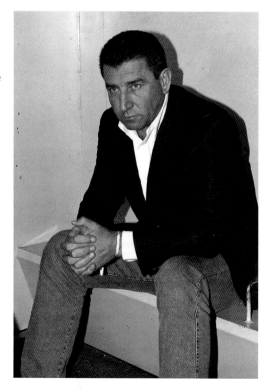

Mosul, Iraq, April 2004: Paul Bremer, effective governor of Iraq during the months following the invasion of 2003, on a tour of inspection guarded by freelance security operators.

Baghdad, 12 November 2005: Kofi Annan, UN Secretary General, protected by freelance security guards.

Baghdad, 19 January 2004: US freelance guard persuades Iraqi demonstrators to back away from the Interim Iraqi Governing Council offices.

Al Asad, Iraq, 18 October 2006: Karl 'Paddy' Moore of ArmorGroup with pet 'convoy cat' at a desert staging area. Moore, aged 35, a former Royal Marine from Belfast, decorated his body armour with the Ulster flag above a warning: 'Stay 100 metres back or you will be shot'.

Road near Baghdad, 20 October 2006: In perspective – the silhouettes of two ArmorGroup operators seen through the bullet-scarred windscreen of an escort vehicle.

Hilla, Iraq, 60 miles south of Baghdad, 15 October 2006: An ArmorGroup convoy escort team rehearses its ambush-response drill.

Afghanistan, 26 July 2003: Afghanistan President Hamid Karzai on an out-of-town tour, protected by US bodyguards.

Kandahar, Afghanistan, 10 April 2004: Local police guard – probably trained by a western security company – protects tractor and driver as they crush opium poppies. Poppy eradication is largely a British responsibility, run by a special Foreign Office team.

professionals, knew a rat run through the backstreets and directed Etherington through it by radio. Baghdad was still many dangerous miles away when, Etherington admits, 'for the first time I realised that we had lost control of the province'.

Yet his team had better luck than a five-man group from Hart Security, a British PSC under siege a mere 500 metres (545 yards) from the CPA compound in Kut. They were there to guard power lines. As the Mahdi guerrillas charged the Hart house, Gray Branfield, a 55-year-old South African veteran of the Rhodesian war, was shot at the door of the building and was then finished off with a grenade. In another version, he retreated up the stairs, firing as he went, only to bleed to death on the rooftop. According to reports, Branfield and his interpreter 'defended themselves for two days and the Hart team called US and Ukrainian military forces so many times during a two-day siege that the battery on their mobile ran out'.[19] The survivors, including civilian technicians and their wounded protectors, finally slipped out of the building, disguised as locals, commandeered a car and drove to safety.

Branfield had served in Southern Africa with Project Barnacle, as an assassin, hired to kill anti-apartheid leaders. He was one of thousands of South African military veterans, most of whom had fought on behalf of the apartheid regime. After the US and Britain, South Africa was the third largest supplier of freelances. The United Nations estimated the number of expatriate guards to be between 5,000 and 10,000, of whom around a dozen were killed in action during the first 18 months of occupation.

A *Sunday Times* report about the battle of Kut quoted an anonymous British freelance soldier to suggest that 'he and his colleagues had often been effectively co-opted into the military. "Sometimes," the man said, "our role has gone beyond guarding our clients to defending whole compounds or districts from armed attack."'[20]

Not surprisingly, someone in the Hart organisation, noting that the CPA permitted freelances to carry only 'small, personal protection weapons' (including some combat rifles), said that discussions were under way with the local government allowing bodyguards to increase their firepower. Nothing came of this, though some operators were already arming themselves with grenades and rocket launchers.

On the same day that the CPA base at Kut was overrun, according to the *Washington Post*,

An attack by hundreds of Iraq militia members on the US government's headquarters in Najaf was repulsed not by the US military, but by eight commandos from a private security firm . . . Before US reinforcements could arrive the firm, Blackwater Security Consulting, sent in its own helicopters amid an intense firefight to resupply its commandos with ammunition and to ferry out a wounded Marine . . . Shiite militia forces barraged the Blackwater commandos, four MPs and a Marine gunner with rocket-propelled grenades and AK-47 fire for hours before US Special Forces troops arrived. A sniper on a nearby roof apparently wounded three men.[21]

Next day the US military spokesman, Brigadier General Mark Kimmitt, when asked about the Blackwater team, replied, 'They knew what they were here for.'

The impact of freelance soldiers on some observers, particularly journalists, was less laconic, and closer to Wellington's comment about some of his allies: 'I don't know what effect they have upon the enemy, but by God they frighten me.' According to Sam Kiley, a Channel 4 reporter, the mercenaries

bustle through the Palestine Hotel lobby in central Baghdad clinking with military hardware . . . The head is crew-cut, the sunglasses wraparound. A Heckler & Koch 9mm submachine gun is *de rigeur*, strapped across a black, Kevlar bullet-proof vest . . . Pockets are stuffed with radios, a hand-held global positioning system, medical trauma pack . . . Another gun, usually a Glock 9mm, is held in a black nylon holster half way down one thigh. Spare clips of 'ammo' and a commando dagger are sheathed on the other leg.[22]

Kiley might have mentioned the ID and weapons card, usually worn in a plastic container on the chest by those whom he describes as 'the hogs of war'.

Experienced Special Forces operators do not share journalists' derision of a bodyguard's tools of his trade. One of them commented, 'Well, OK, the man criticised by Kiley is protecting his principal and himself. He has a crew cut because Iraq is hot, sweaty and dirty; wraparound shades so that he can see clearly what he is shooting at, or who is shooting at him; an HK to kill with; Glock pistol, ditto; Kevlar to help him stay alive under heavy attack (two or more machine guns and AKs for which a Savile Row suit would be no defence); radio to communicate with the rest of the team; trauma pack to save his principal's life. The black nylon holster for the Glock is standard. Spare ammunition is handy as you feel like a cunt if you run out of bullets halfway through a contact. And then you die. The commando dagger, I agree, is a bit over the top.'

'Tak', a Fijian hero of the legendary SAS Battle of Mirbat during the Dhofar war in July 1972, gave a practical demonstration of close-quarters battle skills as a freelance in Iraq more than 30 years later. In the autumn of 2003, a few months after the allied invasion, he and another SAS veteran identified as 'Darren' were driving in separate vehicles on a motorway near Basra after a day spent protecting European engineers. They were armed and in radio contact, but, as Tak later pointed out, he could not drive evasively and shoot at the same time. Even to use the antiquated two-way radio to speak to his buddy, driving the lead vehicle, meant driving with one hand.

Darren overtook a Chevrolet JMC containing the driver and four passengers. Tak started to follow him. 'I looked carefully at the locals as I pulled out. I didn't see any weapons. I thought they were innocent Iraqis.' But the Chevy pulled out, blocking him. He tried repeatedly to pass and was blocked every time. 'I pulled back. I wondered, shall I hit the back of the vehicle [deliberately]? If I do he'll spin and block the road. If I ram it from one side or the other it will probably spin 360 degrees or turn over. I decided to turn off the road and drive a parallel route across the desert.

'Then the Iraqis started shooting at me with AKs. Darren couldn't see what was happening at first and I could not use the mike to speak to him. I was armed, of course. I had an MP5 [Heckler & Koch sub-machine gun] in front, loaded with thirty rounds, a pistol in a leg holster and an AK-47 [long-barrelled assault rifle] just behind me. But, again, I had to concentrate on driving evasively. Eventually I hit a patch of soft sand and, beyond that, a rock wall. I ground to a halt. I was stuck.

'As soon as I did that, the four Iraqi passengers ran across in front of me, firing towards me. They were very quick. I made a split-second decision – a panic decision if you like – to put my hands up. I didn't think about it. They stopped firing and came closer. I now had the MP5 on my lap. It is a short-barrelled gun, useful in a confined situation. I snatched the weapon, aimed it through the windscreen and fired two short bursts. That brought down two men.

'By now Darren had realised what was happening. He returned and shot a third. The fourth man was coming at me from my left. My vehicle was left-hand drive. I was sitting on that side. I flung the door open and went for the man. I whacked him on the jaw with my weapon and as he went down I shot him as well.

'At that point the Iraqi vehicle drove away. I told Darren we had to move out as quickly as possible. It was only when I started to drive away that I realised I was wounded. The last man I killed had got one round off. The bullet passed through my calf. We drove into the UK camp at Basra and I checked into the field hospital for first aid.'

Tak's use of his MP5 as a club played well among the freelance military community. As one of them put it, 'Our friend resorted to "Fijian SOPs" [standing operating procedures – a phrase taken from the original contact report] and used his MP5 to club the proverbial out of the remaining baddy.'

Tak himself cannot explain his sudden decision to fake his surrender, a gesture that did not come naturally but saved his life. 'Put it down to the instinct for self-preservation,' he says. He was one of 200 Fijians recruited by the British army in the 1960s and one of seven to join the SAS. Was this latest encounter his closest call? 'No. It was worse at Mirbat. We were surrounded there.'

Mirbat, on the lonely coast of southern Oman, was a training centre run by 10 SAS soldiers on 18 July 1972 when it came under attack from hundreds of well-armed jebeli warriors swarming down from their mountain base. In a desperate battle, Tak's fellow Fijian, Corporal Labalaba, used a main artillery field gun as a close-quarters weapon, fired down open sights at point-blank range. Tak, wounded three times, lay against a wall still firing his rifle. He recovered and in 1980 took part in the siege-busting operation at the Iranian Embassy in London. Off the battlefield, he is softly spoken and a model of courtesy.

By the time he fought his way out of the Iraqi ambush, in a largely unreported continuation of the initial allied invasion, former SAS soldiers had killed and wounded more than 200 Iraqis in gun battles with 'fanatics still loyal to Saddam Hussein' as well as jihadists inspired by Al-Qaeda. In October 2003, two former SAS men were believed to have killed a tribal warlord and escaped after he captured them and subjected them to a mock execution.

During the first week of the combined uprising in the spring of 2004,

460 Iraqis and 35 Americans died as fighting engulfed eight cities. Some of those who died or were made hostage were carefully targeted by terrorist groups that were well informed and apparently supplied with intelligence from within the Iraqi security forces, unsurprising in view of the penetration of the new police and army units by militias loyal to entities other than a democratic state. The case of Brian Tilley was notorious.

Tilley, aged 48, was a former member of the Royal Marine Special Boat Service, with decorations for bravery. After leaving the service in 1997 he became a security adviser to Nigerian oil engineers and a bodyguard to David and Victoria Beckham. Soon after the fall of Baghdad in 2003 he moved to Baghdad and rented a flat in the luxury Mansour district. He also drove alone around the city dressed as an Iraqi. According to one source, 'He believed in blending in with the crowd. Dark-featured, unshaven and wearing traditional headgear he insisted to friends that "life has no taste without fear"'.

He also acquired a local mistress and became a part of her extended family, sleeping with her in Dawra, one of the most dangerous areas of the city. Soon after 8 a.m. on 14 May 2004 the house was raided by five armed men in Iraqi police uniforms. They shouted, 'Nobody move!' They demanded to know why an Englishmen was living with them. According to one of those present, 'Tilley started to tell the gunmen he was working with the Coalition forces. Suddenly, one of them just turned and shot him in the foot.

'Brian screamed out in pain from the bullet wound but the policemen just started to smash the back of his head with their machine guns, hitting him again and again. Two of them dragged him into the kitchen. I could hear Brian crying out, "No, please!" in English between the noise of them beating him, and then I heard more shots and screams.'

The raiders then shot Tilley's mistress and a girl of 15 who had witnessed what had happened. She survived, against all odds and was taken to hospital. There she saw one of the murderers, still in police uniform. 'The policeman was staring at me. His friends – the four other killers – were behind him. But when he saw there were other policemen standing by my door, he went away.'

Some of Tilley's friends gave witness statements to American officers working with the Iraqi Police Major Crimes Unit. The eyewitness was handed into the custody of Tilley's friends. Three months later the girl identified three of the killers at an identity parade. After four months, no one had been arrested because, apparently, an Iraqi investigating judge concluded that the eyewitness was 'unreliable'. Tilley's belongings, stolen when he was murdered, were not recovered.[23]

Tilley ignored his friends' warnings that he was running an insane risk in his choice of lifestyle. His behaviour recalled that of Captain Robert Nairac, an undercover military intelligence officer in Northern Ireland, who tried to pass himself off as a Republican pub singer in South Armagh, before the IRA caught up with him. Tilley chose not only the wrong place but the wrong time to play James Bond. In the weeks before he was killed, the fashion in hostage taking among Islamic fundamentalists was building to crisis level.

Worse, during the six weeks before his murder, almost 50 freelance soldiers had met violent deaths. It is a grisly catalogue, of which Tilley must have been aware. His murder, like those of prominent Iraqi police officers, judges and other senior officials, also pointed to the penetration of the new security forces by people who were either criminals or active supporters of one terrorist group or another. The British-trained Iraqi police in Basra – 13,750 men – were dominated by Islamic extremists, some of whom were thought to be responsible for the murder of the American journalist Steven Vincent on 31 July 2005.

The CPA in Baghdad, cocooned in the Green Zone, worked on a new constitution. For Rory Stewart, CPA governor on the front line in Nasariyah, it was also business as usual, as RPGs crashed into his head-quarters, occasionally removing limbs from the Italian soldiers responsible for perimeter security. The near-normality of such events belonged to the surreal culture of the London blitz, *circa* 1940. Appropriately, perhaps, Stewart belonged to the culture of an earlier period of British colonial administration: soldier turned scholar, he served the FCO in the Balkans and then spent two years, from 2000 to 2002, walking 6,000 miles across Iraq, Afghanistan, Pakistan, India and Nepal. A good book resulted.

On 11 May, a month after the action at Kut, Stewart and his team, including six bodyguards from Control Risks and an American perimeter guard of six, found themselves cut off. Mahdi guerrillas had seized a crossing over the Euphrates that was their potential escape route. The Mahdis had also taken over police cars, with the complicity of the police, and were working up their bloodlust as they drove triumphantly around the city. A three-day siege of the CPA headquarters followed in which they hit the compound with hundreds of heavy mortar rounds and RPGs, an action described with laconic battlefield humour by Stewart in his memoir *Occupational Hazards*.[24]

An Italian garrison in the front line of the team's security did its best to keep out of harm's way, all but replicating the Ukrainian example at Kut. The allies had no stomach for this renewed war. Repeated appeals by Stewart for air support went unanswered until the very end of the siege, when his team was without water, communications and almost out of ammunition. The position was held from exposed rooftop positions by the CRG team led by Geoff Maberly, and the Americans.

Later, after a C-130 gunship had pounded the enemy positions from a safe altitude of 3,000 metres (10,000 feet), Stewart records,

> I heard a Canadian general say military contractors were mercenaries whose loyalty could not be relied on. I told him these contractors had risked their lives manning guns that soldiers had abandoned. A hundred of them could have brought order back to the province.[25]

Such episodes raised unanswered questions about liaison between free-lance soldiers and the regular Coalition forces. The British company Aegis had as its main task co-ordination between the regular American and British forces and the freelances, to prevent 'blue-on-blue' battle accidents (friendly fire) and arrange relief of teams in trouble.

There was other evidence to suggest that the freelance soldiers were becoming indistinguishable from the regulars. In November 2003, Todd Drobnick, an American in charge of a team of translators working for a defence contractor, was killed in a road accident near Mosul. He was awarded a posthumous Purple Heart and Bronze Star. An extensive study by David Isenberg comments, 'Several other contractors have received battlefield commendations in Iraq, too, but the [US] military says it was a mistake. Only active-duty soldiers are eligible for the awards and those received by civilians are being rescinded.'[26]

After the joint uprising of 2004, freelance soldiers in Iraq found them-selves targeted with increasing enthusiasm. Two days after Branfield was killed at Kut, Michael Bloss, aged 38, a Welshman who had served with the paras, died heroically near Fallujah after ensuring that hydroelectrical engineers in his care had been evacuated. The day before he was shot he sent an email to friends:

I'm in serious shit here. We are expecting to be overrun tonight and we may have to fight our way to a safe haven. Unfortunately all the safe havens are already under attack. I don't wish to alarm you. We'll probably be OK . . .[27]

On 14 April Fabrizio Quattrochi, an Italian security guard, was clumsily executed by an Islamist group two days after being taken hostage. The killing was videotaped but not broadcast by the Arab station Al-Jazeera, possibly because of the defiant manner in which Quattrochi, a 36-year-old former baker, met his end. The terrorists took him to a field and forced him to dig his grave. They then tried to make him kneel with a hood on his head. He challenged them, standing, trying to remove the hood and shouting, 'Now I will show you how an Italian dies!' He was promptly shot in the back of the neck.[28]

Quattrochi was one of four Italian guards seized by a movement called 'the Green Battalion' in an effort to persuade the Rome government to pull out of the Coalition. According to one source, 'In a tragic twist, it turns out that the four guards had their personal-protection weapons confiscated by American soldiers, leaving them vulnerable, just hours before they were kidnapped.' The three other kidnapped guards were rescued by Coalition forces on 8 June.

During the months after Fallujah, approximately 130 contractors were killed by suicide car bombs, roadside bombs, armed ambush, mortar attack or sniper fire. For the freelance soldiers if not others, Bremer's policy of landing the first blow, of 'killing terrorists before they kill us',[29] was not working. On 25 November 2004 four British freelances were killed in an attack on the protected Green Zone of Baghdad. Their identities were not disclosed. Four Americans were killed by a suicide bomber at the Marez base near Mosul almost a month later. In a similar attack on the Green Zone on 3 January 2005, three more UK freelances died. Yet again, their identities were not divulged.

Others – such as Herman (Harry) Pretorius, a South African working for Dyncorp – were wounded, taken prisoner and not seen again. Three weeks after Pretorius was injured by a landmine that blocked the convoy he was guarding, his captors offered to return his body, but at a price. His widow said, 'They have sent photos of Harry's body to his bosses in Iraq to prove that he is dead. The people there identified him from the photos. I don't know if he will ever come home. Apparently the people who caught him want money before they let his body go.'[30]

Some lives ended enigmatically. Paul Chadwick from Nailsworth, Gloucestershire, was a former Royal Marine Commando and judo champion shot while working for ArmorGroup at Taza, near Kirkuk, in October 2004. A spokesman for the firm said, 'We can confirm hostile fire was not involved.' No other details were given.

A sad litany of deaths followed, reflecting new tactics by America's enemies. These included more sophisticated, powerful roadside bombs using shaped charges probably imported from Iran, as well as a wave of suicide bombers. The incidents listed below are no more than a cross-section of the victims, illustrative of a large, more tragic picture. During a two-week period in May 2005, for example, more than 250 Iraqi civilians were slaughtered in an increasingly indiscriminate campaign. On 23 January 2005 the journalist Awadh al-Taee heard two bursts of automatic gunfire on a street in the West Baghdad neighbourhood of Kerada, between the Australian Embassy and a major hotel. Seconds later a convoy of three vehicles, escorting a foreign electoral adviser, drove away.

Askew in the centre of the street sat a civilian car, a neat line of bullet holes piercing its hood and windscreen [he said]. The driver lay some five metres [16 feet] away, wounded in the side and stomach, and going into shock. Later that day, he died in hospital.

Another motorist, who was driving with his two children in the car, stood dazed in the street, his head lightly grazed by a bullet . . . This neighbourhood alone, according to local police, sees one fatal shooting a week by either private security companies or the military.

Under constant threat from suicide attackers driving explosive-rigged cars, coalition soldiers and contractors follow combat zone rules of engagement to protect themselves: warn drivers who stray too close, but if that fails, shoot. With procedures designed to protect the identities of anyone who might be singled out for retaliation, the victim's families may never know what happened, let alone obtain justice.

Al-Taee made a point of examining the entrails of the 23 January incident, though 'scores of Iraqi lives are claimed every month in this way'.[31] He identified the dead man as Abd-al-Naser Abbas al-Dulaimi, aged 29. An unmarried power-station worker, Dulaimi supported his mother, two sisters and the two children of a brother who did not return from the 1991 Gulf war. The police found no weapons on or near Dulaimi's body.

According to the security company involved, the vehicle it fired at 'forced its way through halted traffic to approach our convoy at speed'. The convoy leader attempted to ward off the vehicle with strobe lights and hand signals, then threw a water bottle and fired a flare before shooting into the engine and the empty passenger side of the car to disable it. Security men in the convoy 'saw the vehicle come to a halt, and a driver exit, before they turned the corner and left the scene'. They heard further shooting but do not want to speculate on what happened.

Through an intermediary the security company and the victim's family were put in touch with each other. '*Faisal*' (blood money) is often paid when Iraqi kills Iraqi. Representatives from both sides haggle and normally agree a figure of around $2,500. The US military's standard payout in such cases is also $2,500, that is about five days' pay for a Western ex-military security man, or two years' wages for a mid-level Iraqi civil servant.

Compensation is not the only consideration. When the fatal bullet is fired by a foreigner, national dignity also comes into play. Commenting on the Dulaimi case the *Financial Times* noted,

> In such incidents, the victims have little recourse ... Military personnel and most private contractors working in Iraq cannot be brought before Iraqi courts ... While Iraqis resign themselves to the tribal system of arbitration in the absence of a functioning judicial system, when foreigners get involved the process can become insulting.
>
> Tribal arbitration sessions are meetings of equals, often held in Bedouin-style tents with all the pomp and circumstance of traditional Iraqi society. For a relative of an Iraqi shot by a foreigner even to find out whom to contact for compensation, he must often stand for hours outside the barbed wire of bases and police stations, endure intense questioning and weapons pat-downs. When the money is paid, it seems more like a token payout to make a problem go away.

A knowledgeable observer of such cases, a senior player on the CPA team, offered a counsel of perfection. He suggested that the shots were fired by people employed by the US State Department and therefore 'the person ultimately responsible for the lack of discipline must be the Ambassador'.

What follow are cases in which security operators lost their lives in the aftermath of Fallujah, the suppression of *Al Hawza* and Iraq's first democratic elections.

31 December 2004: The Brookings Institution reports that at least 232 American civilian security and reconstruction contracts have been killed during the year.

12 March 2005: Two security contractors killed by a roadside IED (improvised explosive device).

22 April: An Mi-8 helicopter hired from Canada is shot down at Tarmiya, north of Baghdad. Three Bulgarian aircrew, two Filipino guards working for the British company Global Risk and six Americans employed by Blackwater are killed. The Islamic army in Iraq video the event and added a gloating commentary about the murder, after the crash of a Bulgarian survivor, 'in revenge for the Muslims killed in the mosques of Fallujah'.[32] An Iraqi recognises a vehicle shown in the video. With this rare help from a usually silent community, American special forces are subsequently able to raid a building and arrest six men linked to the attack.

7 May: An attack by two suicide bombers on a contractors' convoy in Baghdad: two American freelances killed, one captured.

8 May: Akihiko Saito, a Japanese veteran of the French Foreign Legion, kidnapped in an ambush in Sunni territory west of Baghdad. Saito, working for the British company Hart, is subsequently murdered by his captors. Their video records a voiceover: 'This is your punishment . . . infidel'. He was then shot.

7 June: Contractors' convoy guarded by a security team ambushed near Habbaniyah, west of Baghdad. At least seven people killed and others disappeared. One analyst, Jon Lee of Middle East Watch, noted,

The incident lasted for approximately forty-five minutes with the insurgents adopting a tactic of standing off beyond the range of the weapons available to the security detail, using light machine guns and RPGs to pick off their targets. Then, when the guards had exhausted their ammunition, the insurgents closed in.

The RPG has an effective range of 500 metres [545 yards] whilst the RPK light machine gun, which is available to insurgents, has an effective range of 800 metres [2,600 yards] . . . If the insurgents use the SVD sniper rifle, the range increases to 1,300 m. The AK, commonly the heaviest 'long' weapon [rifle] used by security details, has a maximum effective range of 450 m, or the M-16 [Armalite assault rifle] 500m.

The ambush, not the first where insurgents have out-ranged a security detail, comes at a time when the private security industry is lobbying for heavier weapons. The use of heavier weapons would radically change the profile of the private security industry in Iraq and is likely to be resisted by the Coalition and Iraqi authorities.

One reason for resistance was that, by openly carrying heavier weapons, freelance soldiers would be more readily identified as mercenaries on offensive combat operations.

30 July: Ken Hull, former RUC officer, is one of two Control Risks guards killed by a roadside bomb while escorting British diplomats in Basra, after which some diplomats never stray from the compound during their Iraqi tours of duty; attack seen as change of tactics by insurgents using more powerful bombs to destroy armoured vehicles.

7 September: A similar attack in Basra kills four US freelances escorting American consular officials.

18 January 2006: Two American freelances, Richard Hickman and Roland Barvels, blown up while escorting a convoy in Basra.

19 January: Stephen Enright, British security guard providing security to contractors disposing of munitions, killed by roadside bomb west of Baghdad.

Some roadside bombs were more easy to detect than others. When they were not triggered by infrared, they were hidden in the carcasses of dead cows left beside the road or concealed inside a crude wooden model of a dog with 'eyes' that reflected vehicle headlights. In the darkness, this canine silhouette was convincing.

As in Northern Ireland, there was a constant battle of wits between the terrorists and their intended targets. The more professional companies engaged intelligence analysts who noted, for instance, that apparently innocuous roadside objects were actually aiming points for Islamic guerrillas using Russian-made RPGs, mortars or machine guns. When the target – a convoy – arrived at the aiming point it was time to press the button. The telltale signs included an old pair of trainers strung across telegraph wires or, in one case, a black VW car with a white stripe painted on the front of the bonnet. This took the risky step of driving past a PMC team.

'We knew what they were doing and blocked them. They grinned back at us and waved,' said one of the team.

In January 2006, as the impact of such attacks slipped down the news agenda in the West, Moqtada al-Sadr switched to another sort of spectacular, kidnapping groups of Westerners, including security guards, in an effort to secure the release of some of his own warriors. There had been an earlier spate of criminal kidnappings in 2004, as a result of which thousands of expatriate workers left the country. The point of the 2006 operations was political. The men whom Sadr wanted free included Sheikh Ahmed Majid Farttusi and Sayyid Sajjad, arrested after an SAS surveillance operation. Basra police then detained two SAS soldiers and prepared to hand them over to the Mahdi guerrillas. The SAS men were freed in a spectacular British army raid on the police barracks.

In this climate, southern Iraq was becoming a no-go area for many foreign civilian contractors who should have been the backbone of the country's reconstruction programme. To make matters worse, regular US soldiers as well as freelance operators were known to be responsible for many civilian casualties. In June 2005 the acting Iraqi Prime Minister Ibrahim Jaafari expressed his concern to the US high command about a number of high-profile cases in which American soldiers shot without challenge. These deaths usually occurred as the victims attempted to pass US convoys, or during search operations. The consequence was a rapid decline in living standards. As Hala Jaber reported, 'With most foreign companies staying out of the south, services have not improved for many Iraqis there, fuelling bitterness towards America and Britain.'[33]

The hostage strategy was underscored on 17 January 2006 when gunmen killed seven security guards and three drivers in western Baghdad and seized two Kenyan telecom engineers in an operation identified by a Western intelligence specialist as 'an incident which bore the hallmarks of complex planning and surveillance'.[34]

The message was repeated on 8 March, when 50 security guards working for al-Rawafid Security in Baghdad were abducted by gunmen in a train of SUVs. The operation took several hours, since the raiders also took away a safe and weapons. They were dressed in camouflage uniforms. The local police, observing what was happening, did not intervene.[35]

On 16 November there was an even more ambitious, and successful, attack of this sort when a convoy of 43 vehicles was halted by guerrillas dressed in Iraqi Interior Ministry uniforms. An expert analysis suggests, 'As the convoy halted, four vehicles carrying around thirty gunmen arrived, overpowering the guards. The gunmen then drove off, taking nineteen semi-trailers from the convoy, one of the escorting gun trucks and the five victims.' This audacious operation happened on a restricted military road leading from the Kuwait border. The raiders then abducted five security guards, four American and one Austrian. Next day there was a confrontation on the same road as Iraqi border guards ordered a convoy including new ambulances, inbound from Kuwait, to stop. One British security operator was killed and three were arrested.

Less than a month later, on 10 December, four South African freelances and five Iraqi security contractors were abducted at a bogus checkpoint in north-eastern Baghdad. Yet again, Moqtada al-Sadr was regarded as the chief suspect.

For every casualty, there were probably several hundred other operators who lived to take the money and return home, or to move on to the next war zone. For some of them, the hardest trial was boredom. A few, including a former Parachute Regiment soldier with long service in Northern Ireland, were struck down by post-traumatic-stress disorder. That individual gave up after three weeks, complaining that 'it was Ulster all over again, wondering whether every garbage bin I passed contained a bomb'.

The experience of many freelance soldiers was that they had more to fear from their US allies than the official terrorists. 'Allen Ferguson' (an Englishman who served in the French Foreign Legion under that name) came under US fire five times in less than two years. He told me, 'There is no telling what the Americans are going to do. We lost two men in Mosul within a week. The first was an attack by .5 calibre machine gun. There was a curfew but we let them know we would be coming out of the gate before dawn. In spite of that they shot at us as we left.

'In another incident we were crossing Saddam Bridge in Mosul. We obtained permission to pass an American convoy. As soon as we pulled out to pass, two clowns in the tail vehicle fired straight at us: ten rounds into the front of the truck that took our front tyre out.'

When he was part of an embedded unit, organically linked to a regular US brigade, Ferguson said, 'We were told that if we killed anyone, even civilians, we would have the backing of the [American] general. If it got more difficult, say a massacre, the Americans would back us and get us out of the country as soon as possible. It was known as "the white card".'

An experienced intelligence analyst who worked in Baghdad recalled, 'A PMC convoy and an American convoy passed in opposite directions. A terrorist booby trap – an improvised explosive device – exploded on the

American side of the road. The US gunners immediately shot up the PMC convoy, in the opposite direction from the source of the trouble. The PMC team were in charge of a VIP passenger, who lost his legs. Their Iraqi translator, a girl aged eighteen, was killed. The bodyguard, an SAS veteran, was refused permission by the Yanks to talk to his legless client in hospital.

'In another case, a PMC convoy of five vehicles was "cleared" – given permission – to pass a US convoy. The American gunner in the third vehicle opened fire. Everybody halted. The PMC commander asked the gunner why he started shooting. The American said he had seen Iraqis in one of our vehicles. The PMC boss protested, "But it is part of our convoy. It is identical with the others." The gunner was not impressed. He said, "My orders are to shoot at any vehicle overtaking me that contains Iraqis." Meanwhile, we noticed that Paul Bremer's motorcade comprised about twenty-four vehicles and two helicopters. The locals always knew where Bremer was. They simply watched out for the escorting choppers.'

There are many anecdotes about such confrontations. On 11 June 2005 two Iraqi security guards escorting a convoy of supplies on its way to an American military base near Fallujah were shot dead by US soldiers who mistook them for insurgents. When a US sentry shot out the tyre of a PMC vehicle manned by four ex-SAS men, they dragged him out of his slit trench and forced him, at gunpoint, to change the wheel. A Chinook pilot who came under fire from a trigger-happy compatriot landed his aircraft and confronted the gunner on the ground. He asked what the man thought he was doing. 'I thought you were an Iraqi,' the man answered. 'Do the Iraqis have Chinooks?' the pilot asked before punching the man on the nose and flying away.

There was a more serious confrontation in May 2005 when a convoy escorted by 16 freelance soldiers and three technicians in white Ford trucks paused to change a flat tyre on one vehicle in Fallujah. The escort was covering an engineering team from a US company named Zapata. As they resumed their journey they were stopped by a US Marine captain who suggested that they were responsible for shots at a Marine watchtower.

The escorts were detained and, they allege, beaten up and humiliated by their captors for three days. The Marines say they were treated correctly in spite of fire aimed at the Marine watchtower from civilians in vehicles similar to those in the convoy.

An analysis by the online news service Corpwatch recalled,

Four former security contractors and retired military veterans told NBC News in February that they had watched as innocent Iraqi civilians were fired upon and one was crushed by a truck by contractors employed by an American company . . . In late November 2004 soldiers in a U.S. Humvee also fired 'six or seven rounds' at the tires of a vehicle carrying foreign security guards on the road to Baghdad airport. Just one day earlier an Iraqi police cruiser opened fire on a white sedan near the Babylon Hotel in central Baghdad. The occupants of the sedan, believed to be British private security guards, fired back killing one police officer and seriously wounding another. [36]

The situation was further envenomed when insurgents disguised as security operators, using similar vehicles, opened fire indiscriminately on Iraqi civilian cars. In 2005, the British company Aegis was blamed for random shooting – filmed from the back of an armed convoy – of Iraqi civilian cars. Aegis ran its own enquiry when video footage of the incident was planted on the Internet. There was no independent confirmation of the allegation and nothing in the video to prove or disprove the story, just the macabre spectacle of civilian cars being shot up by automatic fire from the rear of a Humvee (but see Chapter 13).

Confrontations between regular soldiers and freelances did not always arise from the stupidity of reservist National Guard grunts from the backwoods. The American warning signals were not always clear to non-Americans. Such signals included a white strobe (rather than a more universally recognised red stop light) and a hand signal that is described by an intelligence analyst as 'a sort of flick of the hand from the side of the leg, as sweeping a fly away'.

That sort of confusion, he suggested, might have explained the killing by American soldiers of an Italian government agent escorting the newly freed journalist Guiliana Sgrema on the road to Baghdad airport.

There was also a strict etiquette about overtaking any American convoy. Chris Lister, another Foreign Legion veteran, said in an interview with me, 'The basic rule is not to pass US convoys unless you are specifically authorised. These convoys display large signs saying, "Danger: Do Not Approach", in English and Arabic. Our vehicles are also clearly marked. There is a three-to-one ratio of escorts' to clients' vehicles. The rule is "Don't overtake. Follow at a respectable distance." But if you are on a long trip – say, eight hours from Baghdad to Basra – it can double the time you are on the road.

'You have to wait and hope that, eventually, the man at the tail of the US convoy wakes up to the fact that you are a friendly white face. He can then communicate with his commander and wave you on.'

It was part of the surreal experience of Iraq that some people found themselves embedded with US forces. Allen Ferguson, working for a British company in Mosul, said, 'We were effectively part of the US army's 25th Brigade under Brigadier General Carter Ham. The regular soldiers ran convoys using 19-ton Stryker armoured vehicles. We used stripped-down Toyota four-wheel-drive machines to act as their security screen.

'While the Americans stayed on the road, we drove off-road onto the high ground alongside the route to deter any ambush. We went ahead and signalled when we were in position. We also did road reconnaissance for the American army, taking photographs of bridges and other pinch-points.

'We had good ECM [electronic countermeasures] to detect or block signals used by terrorists to trigger their bombs. On one job, we were the escort for some Americans using Humvees. We were escorting a VIP to Baghdad Airport. The US captain insisted that he should take the lead and, sure enough, his vehicle was blown up. The two surviving Humvees screeched round in a turn and went back. We had stopped in a position to give all-round covering fire to the vehicles. An American female soldier with patches on her uniform but no firearm stood by the side of the road, totally disoriented. We got her into our vehicle. Eventually another platoon relieved us. We drove on to the airport. Then I realised this lassie was still in the back. We sent a signal saying we had kidnapped one of their women. Did they want her back?'

Freelance soldiers who stay the course point out that people working in Iraq should know what they are letting themselves in for. To ensure that they did know, one prominent British PMC arranged induction briefings at Baghdad Airport for men working their first contracts, run by a former Intelligence Corps analyst. In one case at least a former sergeant major, who had spent thousands of pounds to retrain as a bodyguard, concluded at the end of the briefing that Iraq was too risky for his health. He was repatriated.

The atmosphere of threat – for those unaccustomed to the no-peace/no-war climate of Israel, Palestine, Kashmir or Northern Ireland – could grip the newcomer with claustrophobia from the moment he, or she, lands at the heavily defended Baghdad airport. In the bloodbath month of

April 2004 the journalist Andrew Gilligan described how 'on the road in [to the capital] all the palm trees have been chopped down to provide clear fields of fire. The parapets of every overbridge are topped with high barbed-wire fences to prevent the grateful locals throwing rocks at us.

> The terminal itself is a 'sterile zone', with no Iraqi and no civilian motor vehicles allowed within two miles of it. The first port of call, after dropping your bags at the hotel, is the Royal Jordanian [Airline] office to make absolutely sure of your seat out. The scene there is like Saigon say, two weeks before the fall: not quite open panic just yet, but not far off it.
>
> The Coalition loss of the most basic of all possible military necessities – the security of its own supply, not to mention escape routes – says everything about the terrible mess it now finds itself in. After the final collapse . . . of the case on weapons of mass destruction, the events of the last ten days have ruthlessly stripped away all Whitehall's and Washington's other remaining fantasies, deceptions and pretences about Iraq . . .[37]

Against the odds and contrary to the Gilligan analysis, the Coalition weathered the storm of April 2004 and lived to fight another day, but for freelance soldiers, chancing their lives on convoys beyond the reach of friendly forces, it was rough trade. From a corporate point of view, however, Iraq was the dream contract from which it was possible to make millions. While their employees might have resented the label 'mercenary', the companies had a cheerfully uninhibited view of the value of money.

The International Consortium of Investigative Journalists calculated that, between 1994 and 2002, the Pentagon had entered into 3,061 contracts worth $300 million with 12 leading American PMCs.[38] A *Guardian* report suggested in 2004 that 'Iraq has boosted the revenues of British military companies from £200 million before the war to more than £1 billion, making security Britain's most lucrative postwar export to the country'.[39] Peter Singer of the Brookings Institution suggests, 'This is a sea change in the way we prosecute warfare. There are historical parallels but we haven't seen them for 250 years.'[40]

A report prepared for the International Peace Operations Association by David Isenberg also called attention to the political influence exercised by some of the companies in winning contracts.

Several companies, including Diligence LLC, the Steele Foundation and CACI have senior directors or advisors with high-level experience or influence with current or former US and British governments. PMCs also extensively use political campaign donations and employ lobbyists to influence government officials.

In 2001 the ten leading private military firms spent more than $32 million on lobbying, while they invested more than $12 million in political campaign donations. Among the leading donors were Halliburton, which gave more than $700,000 (during 1999–2002), 95 per cent to Republicans and DynCorp, which gave more than $500,000, 72 per cent to Republicans.[41]

There was another, darker, side to some company activities during the first two years of occupation. It was to be found at the military detention centre of Abu Ghraib. The abuses were exposed to the world by some of the abusers, including photographs of prisoner degradation contrary to international law. A handful of low-ranking soldiers were court-martialled. Of the 37 civilians hired as interrogators, only three were linked publicly by official investigations such as the Taguba Report, to abuse. Ironically, only one civilian contractor linked to the interrogation centre fell victim to Iraqi terrorism. He was Ray Parks, an American responsible for the prisoners' often inedible food while working for an obscure catering company. He was ambushed and murdered on his Baghdad driveway 'by three gunmen wearing black robes' on 16 February 2004.[42]

The interrogators had a different story to tell. According to the distinguished American journalist Seymour Hersh, 'representatives of one of the Pentagon's private contractors at Abu Ghraib, who were involved in prisoner interrogation, were told that Condoleezza Rice, then the President's national security adviser, had praised their efforts.' Hersh added, ironically, 'It's not clear why she would do so. There is still no evidence that the American intelligence community has accumulated any significant information about the operations of the resistance, who continued to strike US soldiers and Iraqis.'[43] Isenberg's analysis, meanwhile, concluded that, although investigation of the Abu Ghraib scandals was still incomplete, 'most of the abuses were carried out by regular military forces'. The CIA also had an interest in 'keeping certain prisoners off the books'.

Given the culture of counter-lawlessness introduced by the US after 9/11 – including the CIA's invention of 'ghost' prisoners; the effective sanctioning of torture in third countries after terrorist suspects were flown secretly out of the US; the redefinition of 'torture' by US government lawyers; the UK's acceptance of an intelligence product of torture – the surprise was that so few of the thousands of foreign military advisers and employees in Iraq were caught up in the Abu Ghraib scandal.

On the ground in Iraq during the first years of occupation, regular Coalition security forces were placed by their political bosses in a situation similar to that of the French army in Algiers in the 1950s. Ordered in 1957 to halt a terrorist campaign 'by every means possible', the soldiers did just that, only to be scapegoated by politicians when the use of torture was exposed by the media.

While the French won their military battle against terrorism (and lost the political war) neither the British in Northern Ireland (who discovered that internment and interrogation of the wrong people acted as the IRA's best recruiting sergeant) nor the Americans in Iraq made any visible progress against their invisible enemy by relying on repression.

Sent by governments of Washington and London in insufficient numbers, without the necessary funding or planning for rapid reconstruction after the invasion, the occupation forces were handed a poisoned chalice. The use of freelances was unavoidable. With that innovation came another: CPA Order 17, effectively a licence to kill in some circumstances, without further legal inquiry.[44]

Before and after Abu Ghraib, the anxiety expressed among the military cognoscenti was not that some bodyguards and interrogators came from the private sector, but that some of the civilians were insufficiently trained and experienced. But the security forces' failures – though sometimes serious – were not in the same league as those of the Pentagon's intelligence agencies and Britain's SIS, both of which, genuflecting before a political imperative ahead of the invasion of Iraq, got it tragically wrong.

The image of private security operators in Iraq was, nevertheless, damaged internationally on 16 September 2007 when a Blackwater team escorting US diplomats opened fire in a crowded Baghdad square. The firm and the State Department claimed they were acting in self defence after a bomb attack. Civilian eye-witnesses and journalists asserted that the explosion was too far away to be a danger to the Blackwater convoy. Estimates of the civilian dead ranged between eight and 28; many more innocent people were wounded. Blackwater convoys were suspended.

12

IRAQ 2005:

The thirty-two-second ambush

Insufficient firepower was probably one of the deadly ingredients in the deaths of three operators working for Edinburgh Risk & Security Management, a Virginia-based security company, who were pinned down in an insurgent ambush on 'Route Irish',[1] the road to Baghdad Airport, on 20 April 2005. They belonged to a seven-man team in three vehicles on their way to the airport to pick up two passengers as part of Operation Apollo, responsible for Iraqi elections.

The night before, according to the company, 'the team reviewed video footage taken of Route Irish during previous moves in order to identify choke points, danger areas and likely areas of enemy attack'. The team was also alerted to be prepared to identify itself 'to avoid blue-on-blue incidents with Coalition or other PSCs.' Next morning the team received detailed orders at an operations group conference led by the team leader Allan Johnson, a former British army medic, 'to identify danger areas and to brief the team's scheme of manoeuvre during the movement'. Two other members of the team, also British army veterans, were Simon Merry and Stef Surette. They 'briefed with the drivers in regards to the route and actions on when approaching danger areas, Coalition or other PSC call signs' (vehicles).

The convoy rolled out of the heavily defended International Green Zone's Gate 12 at 11.40 after confirming with the Regional Operations Centre (run by Aegis) that the Route Irish was open. The lead vehicle was a soft-skinned BMW sedan driven by James Yeager, described as 'an American weapons instructor'. The vehicle was under the command of Surette, with Mark Collen double-hatted as rear gunner and team medic. In the centre, Simon Merry was driving an armoured Mercedes, accompanied by Ian Harris, the mission's second-in-command.

The rear vehicle was another soft-skinned BMW sedan driven by Chris Ahmelmen, an Australian ex-infantryman (nicknamed 'Camel') accompanied by Allan Johnson, the mission commander, with James (Jay) Hunt, a former US army ranger, as rear gunner. Each man was allocated an arc of fire in the event of an attack.

The team movement was going according to plan until the team reached RV [rendezvous or rally point] 5 . . . the last footbridge/flyover heading west just prior to the checkpoint leading into BIAP/VICTORY [that is the Baghdad Airport exclusion zone and the sprawling US military encampment nearby].

As the team reached RV5, traffic was coming to a halt and the team was halted just beneath or just outside of RV5 with the main body vehicle [number two in the convoy] coming to a halt just beneath the footbridge. The team was halted at approximately 11.55 hrs.

Traffic to the front was halted due to Coalition Forces, closing the road in response to an incident on the road.

The Coalition Forces were located 300–400 metres (328–437 yards) to the front of their position. There were about ten civilian Iraqi vehicles to their front which left the scene by either driving backwards onto a slip road to leave the area, or by crossing the central reservation after making a U-turn.

Johnson ordered the team to move forward in order to create depth between his convoy and Iraqi civilian vehicles behind them. He also wanted a safe distance between the convoy and the footbridge/flyover, since it opened the possibility of attack from above.

The motorcade moved forward approximately 300 metres [328 yards], giving the rear gunner, Jay Hunt, in the rear vehicle enough clearance to cover the footbridge with fire if required whilst also allowing the team to cover and close the slip road located to the right-front of the motorcade so as to prevent enemy attack from that location.

At this time the three vehicles were spaced with approximately 100 metres between vehicles and with the convoy occupying an area estimated to be 300–400 metres (328–437 yards) between the front and rear vehicles.

'During the halt Al Johnson and Ian Harris discussed crossing the median [central reservation] in order to leave an area where they felt they were exposed.' They decided not to do so, since the central reservation contained an obstacle.

While the team was halted Mark Collen identified a suspect vehicle along the slip road to the right flank, north, of the motorcade at a distance of approximately 500 metres [547 yards]. He took the vehicle under surveillance using a scope mounted on his M4 [assault rifle].

Collen saw only one man, an Iraqi, in the vehicle, apparently uninterested in the convoy. Collen concluded that the suspect was not a threat and informed the team accordingly.

The team remained static for approximately ten minutes while it waited to see if Coalition Forces would open the road. At approximately 12.00–12.10 Al Johnson decided to abandon the position and was ordering the team to move when the team came under intense heavy automatic weapons fire.

The attack was from north of their position,

along the slip road bordering Route Irish. All three vehicles sustained damage and casualties during the initial burst of gunfire. It is assessed that the team was engaged by two or more PKM belt-fed GPMG [Russian general-purpose machine guns] firing armour piercing ammunition.

The armoured sedan would have normally defeated standard ball ammunition. But that did not happen in this case. During the initial burst of gunfire, lasting thirty-two seconds, the team suffered three casualties: Jay Hunt, Chris Ahmlemen and Stef Surette. Hunt and Surette were wounded in the hip/groin area and suffered severe trauma to the femoral artery while Ahmlemen was shot in the hip and head, the head wound killing him outright.

As the shooting started, Yeager tried to drive out of the killing ground. His BMW, fitted with an automatic gearbox, could not move because, the company says, he 'had taken the car out of "drive" by placing it in "neutral" and had set the emergency hand brake'. Since they could not drive away, Yeager, Collen and Surette leaped clear of the car. Surette, already wounded, lay beside the vehicle,

> though he was attempting to remain in the fight. Yeager fell to the rear of the vehicle in order to return fire . . . According to Yeager he could not identify enemy forces and thus he attempted to suppress [shoot at] the general vicinity of where he suspected enemy fire was coming from. Having fired off half a magazine, Yeager broke contact and moved to the central reservation. Collen, who was also at the rear of his vehicle, identified enemy forces firing from a white suburban vehicle and engaged it with approximately 100 rounds of 5.56mm from his M249 Minimi.

His gun then jammed. Unfazed, 'he switched to his M4, with which he continued to engage the enemy forces within the white suburban . . . which drove out of sight'. Collen then gave first aid to the injured Stef Surette.

While this was happening Simon Merry in the second vehicle in the convoy, the armoured sedan, tried to drive forward to give cover to the lead car. He was going nowhere, however. 'The car was unresponsive . . . The initial burst of GPMG fire caused catastrophic damage to the transmission.' Ian Harris, the commander, got out of the vehicle under heavy fire and ran to the front bonnet of the lead car,

> to provide suppressive fire in support of the team. Ian was able to identify enemy forces located within the white suburban and fired semi-automatic, well-aimed fire into the rear of the vehicle. He reported that his fire seemed to be 'bouncing off' the rear of the vehicle.

Other members of the team confirmed that their fire also had no effect on the enemy vehicle. They concluded it was armoured.

Having failed to get his vehicle to move, Merry got out and provided covering fire for the third vehicle in the convoy from the rear of his own car. He also fired a smoke grenade to the front of the convoy to mask the crippled lead vehicle.

In the third vehicle, the driver, Ahmlemen, was dead. His companion

Hunt, also hit in the first burst, dismounted but 'was almost immediately out of the fight because of the nature of his wounds'. His femoral artery had been slashed open and he was now in danger of bleeding to death. Johnson, in command of the vehicle, moved him to cover behind the car's left front tyre, then checked Ahmlemen. Satisfied there was nothing he could do for a dead comrade, he returned to Hunt.

The attack was recorded by a video camera mounted on the dashboard of Johnson's vehicle. The initial hail of fire, timed by the video, lasted 32 seconds. Within that time, the company reported that 'three operators were combat-ineffective due to enemy fire . . . and all three vehicles were disabled either through mechanical failure and/or driver errors and wounds'. The report continued,

> All three vehicles were under fire almost simultaneously, which leads to the belief that there was more than one enemy element engaging the motor-cade though only one enemy element was ever identified . . . The volume of enemy fire and the consistency and accuracy of that fire on a callsign that was spread out over 300 metres [328 yards] indicates either a very proficient enemy operator or the presence of more than one GPMG . . . Enemy forces engaged the motorcade for no more than one minute and ten seconds.

At this point they escaped. As it became clear that the immediate threat had passed, Collen and Johnson continued to provide first aid to Hunt and Surette, while the rest of the team covered them. Merry, meanwhile, signalled Coalition Forces, a mere 300 metres (328 yards) to their front (west of the killing zone). The Coalition team, regular soldiers, 'responded to the signals by approaching the engagement area slowly with three Humvees'.

At the rear of the third vehicle, Yeager noticed a local civilian vehicle driving towards them from the opposite direction, on Route Irish. He thought it might be a suicide bomber and fired two shots into the vehicle, which stopped and kept its distance.

While the Coalition Forces took responsibility for evacuating the wounded, Harris and other survivors travelled in the first and third vehicles to the casualty hospital at Camp Victory. Another freelance team, from the British company Olive, arrived and collected Ahmlemen's body. 'At the hospital, Chris Ahmelmen and Jay Hunt were pronounced dead and Stef

Surette was undergoing treatment during which he died.' Johnson – who was himself wounded in the buttock – 'continued to stay with the casualties until he was ordered by the military to receive treatment'.

Analysing the event with the benefit of hindsight, the report concluded that the team should not have remained static 'for a protracted period of time in a canalized area such as Route Irish'. While it was understandable that the team tried to create space between themselves and the traffic around them, 'this also resulted in the team unmasking from the concealment provided by low profile saloon vehicles within the main body of local traffic'.

Once the ambush began, the team followed standard operating procedures, attempting to break contact by driving out of the killing zone, 'but this was precluded due to operator error for vehicle one and mechanical failure due to enemy fire with vehicles two and three'. The team then left their vehicles and tried to establish 'a base of fire to suppress enemy forces . . . to break contact'. But that option was also damaged by 'the fact that the team suffered fifty per cent casualties in the initial volley of fire'. As a result, 'Ian Harris and Mark Collen, each under heavy enemy fire, were the only two individuals . . . who attempted to suppress enemy forces.'

Merry was trying to manoeuvre his vehicle into a position where it could support the other vehicles while Johnson was treating the dead and dying. Yeager, at the 'median' (central reservation), 'could not engage enemy forces as he did not have a line of fire from his location'.

'Lessons identified' in the report included:

1. Immediate evacuation if conditions force the convoy to halt on Route Irish (though how that could have been accomplished on this occasion is not made clear).

2. The imperative need for the team coming under fire to 'establish fire superiority prior to breaking contact' and to ensure 'that team members who have eyes on the enemy call out fire direction, distance and description so as to alert other team members to the enemy location' since 'you cannot manoeuvre until you have established an aggressive base of fire'.

3. 'Team leaders should have no additional duties other than that of team leader.'

4. 'Crew-served weapons must be kept running during the course of the fight. If one goes down due to a wounded or killed operator then that weapon must be immediately put back into action by another team member.'

5. Every convoy movement 'needs to include at a minimum one weapons system utilizing 7.62mm NATO [firepower] in order to defeat enemy forces employing hard and soft skin vehicles.'

It is perhaps surprising that the team depended upon the lighter impact and range of 5.56mm weapons. But that raised again the broader issue of the fighting environment and the level of threat that freelance soldiers might be expected to encounter. The report's final conclusion, signed by the firm's managing director, Christopher Farina, underscored this difficulty. He wrote

PSCs have experienced countless attacks on Route Irish as well as on other MSRs [main supply routes] within Iraq. PSCs, while having the ability to defend themselves and their clients to a degree, will only be as successful as the conditions established by Coalition and Iraqi security forces [allow]. The fact that enemy forces can mass and execute operations in the vicinity of Route Irish as well as throughout Iraq is a testament to the current conditions within Iraq. PSCs, in order to operate successfully, must swim in a sea of security established by 'green army' [regular forces]. If general security is not established by Coalition and Local National security forces to a degree that precludes the enemy's ability to operate in strength across Iraq then PSCs and their clients will continue to become a collateral target of an insurgency that operates with impunity.[2]

In a separate account of the incident, posted on the Internet,[3] Yeager – a US police firearms expert – said that the US army had stopped the traffic because a roadside bomb had severely damaged a sport utility vehicle (of a type used by freelances in the country). The BIAP road is dual carriageway, divided by a 'median strip' with access roads on ramps, on this occasion blocked by a temporary halt sign.

There were also two or three Humvees with at least one of them pointing a .50 calibre heavy machine gun, which I knew would go through an armoured car, in our direction to make sure no vehicles got close.

Since we had made a conscious decision to drive cars that looked like the locals and dress like the locals I hesitated to get closer than 200–300 yards [183–274 metres]. There have been more incidents of the Military shooting at PSDs [private security details, that is, convoy escorts] than terrorists which is completely understandable, because as a group we tend to drive aggressively, try to blend in with local vehicles, dress like locals and carry weapons often times in plain view if not sticking out of the windows.

When they stopped, Yeager, at the wheel of the lead vehicle, moved his rifle from the console in front of him, onto his lap. His potential arc of fire was from dead ahead, ('12 o'clock') clockwise to around 8 o'clock. Jay Hunt, the rear gunner, had an even wider arc: from the vehicle's 9 o'clock to around 3 o'clock.

As they remained stationary, the team leader, Johnson, left his vehicle (at the back of the convoy) to fire repeated bursts from his MP-5 sub-machine gun as warning shots to other cars not to get too close. After the second warning fusillade, said Yeager, 'I removed my "Haji" dress because there was nothing between those US army .50 calibre machine guns and us.' He did not want the fact that they were wearing local clothing, including shemags (desert scarves), to provoke a friendly-fire incident. So far as the locals were concerned, however, he felt that their cover was blown.

After ten tense minutes beneath the underpass,

we pulled forward about 100 metres [110 yards] to where the final on-ramp [access slip road] to the BIAP road entered. I pulled my number one vehicle far right, as instructed . . . to block traffic from coming onto the roadway. After about 10–15 minutes I took the car out of gear and pulled on the emergency brake because my calf was beginning to ache. I would end up regretting that decision.

To their right there was a slip road about 68–91 metres (75–100 yards) away, parallel to the BIAP road, and houses on the other side of it. At this point Ian Harris, in the second vehicle, spotted a small white sedan on the slip road. He asked someone to look at it through binoculars.

We didn't have any but Mark [Yeager's rear gunner] had a telescopic sight on his rifle. He stated it was parked and the sole occupant was talking on the phone, wasn't paying any attention to us and wasn't a threat. I said aloud, 'He is a fucking "dicker"' [a lookout].

Meanwhile, both the other people in his car – Surette and Collen – had seen a large white SUV, with black tinted windows,

rolling down the frontage road heading the same direction we were pointing. They apparently drove a short distance and whipped into an intersection, did a U-turn and stopped momentarily, pointing their vehicle in our direction. This event took several minutes. Mark said later that the passenger window was down in the SUV but he could not see inside and he kept looking in other directions because he didn't consider the vehicle to be a threat.

Within three to five minutes of spotting the Dicker, Yeager heard another volley of fire. He thought this might have been another warning burst from the back of the convoy. Instead, 'I felt rounds hitting the car and I heard the distinctive supersonic crack of a round pass through our car, inches in front of my face, from right to left, missing Stef and I. Stef yelled, "I'm hit!" and he began emptying a 30-round mag out his window.'

Yeager hit the accelerator. The engine roared into high revs, but the car would not move. Yeager assumed it was disabled by gunfire. 'After what seemed like an eternity but was a couple of seconds, I grabbed the door handle and began implementation of our ambush SOP [standard operating procedures] for a disabled car.' The first step was to get out. He scurried to the rear wheel and instantly emptied a 30-round magazine in a single burst of automatic fire. Then he fired aimed shots into barriers beside the slip road, since there were signs that someone was behind them.

By now he sensed that Mark had got out of the rear door. He followed the next SOP: put distance between a vehicle under attack, and yourself. He yelled 'Move!' and ran towards the central reservation some 12 metres (40 feet) away. He fired towards the houses, believing that the enemy machine gun, a PKM, was in that direction somewhere.

I felt useless but I thought I might be able to keep their heads down.

'SHIT!' I thought . . . I had forgotten to deploy a smoke grenade. When Mark resumed firing I ripped it out of the pouch, peeled off the 100mph tape, put the spoon in the palm of my hand, straightened the ends of the pin out and pulled the ring. I kept thinking about my instructor course for and teaching the proper deployment of flashbangs, smoke and CS. My mind was racing. I forced myself to focus. I wanted to obscure Mark and Stef and so I heaved the high concentration smoke as hard as I could and managed to get it on the far side of their car.

There was still sporadic outgoing fire from the other cars. This was good news, a sign that his comrades were still alive. As he reloaded his gun, he studied the opposite side of the road and the overpass. They were clear. Then he looked at car number three.

I saw Jay Hunt with blood all over his crotch. I heard him tell Johno [Johnson], 'I'm hit in the femoral, buddy.' Very calmly. He slid himself towards the front of the car so that Johno could apply first aid from behind the engine, which was the safest spot. I looked at Chris. He was still in the driver's seat, slumped helplessly to the left against the door.

I checked car two, the armoured Mercedes. Simon and Ian were uninjured and now in the fight. I was glad to see them . . . I looked at car one and saw Stef was out of the car but he was going down. Although I knew he told me he was hit he had still been in the fight and got out of the car under his own power. I did not realise the extent of his injuries.

Johnson, treating Hunt's injuries, called for help since he could not give first aid and remain in the fight. Yeager joined him. As he guarded these two, 'a car drove towards us from the rear. I wave them off but they do not stop. I fired twice and they stopped.' Johnson was now running out of bandages and Hunt was hyperventilating. Yeager motioned towards his medical pouch and Johnson snatched additional wound dressings from there.

At this point, US army Humvees drew towards them from one direction, while a European, dressed like a PSD operator but carrying no weapon, walked towards them from the other. 'I yell, "Do you have any bandages?" He holds up his finger in a "wait-a-minute" fashion as he strolls my way.' Yeager repeated his shouted request for bandages.

He replies in what I think was an Australian accent, 'Can we drive through?' I was simply stunned that he had the nerve to ask to drive through. He was within 20ft [6 metres] now. I said, 'Do you have any fucking bandages?' He ignored me and walked past to one of the just-arriving US soldiers and asked if he could drive through.

According to Yeager, the regular soldier ordered the newly arrived freelance operator to pick up Chris Ahmelmen's body, still slumped in the car of vehicle three.

'As I opened the door and caught Chris, he had begun to fall out. The car, an automatic, was still in gear and when I pulled Chris out, the car began rolling way toward Jay' – as he lay fighting for life. Johnson pulled Hunt clear.

If Johno had not reacted quickly, Jay would have been crushed by the car. I had to drop Chris's body and run around the opposite side of the car to get inside. Luckily a soldier on the other side was able to get in and switch it off before it crashed into a Humvee that was backing up to avoid the collision.

The rest of Yeager's account confirms the company's official report. He added a postscript, however, in which he remarked,

Everyone that was wounded was wounded by the initial volley of gunfire. Stef and Jay received wounds to their pelvic/upper thigh region that severed their femoral arteries . . . Even though they were injured they stayed in the fight . . . Stef emptied a 30-round magazine (loaded with 28) and reloaded and fired an unknown number of rounds from the second magazine.

I never knew during the firefight which vehicle (or house, or person etc) was shooting at us and I was the first one in position to deliver accurate, sustained and deadly return fire and I didn't know where to aim my gun . . . As soon as our group started shooting, the terrorists became disinterested in staying in the fight, which is their modus operandi.

13

THE ONLINE DIALOGUES:

Grunts, muppets and the civvy bodycount

On 12 October 2005 Andrew Joscelyne, a senior member of the Aegis Defence Services team circulated an Internet notice to its 916 operators in Baghdad, Basra, Diwaniya, Fallujah, Mosul, Tikrit and 'Victory', the main US camp adjacent to Baghdad Airport, at Saddam's former lakeside villa. Joscelyne was acting as a messenger for his prophet, the firm's boss, Tim Spicer OBE. Spicer had taken note that some of his men had created their own website (*Aegis Iraq PSD Teams*) and he wanted to suggest some ground rules for the message board that would soon emerge as the voice of the grunts.[1]

Spicer said,

I am fully in favour of good-natured banter and a light-hearted view of life and its difficulties in Iraq. I encourage anything that takes the pressure off and improves motivation.

I would not be in favour of a site if it was in any way libellous to anyone, downright nasty or detrimental to anyone's morale. My major concern is one of OPSEC [operational security] – either that of our clients or our own individuals – posting unblanked photos may not be so clever. Anything that is of use to AIF [Anti-Iraqi Forces, a.k.a. 'insurgents'] should not be allowed to flourish.

I am also concerned about media interest in this site and I remind everyone of their contractual obligation not to speak to or assist the media without clearing it with the project management or Aegis London. This site could be construed in this way. I remind everyone that there is a proper chain of command for airing concerns, grievances, etc.

Please think twice about posting your happy snaps and whilst I am not concerned about this site as yet, if it develops into something other than a light-hearted pressure valve I will take a much greater interest. Remember that your job and those of your colleagues indirectly relies on the maintenance of our contract. Refrain from posting anything which is detrimental to the company since this could result in the loss or curtailment of our contract with resultant loss for everybody.

There was much at stake. Thanks to US and UN contracts in Iraq, the firm's sales topped £62 million in 2005, after a leap to £15 million (and a profit of £772,000) the year before. But the style and content of Spicer's advice did not sit easily with the culture of the private security details, the front-line operators known as PSDs. Spicer's world of fair play combined with discretion, perfumed with the decent values of a good public school, was not that of his angry, aggressive, sceptical and sometimes unlettered men.

The site would also soon provoke an inquiry into allegations that an Aegis team had indiscriminately shot up civilian Iraqi cars on public roads and, to round off this public-relations disaster, had videoed the crimes before posting them on the Internet.

As with many old soldiers' tales, the precise truth of the anonymous posts on the Aegis-Iraq message board is beyond proof. The vigorous style and language and cultural values of the posts, however, are entirely convincing.

There was also good reason for anonymity. 'The Doc', in one of the first posts, pointed out that,

The company as a whole may operate overtly but I would have thought that the individuals may want to hide their identities. I certainly do. There are reams of documented evidence to show that both AIF [Anti-Iraqi forces, or insurgents] and HIS [hostile intelligence services] and FIS [foreign intelligence services] for that matter are busy collating intelligence on how the military and civilian companies are operating. Sharing laughs and experience between the outstations can be extremely entertaining and valuable, but sure a safer way to do it is to share email addresses.

Methinks that testosterone-fuelled bravado and shocking operational naivety has got the better of some people. Some of you will be surprised to know just how much you can pick up about operational practices and IDs just from a good look at the photos.

To this and similar anxieties, the operator who started the site replied,

You seem to think we are bigger fish than we actually are. Although we are professionals . . . we are by no means CIA or MI5. Please come back to Planet Earth. With regard to giving away our kit secrets, we have the same as every other PSD: a Long weapon [rifle, machine gun, etc.], a secondary weapon [personal pistol] and a four-wheel drive SUV. Duh, I think the enemy are well aware of this and that's why they keep blowing us up.

As well as discussing the video scandal, the posts meandered around a potpourri of grumbles about working conditions, including allegedly incompetent middle management, inappropriate, often petty discipline, mutual recrimination and allegations of widespread drink and drug abuse. At the very least, these 'Aegis Dialogues' convey the fear, anger and frustration of the grunts in a uniquely candid fashion.

They also offer a rare insight into the insiders' debate about the techniques used by different operators to stay alive in a new type of conflict. It is one in which freelance soldiers fight suicide bombers, where one side seeks martyrdom and the other a well-paid job to clear the mortgage back home. In spite of the often foul language and sometimes dislocated thought, the grunts' debate is the perfect paradigm of militant mysticism versus militant capitalism.

As one anonymous contributor posted on 11 November 2005: 'Nobody has the perfect solution for tactics over here. This place is nothing like Northern Ireland. Nothing like South Africa. Nothing like the US has been involved in.'

The controversial video oozed into the public domain just a month after Spicer's rules were gazetted. Soon after that, a DVD copy was sent to *The Times* in London.[2] This copy, like the video version,

shows the view from the back of an armoured vehicle driving in Iraq. One of the roads appears to be a section of western Baghdad and another the notorious airport road that has been the scene of numerous attacks on US forces.

The footage shows four incidents when live rounds were fired at motorists. In one case a car is hit and collides with a stationary taxi. In another, a car drives off the road after apparently being raked by automatic fire.

None of the people involved in the incidents is identifiable, nor is there any evidence that Aegis employees were responsible, although the footage was initially released on a website connected to the company. Security experts in Baghdad who have seen the film said that it was most likely shot at least a year ago [November 2004] when there were far fewer controls on the activities of thousands of private security guards employed by the Pentagon to protect contract workers, escort goods and defend installations such as Baghdad International Airport.

In its statement, Aegis said that it was contracted by the American authorities to protect civilian and military personnel travelling throughout Iraq. It said that its staff observed strict rules of engagement that 'allow for a structured escalation of force to include opening fire on civilian vehicles under certain circumstances'. It said all such incidents were investigated.

Foreign contractors are supposed to obey the same rules as the military in warning civilian motorists not to approach convoys by waving them away and firing warning shots. Only if a vehicle accelerates towards them are they allowed to use deadly force. Because of the regular attacks against US forces and their allies by suicide car bombers, protecting convoys requires split-second decision-making. Scores of Iraqi civilians have been killed and injured by mistake.

One British security guard currently working in Iraq for another company said that he had witnessed at least two instances of innocent Iraqis being killed by poorly trained defence contractors who left the bodies by the side of the road and drove off. But the Foreign and Commonwealth Office said that its experts had viewed the footage and found no evidence that Aegis staff were involved.

Aegis, *The Times* added, had won, just one week earlier, the 'Small Consultancy Firm of the Year' award after picking up the largest security contract ever awarded by the Pentagon in Iraq, worth £220 million.

The embarrassment was worsened by the addition to the video of a soundtrack, the Elvis Presley song, 'Mystery Train', playing a jaunty, mocking tune as Iraqi civilians are seen fleeing after a targeted car swerves and crashes into another vehicle. The lyric includes such lines as 'Well, that long black train got my baby and gone . . .'

Release of the video prompted an outcry by some well-organised lobbies opposed to the occupation of Iraq. Mike Lewis of the Campaign Against the Arms Trade said the video showed that 'private military companies are even less accountable than regular armies. Privatizing war makes it even harder to stop the abuse and killing of civilians.'

Aegis itself announced a formal board of inquiry, in co-operation with the US military authorities, to investigate

> whether the footage has any connection with the company and, should this prove to be the case, under what circumstances any incident took place. Aegis is contracted in Iraq by the US government to provide a wide variety of services including, critically, the protection of both civilian and military personnel travelling throughout the country, in a very hostile environment under circumstances of great personal danger. Typically in one week Aegis carries out over 100 escort assignments covering approximately 18,000 miles.
>
> Aegis's personnel have substantial military and peacekeeping experience and all operate under strict and accountable Rules of Engagement of the Coalition Military and the US Department of State, as well as Coalition Provisional Authority Order Memo. 17.
>
> These Rules of Engagement allow for a structured escalation of force to include opening fire on civilian vehicles under certain circumstances. All incidents of the use of such escalation of force which includes the use of firearms are logged and investigated to ensure that there has been strict adherence to the Rules of Engagement. Should any incident recorded on the video footage have involved Aegis personnel, this too will be subject to scrutiny by the Board of Inquiry.[3]

Order 17 was not a universally joyful experience. On 28 October, some nine days after the website opened, 'PSD Team Member (Resigned)' revealed,

> I was forced to jump before I was pushed for just doing my job as a rear gunner. I followed all the rules of engagement and stopped an

incoming vehicle that I deemed to be a threat to the team and most importantly the client. The vehicle was stopped with two rounds into the engine block and nobody hurt. This incident was blown out of proportion . . .

I have seen footage of other AEGIS teams stopping incoming vehicles with a lot more than two aimed shots to the engine block. Why are there rules for one region and not another? The answer I feel is that the Regional Directors make their own rules.

The grunts, by way of the 'Aegis Dialogues', ran their own public discussion of the affair, until the site was closed and reopened in a more muted style after about six weeks. Some contributors, unsurprisingly, supported the gunner involved, some with reasoned argument or, more frequently, with knuckles touching the ground. At least as many denounced the shootings as counterproductive, illegal and immoral. Another group withheld judgement, reasoning that the provenance of the video was uncertain, and that it was probably not the whole story. A few were clinically analytical.

What follow are some sample comments (complete with spelling errors) from the antis, who disapproved of what was done. From 'Way Out Station', 11 November:

Jesus, it must be bad if all cars that advance towards you at speed get the hell shot out of them . . . How many cars have been shot up where a husband has been trying to get his wife to the hospital in the process of dropping a sprog? What an existence . . .

From 'Fmed,' 13 November:

That is the most damaging footage of trigger happy body count hunters that I have witnessed. It has done nothing but show the company and the lads it employs in a bad light . . .

From 'Anonymous', 13 November:

The footage of the rear gunner is quite simply a disgrace. [Neither] myself nor a single person I have spoken to agrees with the actions carried out . . . If that guy was in my team then he would definitely get the beating of his life . . . the fuckwit would not make it anywhere near the important role as rear gunner . . . he should have been booted into touch after the first one and to let him carry on waxing the fuck out of who he feels like is disgusting.

The video is circulating all over the net and all it shows is a complete fucking trigger happy idiot who is inept at his job and possibly scared shitless of any vehicle coming within 200 metres of him . . .

From 'Disgusted', 25 November:

The word is out. That despicable video of a rear gunner shooting up innocent Iraqi drivers, no, murdering Iraqi drivers, is circulating on the WWW and it won't be long before it gets into the hands of the PCO [Project Co-ordination Office] . . . There will be a lot of people jobless and gunning for you [the website controller] . . . The murdering idiot who filmed the terrible murderous acts needs hanging out to dry . . .

From 'Iraqi,' 27 November (to underline the case for not making unnecessary enemies through a too-ready use of firepower):

Shooting at civilians for fun are we? I'm sure there are some nice IEDs [improvised explosive devices] waiting for you on Irish [that is, Route Irish, the main route from the Baghdad Green Zone to the international airport].

A day or so later, 'Iraqi' returned to the attack:

You are a bunch of cowards hiding in your bullet proof cars wearing bullet proof vests firing at innocent civilians.

'Low Profile', on 27 November, posted,

All this plays into the hands of those that see us as mercenaries/baby killers/whatever . . . It makes you all (and reflectively all of us in the AOR [Area of Responsibility]) look like cowboys. And it's a pretty bad clip, let's face it (er, how many 'warning shots'??)

The same day, Fmed suggested,

If they ignore hand warnings, put a round off in front of the vehicle [as a warning shot]. If that fails, in the bonnet, until they do stop or you are sure that it is a suicide bomber. But just to 'light up' a vehicle for speeding is extreme to say the least.

'SET Member' (presumably one of a security escort team) proposed,

How about circulating the names of all the members of the team involved in murdering the Iraqis on the footage to all the security companies working in Iraq, so we won't have to work alongside these maniacs in the future . . .

On 28 November 'Tractorface', whose allegiance was unclear, wrote, ironically,

Thank you for the shooting-civilians-in-their-cars video. America has no clue what it means to have a war where you can't distinguish enemies from civilians, and this video is a slap in the gut. Whoever released this was either saying 'fuck you' to Aegis and the war in general, or they were ignorant about how this would be seen. Let me explain how the public is going to see this. It looks like adolescent jerkoffs playing Grand Theft Auto and killing people that try to pass their truck.

There is no indication in the video that they are escorting a convoy, or that targets are given any sort of warning besides flying lead. When the convoy comes to a stop on the empty highway and still shoots at people approaching way too fast to read any warning signs or even know what the fuck is going on, it looks like the Aegis guys are intentionally slowing down to fuck with these people and do them harm. But the cream of it all is the soundtrack. Music that says, 'Just another day at the grindstone, shooting at people taking their kids to school'. I didn't start this post to rip you guys up but it just occurred to me. You're being paid to INCREASE security in Iraq?

Two days later, someone claiming to have worked for Aegis wrote,

The whole team is guilty of murder and by stupidly airing this piece of rubbish they will be prosecuted eventually. Aegis should be kicked out of Iraq whole scale for employing these muppets and murderers. This will effect us all eventually. I'd like a few minutes alone with this cowboy to see if he is as brave as he thinks he is.

Other voices expressed sympathy, if not support, for the tail gunner involved. In an early contribution on 15 November an anonymous operator wrote,

> Unless you can sit in the rear gunner's shoes . . . you will never know. I've been in the sandpit [Iraq] for two years, my first nine months as a 'trunk monkey'. It's the loneliest job on the planet . . . You alone have to make the decision whether to open fire or not . . . Shit happens, but at least you and your team get to go home. We don't want guys too worried about repercussions and failing to open up when they need to. When some nutcase slams a car full of explosives into your convoy!

'Admin' on 16 November agreed:

> Unless you were there . . . who is anyone to judge the duties of the rear gunner? The headshed [high command] has scared a lot of rear gunners and some have had to resign before being sacked and all for carrying out their duties. What is the point of a rear gunner who, because of the possible ramifications, is too scared to stop a fast-moving incoming vehicle in a land where any of them could be a VBIED [vehicle-borne bomb]? . . . A rear gunner has to have the courage of his convictions.

Admin referred to two cases in which 'it was the rear gunners that were returning fire, putting their lives on the line for the safety of their team and the clients'.

On 19 November an anonymous operator also challenged critics of the mysterious tail gunner:

> If you think it's a bad idea to have a belt fed [machine gun] and firing ports in the rear wagon I'd advise you to go out on the ground up north for a bit. And just cabby away at vehicles because they come TOO CLOSE? It's to stop nutcases driving in and detonating up the backside of your convoy! Check the stats, back in late 2004 there was reckoned to be at least 1 suicide bomber on the BIAP [Baghdad International Airport]

every couple of days! Would I fire warning shots to keep traffic back? Fucking right I would . . .

When has Iraq ever been a 'low threat' environment? Every time you roll out [beyond] the wire expect the worst. Theres one drill, if it looks dodgy and its approaching at warp factor 9, hand signals – warning shots – brass the fucker into the stone age.

Criticising those who advocated using routes off the MSR (main supply routes), the same correspondent suggested that wherever they went,

we are going to be pinged [targeted] . . . shit happens, you get pinged – deal with it, fight through it, endex. What are the three principals of BG/CP [bodyguard/close-protection] work? 'AVOID, ESCAPE, CONFRONT.' When did it become 'take as much kit as you can so we can CONFRONT? What about basic military skills of 'adapting' and 'improvising' etc.

This is without a shadow of a doubt the most high risk environment to conduct BG/CP work. We should not be following the DS [directing staff] solution laid out by a course back in old Blighty. They should be following OUR drills . . . Most European CP courses are about as useful for work in this environment as tits on fish. I've been out here in Baghdad for 2 years, I started as a rear gunner and now command my own team. I don't sit in an office I roll out of the wire each day . . .

I'm sick and tired of so called experienced 'London BGs' deploying out and trying to tell you how best to do the job. I rely 110% on my prior military experience, because let's face it when did this war ever end?

On 20 November, 'Guest' said he was worried about the suggestion that anyone should 'brass the fucker into the stone age'. 'Guest' claimed to have been a freelance operator in Iraq, Afghanistan, Eastern Europe and the UK after 15 years' regular soldiering.

The one thing that worries me is I know from experience in NI [Northern Ireland] and other places as soon as you start to piss locals off in THEIR back yard you loose respect and you end up as recruiters for the bad boys. Piss some one off and they will tell 15 people. Do something good and they will tell three. How many teams do you think are working out here without having to brass the fuckers? Take care and stay safe.

The anonymous advocate of 'brassing' surprisingly apologised to 'Guest' for an inappropriate choice of words. 'That's what happens when you mix alcohol with internet.' He went on:

> I don't mean 'brassing' everything to pieces within 300 metres. But you do need the ability to be able to stop a vehicle intent on either detonating or spraying your team up from the rear. You need to trust the rear gunner to do his job and the vast majority do, though there's always one or two who fail in this . . .
>
> I've been hit 7 bloody times out here, 5 during a 6 month period in 2004. Although 4 were Ied's [improvised explosive devices] which I'm sure most people have gone through a few of those. 3 were SAF [small-arms fire] 2 quite bad and 1 involved the death of a comrade.
>
> I was also a 'teeth arm' [regular soldier with a fighting regiment] serving for ten years but nothing prepared me for the roads around Baghdad. Certainly not a CP [close protection] course. The majority of our drills are 'bastardised' to fit the current environment . . . Having a rear element keeping traffic away from the principal is part of this. There's the right way and wrong way of course, those muppets from Zapata engineering . . . made life that bit more difficult for all of us after they drove around Fallujah having a go at anything that moved . . .

'Just Another Brit PSD' weighed in on 21 November to suggest that 'there are plenty of teams out there who don't run Gun trucks and have never been pinged' (targeted). The writer, after 18 months in Iraq, had encountered two incidents while operating in high profile, 'and we don't employ Trunk Monkeys' (tail gunners).

On 21 November, 'Trunk monkey Baghdad' commented,

> You are either LP [low-profile] or not. If you are LP stay LP and don't close in flashing your lights as I've seen a lot do. You draw attention to yourselves not just from High profile PSD teams but from the locals. Also if you are LP stay with the local traffic and create the bubble, just look at the example set by Edinburgh Risks for that one. [Trunk Monkey's reference to Edinburgh Risks was to reopen memories, and wounds, resulting from a controversial episode in which three operators were shot dead after being boxed in by a traffic jam.] Stick to the established PSD proto-

cols of not closing in on another PSD team and all should be ok, but then you should know this already.

There was further advice along the same lines:

Different companies operate different profiles. LP don't need [armed trucks]. They blend in, or should. The profile my company operates cannot be considered anything other than high profile. A gun truck is a logical step.

At the end of the day we are all on the same side. We think alike but because of company profiles or policies we operate differently. This should not be a hurdle to joint learning about critical issues.

Others agreed:

Low profile is LOW PROFILE. This doesn't involve trying to squeeze past coalition convoys and other PSD teams. You can't have your cake and eat it. It might be slower but I'm sure anyone that has worked that way will agree it's the safest way to travel. It's all very well saying 'What if the rear gunner engages another PSD team?' Well any team operating LP will not bloody well attempt to zoom past a PSD team knowing full well they run the risk of being opened up on. The object of LP is to blend in. You don't see the local population attempting to zoom past PSD teams, bar a few with an obvious agenda, so why try it in an LP convoy.

On 22 November 'Just another Brit PSD' implied that the problem was not a potential blue-on-blue contact but

the engaging of civvies that's causing the Iraqi Interior Ministry to begin to scrutinise the actions of certain PSD companies . . . There are plenty of High Profile teams out there without rear gunners pissing off the local population. In 20 months in Iraq 12 of them in Baghdad last year we never employed rear gunners and it worked for us.

If locals keep getting killed, then guess what's going to happen? The Iraqis will remove the Support [medium/heavy] weapons from us, the Minimis [Belgian machine guns] and GPMGs [UK general-purpose machine guns] and RPKs and PKMs [Russian machine guns] will all go.

It's their country and we will have to respect their laws. And where will that leave us? Tensions are already high between Officials and PSD teams. Why heighten tensions? It's the slip roads where these guys can merge in from, or the defilade of overpasses, and if a SVBIED [suicide car bomber] rolls down an embankment a trunk monkey isn't much use!

'Disgusted with disgusted' hit back:

> You are a moron. A blind idiot. Making presumptions about a video that you have no idea about. Probably some scared ass office pogue that doesn't have the bollocks to get out from behind the desk.

Two days later another anonymous contributor (but, like others, identified by his remote location identity) argued, 'A video is only a PIECE of the story, not the whole thing. And somebody who makes comments or slanders based solely on the video is as blind and unthinking as most of the media.'

To this, 'P.S.D. Member' added,

> We all know that our good and honest company had nothing to do with that video. We have the rules of engagement that we all obey to the letter. We all know that the video was shot by a company trying to frame us. We at Aegis have respect for civilians and for our company. We also have respect for the rules of engagement and for Mr Spicer. Your not going to fuck up the good work we have done here so take your trumped up charges and stick them up your ass side ways . . . The video was not of Aegis personnel or on route Irish . . . I ask all Aegis PSD members to boycott this site and leave the scum of the press to swim in their own shit.

Was the video, after all, a piece of black propaganda? One of my sources, with intimate knowledge of the area, having watched the video, said, 'It definitely *was* Route Irish. I have travelled up and down that route enough times to recognise individual palm trees.' Although this doesn't mean that Aegis was the organisation in the video, it does detract from the plausibility of the posting by 'PSD Member'.

There is another possible explanation for why the video was made. 'Rear Gunner Zulu', on 15 November, revealed

I myself used to film from the rear and turn in the footage at the debrief if anything happened. I nearly got into trouble for one incident but was cleared of any wrongdoing. The footage had been viewed months after the incident by people in an office with little or no actual time on the ground and they failed to take into account the events and intel [intelligence] at the time. Needless to say, I do not make videos for the headsheds/ops/int any more . . .'

Perhaps the most perceptive comment was an anonymous post on 27 November:

The issue is not that there are trigger happy bozos lighting up Iraqis. It's that the powers that be want to pretend that you can run private security in a war zone under peacetime rules. Could any of these cars [in the video] have been loaded with explosives? And would a car full of pop guns stop them? No.

Aside from the video debate and grumbles about petty rules concerning permission to grow a moustache, among other matters, the 'Aegis Dialogues' focused attention on Tim Spicer's turbulent earlier career as a military contractor (Papua New Guinea, Sierra Leone) and efforts in Washington by the Irish lobby to challenge the $293 million contract awarded to Aegis by the Pentagon through which, as well as running its own protective convoys, the firm co-ordinated the activities of the 60 other security companies in Iraq with the US military.

It is significant, perhaps, that – as the *Nation* pointed out in an article reproduced on the Aegis-Iraq site – 'one of Spicer's most vocal critics is the Rev. Sean McManus of the Irish National Caucus, a Washington-based lobbying group. His group has a special section on its website devoted to the [Iraq] contract and Spicer's misdeeds.'[4]

Spicer made enemies with long memories, particularly while commanding his battalion of the Scots Guards in Northern Ireland in 1992. Two of his soldiers, believing they were chasing a grenade thrower, shot and killed an unarmed man. The facts of the case suggest ambiguity. Why would an innocent man, armed only with a swimming suit in a plastic bag (the bag was never found) run? Why would two soldiers kill someone who offered no threat?

The soldiers were convicted of murder. The affair was regarded as a travesty of justice by most British soldiers and much of the UK press. The Irish Republican community saw it as further proof of a shoot-to-kill policy by the army.[5] Thirteen years later, in 2005, given the opportunity, the American Irish Caucus was not prepared to bury the matter even if the IRA had now given up its armed struggle. Haunted by such ghosts, the last thing Tim Spicer needed was a further accusation that men under his command had killed innocent people for sport. In November 2005, the firm announced that it was running an inquiry 'to see if any of their employees were involved'. The Foreign Office confirmed that it was investigating the video 'in conjunction with Aegis.'

But at that time an Aegis spokesman also told the *Sunday Telegraph*, 'There is nothing to indicate that these film clips are in any way connected to Aegis', while an FO spokesman said, 'Aegis have assured us that there is nothing on the video to suggest that it has anything to do with their company. This is now a matter for the American authorities because Aegis is under contract to the United States.'[6]

The careful wording of the two statements – notably the phrase 'nothing on the video to suggest . . .' etc. – was put into a somewhat different context three months later, when the owner of the Aegis-Iraq website – Rod Stoner, a former British soldier – identified himself in a television interview. Next day, on 7 April 2006, Aegis was granted an injunction prohibiting Mr Stoner from speaking to the press or disseminating in any way the company's rules of engagement, or other company-confidential information.[7]

Meanwhile, Aegis passed the unpublished findings of its own inquiry to 'the US authorities', while still not confirming that its employees were involved in the incidents shown in the videos. Channel 4's subsidiary, More4, asserted in its news programme that their source had been employed by Aegis between 2004 and 2005.

The Iraqi authorities seemed to have only a walk-on part in this drama. Captain Adnan Tawfiq of the Iraqi Interior Ministry, which dealt with compensation issues, told the *Sunday Telegraph* that he had received numerous claims from families alleging that relatives had been shot at by private contractors travelling in road convoys. He said, 'When the security companies kill people they just drive away and nothing is done. Sometimes we ring the companies concerned and they deny everything. I would say we have had about 50–60 incidents of this kind.'[8]

More4 News, in its coverage, quoted Stoner: 'We never know whether that was an innocent civilian or an insurgent. We don't know because we never stop. Because we are carrying a client out, our mission is to get from A to B.' The programme also interviewed a diplomat from the Iraqi Embassy in London, Ali Al-Biati. He was asked, 'Do you know who's responsible if British civilians are going around shooting Iraqis?'

He replied, 'What we know is that [UN] Resolution 1546 states that the security of Iraq is under the multinational forces and the Iraqi government at the same time. There is a contract between some of the multinational forces and some companies. There is a law for that. And that is clear within the law of the resolution. Those laws should be respected and those people that are abusing the power that they are given should be accountable, investigated and brought to justice . . . People are investigating it but it takes time. Once there is a report come out we will wait and see.'[9]

On 28 June 2006, the Aegis website published its own, definitive account of the affair. It said,

Aegis Defence Services is pleased to announce today the positive outcome of the investigations into the so-called 'trophy video'. The video purporting to show its security contractors shooting at civilian vehicles on the highways in Iraq came to light in November last year. Aegis launched an immediate enquiry under the auspices of an independent review board which included a British Barrister and Recorder of the Crown Court and a former senior British police officer. It was a thorough and conclusive investigation which reported back before Christmas.

Its findings were that the films were recorded during Aegis' legitimate operations in support of Multi-National Force Iraq and the incidents recorded were within the Rules for the Use of Force. There was no evidence of any civilian casualties as a result of the incidents and the images published were all taken out of context and were therefore highly misleading in what they represented.

The report was handed over to the US Military who launched its own enquiry through the Army's Criminal Investigation Division. This enquiry is now closed with confirmation that no further investigation or action is warranted. The speculative allegations made at the time of the video are therefore entirely unfounded.

Colonel Spicer, CEO Aegis, said today: 'We are very pleased that the

US Military concurs with our findings. It is regrettable that the actions of one Aegis contractor, who has been the subject of separate court action in the UK, brought into question the high standards of behaviour achieved by our team in Iraq. Aegis is a prime contractor to the US Government with an exemplary record of performance working in very difficult circumstances and observes the strictest protocols for standards and ethics.'[10]

Spicer and others on the Aegis team would share the DoD's anger about colourful reports that do not entirely stand up. Yet during its brief life, the Aegis-Iraq website also shed light on other aspects of private security, such as the economics of getting into the business (one man paying £4,000 for close-protection training in Britain before being hired), attitudes to money, and weapon-handling. On 3 November 2005, before the video controversy began, an anonymous post entitled 'Team Loyalty' reflected

This is still a war zone and it should be treated as such. There has been enough death and destruction in this country to last a lifetime . . . Money is money . . . but PSCs [private security companies] should respect due diligence to their employees . . . I resigned from Aegis as my life was being put in danger by the incompetence of a team leader . . . . Wake up, people. If you are here for the money, good. But remember this: money does not bring people back from the dead . . .

'Guest,' next day, in a long post noted, 'The $ is king'. He added later,

When the risk is too much, WALK. So how much money is enough? The answer is simple. How much do you value your worth? That is a personal thing . . . I am alive and I know of guys who work for shit money in shit conditions who are now DEAD. Be under no illusion. PMCs [private military companies] have a LEGAL DUTY of care for all their guys and I know they are breaking the law so often it is incredible . . .

'PSD Member' wrote on 10 November,

I believe one of our boys who was caught in an IED [roadside bomb] . . . is now at home in Ireland, after being seriously injured on the job . . . I have only just realised, most of us aren't covered against serious injury. I was told . . . that our fellow operator is now at home after only receiving a £1,000 cash pay out, full stop . . . nothing else.

'Just Another Brit PSD' replied, 'Surely you were not naïve enough to believe what the Headshed told you about insurance policies? . . . £1,000 is nothing when you can no longer wipe your own arse!' In another post on 14 November he wrote, 'If you've all signed contracts then take them to a lawyer as they're obviously not worth the paper they're written on . . . It's called "Duty of care".' And on 21 November an anonymous contributor suggested, 'The companies out here are here for one reason: to make as much money in as short time as possible. Isn't that why we are all here? Grow up!'

14

AFGHANISTAN 2001–FUTURE INDEFINITE:
'In Talibs' fields, the poppies blow'

The catalyst for the global War on Terror was the Twin Towers attack of 11 September 2001. America wanted Osama bin Laden dead or alive. The UN wanted him alive, but on trial. In early October, as a preliminary to invasion, US and UK Special Forces infiltrated northern Afghanistan to make contact with the remnants of the Northern Alliance – an awareness-raising mission to make diversionary attacks on the government and to spot targets for air attack. Air assaults on Kabul, Kandahar and Jalalabad were made from an altitude beyond the reach of the Stinger missile.

During the major two-year war against the Taliban that ensued, the US devised an apparently winning formula to minimise American casualties This combined massive air power with 'friendly' Afghan ground forces, linked through US and British Special Forces. Thousands of the 'friendly' Afghans were mercenaries belonging to private armies paid in cash by the CIA.

They were known as the 'ASF', or Afghan Security Forces, something other than a police service or regular army. Their leaders often became corrupt warlords or, worse, turned out to be allies of Al-Qaeda. As a result, an essential ingredient of the strategy – to drive the Taliban into a killing ground on the border with Pakistan – failed. The reason: border states such as Waziristan, technically part of Pakistan, were more loyal to the enemy than the friendly government of President Pervez Musharraf in Islamabad, so much so that some of them became known as 'Talibanstan'.

The problem was painfully obvious during Operation Anaconda in March 2002, to clear enemy survivors from caves above 3,000 metres (10,000 feet) south-east of Gardez. It was a battle in which Australian and New Zealand SAS soldiers were prominent. In theory, there was no escape for a bottled-up enemy, since the Pakistan army would block any retreat. In practice, as the Italian analyst Antonio Giustozzi has pointed out, during Anaconda, in the post-Taliban period, 'allegations started to surface that Hazrat Ali's militiamen had let the [foreign] Arab fighters slip through the net into Pakistan.

'Similar allegations would later hit Gul Agha Shirzai of Kandahar, while another US ally, Padcha Khan Zadran, discredited himself by turning against President Karzai and forcing the Americans to dump him.'[1]

The body count resulting from this phase of the War on Terror varies between 1,000 and 50,000. The purpose, to bring Osama bin Laden and his friends to justice, was not accomplished. There was a clear case to remain focused on the porous border between Pakistan and Afghanistan. Instead, in 2003, influenced by the oil lobby, President Bush sent an army to invade Iraq, on a wild-goose pursuit of non-existent weapons of mass destruction. During the next two fatal years, the US and Britain effectively abandoned Afghanistan as the Taliban returned to take control of much of the country outside Kabul. How could the West make such a mistake?

The answer, according to Steve Coll, a *Washington Post* journalist with intimate knowledge of the region, was that most of the American Establishment was prepared to accept the case presented by influential Saudis and Pakistanis, that 'the Taliban will mature and moderate'.[2] This was a lie. In Islam, one size does not fit all, in spite of the apparent uniformity of dress. Far from 'maturing', the Taliban regressed into a medieval culture, and the seeds of a new conflict were sown in Afghanistan.

Had Western promises to develop the country been kept promptly, that might not have happened, but the brief window of opportunity, the honeymoon that followed the reintroduction of music, dance, kite-flying and girls' schools, was thrown away. Aid was slow to arrive and, when it did, much of it – handed over to the Afghan authorities – disappeared on the way. By 2004 a resurgent Taliban was tightening its grip on much of the country and security contractors were no longer the predator but the prey. In May of that year two operators working for the British firm Global Risk Strategies in Nuristan, 85 miles east of Kabul, were shot dead with their translator. They were in the country to help the United Nations to register voters for forthcoming elections. A Taliban commander, Mullah Momin, telephoned Reuters to say, 'We are killing all locals and foreigners who are helping the Americans to consolidate their occupation of Afghanistan.'[3] In the preceding nine months, terrorists had murdered about 700 people. Twenty-two were aid workers, including a French woman with the UN and a representative of the International Red Cross.

Global Risk Strategies was run by Damien Perl, aged 36, a former Royal Marine, and Charlie Andrews, aged 34, a retired Scots Guards officer. The *Guardian* reported,

> Global Risk Strategies has developed an entrepreneurial edge . . . Where British or US ex-special forces can command more than £300 a day – sometimes a lot more – Global need only pay around £35 a day to its 1,300 force of otherwise unemployed Fijians and Gurkhas . . . The company does not like its employees to be called mercenaries, or to be known as private military or security company. It says, 'We are a risk management company who don't always operate armed.'[4]

The firm's evolution illustrates how the industry as a whole mutated. Its first innovation was an air bridge from Manston, Kent, to Afghanistan, for journalists and NGO staff. It branched out to build secure compounds in Kabul. Impressed, the CIA hired it to transport currency in the country. It was, inevitably, risky work. In November 2003 three of the company's Fijians were seriously wounded by a roadside bomb. Two more were injured in an exchange of fire soon afterwards. The following February, another was killed by mortar fire.

In 2007 the Department for International Development (DFID), the UK agency responsible for distributing £217 million of aid, claimed that it was monitoring the situation but the Governor of Helmand, Mohammed Daud, said, 'Promises to get projects up and running have not been kept. There hasn't even been a DFID representative in Helmand for two months'.[5]

Norine MacDonald, Canadian president of the Senlis Council, one of the leading agencies, described the situation in Helmand as 'a famine in which children are starving to death. There is no food and virtually no foreign aid. People here are being left with a choice: either join the insurgency and get money to feed your family, or watch them die.'[6]

An equally fatal gap was the West's failure to create a viable police service in a country more ready to learn the arts of war rather than the ways of peace. As a *New York Times* team put it in December 2006,

> For the first two and a half years after the fall of the Taliban [in late 2001] no systematic police training program existed outside Afghanistan's capital . . . The US focused on training a new, multiethnic army and paid little attention to the need for policemen.[7]

Admittedly, this was not an ideal environment for such an experiment. In a country the size of Texas with virtually no infrastructure and a pitiless climate, at least 70 per cent of the population of 31 million are illiterate. The only sources of wealth are the opium poppy and the gold-rush economy that descends from heaven with an international community determined to build a new nation as in Bosnia, Kosovo, Sierra Leone and many other places.

Afghanistan is a tougher nut than any of them. Almost three-quarters of the police, like their civilian brethren, cannot read or write. That includes police recruits who, even if they wish to do well, have had no legal system – no courts, no prison service – within which to function. In any case, to act as guardians of the rule of law – that is, Western law – would put most of them on a collision course with sharia, their religion and their tribes.

As an inquiry team sent from Washington concluded,

> Until the Afghan criminal justice system, including law enforcement, judiciary and corrections has matured . . . coordinated from the national to the local level such that laws are standardized and uniformly applied, the Afghanistan National Police (ANP) will function more as a security force than as a law enforcement organization.[8]

In April 2002 the German government gallantly agreed to train a police force, starting (and finishing) with a National Police Academy in Kabul. The serious business of raising a force of 62,000 was left to the American DynCorp International company, which supplied just 245 trainers, mostly ex-city cops from the US. The budget matches the scale of the task: an estimated $600 million a year – on a contract valued at $1.1 billion at least until 2010 and probably indefinitely. There was also a blood price. More than a hundred DynCorp employees were killed in Iraq. Dozens more met an untimely end in Afghanistan, the Balkans and Colombia. As one of the company's team leaders puts it, 'It really is a huge gamble. The dice rolled very badly during my fourteen months in Iraq.' During that tour, 13 US police trainers and eight DynCorp bodyguards were killed.[9]

In Afghanistan during the first five years or so, progress in training the local police force was, well, laboured. The Washington inquiry, published in December 2006, noted,

> In the past, a DynCorp contract included an initial and one-time issue of uniforms and non-lethal equipment at graduation to ANP students attending the training centers. Uniform issue included uniforms, web belts, batons and handcuffs. The program was terminated after 2004 [as] ineffective. After graduation many students sold their equipment before they reached their duty stations.

Uniforms were not the only items to disappear. Out of 5,000 motor vehicles supplied to the ANP, the whereabouts of 3,000 was unclear. As the report says, 'Equipment lost to corruption after initial issue is not replaced.' There were also supply problems. As of 1 June 2006, most police units held less than 50 per cent of their authorised equipment. In view of doubts about exactly how many officers were actually employed, this might not have been a problem. But, 'Reports on actual numbers of police are unreliable. They are inflated and there is no personnel accounting system in place. Numbers of on-duty police are determined by the salaries delivered to police stations according to the number of patrolmen listed on the roles.' And this in a country where the absence of banks means that all transactions are in cash.

Two groups of police officers were more than usually blatant in the rackets they ran.

> Often higher ranking officers will take a portion out of each patrolman's pay [£37 a month] before paying the policeman. In one instance, a police colonel boasted to his ... counterparts that he always took a portion from the pay of every policeman in the province ... Salaries actually reaching ordinary policemen are routinely reduced because of salary skimming by more senior police.

The source of these funds is the international, largely Western, community. 'International donors have financed the bulk of the Afghan budget. The

Afghan government does not have the revenue to pay its police.' The US contributed $20 million in 2004; $40 million in 2005 and $9.5 million in 2006.[10]

The second group on the make was the 3,400-strong Highway Police, 'so poorly organised and corrupt that the best solution is to draw that organisation down while retraining and reassigning its manpower to . . . the uniformed and border police'. Since courts do not function, the Highway Police often become highway robbers and practise their own system of justice known as 'bribe and release'.

An Afghan journalist – Sayed Yaqub Ibrahimi – revealed in June 2006 that,

> Afghanistan's police stand accused of extorting money from drug smugglers, gun runners, brothel owners and gamblers in return for looking the other way. Those who refuse to pay can be arrested as part of an apparently virtuous clean-up campaign, then released once they hand over the cash.[11]

Ibrahimi and others believe that many police officers are mujahedeen veterans. Others double as militia commanders. There was little that DynCorp or other PSCs could do to arrest what was seen in the West as corruption and in Afghanistan as simple street wisdom.

But beyond the shambolic official police service and the flimsy official judiciary, there was an alternative system of justice. A State Department inquiry into human rights in Afghanistan identified places where shipping containers were used to pack in prisoners who were reportedly 'beaten, tortured and denied adequate food'.[12] There were also private and illegal prisons. The Afghanistan Independent Human Rights Commission, taken seriously by State, claimed that the country's own intelligence agency – following the CIA's example in 'rendering' inconvenient people – ran at least two of them.

Yet another layer of 'justice' included interrogation centres operated by the US army, the CIA and even private entrepreneurs. Some of the interrogators were civilians, hired individually by the CIA for paramilitary duties without the involvement of companies. One of them was David Passaro, a former Army Ranger (commando) working at a base near Asabad in Afghanistan in 2003. In June 2003 a local farmer named Abdul Wali, a veteran of the anti-Soviet resistance, gave himself up to the Americans.

Having been repeatedly beaten by Passaro, he died in custody three days later. It was claimed that he had a bad heart.

The following year in the US, Passaro was charged with assaulting Wali. He was convicted on four counts and sentenced to eight years and four months in prison. He was the first civilian to be accused of brutalising a prisoner either in Iraq or Afghanistan. By that time, the use of civilian interrogators – known as '97 Echoes', since 97E is the official code for interrogation training at American military bases – was becoming a habit in both conflicts. The emerging industry leaders were Lockheed Martin, CACI (three of whose former employees were linked to abuse at Abu Ghraib prison in Iraq) and Sytex, a Lockheed Martin subsidiary, which supplied four interrogators to the US base at Bagram, Afghanistan, notorious for the brutality of some of its regular military guards. Commenting on the Passaro case, Priti Patel, an attorney with Human Rights First, alleged that at least 20 cases of CIA agents and civilians involved in prisoner abuse had been referred to the Justice Department for prosecution but 'nothing has happened'.[13]

The most colourful of the freelance interrogators was Jonathan ('Jack') Idema, a former Special Forces soldier turned bounty hunter. He and two others ran a private, secret interrogation centre at a house in a Kabul suburb until July 2004, when it was raided by Afghan police. The agents were surprised to discover several local men inside, three of whom were 'strapped to the ceiling and hanging by their feet'. Idema's eight captives included a judge.[14] After he was sentenced in Afghanistan to 10 years in prison, NATO officials admitted that they believed he was an American soldier. Coalition soldiers had even searched buildings at Idema's request. The Idema team's credibility 'was such that with their uniforms, their approach, our people believed they were what they said they were. It was a mistake.' Idema and a partner were sentenced to 10 years' imprisonment, reduced on appeal to three.

There were other adventurers, pseudo agents and possibly genuine deniables at work in Afghanistan. On 31 August 2005 ex-Colour Sergeant David Addison, aged 46, a former British military intelligence agent working for US Protection & Investigation (USPI), was taken prisoner when Taliban guerrillas ambushed an armed convoy at Farah, on the road between Kandahar and Herat. Three days later, following high-level intervention from the British government, a joint Coalition assault team tried to rescue him. The mission went disastrously wrong. On 3 September

Dr Kim Howells, Minister of State at the Foreign Office, interrupted his weekend to issue a statement about the affair. 'With great sadness, I have to report that in the course of the operation [to locate and, if necessary, to rescue David Addison] they found a body, which is presumed to be that of David . . . We do not yet know precisely how and when he died.'[15]

A few months earlier, USPI had been criticised by the International Crisis Group for paying high wages to commanders of the Highway Police – discredited by the State Department – in an arrangement 'fraught with risks, not least because it facilitates narcotics trafficking by commanders'.[16]

Not surprisingly in this madhouse, where reality and deception are bedfellows, senior American generals and British ministers speak not of 'success' in Afghanistan but 'progress', which one US general defined as a situation in which 'there are no women being taken to the [Kabul] football stadium to be executed'. He was apparently unaware of a State Department report concerning a village in Badakhshan province where, on 29 April 2005, Amena, a 29-year-old woman, was stoned to death 'for allegedly committing adultery'.[17]

Des Browne, Britain's Delphic Defence Minister, gave a less defined answer to the future of Afghanistan: 'Let us be clear – success will not be what we understand by security and prosperity and proper governance. It will instead be progress and it will be massively worth achieving, both for them, the Afghans, and for us.'[18] He did not define 'progress'.

Admittedly, there was the new fact of an elected, if indigent, government in Kabul, whose writ did not run through 80 per cent of the country. Hopefully, much of Afghanistan, if not the border area including parts of Pakistan, would cease to be a haven for terrorists hoping to repeat 9/11. But much of the Afghanistan National Army, being trained by US soldiers in 2006 but still riddled with nepotism and graft, had yet to prove itself.

An exception was the three-week battle to take and hold the hill position known as Sperwan Ghar in September 2006, during Operation Medusa. Two companies of ANA soldiers on a training operation won the grudging respect of three SF ODAs (Operational Detachment Alphas) leading the attack. Medusa was a two-week battle in which NATO fought to prevent Taliban forces from overrunning Kandahar. Lieutenant General David Richards, the British commander of NATO forces in Afghanistan, asserted that it marked 'the turning point of the whole campaign . . . If I had had a reserve [force] I could have made it a more conclusive victory.'[19] The victory cost 500 lives including at least 22 civilians bombed by NATO.

But elsewhere, as the Taliban returned to the area, the allies' use of local mercenaries disguised as an auxiliary Afghan Security Forces unit had not sealed the border and the Pakistani army had failed to tame the wild men of Waziristan.

As the situation worsened during the summer of 2006, it was business as usual for the 25 private security companies (American, British, Australian and South African) on the ground in Afghanistan, providing convoy escorts, close protection of diplomats, reconstruction experts, journalists and mine clearance in a culture where the only law was the law of the gun. They sometimes received a bad press from their natural allies. General Richards complained that 'the preponderance of unethical, poorly regulated Private Security Companies, often all too ready to discharge their easily-sourced firearms, is a serious additional source for concern'.[20]

He was not the first to voice concern. In 2004, the US State Department had rebuked DynCorp for the aggressive behaviour of President Karzai's bodyguard. A BBC correspondent saw the Afghan transport minister being slapped by American heavies during a visit to Mazar-e-Sharif.[21] The guards might have been feeling less than cool after the death of three US citizens when a bomb exploded outside their Kabul office in August that year. DynCorp's men were also complimented by State for keeping Karzai alive but, coincidentally, he replaced them with Afghan bodyguards.

The unique task facing the PSCs in Afghanistan – the major difference between this environment and everywhere else – was the pursuit of the poppy, and its eradication. The policy was made in the USA, largely fought by British soldiers in the poppy garden of Helmand, in opposition to both the British Medical Association in London and common sense. One British company had a team dedicated to the close protection to diplomats (headed by an SIS representative) attempting to turn off 92 per cent of the world's illegal opium. As well as Foreign Office staff, experts from the British tax and customs department (HM Revenue and Customs) also needed protection. Why were they involved in this new opium war? Possibly to follow the money trail attached to a global industry worth £1.5 billion in 2005, most of it grown in Helmand province, an essentially British battleground.

The West's dilemma, as some commentators repeatedly noted, was that by attacking the poppy, NATO, the US and Kabul's own poppy eradication teams alienated a population dependent on it for survival, who then turned to the Taliban and its handouts in exchange for guerrilla activity as the only alternative. Nick Higgins, a security consultant who had spent nine months in Helmand on US aid projects pointed out, 'The Taliban pays $200 a month with a bonus scheme for successful attacks.'[22]

The guerrilla movement also offered new volunteers a golden hello, City-style, of $200 (£101) when they joined the insurgency. The closure of one aid project, said Higgins,

> threw 14,000 men back into unemployment with no relief in sight . . . This sudden upsurge in Taliban numbers is not some vast influx of men from across the Pakistan border, not an upsurge of popular support against a foreign invader. It is quite simply a question of economics.

The West's strategy, combining civil development and military superiority, should have been a twin-track policy. In practice, the two tracks ran in opposite directions. It was an object lesson in losing, not winning, hearts and minds, a potential victory thrown away in the interests of political correctness. A *Times* writer, Camilla Cavendish, reported: 'Eradication [of the poppy] is being carried out mostly by local police who cannot believe their luck at being handed a perfect opportunity for bribery . . . The poorest farmers are incensed that their crops are being obliterated to enrich others.'[23]

Her solution – and she was not alone – was to buy the 6,700 tonnes of opium produced in Afghanistan each year so as to reduce a world shortage of 10,000 tonnes required for legitimate medicine, as in Turkey, where 600,000 farmers earn a living from controlled poppy cultivation. Her diagnosis was confirmed by Dr Vivienne Nathanson, head of science and ethics at the British Medical Association. She pointed out that diamorphine (a.k.a. heroin) – a derivative of opium – was a popular remedy for pain, on prescription, in Europe and there was 'a dramatic shortage' which the Afghan crop could relieve.[24]

Why was there a shortage? Because 'there is quite a global move led by the United States to not use diamorphine medically'. There were 'those of us in Europe who disagree. We think diamorphine is a better drug than alternative painkillers because it has other effects physically when given, for example, to people with certain respiratory conditions or after heart attacks . . . We need it even though the Americans are trying to reduce the amount that's available.'

A report published by European Addiction Research in 2005 suggested,

'The routine clinical use of diamorphine in medicine is unique to the UK, but this is not well known outside the UK.'[25] Paradoxically, in spite of a shortage of the drug in Britain, the Foreign Office committed itself to spending £270 million, an increase of £115 million, on a three-year programme of drug eradication. The money was to be passed to the Kabul government. President Karzai and its Counter-Narcotics Minister Habibullah Qaderi, were very grateful. The additional money would 'greatly help our efforts to tackle the narcotics problem.'[26]

What was clear from this debate was that the opium poppy was another victim of a political debate waged by powerful interests far away from the front line. British policy in this, as many other matters, came down on the side of America in spite of doubts by senior military officers, including Lieutenant General Richards, who believed that Afghan farmers had 'no viable alternatives to opium'.[27] The fighting in Helmand was as much an opium war as an anti-Taliban campaign.

Meanwhile, a substantial force of PSC operators worked alongside the Afghanistan police in the anti-opium crusade. The American enterprise USPI (US Protection & Investigations), having trained President Karzai's bodyguard at a cost of $82 million, was paid another $290 million to train the officers in poppy eradication. In 2006 it employed 800 expatriates, most of them American, with starting salaries of $100,000 a year. An Afghan policeman was paid between $500 and $700, plus bribes, for taking part in the alternative, non-eradication programme. As Christian Aid reminded the world, by July 2004 the US had spent $40 billion on military operations while international spending on aid was $4.5 billion, much of which, it might have said, but did not, was stolen.[28]

One source of blight on the poppy-eradication programme was the difference between the British approach – to plough up the crop – and the Americans, who believed it was better to use aerial toxic spraying from January 2007. Ever since the use of Agent Orange in Vietnam, this form of chemical warfare had had a poisonous history, and outcome, whether to eliminate ground cover in Asia or coca in Colombia. The auguries for hearts and minds were not good even if, in the short run, President Karzai, backed by ten of his ministers, rejected the plan.[29]

Undeterred, an eradication force of Afghans with their international 'advisers' from DynCorp drove into Helmand's main city of Lashkar Gah on 30 January protected by helicopter gunships. They came under attack every night they were in the town. In the eyes of a disillusioned population in conditions of abject poverty, while 800 foreign NGOs lived well, alongside the isolated Karzai government, in Kabul, all foreigners were the enemy. The experience of an ArmorGroup close-protection team was typical of the war in southern Afghanistan. In September 2006, one of the firm's B6 armoured vehicles was taking an FCO diplomat, a development expert from DFID (the development ministry) and an RAF intelligence officer to meet the provincial governor of Lashkar Gah. The ArmorGroup team leader and driver were in the same vehicle, which was followed by a backup counterattack B6.

'As the convoy reached the gates of the governor's residence, there was some sort of kerfuffle and a suicide bomber broke through the local police cordon,' an ArmorGroup spokesman said. 'The man laid himself against the side of the vehicle, blowing off the front wheels. The people inside were uninjured but shaken. The escort immediately drove up alongside to provide cover. The team inside put down a smokescreen. The five people in the disabled vehicle were transferred and everyone driven to the company compound nearby. From the attack to arrival in the compound took just three minutes.'

According to one British operator, a former undercover military agent who served with 14 Intelligence Company in Northern Ireland, not all suicide bombers choose martyrdom. It is wished upon them. 'An illiterate bomber is paid $100 to deliver a "vest bomb" or a car bomb to a particular contact. He doesn't know it, but his controller has followed him in another car, with a button-job device to detonate the bomb. When the human bomb is close to some foreign soldiers, he blows up. It helps to explain why many of them seem to miss the target.'

The same source told me that the movement of foreign aid workers, training teachers, and their protectors, was increasingly by air to avoid the threat of extortion and murder on the ground outside the capital. This was no guarantee of survival. The US government hired the services of private airlines for some routine internal flights. On 27 November 2004, three soldiers – Lieutenant Colonel Michael McMahon, Chief Warrant Officer Travis Grogan and Specialist Harley Miller – were passengers aboard a turboprop aircraft that crashed on a remote mountain. All three, as well as three aircrew, died. The soldiers' relatives filed a civil lawsuit, alleging that the aircrew were newcomers to the theatre, unbriefed and not properly equipped. They believe that no flight plan was lodged, resulting in a two-day delay before the wreckage was found. Miller, it is thought, survived the crash but died of exposure.[30]

By the spring of 2007, southern Afghanistan was a no-go area for most private security teams. Local civilians had to take their chances. On 25 September 2006, Safia Amajan, aged 63, the head of the department of women's affairs in Kandahar, was assassinated in front of her home by a gangster contracted by the Taliban. During the period of Taliban rule from 1996 to 2001, she had taught girls privately, and – contrary to the Taliban's interpretation of sharia – illegally.

A few weeks later, Ghulam Sakhi, a driver, got his big career break when one of his friends was shot dead by the Taliban on the modern highway linking Kabul to Kandahar. The road was the country's multimillion-dollar showpiece of Western reconstruction (a million dollars for every one of 242 miles). Sakhi was paid up to £645 to transport military supplies for the Americans in a 10-hour round trip from Bagram air base to US soldiers in the eastern Afghanistan. There was one negative. The vehicle he drove was his late friend's. The blood had been wiped away but the bullet scars remained on the windscreen. Sakhi was frightened, but, he told a reporter, 'I haven't got much choice. I have a family to feed.'[31]

Burned-out trucks and beheaded bodies were left like grotesque milestones to remind travellers of Taliban power. One Western construction company lost five staff, while its guards had killed 34 people in a single month. Meanwhile, in another part of the forest, in the calm, reassuring, panelled lecture halls of the West, whether in London or Washington, military top brass, diplomats, academics, NGOs and politicians talked to selected audiences about the long-term future of Afghanistan. Their first message was that there could be no resolution of the security problem until the hungry poor had viable jobs and good governance. The second was that there could be no jobs or good governance until the security problem was resolved. The third, and most bleak, conclusion was that there could be no solution of any sort before 2010 and probably long beyond that. The alternative, they feared, was that Al-Qaeda would enjoy the same immunity in the very power base that enabled it to launch its war on the West, in the West, from 11 September 2001.

Since the responsibility for retraining Afghanistan's army as well as its police force increasingly depends on the private sector, it seems that the West is in the country for the long haul, but arguably for the wrong reasons. A long war of attrition is the most likely, perhaps the inevitable, outcome. Will military force levels ever be sufficient to hold down a rebellion driven by religious conviction, starvation, resentment and the international drug industry? Do PSCs, essentially profit-seeking corporations, have the resilience and do Western governments have the will required?

Perhaps they should keep in mind the considered view of Terence MacSwiney, Lord Mayor of Cork, as he starved himself to death for Irish freedom in 1920: 'It is not those who can inflict the most but those who can suffer the most, who will conquer.' The Afghans, unfortunately, are accustomed to suffering. Even Prime Minister Tony Blair had to admit, during a one-day visit to Afghanistan in November 2006, 'We are wiser now to the fact that this is a generation-long struggle.'[32] Some of his military advisers suggested that 20 years would not be unduly pessimistic. This was good news for the security companies, aware that the Iraqi gravy train was slowing down, even if it was not about to hit the buffers.

Or was it such good news after all? From mid-2007, tensions between the Kabul government of President Karzai and his western allies increased as the Afghani Interior Ministry cracked down on private security guards armed with unlicensed firearms. Western critics suspected an attempt to take over a multi-billion dollar business in which 60 companies employed 30,000 people, including 10,000 foreigners – many more than the regular British garrison. By arresting foreign security guards, some of them British, the Ministry paralysed many of the international military and civilian operations requiring their services. A crisis meeting between Karzai and the US Ambassador to Kabul, William Wood, attempted to break the deadlock even as there were signs that both British and American governments intended to involve more, not fewer, private security companies in the region, including the training of Pakistan's security forces on the border with Afghanistan.

It might have been a coincidence that the most experienced, multilingual British operator was assassinated in Kabul in August 2007. Richard Adamson, aged 66, a former SBS commando who joined a covert team to train mujahedeen fighting the Red Army in 1986, was working for Armor-Group when he was killed with a single shot. At the time, robbery seemed the most likely motive, since he was carrying $200,000 when he was murdered. As local interests targeted the security industry, however, this seemed less certain.

15

LICENSED TO SAVE:

The unarmed warriors

oldiers, wrote that great war poet and war veteran Siegfried Sassoon, are 'citizens of death's grey land'; but no longer, not exactly. In the twenty-first century, the art of war and the ways of peace pirouette ambiguously around one another in a shrinking world. It is difficult to distinguish between good news and bad, the good guys and the bad. In part, perhaps, this is because the idea of nationality – a safe haven, 'home', a repository where individual identity and national culture are safely locked away with the comforting, immutable private life of the teddy bear – is no longer what it was in our shrinking, overpopulated global village.

There are freelance soldiers who – largely unnoticed by media instinctively hostile to their profession – venture forth, idealistically, into this new-world community simply because they think it is the right thing to do. They risk and sometimes lose their lives clearing minefields, removing cluster bombs, verifying ceasefires, monitoring insecure peace agreements, containing conflict, protecting aid workers, destroying weapons, challenging corruption, evacuating (often covertly) victims of war and natural disaster, freeing hostages, negotiating ransoms downward and even running private intelligence services that also save lives or reputations.

Some freelances cheerfully admit that they are romantics in search of adventure rather than profit. As one practitioner put it, 'During the Middle Ages they got rid of the middle class by sending them off on Crusades. In Victorian times they went off to Empire. We are the sort of people who do not quite fit in at home so we go out and work for NGOs and take on those challenges there.'

As well as mines, they decommission guns. When a war finally burns itself out, in theory, the warriors hand over their weapons to be chopped up before their eyes, by a hydraulically powered guillotine mounted on the back of a truck. There is a reward for those who hand the guns over, a 'buy-back' scheme that is open to abuse, but a necessary, tangible sign that there is, and will be, a peace dividend.

An unlikely pioneer of this damage-limiting community was Colonel Colin Mitchell, late of the Argyll and Sutherland Highlanders, nicknamed 'Mad Mitch' thanks to his high-profile, bagpipe offensive in the Crater district of Aden city in 1967. The Establishment did not care for his style. In January 1968, medals were awarded for a campaign that foreshadowed Northern Ireland: 10 DSOs, 10 MCs, eight MMs and, for Mitchell, a modest 'Mention in Despatches'. Soon afterwards, the Argylls were disbanded and Mitchell resigned his commission.

For a time, from 1970 to 1974, he was a Conservative MP. There were blanks in the story of his life. He was also, it was rumoured, a freelance warrior in Vietnam and Rhodesia, 'using counter-insurgency methods learnt during military service in Palestine, Cyprus, Kenya and Borneo'.[1] In 1983, in his late 50s, he spent months with the mujahedeen in Afghanistan, fighting the Russians. There he witnessed the appalling and indiscriminate damage done by Russian anti-personnel mines that turned his idealism towards protection of the innocent.

In 1986, 10 years before his death at the age of 70, he founded the HALO ('Hazardous Area Life-Support Organisation') Trust. His son, Angus, told the *Daily Mail*, 'In his final years he chose to do the dirtiest and most dangerous job left on earth: clearing up the lethal debris of war. It became an obsession with him and it is something the British can be proud of.'

HALO was the first international humanitarian mine-clearance NGO. Mitchell worked with his wife and a friend, Guy Willoughby, a former Guards officer (later to become director of the Trust) to create what he called 'a 20th-century version of a medieval order of chivalry'.[2] With some financial backing from the UK Overseas Development Administration and a few charities, Mitchell gave priority to Afghanistan. There was no func-tioning Afghan army to clear the mines. Soviet troops were unable or unwilling to do the job before they left.

Mitchell, whose own experience of mine clearance began when he was a 19-year-old officer in wartime Italy, when his soldiers used bayonets and sticks to lift or mark anti-tank mines, was a romantic with a practical streak. His organisation recruited 14 young British officers who had taken early retirement and were willing to serve without pay. Having been trained in the dangerous arts of clearance, they trained 1,200 Afghans. Mitchell taught his teams not to be daunted by the formidable number of mines littering the countryside, but to concentrate on 'the much smaller number, possibly around one million, located where they pose a real threat to civilians trying to rebuild their livelihoods'.[3]

HALO, saving lives, suffered casualties. During its first eight years, 43 of its staff were killed or maimed. The work continued. The need remained. Between 1988 and 1992 clinics set up by the International Committee of the Red Cross (ICRC) to serve wounded Afghans brought into Peshawar and Quetta, on the Pakistan side of the border, found that 44 per cent of the casualties – 1,530 people – were landmine victims. By early 2006, the organisation had cleared 5 million landmines and other unexploded ordnance. It was employing 6,000 deminers in former war zones from Africa to Asia by way of the Caucasus. As Mitchell's partner Willoughby points out, they cleared 'more mines, more hectares and using more equipment than any other demining agency'.

HALO became the point of entry for many deminers who later made it their profession elsewhere. Simon Conway, director of the London-based charity Landmine Action, was living on a Hebridean island in the 1990s, after a brief army career, novel-writing in New York and a failed marriage. A friend suggested he join HALO. 'It just fell into my plate,' he told the BBC interviewer Olivia O'Leary. Within a very short time he was in Cambodia, talking to a village headman who had survived seven mine explosions. The headman's prosthetic leg had been blown up two or three times and he had lost fingers. The village was in a political limbo because of mines. 'It didn't exist, officially. When we started clearing the mines they got voting rights and a teacher.'[4]

His friend Paul Heslop, later chief of staff at the UN Mine Action Office in Khartoum, was bored with a well-paid City job. Eight days after an interview with HALO, he was in Mozambique learning how to clear mines. 'I joined the army to do operational tours. [Instead] I did the equivalent of thirteen back-to-back operational tours with HALO in Mozambique, Angola, Cambodia, Afghanistan, Kosovo and Laos.'[5]

Like most deminers, he has had some close calls. In Mozambique he was trying to coax a tripwire out of the earth before the mine exploded. 'The wire started to twitch . . . I stood still. The wire continued to twitch. The village chief had come to see what I was doing. He had his leg in the wire and he was doing a jig to get it off his leg. I started to speak Portuguese very quickly, extracted him from the tripwire and sent him back. Then I returned to the site, cut the wire, disarmed the mine and took it back with me . . . Had he continued to jiggle the wire he would have pulled the pin on the fuse. The mine would have gone off and we would both have been pink mist.'

It is the sort of experience to generate nightmares in which the mine clearer is lost, disoriented in a minefield surrounded by tripwires, from which there is no way out.

As Mitchell and Willoughby created HALO, another former soldier working in Afghanistan – Rae McGrath – was working on agricultural and reconstruction projects in the same country. His epiphany was the moment when 'we found the remains of a young herder up in the hills. He was a kid and his foot had been blown off. He couldn't walk away, so he just stayed there and bled to death, and it probably took him a long time.'[6]

The herder was the victim of an anti-personnel mine, the sort dropped by armed forces in many areas of the world. These include the RAF (using a BL-755 cluster bomb) and the Israeli army, dispersing them with artillery. The anti-personnel mine is an area-denying weapon and it is indiscriminate. McGrath told the ICRC journal, 'It became obvious [in Afghanistan] we were dealing with a quite different weapon. These things had been used quite literally in their millions and had been randomly laid over huge areas.'

McGrath founded the Mines Advisory Group (MAG). What distinguished it from the HALO organisation was that it became an international campaigning unit to press for the abolition of anti-personnel weapons, as well as clearing mines in many parts of the world. It took part in the International Campaign to Ban Landmines. McGrath was made a co-Nobel Peace Prize Laureate and worked closely with Princess Diana on the proposed ban. Britain finally abandoned cluster bombs in March 2007.

One of his colleagues in MAG was Christopher Howes, aged 36, a Royal Engineer for seven years and a veteran of the Falklands war. Howes joined the team in November 1995 and, after working in northern Iraq, was sent to a remote area of northern Cambodia, to run a team of 20 local mine clearers. An official account of what happened to him says:

On the morning of 26th of March 1996, his team was preparing to start clearance work in a village in the province of Siem Reap . . . A group of thirty armed Khmer Rouge guerrillas emerged from the nearby forest. The [demining] team were surrounded and under threat of armed force, ordered to their vehicles. They were driven to the end of a dirt track where the vehicles were stripped of equipment. Mr Howes was then told by the Khmer Rouge leader to return to MAG for ransom money.

It was clear that his local workers would be kept as hostages until he obtained a ransom. But, says the official citation,

Through his interpreter, he refused, pledging to remain with his team and urging their release . . . Mr Howes continued his efforts to urge the guerrillas to release the other team members and eventually they agreed. However, the guerrillas kept Mr Howes and his interpreter hostage and two days later the interpreter was killed. Mr Howes was taken to the Khmer Rouge headquarters where he was held for several days before being shot dead on the orders of the Khmer Rouge General.[7]

The truth of his fate was not known for two years, until a mutiny within the Khmer Rouge precipitated witness statements to Scotland Yard officers sent to investigate the murders. During that time, a rumour mill regularly leaked false claims that Howes was alive. On his behalf, a ransom, reputed to be £44,000, was paid to an individual who convinced Howes's colleagues that a deal could be done. The money was apparently handed over in a carrier bag to an unknown man in Phnom Penh, who was never heard of again. The alleged murderers were later granted an effective amnesty by the Cambodian government.

Howes was awarded a posthumous Queen's Gallantry Medal. At a memorial service in his native Bristol, the Reverend John Wright said, 'He was an example of something now thought old-fashioned: a fine English soldier. He died doing good work in a part of the world gone bad.'[8]

MAG was to lose other good men, notably Ian Rimmell BEM, ambushed and assassinated near Mosul by a Saudi-based terrorist unit. He was travelling in a clearly marked mine-clearance vehicle when he was murdered on 24 September 2003.[9]

ArmorGroup is a British company that distinguished itself in mine clearance. It is the biggest 'mine action' commercial operator. By 2006 it had sent its teams to 22 war zones in 10 years, including Bosnia, Slovenia, Cyprus, Lebanon, Iraq and Sudan. One of its most extraordinary contracts was on Sakhalin Island, off the Siberian coast of Russia. As a preliminary to extracting oil, ArmorGroup extracted ordnance – some of it very old, souvenirs of antique wars – under the sea. The programme, worth little until oil was spotted, was worth $32 million to the US Defense Threat Reduction Agency.

A member of the firm explained, 'We do "mine action": 60 per cent of this is mine clearance, 30 per cent weapons reduction, when we take out ordnance. In Sakhalin – the most mined island on the planet – we are taking out Japanese naval shells dumped after the Sino-Japanese War of 1911, to allow underwater oil exploration.' Former Royal Navy divers work from a dive ship in seas that are frozen for five months out of twelve.

From the early nineties, ArmorGroup trained local mine-clearance trainers for the European Union in the Balkans. On the Cyprus Green Line (separating, since 1974, the front line between Greek and Turkish invaders) 'we had to send in the gardeners to clear a jungle of vegetation before we could get to the mines'.

There is no shortage of work. As mine clearers repeatedly point out, 'more mines are being laid today than the combined mine-clearance operations can lift'. In other words, there is a creeping, global pollution arising from this hardware, much of it spread by cluster bombs. 'In Iraq, in 2005, we lifted a million bits of unexploded ordnance.'

After the Israeli blitz against Lebanon in 2006, one of ArmorGroup's operators joined a clearance team near Tyre. The team came upon a local farmer in a state of hysteria, in a field 'surrounded by dead goats'. ArmorGroup's operator now faced the EOD (explosive ordnance disposal) officer's toughest moment: the decision to take 'the long walk', alone, into the danger zone. In this incident, the operator 'cleared a route into the field, believing he was dealing with cluster bombs, which are usually on the surface and easily spotted.' Then something exploded under him. He had stepped on a landmine and lost a leg. A company spokesman said, 'The farmer ran away, unhurt. Another British operator pulled him out, unconscious. A Lebanese medic working for the UN also lost a leg in the same incident. A UN enquiry determined that the damage was caused by Israeli Number 4 landmines in an unmarked minefield. We do not know who put them there, the Israeli army or Hizbollah.' What happened to ArmorGroup's mine clearer? 'He is back at work, doing the same job, with a prosthetic limb.'

The Israeli onslaught demonstrated that more mines and other explosive devices are being let loose upon the world than the number retrieved by deminers. At least 25 per cent of cluster bombs sprayed indiscriminately by artillery in Lebanon did not explode immediately. During the first 13 days after the ceasefire, cluster bombs – which can be mistaken for toys – killed eight people including two children. Yuhmur, five miles from the Israeli border, was 'highly contaminated, including all the houses and gardens', said Sean Sutton of MAG. In one week, his team had made safe more than 1,000 of these devices.

But a *Sunday Times* report by Hala Jaber was reassuring. Jaber, a brave, front-line journalist, noted, 'The US State Department opened an investigation last week [in August 2006] into whether Israel's use of American-made cluster bombs violated an agreement that they would not be used in civilian areas.'[10]

Freelance soldiers working in the devious world of K&R – kidnap and ransom negotiation – often achieve a happier outcome than their mine-clearing brethren, with less risk. Since 1985, when three former SAS officers invented a new profession on behalf of Lloyd's and KMS, hundreds of kidnap victims have been secretly returned to freedom, at a price, by free-lance soldiers. Their experience in sifting intelligence; second-guessing an opponent's motivation, strategy and state of mind; the use of psychological pressure to achieve dominance; deception planning; manipulation of the media; and – as at Prince's Gate in 1981 – ending a hostage siege by force if necessary; gave soldiers with Special Forces experience a unique preparation for the sinister world of kidnapping.

The Falklands war ended when psyops (psychological operations) combined with coercive diplomacy, sometimes called coercive bargaining, by the SAS commander Michael Rose persuaded the Argentine commander General Mario Menendes to give up the fight.[11] It saved lives. Other significant lessons were learned during the first 10 years of Control Risks' exploration of this field, years in which, by coincidence, kidnapping became a major criminal enterprise as a well as a high-profile political gambit among terrorist groups around the world. The first lesson was that the victim of a terrorist group, on balance, is at greater risk than the captive of a criminal enterprise. Though some terrorist groups, such as the Colombian FARC, occasionally demanded a financial reward, the benefit they usually wanted was political.

Often the demand was far beyond practical fulfilment, for terrorists are dreamers. A case in point was the spate of Moluccan hostage spectaculars in the Netherlands in the 1970s. The Moluccans – second-generation immigrants from Holland's former colony of Indonesia – wanted their own homeland. They had less chance of getting it than Native Americans in establishing their land rights in the USA. The best the Dutch authorities could offer was to publish the terrorists' 'just demands' as a surrogate achievement, as at Prince's Gate.

The political hostage was often seized as a symbol of power and wealth at a time when government was vulnerable, including election campaigns. The drama was – and is – played out in public, and often ends in blood-shed, as at the Munich Olympics in 1972 or the Beslan School massacre in southern Russia on 1 September 2004. The role of the freelance in opera-tions of that sort is variable, highly classified and almost certainly less frequent than his part in reducing the damage of a criminal kidnap.

A standard operational procedure has emerged for managing a crim-inal kidnap. The professional adviser limits his role to advice, if only to avoid allegations of complicity in the original crime and its outcome. He monitors the situation and advises the client. He will encourage the family or company affected to create its own crisis-management committee (the CMC), including someone with the nerve and acting ability to work as the negotiator with the kidnappers, usually by telephone.

The professional freelance is the producer in this drama, unseen by the players. One reason for this is that police forces do not always smile upon those who do deals with criminal gangs. Their priority is a high-profile success in court, or public surrender after a siege. Sometimes they get it tragically wrong, as did the FBI at Waco, Texas, in 1993. The K&R nego-tiator, like the victim's inner circle, aims to secure the victim's release but – exercising detachment as well as judgement in a deadly poker game – at a realistic price linked to the underworld's equivalent of the Stock Exchange, known as 'the going rate'. The going rate varies from place to place, from time to time.

The former SAS officer Mark Bles (a pseudonym) and his amanuensis Robert Low, in their entertaining book *The Kidnap Business*, describe five cases in which Bles and his colleagues pick over the fine detail of every message, the vocal nuance of every telephone call (including the dura-tion of each call), the timing and level of the demand to determine whether the kidnappers are stable, disciplined individuals or unstable, impulsive gangsters.[12] The kidnap gang – sometimes the number runs into double figures – are played along like exotic fish on a line, until their ransom demand is brought down to that Plimsoll line, the going rate.

There is also the second lesson: the small matter of determining that the hostage is still alive when the ransom is paid over. It is not unknown for kidnappers to keep the now-dead hostage in a deep freeze, bringing out the corpse from time to time to be photographed holding a copy of the latest copy of the local, latest newspaper. Negotiating some cases can last two years. Intelligence, as one veteran of the business reflected, is a waiting game.

There are also some cases that baffle even the experts. In 2006 the German government paid $5 million (£2.8 million) to obtain the release of Susanne Osthoff, an archaeologist, held by one of the many kidnap/ransom gangs in Iraq. The Germans, thorough as ever, have an official fund reserved for such events. However, *The Times* reported,

> Immediately after her release $2,000 of the ransom money was found concealed in her clothing. The popular mood against Frau Osthoff was so strong that she refused to return to Germany. Much to the irritation of the [Berlin] government, she has vowed to return to Iraq.[13]

The arts of diplomacy, coercive and otherwise, are practised on the outer reaches of risk by such people as Tony Hunter-Choat, a remarkable Englishman who began his military career when – bored with studies as an architect in Surrey – he crossed to Calais and joined the French Foreign Legion. He served five years with the Legion's First Parachute Regiment, fighting in Algeria, and almost lost a hand in combat. Later, after service as an SAS commanding officer and leader of the Sultan's Special Force in Oman, he became the Aga Khan's security chief. In 1998–9 he was one of a few hundred 'peace verifiers' working in Kosovo for the OSCE (Organisation for Security and Co-operation in Europe), an international NGO backed by 55 European governments.[14]

Following the savage Balkan wars of the early 1990s, an American-imposed peace in 1995 created an ambiguous, temporary peace in the former Yugoslavia. In the southern province of Kosovo, the home of a majority Muslim, Albanian population, Serbia's Christian security forces and their equally ruthless Albanian enemy, the Kosovo Liberation Army, had to be kept apart. On paper, this was achieved by an agreement at

Dayton, Ohio, between the then Yugoslav president, Slobodan Milosevic, and Washington's human bulldozer, Richard Holbrooke. The peace verifiers, most of them freelance soldiers, went into the field armed only with their knowledge of soldiering and strong nerves.

An official US government account describes how Hunter-Choat

> was responsible not only for verifying the agreed ceasefire between the Serbs and the Kosovar Albanians but, more importantly, for maintaining and prolonging that ceasefire. Working in an environment that was always dangerous, persuading both sides to exercise restraint in the face of continued provocation, required nerve and co-ordinating the human-itarian activities of the many NGOs in his area of responsibility, Brigadier Hunter-Choat also served as a security consultant and lecturer on lead-ership.[15]

After the invasion of Iraq, Washington made him security director for the Programs and Contracting Office (formerly the Program Management Office) running the $18.4 billion reconstruction operation in that country. He is identified by the writer Robert Young Pelton as the author of the rules of engagement for private security operators in Iraq.[16]

During the twilight period between the Dayton Accords and the ethnic cleansing of Kosovo in 1999 that led to NATO's (probably illegal) bombing of Yugoslavia, the *Washington Post* reported,

> Only the courageous efforts of the Kosovo Verification Mission have so far prevented a return to open warfare … The mission … is being loaded with the tasks that normally follow a political settlement: maintenance of the ceasefire, separation of the military forces, mediation of disputes, protection of human rights, collection of war crimes evidence, building up democratic institutions and holding municipal elections.
>
> The 'mission gallop' has occurred under conditions that would not be regarded as safe for a heavily armed military force many times the size of this unarmed civilian effort, which is projected eventually to reach 1,600 'verifiers'.[17]

Typical tasks included negotiating the release of five Serb civilians who were held in captivity near Vucitrn. Nine ethnic Albanians were released by the Yugoslav army on the same day. The verification teams were regularly shot at by roadside snipers. The OSCE *Newsletter* for January 1999 noted that its human-rights officers were investigating suspicious deaths, allegations of torture, abductions and the plight of refugees.[18]

The uneasy peace of Dayton started to crumble at the village of Racak, a village penetrated by KLA Albanian guerrillas, on 15 January 1999. During the preceding days, OSCE records, 'verifiers had reported what appeared to be "a wholesale violation" of the ceasefire by Yugoslav army and police forces'. According to other sources, OSCE verifiers tried to get into Racak but, in spite of their protests, they were kept out.

> Instead they watched the fighting from a nearby hill. They later gained access to the village, where they found one dead man and a number of injured people and received reports of other deaths and of people being taken away by the Yugoslav security forces. They were denied permission to interview the villages or explore the area around the village.

The following day the verifiers did get in, accompanied by foreign journalists and members of the EU's Kosovo Diplomatic Observer Mission. An OSCE report records:

> On arriving at Racak, KVM (Kosovo Verification Mission) personnel discovered thirty-six bodies (later confirmed as forty-five), twenty-three of which were lying in a ditch. According to a statement made by the American Head of Mission, Ambassador William Walker, who visited the site, 'Many of the victims were elderly men, many shot at extremely close range, most shot in the front, back and top of the head.'

Other reports suggested that five bodies had been removed by family members. A total of 45 dead were said to include a boy aged 12 and three women. Some bodies had been decapitated.

Walker told a news conference, 'I do not have the words to describe my personal revulsion, or that of all those who were with me, at the sight of what can only be described as an unspeakable atrocity . . . Although I am not a lawyer, from what I personally saw, I do not hesitate to describe the event as a massacre, a crime against humanity. Nor do I hesitate to accuse the government security forces of responsibility.'

Until then, the OSCE chairman-in-office, Knut Vollebaek, believed that thanks to the verification mission, 'a humanitarian catastrophe has been avoided.' The Racak massacre and the role of the verifiers first in trying to prevent the atrocity, then acting as witnesses of a war crime, were to take on major significance. The event led within two months, amid ethnic cleansing in Kosovo, to NATO's (possibly illegal) bombing of Yugoslavia and the loss of many more lives.

An equally challenging task (which proved to be a mission impossible) was set for the Iraq Survey Group, looking for Saddam Hussein's mythical collection of weapons of mass destruction from April to September 2003. One of their number was Brigadier John Deverell OBE, a former SAS commander, who later reported that the 1,500 hunters under military command 'included interpreters, scientists, specialist searchers (not least British soldiers equipped with ground-penetrating radar), ex-UN inspectors and intelligence specialists both military and civilian'.[19]

There were other, more proactive – and more enigmatic – groups exercising the techniques of silent, non-violent strategies, in some cases adopting the centuries-old philosophy of Sun Tzu, who advocated persuasion, combined with minimum force, to induce an opponent 'to submit of his own accord'. In August 2006 a Muslim cleric named Omar Bakri Mohammed was excluded from the UK on the grounds that his presence was 'not conducive to the public good'. He had been linked to a radical group in London called Al Muhajiroun. His status as an undesirable in Britain was confirmed when he was entrapped by his praise of the London 7/7 bombers on the Internet. The material was used by the BBC's *Newsnight* television documentary team. Bakri Mohammed, in practice, was the victim of a sting set up by a privately run intelligence organisation called Vigil.

Vigil was created by a City financier and a retired soldier as an act of patriotism to make Britain a safer place. It is not run for profit. It collaborates with official security agencies on both sides of the Atlantic. Its director Dominic Whiteman told the *Sunday Telegraph*, 'Vigil was formed because we realised that there were a lot of recently retired ex-military and intelligence personnel who had a stack of contacts around the world and who knew a lot about the war on terror . . . We felt some of this expertise was being under-utilised.'[20]

Around 70 per cent of its work uses the Internet to monitor the activities of suspect groups. It sends Arabists to fundamentalist rallies. Its financial experts follow the money trail linked to the groups coming under its eye. One of its operators was Glen Jenvey, aged 42, and a veteran counterintelligence operator who 'infiltrated the Tamil Tigers while working for the Sri Lankan High Commission in London in the 1990s'.[21]

This is potentially dangerous work, which is why the founders of Vigil remain anonymous. It is not the only potentially lethal pond in which some freelance soldiers go fishing. Another is commercial intelligence. Investigations known as 'due diligence', to establish the bona fides of wealthy, powerful people by others with whom they are dealing, have been a function of private security companies for more than 20 years. The assassination of Alexander Litvinenko, a former Russian agent settled in London in 2006, triggered an inquiry that – among many other leads – pointed to Litvinenko's work as a due-diligence investigator, notably a report he wrote about organised crime in Russia, as a reason for his death. Litvinenko was murdered with a radioactive poison, polonium-210.[22]

Vigil is not the only privatised intelligence service. The New York-based Diligence was founded in 2000 by Nick Day, a former MI5 agent who also served with the SBS, together with veterans of the CIA and Soviet military intelligence. In 2006 the latest recruit was Michael Howard, former leader of the Conservative Party. In New York it was led by Richard Burt, a former US ambassador to Germany. The company's advisory board included Lord Powell of Bayswater and Britain's former Prime Minister John Major.[23]

Kroll, a leading company in the due-diligence business, has employed a number of former British Special Forces officers. Kroll's managing director Ernie Brod identifies 1984 as the year when the due-diligence business took off. It did so as a result of an air-transport scam. As Brod tells it, a Los Angeles investment bank was hired to raise funds for a private airline called Flight Transportation. The bank arranged for one of its staff to test the air company's claims by flying to every destination served by its fleet. The airline attached just one condition to the test, as in the best fairy stories: the token passenger must always fly on a Tuesday.

Just 30 days after the funds were released, some of Flight Transportation's senior executives were arrested when the FBI learned that the firm's 'fleet' comprised just one aircraft, repainted to order to simulate many others.[24]

Most major security companies are now multidisciplinary. They run due-diligence enquiries using, for example, former investigative journalists as well as intelligence veterans alongside more traditional military operations. Control Risks is one example. But, alongside its forensic accountancy, it extracts VIPs from danger employing techniques that were developed by the British escape organisation MI9 during World War Two.

After Saddam Hussein's army invaded Kuwait in August 1990, the Iraqi dictator adopted a strategy of human shields, comprising foreigners including at least one English child. During the four-month stand-off that preceded the Allied counterattack in January 1991, Control Risks created an imaginative plan to extract its 200 clients held in Iraq. A company spokesman told me, 'Many of our clients were held at their sites all over Iraq. They might be at building sites, retail outlets or oil installations. Initially, we set up a team to identify the places where the clients were . . . We then decided this was not enough. No one could guess how far Saddam would go in playing with the lives of these people or whether the human shields would be in the firing line when [Western] retaliation came in. They might be killed [as collateral casualties] by the Allies.'

The company hit upon a plan that enabled their hostage clients to opt for an escape attempt, or not, 'based on information we would give them, about where it would be safest for them to escape'. First, Control Risks 'set up an agreement with the Iranians. Tehran would allow our groups to cross the mountains out of Iraq to be flown out of Tehran by private jet.' On the Iraqi side of the border, the company had help from an influential Iraqi/Kurdish group, the Patriotic Union of Kurdistan, whose secretary-general became the President of Iraq, Jalal Talabani.

As a company representative revealed, 'Talabani was one of our Middle East analysts. We co-ordinated with him to provide Kurdish guides to take the escape parties of our clients across the mountains into Iran . . . Then we sat down and wrote an individual escape plan for each client.'

Communication with the clients was established by radio, co-ordinated from a flat in Pimlico. The company employed an amateur radio 'ham' to broadcast on agreed frequencies. Through devious back channels into Iraq, the firm also 'provided short-wave radios to the clients via embassies and other means'. With the package came a set of codewords 'like old-fashioned World War Two plans'. The first of these codes included an assessment of the transition from peace to war – indicators of what soldiers know as 'TTW', or transition to war. Differing codes would inform the clients of the likely time left before the start of a massive Anglo-American blitzkrieg. 'We produced the assessment in September 1990. The indicators were right to within two weeks.'

This was more accurate than might have been expected. At that time I was back on active service in the Gulf and regularly received hints from the UK high command that the Allied offensive was imminent. Usually, the hints proved to be a false alarm.

A second set of codewords informed each CR client when and where their Kurdish guides would be if and when the threat level reached a critical point. It was assumed that the clients would have a hard journey out of Iraq during the winter of 1990 when mountain passes would be deep in snow.

In the autumn of 1990, the first party of clients tiptoed away from their places of work and homes at dead of night to a rendezvous near Sulaimanya in northern Iraq. 'Although they were potential human shields on their work sites and at key points near Kirkuk, they had some freedom of movement. They were allowed to drive within limits. We instructed them to drive along certain routes to reach their rendezvous. The operation was 100 per cent successful. A small party walked across the mountains to Tehran and the clients' own corporate jet took them out. They were all Europeans.'

On 6 December 1990, before other parties could follow, Saddam Hussein, under diplomatic pressure, agreed to release the foreign hostages. 'We were disappointed. So was one German in the second party, preparing to leave. He wanted to go ahead anyway and have his adventure.'

During the Second Lebanon War in 2006, the company set up an extraction group that employed guides to lead clients including journalists out of beleaguered Beirut to Damascus by road. Another group used a client's ship moored off the Lebanese coast. Control Risks was not the only team engaged in such rescues. In July 2006 two former Special Forces medics, Dave Connell and Ged Healey, crossed into Lebanon from Syria in the knowledge that during the preceding fortnight 411 people, including International Red Cross workers and UN observers, had been killed during the Israeli invasion. Their firm, Ex+med UK Ltd, specialises in providing medical care in remote and hostile areas.

According to one account, they picked up 60 clients from secret locations in Beirut, put them on buses and drove towards Syria. 'Intelligence from colleagues outside Lebanon warned them of Israeli attacks and prompted the convoy to take a longer, but safer, route back,' Connell said later: 'Our evacuees were mainly women and children who were family members of an international insurance company from Beirut. They had dual [British/Lebanese] nationality but many of their friends, work colleagues, maids and cleaners had no option but to stay and it was very difficult for them to say their goodbyes.'

Although many of the elderly evacuees were accustomed to the violence of war, children were visibly shaken to see their schools reduced to rubble and one young woman suffered an anxiety attack on the bus journey to Syria.

In spite of the dangers, Connell said, 'We will return there if required. That's what we are trained to do.' Or, as the mine clearer Paul Heslop remarked, 'I love the job. It is fantastic. It is very challenging.'[25]

PART IV

■

REGULATION

16

THE FOREIGN ENLISTMENT ACT 1870–PRESENT:

Lying in state at Westminster

The history of Britain's attempts to pass laws governing the activities of freelance soldiers, as might be expected in a culture that bred Francis Drake and Cecil Rhodes, is colourful, but not a model of jurisprudence. Like other venerable institutions, UK law in this matter is there because it is there, not because it ever served a useful purpose. It really belongs to the England of Gilbert and Sullivan as portrayed in *Iolanthe*:

> *The House of Peers, throughout the war,*
> *Did nothing in particular,*
> *And did it very well.*

This institution is called the Foreign Enlistment Act 1870 and it is still the rock upon which ministers still stand, even if they wobble sometimes.

Britain's first Foreign Enlistment Act, in 1819, was a statement of international neutrality based on self-interest rather than virtue. It provided that 'No British subject ... could engage in equipping ... any ship or vessel, with intent or in order that such ship or vessel shall be employed in the service of a belligerent.'[1]

During the Peninsular War of 1808–14, Spain was a vital ally in Britain's war against Napoleon. After Napoleon's defeat at Waterloo in 1815, Spain remained a key player in a process of collective European security constructed by the British to contain France. This policy collided with the uncontrolled idealism of British and Irish volunteers, who sailed in their thousands to join wars of liberation being waged by Spain's colonies in South America. In 1817 Spain's ambassador to London, the Duke of Carlos, persuaded the Prince Regent to impose a ban on such volunteers, who were threatened with loss of any rights they might have to rank or pension.

But even as the new law against foreign enlistment was passing through Parliament, an Irish Legion of 1,700 was being raised in Dublin to fight for Simon Bolivar. Some fought gallantly, others less so, and virtually all the volunteers – supplied with liquor as a condition of service – saw the world around them through an alcoholic haze. The sacking of the Colombian port of Riohacha in 1820 by drunken Irishmen obscured the idealism.

Britain had accepted another diplomatic hostage to fortune in Washington, as part of its war on France. In 1794, under pressure from London, the US Congress passed its own Foreign Enlistment Act to control American citizens assisting the French war effort. Some 70 years later, as the US was torn by the civil war of 1861–5, Southern (Confederate) forces found allies in England prepared to help build fast raiders that would ravage the merchant trade of the Unionist North. This clandestine programme (similar to the covert release of gunboats for Israel from Cherbourg on Christmas Eve, 1969) led to a near-breakdown in Anglo-American relations.

From the beginning of the Civil War, the North imposed a blockade on Confederate harbours, halting the export of cotton destined for the mills of Lancashire. In November 1861 a Union warship intercepted a British mail steamer in international waters off Cuba and detained two Confederate commissioners, bound for Britain and France. Britain demanded the release of the two and, as war threatened, Lincoln gave way, commenting, 'One war at a time is enough.' He was less ambitious than President Bush.

The Confederate answer to the blockade was to commission shipyards in Liverpool to build vessels that would attack the North's extensive merchant fleet on the high seas. A Liverpool solicitor, F. S. Hull, advised that the Foreign Enlistment Act was concerned with 'warships', that is, ships carrying guns. It would be lawful to sell an unarmed vessel to a belligerent regardless of its intended use. The guns could be added later, beyond British jurisdiction. The advice undermined Queen Victoria's Proclamation of Neutrality, limiting the help that belligerent ships could receive in UK ports.

As the first vessel was laid down, the Unionists hired a private detective to spy on the operation. Washington complained that the ship would have the attributes of a gunboat. The builder claimed that the vessel, a propeller-driven wooden cruiser named *Oreta*, was contracted to Italy. Lord Russell, the Foreign Secretary, was advised that the builders had broken no law. Hastily, the *Oreta* was prepared for 'sea trials', and on 22 March 1862, she slipped out of Liverpool. Off Nassau, she made rendezvous with the steamer *Bahama*, and the guns were loaded, along with her Confederate commander, John Maffet. The *Oreta*, renamed CSS *Florida*, a 'commerce raider', now went hunting.

Meanwhile, plans were laid for a second raider, built at Laird's shipyard, Birkenhead, under the codename '290'. Over two piratical years, as the CSS *Alabama* under Ralph Semmes, she sank hundreds of tons of merchant shipping between America and Europe until a Union man-o'-war, the USS *Kearsage* (Captain John A. Winslow), sank her after a two-hour battle off Cherbourg, watched by spectators ashore. Captain Semmes was rescued by a British yacht.

As other raiders, including a three-master named *Alexandra*, were built or planned in British yards, Richard Cobden MP, an advocate of free trade, told Parliament in April 1863, 'There is no other country [than Britain] in the world that has a quarter of the interest in upholding the system of international law, of which the Foreign Enlistment Act is the basis.'[2] Essentially, Cobden had identified an issue that would haunt the British arms industry into the twenty-first century: the merits of a quick profit from arms manufacture and human support set against the potential long-term damage of supping with the Devil.

Cobden reminded the Commons that Washington had repeatedly acted to protect its neutrality, often to British advantage, whether in dealing with a Canadian rebellion or the supply of hostile Russian ships during the Crimea War.

'Can we, I would ask, look for the maintenance of the law relative to foreign enlistment in America or elsewhere, unless we ourselves set he example of good faith? You have not only in America, but in France, a most stringent law on this subject . . . What both France and America will require is this: that you will, in the event of war, as far as lies in your power, prevent privateers from going out and preying upon their commerce.'

The Foreign Enlistment Act, he concluded, would become a dead letter if 'ships of war, sailing from your ports, built in England, manned from

England, armed and equipped from England, that were never intended for any destination, are roaming the seas without any fixed goal and marking their track by fire and devastation'.

The outcome, after the defeat of the Confederates in 1865, was the Foreign Enlistment Act of 1870. Like its predecessor, it was to become a political fig leaf to cover the embarrassing consequences of unauthorised military operations for which the London government might be blamed. As the 2002 Green Paper noted, the case for regulation was strengthened by the chance that 'activity in this area by individuals or companies could cut across Britain's foreign policy objectives'.[3] Furthermore, 'activity by British companies will also reflect on Britain's reputation' or put British lives at risk. *Plus ça change* ... Another 26 years passed before the 1870 Act was put to the test. It was a *cause célèbre* that marked the beginnings of a whole new war in Africa, prompted by some wild spirits known as 'Jameson's Stock Exchange Heroes'.

The shooting on the veldt was over. The dead were buried, some so carelessly that their boots protruded from the red soil of Africa. Now the ringleaders, products of the best English schools and some very good regiments, were on their way to Bow Street court up the Thames aboard the tug *Corruna*. The tug had collected them downriver, after their long sea voyage by way of the Suez Canal. It sailed past Traitors' Gate and the Tower, before depositing them at Temple Pier on a cold, damp February evening in 1896.

The prisoners still wore the light linen uniforms and broad-brimmed slouch hats in which they had surrendered to the Boers. That night they went immediately before the magistrate, accused of fitting out a warlike expedition, within Her Majesty's dominions, without permission, and invading the territory of the South African Republic. Specifically, they were in breach of the Foreign Enlistment Act 1870, upon which the British government still depended in 2007 to deter freelance military adventures.

As the Lord Chief Justice, the Irish Lord Russell of Killowen, would later explain, *if* the expedition was on the Queen's authority, 'it would be an act of war'. But, 'if done by unauthorised subjects of the Queen, it would be an illegal and filibustering raid', even if its ostensible purpose was humanitarian.[4] At the time, the Transvaal, an Afrikaans Eldorado heaving with gold and diamonds, was designated 'friendly'. Within a very few years, Britain would indeed be at war with the republic, but, for the moment, the attack of which its aristocratic leaders stood accused was as premature as it was politically inconvenient. Germany, led by Kaiser Wilhelm, publicly supported the Boers, a matter that enlarged a little local difficulty into a potential European war among what were called 'the Great Powers'.

As the 15 prisoners entered court, however, spectators cheered and clapped. As every red-blooded Englishman knew, these were heroes defeated by ill luck, lack of numbers and betrayal by the expatriate (largely English) Fifth Column in Johannesburg that should have risen up as the intruders' force of 478 men galloped across the border from British territory 180 miles away. Now, five months later, six men were on trial before a special tribunal headed by the Lord Chief Justice.

Their leader was Leander Starr Jameson, whose name would for ever be linked to 'the Raid'. Jameson was not a professional soldier. He was 'Dr Jim', a popular Scottish doctor, who had fallen in love with Africa and had come under the spell of Cecil Rhodes. The others were Colonel Raleigh Grey, Major Sir John Christopher Willoughby (Royal Horse Guard), Major Bobby White (Royal Welsh Fusiliers), Major the Honourable Henry White and Major the Honourable Charles Coventry.

Coventry, son of the Earl of Coventry, had been given up for dead after their last stand at Dornkoop. The reports were premature enough for him to read his own obituary, which might have explained the fixed smile on his face throughout the trial. The rank and file, by contrast, were a very mixed bunch. One witness said that they were 'all sorts of people including two sailors and some waiters'. Many – around 200 – belonged to the Bechuanaland Border Police, a white-skinned force now reorganised as the enforcement arm of Rhodes's Chartered Company of Rhodesia (the British South Africa Company) modelled on the East India Company. The rest were untried white Rhodesians.

Not for nothing were some of the officers and gentlemen involved in the invasion known as 'Stock Exchange Heroes'. The company had fattened itself on Bechuanaland, a protectorate the London government had privatised to oblige Rhodes. Not everyone switched his allegiance. Sergeant John Thomas White, invited to join the invasion of Transvaal, declined, explaining, 'I was a married man and could not afford to knock about in those irregular corps.'

Most of the refuseniks were formed up as 'F Troop', anyway, and obliged to mount and follow the rest some 275 metres (300 yards) behind the main column, into alien territory. They did not know their destination. Colonel Grey harangued them. 'What's the matter with you men? Why don't you come?' One had the temerity to ask, 'Are you going to fight for the Queen?' It was a good question. The blacks of Bechuanaland who had welcomed the protection of the great mother Victoria were less sure about Rhodes's corporation.

Grey replied, 'No. We are going to fight for the supremacy of the British flag in South Africa.' That, surprisingly, encouraged some of F Troop to change their minds. There were other blandishments. One witness recalled that Jameson had delivered a speech to the men, telling them they were going to Johannesburg 'to protect the [non-Boer] women and children'. The cover story, a moral pretext for an immoral action, depended on a letter that Jameson had inspired. It was signed by five leaders of Johannesburg's expatriate business community, claiming that

> a foreign corporation of Hollanders is . . . controlling our destinies . . . What we have to consider is, what will be the condition of things here in the event of conflict? Thousands of unarmed men, women and children of our race will be at the mercy of some well-armed Boers . . . We are justified in taking any steps to prevent the shedding of blood . . . We feel constrained to call upon you to come to our aid, should a disturbance arise here.

In practice, Rhodes and Jameson had seen to it that the dissidents had an armoury including 3,000 rifles. Detailed maps had been drawn up for the invasion in October, more than three months before the attack happened. Jameson's column, it was planned, would go to the rescue of the women and children on 28 December *after* trouble had been stirred up in Johannesburg, not before.

The public illusion of a spontaneous rescue, however, was dented by secret warlike preparations made by Jameson and Rhodes months before the 'women and children' letter. It was further, and fatally, damaged at the last moment when the expatriate dissidents (the 'Reform Committee') changed their minds about manning the barricades.

Like those attacking Horatius on the bridge Macaulay built over the Tiber, those behind cried 'Forward!' while those before cried 'Back!' They sent a message to Jameson, asking him to hold off. Undeterred, Jameson clumsily forged the date on the 'women and children' appeal he read to his troops (originally drafted on 20 November 1895, redated 20 December, then amended again – by Rhodes's agent Dr Rutherfoord Harris – to read

28 December) so as to retain its current credibility. Naturally, in the naïve jingoism of the time, Jameson's raiders cheered and sang 'God Save the Queen'. On 29 December, the vanguard – around 300 men formed up in troops A, B and C – crossed the border into the Transvaal Republic.

C Troop was equipped with eight Maxim machine guns, weapons that had acquired a legendary status since Jameson had used five of them, and 50 Company soldiers, to mow down 5,000 fierce Ndebele warriors in the Matabele war twelve months earlier. As Hilaire Belloc's mocking doggerel put it later:

> *Whatever happens, we have got*
> *The Maxim gun, and they have not.*

To reinforce this superiority in firepower, if not numbers, the invaders also brought along two artillery pieces: a 12-pounder and a 7-pounder. The order of march was scouts in front, an advance guard, a rearguard and flanking columns. Thirty miles inside Boer territory, the vanguard was joined by 120 men of the Bechuanaland Border Police column from Mafeking. Jameson let it be known that they had the support of the British government. He might have been telling part of the truth. The collusive role of the Colonial Secretary in London, Joseph Chamberlain, has been debated ever since. Jameson also believed that by riding light, using pre-position stocks of food and fresh horses, he could cover the 180 miles to Johannesburg in three days. His calculations were wrong in almost every respect.

The invaders marched for two days with one overnight stop. Soon, their column was being shadowed at a respectable distance by Boer scouts. The Boers knew the invasion was happening because Jameson's people had failed to cut all the telegraph wires between the border and Pretoria. The wire that was left intact was now a metaphorical tripwire, costing Jameson the element of surprise on which he depended. It was one of many examples of sloppy planning combined with born-to-rule arrogance. At intervals along the way, Jameson received couriers who brought clear messages from the British government, ordering him to retreat, and ambiguous messages from the Johannesburg expatriates, one of which was fatally misinterpreted as a promise of several hundred men who would ride out to fight alongside the invaders.

The first contact was low profile. Lieutenant Eloff, a young Boer, came

out to meet the invaders, alone, ordering his nine troopers to wait. Eloff
was the well-mannered grandson of the Transvaal president, Paul Kruger.
The raiders halted him at gunpoint, and took his rifle and horse. He got a
receipt for the horse and was told he would get mount and rifle back in
Johannesburg, or Pretoria, the Transvaal capital. Was this, as the prosecution would claim, a sign that Jameson, backed by Rhodes, was not on a
rescue mission but an invasion?

A few months later, Eloff was in the witness box at Bow Street, giving
evidence. He had asked to meet Jameson and, reluctantly, was given an
audience. 'What did you say to him?' asked counsel.

'I asked him if he had any right to arrest me, a Transvaal officer, when
no war had been declared.'

Jameson had not answered him directly, but had said, 'You shall have
your horse back again, but we will keep your arms.'

As the column moved on, Eloff – having been paroled – agreed to wait
for two hours from the time the rearguard left, at about 9 p.m. on
31 December, before returning to his own force. This was, so far, a gentle-
manly conflict. After dark, Boer commandos exchanged shots with the
intruders, wounding one of them. Jameson's column was riding south-
east, towards Krugersdorp, a dusty gold-rush town and the railhead of a
line that led to Johannesburg. It was also the birthplace of Transvaal resistance to British rule and would later become the site of a British
concentration camp for Boer women and children.

Alerted by Eloff, a 300-strong force of Boers rode through the night to
intercept the British force. It reached a mine named Queen's Battery, 20
miles from Krugersdorp, at about noon on 1 January. Jameson's men came
across the horizon three hours later. They halted, and sent an unarmed
messenger forward with a chilling message, to the effect that the town
would be shelled if any resistance were offered. It also suggested that
women and children be removed to a place of safety. The shelling began 30
minutes later and continued until dusk. Then, unwisely, the raiders
charged the Boer lines, only to run into heavy rifle fire. They retreated,
leaving several men and many horses as they went.

Jameson was still determined to 'go through' the Boer positions at
Krugersdorp. He was influenced by a message he received from the Johannesburg expats in unusual circumstances. The expatriates had sent two
cyclists, ostensibly on a fun ride, to meet him. The messages were
concealed inside the saddle stems of their machines. On their way through

Boer positions, they had convinced local commanders that they were harmless. So the Boers entrusted the two – Arthur Rowlandson, the son of London cleric, and Cellier, an Afrikaner – with messages for their own front-line commander, as well as security passes to help them on their way. Before delivering the Boer material, Rowlandson committed it to memory. Then he and Cellier used their local passes to cross the lines into the path of Jameson's column.

One of the messages for Jameson was from Rhodes's American friend, Dr Woolf, confirming that the best route to Johannesburg was through Krugersdorp. This was not good advice. A second, from Rhodes's brother Frank, said that the expatriates had done a deal with the Boers and the war was off. A third ambiguously implied that a party of some sort was riding out of Johannesburg to meet Jameson. This never happened but it added to Jameson's deluded belief that a mere show of strength would see him through even if there were now no *casus belli*.

As the invading column climbed an incline near Krugersdorp at 4 p.m. on New Year's Day, it faced a force of several hundred Boers, well dug into ambush positions from which accurate sniper fire was aimed at the British. Jameson's firepower was impotent seed upon the earth. (The Boers, unfairly, were soon to fight bigger battles than this from *trenches*, to the annoyance of their atavistic enemy.) As the artillery failed to do the trick, Sir John Willoughby led a futile charge in which he lost 60 men. The game was up. In darkness, Jameson's column probed this way and that, seeking a way out of the trap. Instead, it was nudged by the Boers into a natural cul-de-sac – and killing ground – at Doornkop. This time, the Boers also had artillery, as well as the high ground. It was a hopeless last stand in which the Maxims started to jam and the guns ran out of ammunition. After sustaining another 30 casualties, Jameson found a white flag: a grubby apron borrowed from a Hottentot matron. It might have been worse. After Custer's last stand, the survivors were slaughtered. At Doornkop, the Boers showed mercy, assisting the wounded, burying the dead.

The survivors were incarcerated for a time in Pretoria, then handed over to the British in Natal, for shipment home, to a prison where they encountered a better class of cockroach. Kruger's government was paid £1 million in compensation by the British South Africa Company, a reminder of the cost of such adventures if they went wrong, and an echo of the £3 million compensation the London government had to pay the

United States for British complicity in Confederate raids on American merchant ships in the 1860s.

As Jameson and his officers faced trial another hostage to fortune emerged, thanks to their amateurish approach to security. In court in London, Boer witnesses identified two battered boxes, one tin and yellow, the other black. The boxes were war booty containing a collection of secret documents belonging to Captain Bobby White, including coded material, lists of men on Jameson's payroll and, most compromising of all, a list of the Johannesburg expatriate Fifth Column. It was further evidence that an exercise in provocation, rapidly followed up by Jameson's 'rescue' mission, had been carefully planned for months beforehand. Much of this material was read aloud, in public. What was not disclosed was that the person responsible for the compromise was not Bobby White but his commanding officer, Willoughby, who had insisted on taking White's box of goodies along for reference, regardless of the risk of capture.

It seems possible that the authorities had wind of what was about to happen, for on 11 November the British authorities had formally proclaimed the Foreign Enlistment Act to be in force in the Cape and other South African territories under their control. As the trial progressed, it became clear that the only serious defence that eminent lawyers for Jameson and his men could advance was that the territories from which the raid was launched – notably parts of Bechuanaland ceded to the British South Africa Company – might be beyond the jurisdiction of the Act. It was a tenuous, lawyer's manoeuvre and a shoddy thing in the light of the death and destruction the raid had caused.

Jameson's counsel, Sir Edward Clarke, suggested, 'The [company] charter excluded the authority of the Crown within the limits of the Company's foreign jurisdiction act.' The Lord Chief Justice, Lord Russell of Killowen, turned a basilisk eye on him, asking, 'You don't suggest the company assumed sovereign rights?' Suddenly, the freedom of the veldt, where anything goes, was constrained and deflated within the legalistic nit-picking confines of a London court.

'Oh, no, my Lord!' he said apologetically. It was the moment his client's case was lost.

Russell reminded the jury of the military nature of the column, the Maxims, the artillery, and the fact that Jameson was the first to open fire on the Boers at Queen's Battery. If Jameson honestly thought he was out to save women and children, one of the most obvious means of deterring alleged 'desperadoes' in Johannesburg 'would have been to let it be known that such an expedition was approaching, but the wires were cut, not to prevent the desperadoes from getting any warning but to prevent the Boers from getting warning'. The notion that Jameson was protecting the women and children was 'absurd'.

'Was it an expedition prepared to proceed against the dominions of a friendly state, that state being called the South African Republic? . . . Marching into the Transvaal was an act which violated the peace of that friendly state. Was it intended that, if the march was resisted, it would meet resistance by force? We know that it did so. Was it so intended? There were scouts with it, an advance guard and flanking parties . . . force was in contemplation and measures were taken to resist force by force . . . I direct you, in point of law, that an expedition is not less an expedition against the dominion of a friendly state if it was not aimed at over-throwing the government, or if it was prompted by philanthropic and humane motives.'

The jury was still reluctant to convict. It had answered Russell's questions about jurisdiction and concluded that the Foreign Enlistment Act did apply in this case. That, said Russell, amounted to a finding of guilty. But, said the jury foreman, 'There is one objection to that, my Lord. We have answered your words categorically, but we do not agree absolutely upon a verdict of guilty or not guilty.' Russell had been summing up for six hours. He replied, 'This is a most unhappy state of things, gentlemen . . . These questions, answered as they are, amount to a verdict of guilty . . . The answers are capable of no other construction. Therefore, I direct you . . . to return in accordance with these findings a verdict against the defendants.' The jury whispered briefly, then cracked, and convicted.

Jameson was sentenced to 15 months' imprisonment without hard labour, Willoughby to 10 months, Major White and Colonel White, Colonel Grey and Major Coventry to five months apiece. They were not obliged to clean their cells or wear prison uniform and could receive visitors, who were allowed to bring comforts with them. As they left the court to begin their sentences, the crowd called, 'God bless you, Dr Jim!' Coventry was promptly pardoned by the Home Office. Jameson, too, was pardoned after less than five months in Holloway Prison and returned to South Africa. Only one consequence cut through this featherbedding, to lash aristocratic hides. All the officers lost their commissions. Willoughby sent a whingeing letter to his regimental colonel-in-chief, claiming that

Jameson had misled him into believing that the raid was sanctioned by the British government. It did not wash.

The drama did not end there. There was a prolonged public, parliamentary inquiry in which Joseph Chamberlain, the Colonial Secretary and suspected puppet master behind the operation, was one of the inquisitors as well as a witness; a prominent member of an inquiry that was, in part, inquiring into himself. Evidence the MPs did not see included a collection of 'missing telegrams' as well as material censored by the committee chairman in a way that was not unhelpful to Chamberlain. The missing and censored material amounted to a narrative of negotiations prior to the raid between Chamberlain and Rhodes's representatives in London. Some of the cables were ambiguous, others compromising to a deadly degree. The inquiry found no one guilty of anything. No one was to blame.

One critic of the inquiry, to international applause, described the outcome as 'The Lying in State at Westminster'.[5] But then, as Chamberlain himself put it, there is, sometimes, 'a very thin partition wall between legitimate and illegitimate actions'. It is an excellent mantra for all deniable operations employing freelance soldiers, particularly those that do not quite achieve the right result. In this case, the not-so-eventual outcome, four years later, was what all convinced imperialists, including Chamberlain and Rhodes, would have wanted: British occupation of the whole of South Africa.

The Foreign Enlistment Act was never used again as an instrument of justice, but it was employed politically in 1937 in an attempt to deter or intimidate British volunteers joining the International Brigades in Spain. The volunteers fought for a legitimate government against Franco's rebellious military junta. They were the first to confront the emerging fascism of Hitler's Germany as well as Franco's Spain. Many were dedicated communists, and therefore perceived as a threat to Britain's internal security. The attempt to bluff them into turning back, using the 1870 Act, became a political farce. It proved only that national legislation in this international arena is unenforceable.

As Professor Simon Mackenzie has pointed out, to use the Foreign Enlistment Act in 1937 would have required some form of recognition of Franco's insurgency – an acknowledgement that it enjoyed equal legitimacy with the elected Republican government – since the statute required that a neutral Britain be at peace with both belligerents.[6] In September 1936, as volunteers controlled by the British Communist Party began a movement that would grow into a force of 2,000 commenced their stealthy journey to Dover, Paris and the Pyrenees, the Foreign Office put its money on a formula that 'once we issued a warning that the Foreign Enlistment Act would be applied . . . we should be faced at the worst only with a small trickle of British subjects going abroad for enlistment'.

The Communist Party of Great Britain was unimpressed. Volunteers arriving at the party's headquarters at King Street, Covent Garden, were screened by party officials and, once accepted, provided with away-weekend tickets for the boat train to Paris, for which no passport was required. The government countered with a press release in January 1937 asserting that anyone recruiting or volunteering for the Spanish war would be in breach of the FEA, and liable to imprisonment for up to two years, or to a fine and imprisonment. The Foreign Secretary, Anthony Eden (later as Prime Minister to preside over the Suez disaster), justified the policy by alleging that many of the volunteers were juveniles or drunk when they agreed to go to war. He also fell back upon that well-tried formula, the Attorney General's (undisclosed) legal advice. The *Daily Mail*, predictably, suggested that unemployed workers were duped into joining the Spanish conflict.

Dogged and loyal as ever, the Special Branch posted officers to Victoria Station, the Channel ports and on the ferries themselves to intercept the volunteers. This was not difficult. As Professor Mackenzie's paper 'The Foreign Enlistment Act and the Spanish Civil War, 1936–1939' points out, they were easy to spot 'since they tended to bunch together (despite warnings . . . not to do so), carried little in the way of luggage and were for the most part dressed too poorly to appear credible as Paris-bound tourists'. Many were unemployed miners.

The volunteers blandly denied they were going to war. They were off to an exhibition in Paris, or away for a jolly weekend. Some were released with the Branch's compliments: 'Go on, you bastard, and I hope you won't come back.' Some were arrested on arrival in France and returned to England, only to make another, more successful, attempt.

There were no arrests under the Act. The problem then, and now, was that a viable case could not be brought without corroborative evidence, short of a plea of guilty by one of the participants. Mackenzie's conclusion is that the use of the Act was both a failure and a success. It did not accomplish its legal purpose. It was not even a deterrent. But it 'demonstrated to the world that Britain – in theory if not in fact – was living up to its announced goal of non-intervention'.

The role of the FEA was again under scrutiny after the massacre of British mercenaries by some of their psychopathic fellow countrymen in Angola in 1976. Harold Wilson, then Prime Minister, promised MPs an inquiry headed by Lord Diplock. The terms of reference would include 'possible amendment of the Foreign Enlistment Act'.

Margaret Thatcher, then Leader of the Opposition, asked the Prime Minister to make it clear that the inquiry would be about 'the general question of the suitability of the Foreign Enlistment Act 1870 in the circumstances of today'. She argued, 'As British citizens have within present recollection fought for many different causes overseas' – MPs interjected, 'Not for money' – 'any Act of this kind can be operated not according to whether the Government approve or disapprove of the cause but only according to objective tests laid down by law about British interests. Will the Right Hon. Gentleman confirm that the Foreign Enlistment Act makes no distinction between whether those who fight overseas are paid or are volunteers?'[7]

She could not have anticipated that, almost 30 years later, her son Sir Mark Thatcher would plead guilty to an offence against the 1998 South African Regulation of Foreign Military Assistance Act as a result of his involvement in an alleged coup plot in Equatorial Guinea. His help in providing helicopters, he asserted, was to provide an air ambulance rather than a gunship.

The Diplock team did not endorse Margaret Thatcher's implied distinction between 'good' and 'bad' freelance fighters. 'Mercenaries', they reported, 'can only be defined by reference to what they do, and not by reference to why they do it.' Diplock's definition, for the purposes of UK legislation, was, 'Any person who serves voluntarily and for pay in some armed force other than that of Her Majesty in the right of the United Kingdom.'[8]

As for the Foreign Enlistment Act, changes over the preceding century

have resulted in there being important omissions from the Act and a number of obscurities in the statutory language affecting most of the ingredients of the offences. These make the application of the Act to UK citizens who participate in a particular internal conflict in a foreign state a matter of grave legal doubt and the commission of an offence almost incapable of satisfactory proof.[9]

It is all the more surprising, therefore, that 30 years later, Hazel Blears, a Minister of State at the Home Office in Tony Blair's government, was able to confirm that 'under Section 4 of the Foreign Enlistment Act 1870 it is an offence for a British subject to enlist in the service of a foreign state which is at war with another foreign state which is a friendly state. The maximum penalty is two years' imprisonment.'[10]

The hole in this argument had long been identified by Diplock: 'The offence of leaving the United Kingdom in connection with illegal enlistment is restricted to leaving by ship – a means of travel unlikely to be used by a mercenary in modern times. The offence does not cover anyone leaving the country by air' – perhaps because that was possible, in 1870, only by balloon. There was another difficulty: the crime was one of illegal *enlistment* in an armed force and not *service* in it.

As for Angola, 1976,

> until the status in international law of each of the parties to the struggle was clear, the United Kingdom government had no power in law to stop the enlistment or recruitment of mercenaries for service on behalf of any of those parties ... We think the provisions of the Foreign Enlistment Act, 1870, which relate to illegal enlistment have become thoroughly unsatisfactory in modern conditions. They should be repealed and a fresh start made.

But how and where? Would new legislation jeopardise deniable freelances acting covertly on behalf of the British government, as in Yemen, 1962–8? Diplock was not optimistic about finding a legal solution to the task of regulating mercenaries. As he put it,

> No device of draftsmanship can overcome the practical difficulty of obtaining the evidence to justify a conviction in a criminal court for an offence which consists of acts which the accused is alleged to have done abroad. We do not think that it would be acceptable to seek to overcome the prosecution's difficulties of proof by transferring to the accused the burden of proving his innocence of the offence once the prosecution had been able to establish that he had been seen in company with persons bearing arms in an area where armed conflict between opposing forces was prevalent.

Under such a reversed onus of proof it would be the accused instead of the prosecution who would be faced with the practical difficulties of obtaining evidence from abroad. So radical a departure from a basic rule of criminal justice in this country could, we think, never be acceptable.

Those words, written in August 1976, came from a more liberal perception of basic liberties than existed in Tony Blair's Britain of the twenty-first century, one in which embarrassments as vague as 'glorifying terrorism' were to be criminalised. But since Hazel Blears, the minister responsible for control of terrorism, should still pin some faith on the rusty Foreign Enlistment Act, it was clear that the practicalities of defining mercenary work as a crime continued to defy even the most repressive imagination.

17

LEGAL REMEDIES 1976–PRESENT:

The utopian in pursuit of the uncontrollable

n January 2005 the campaigner George Monbiot, in his *Guardian* column, asked,

> What is the legal difference between hiring a helicopter for use in a coup against a west African government and sending supplies to the Chechen rebels? If there isn't one, why isn't Mark Thatcher in Belmarsh? Conversely, why aren't the 'foreign terrorist suspects' in Belmarsh prison free and, like Mark Thatcher, at large in London?[1]

His answer was that, thanks to UK government policy, 'You cease to be a mercenary by sending £20 to Companies House.' What he had in mind was the Spicer Effect, the rebranding of freelance soldiers as 'private military companies'. Monbiot himself had no solution to the dilemma of how to regulate the trade. As he conceded, 'If the government banned British subjects and residents from engaging in any foreign conflict, no one would be able to assist the armed opposition to the Burmese junta, or enlist to fight in another Spanish civil war.' The UK could also become a launch pad for operations to overthrow democratic governments. So, 'there needs to be some means of choosing'.

He did not like the way the Foreign and Commonwealth Office was moving, flagged up in a discussion document (a Green Paper) in February 2002, which he summarised as 'preparing to license only operations that make money and assist Western strategic interests'.

For its part, the Green Paper (*Private Military Companies: Options for Regulation*), signed off by the Foreign Secretary Jack Straw, observed,

> There is nothing wrong with governments employing private sector agents abroad in support of their interests; but where such links are transparent they are less likely to give rise to misrepresentation. Some might consider this an argument for a licensing or other regulatory system.[2]

Monbiot did not need to worry. Parliament's efforts to catch the slippery eel of freelance military activity, and tame it, went nowhere. Five years and three Home Secretaries later, a dedicated FCO team was still waiting for the Blair Cabinet to make up its mind. This quadrille of planning, analysis and debate, followed by silence, replicated the history of the UN's doomed efforts to accomplish the same task. Meanwhile, the trade in privatised military skills was booming as never before.

British torpor in this matter was pricked from time to time by scandalous events overseas and scandalised headlines at home. The macabre adventure that was Angola, 1976, prompted Lord Diplock's call for root-and-branch legal reform. The delivery by Sandline of 35 tons of weapons to Sierra Leone, apparently in breach of UN sanctions, in 1998, prompted the first Commons Foreign Affairs Committee inquiry and report in February 1999.[3] The committee suggested that the FCO produce a Green Paper within months.

A powerful interdepartmental team – the Whitehall PMC Group – met on 16 November 1999. It is clear from a record of this gathering – attended by 15 civil servants, including representatives of the Secret Intelligence Service, MI5 and the Defence Ministry's Intelligence Secretariat, as well as the Foreign Office – that different policies were already being pursued by different ministries.[4] The MoD, for example, owned up to running its own database on freelance soldiers operating in Africa. This was probably a hangover from the Angola operation in 1976.

Much of the meeting was concerned with keeping track of private military companies, and their employees, without tripping over the Data Protection Act or European human rights legislation. The problem of gathering information about the PMCs was apparently complicated by cut-throat competition among them as a result of which companies might spread damaging rumours about one another. The group was also advised that some PMCs were off-limits to Whitehall's surveillance, particularly if they were registered in the territories of friendly intelligence states such as the US. The near-impossibility of legislation was clear from the outset, yet the Green Paper, when it appeared in February 2002, reflected none of these concerns. A second Commons Foreign Affairs Committee investigated the issue yet again and in July, it sent back to the FCO 27 recommendations for legal reform.[5]

The essential thrust of the new Commons report was that private military companies are a fact of life and that they can perform a useful if limited role subject to stringent control through licensing and monitoring. If the proposed controls were too expensive and complicated, the MPs suggested, then a new, third force comprising British military veterans under public authority should enter the market.

In October 2002 the FCO published a seven-page reply to the 27 recommendations by MPs to control the industry.[6] The replies were a less-than-complete endorsement of the proposals. The government 'agreed' with just five. It 'agreed, but . . .' in reply to one. It 'noted' the contents of two. It 'will consider' nine while 'considers there is a case for' one other. It found that two proposed limits on PMC activity were covered by existing legislation. It gave vague – 'if', 'but', 'would', 'could', 'should' – replies to seven more.

The five proposals the government accepted unconditionally were as follows.

1. To identify contracts between government departments and private military/security companies. (The MPs said that the lack of centrally held information in this area was 'unacceptable'.) However, the Ministry of Defence was left out of the exercise.

2. The UN Convention on mercenaries 'was unlikely to provide a workable basis for regulation'. That, said the government, was unlikely to change, so it would 'continue to develop UK policy'.

3. There would be value in promoting a common European Union approach to PMCs. It promised to consult the EU and report back to the Foreign Affairs Committee.

4. 'PMCs have the potential in some circumstances to play a positive role.' No surprises there.

5. 'An outright ban on all military activity abroad by private military companies would be counterproductive.'

As for the Commons proposal that PMCs should be 'expressly prohibited from direct participation in armed combat operations, and that firearms should only be carried – and if necessary, used – by company employees for purposes of training or self-defence', the government promised only to 'consider this carefully'. It then quoted the MPs' own report, that 'PMCs may have a legitimate role in helping weak governments to secure revenue streams, for example by protecting border points and highways'. This, the government added, 'may require the use of firearms'.

What happened next? To the embarrassment of Whitehall, the minutes of its PMC Group meeting of 16 November 1999 were published verbatim on an American website on 21 November 2002 along with more damaging material. The government, meanwhile, proposed to seek further information about regulating PMCs from the UN, the EU, the United States and other governments 'as part of its further consideration of the issues, before taking any view on the way forward'.

By 2006 another year had passed since Monbiot's confident prediction that the Green Paper was expected 'to propose a licensing scheme for mercenaries within months'. Extensive consultations by FCO officials among the moguls of the security industry, academics who had written learned papers, diplomats and soldiers had provided the basis for the next stage in regulation, a White Paper. So, having done its staff work, the FCO's Conflict Issues Group passed its favoured options on to the Foreign Secretary Jack Straw (and via him to the Cabinet), and waited. Nothing happened.

In 2007, still fiddling while Baghdad burned, the British government was pondering the means by which an entrepreneur-friendly regime could appear at a stroke both to regulate and recognise this massive new industry. The government's political instinct, perceived from outside Whitehall, seemed to point to a search for some sort of Pontius Pilate Enabling Act. According to one insider, the Foreign and Commonwealth Office was 'still pressing on with the idea of co-regulation, whereby the British Association of Private Security Companies do the work. It would put together a code of conduct and be recognised as the body to control the industry. It would be responsible for company approvals. The government would extend its arms control legislation to cover the approval of contracts. Or again, the government could simply do nothing while they wait to see how things develop.'

Whitehall was also considering a mechanism for procrastination that would defy a *Yes, Minister* script. The Department for Trade and Industry (famous for identifying what might be a good day for burying bad news, such as 9/11) would be responsible for regulation in some form while the Foreign and Commonwealth Office (the lead agency for the preceding seven years) would foot the bill for the DTI's activities. A further level of bureaucracy was to be the Better Regulation Executive, an entity within the Cabinet Office, which would hammer out the final policy to be presented to the government of the day, and Parliament. This cut no ice in Baghdad or Kabul, where, according to some insiders, governments were at last making plans to license military companies but only if (in Iraq) each firm was prepared to pay up to £2 million for the right to operate in the country.

Another layer of regulation was emerging in Britain, where anyone wishing to work in close protection overseas found it increasingly necessary to obtain a domestic qualification provided by the Security Industry Association (SIA) for men and women working in the security industry at home. The SIA resulted from an Act of Parliament in 2001. Meanwhile, the British Association of Private Security Companies (BAPSC) – that exclusive club for contractors offering armed defensive services outside the UK – was preparing courses in international humanitarian law for its members in partnership with the British Red Cross. As a result of these private initiatives, the British industry was building its own framework of regulation without the government's help. None of those initiatives, however, could prevent an individual from working offshore, outside everyone's jurisdiction.

If there was too little action in London, there was too much legislation coming out of South Africa. The government of President Thabo Mbeki approved a grandiose law to halt mercenary activity claiming international jurisdiction over its citizens and, possibly others, in conflict zones. Yet it would permit South Africans to support 'national liberation; self-determination; independence against colonialism, or resistance against occupation, aggression or domination by foreign nationals or foreign forces'.[7]

Only a handful of prosecutions were successful as thousands of South Africans flouted the new law around the world. Others used a humanitarian exception to the law to claim, untruthfully, to be engaged in mine clearance. Possibly it was this situation, in Kosovo, that led the Secret Intelligence Service to suspect that some deminers were implicated in covert intelligence activities. The South African cases that did produce a result succeeded only because the accused, one of whom was Sir Mark Thatcher, agreed to plea bargains in return for token fines. As a result, the law – the Regulation of Foreign Military Assistance Act – was vividly counterproductive and a further reason for caution in London.

There were other quixotic attempts to contain the burgeoning international security industry. The Brookings scholar P. W. Singer thought he detected a solution, thanks to five words added to the 2007 US Defense Budget Bill making freelance soldiers subject to military law, along with embedded war reporters.[8] To be subject to court-martial justice, however, the freelance would have to be 'serving with or accompanying an armed force in the field'. The semantics had yet to be tested. What, for example, is the meaning of 'serving with'?

Several years earlier, in 2000, Congress passed the Military Extraterritorial Jurisdiction Act (MEJA) because they acknowledged the virtual impossibility of putting freelances before courts martial. MEJA, however, covers only civilians working for or connected – legally connected – to the Pentagon. Most freelance soldiers are employed by other entities. Iraq is not only a sandpit. It is also a pit of legal ambiguities.

France, whose own Foreign Legion is regarded by its critics as a mercenary force (some recruits serve under pseudonyms), passed a new law in April 2003 making it a crime to serve as a soldier anywhere in the world 'in exchange for personal advantage or compensation, without being a citizen of a state involved in the armed conflict, a member of [local] armed forces or envoy of a state other than those involved in the conflict'.[9] Four months later, 11 people were arrested in Paris for an alleged plot to run a coup in Ivory Coast.

Coincidentally, or perhaps not, a naturalised French-born South African, François Roger Rouget, was the first person to be convicted under South African law a few months earlier, for trying to recruit mercenaries to fight in Ivory Coast's civil war, a conflict in which South Africans and British freelances are reported to have fought on both sides. Rouget, a former French Army officer and professional hunter, received a five-year suspended sentence.[10]

The world was not short of gestures similar to South Africa's, with even less impact. In November 2006 the Swiss Foreign Ministry and the International Red Cross set up a conference at Montreux attended by delegates from 16 countries and a handful of experts from the security industry.[11] The objective was to construct a code of conduct to which three entities could contribute: the companies, their governments and 'the states on whose territory they operate'.

Flying in the teeth of the history of deniable operators who run black operations on behalf of democratic governments, the conference communiqué said that participants shared the view 'that states have to respect international law when using private military and security companies and cannot circumvent their international legal obligations by resorting to their services'.

Back in London, mired in the renewed Iraq war, the British government groped its way towards an obvious conclusion, that this was not the best political moment to give official, public blessing to a scheme providing freelance operators with the sort of privatised licence to kill represented by Bremer's Order 17 in Iraq.[12] Throughout the period of allied occupation, the legal status of freelance soldiers there remained a model of ambiguity. In his attempts to legitimise the activities of the new private army Bremer, the American governor of the country from May 2003 to 30 June 2004, had to fill a legal void: the absence of a clear legal and moral framework within which freelance military operators could now function.

Bremer and his team handled the first difficulty through a vetting system. No one, in theory at least, could become a hired gun in Iraq if he had a criminal record, though in practice at least one hardened assassin got through the net. Moral legitimacy took slightly longer to accomplish, since it is a blend of public morality and perceptions, politics and law. All these considerations were shaped by the inconvenient fact of the United Nations Organisation, a body created to ensure international order and morality as well as an increasing number of ad hoc war crimes tribunals.

Fortunately for Bremer and his Coalition Provisional Authority team, but bad luck for the amputees and other sorts of victim, the UN had failed spectacularly to halt genocide in Rwanda, massive slaughter in Sierra Leone and Bosnia and near genocide in Darfur. These events produced some grotesque results, such as amputee football in Sierra Leone, with rules devised by FIFA. The degradation of Rwanda and well-publicised corruption among many UN officials destroyed the credibility of blue helmets in much of Africa.

By contrast, freelance operations in Angola and Sierra Leone had demonstrated that swift action by mercenaries could end anarchy and save life even if, in the process, rules governing arms exports were broken and Kofi Annan, the UN Secretary General, provoked to wrath. No one needed to beat any drums to make the point that, in the world of the warlord, the UN writ did not run; and that mercenaries who fought fire with fire sometimes won.

What of the law? Bremer might have been expected to take a robust approach, in view of his assertion back in 1996, years before the Twin Towers attack:

> We must take significant new steps to fight terrorism . . . to show the American people that their government will not tolerate attacks on her citizens here [in the US] or abroad. For too long the terrorists have had the initiative . . . We must make the terrorists themselves worry that they are not safe from our reach, no matter where they are.[13]

No surprise, then, that Bremer and those working for him in the CPA appeared to act with the thoroughness of a Roman consul in promulgating, on 26/27 June 2004, an elaborate code known as Order 17, later embodied in the new Iraq constitution. The significance of Order 17 was that it licensed freelance soldiers from whatever nation they came, while imposing a code of conduct and rules of engagement on them, as if they were regular servicemen. It was a new benchmark for freelances, acknowledging that 'states are contributing personnel, equipment and other resources, both directly *and by contract*, to the Multinational Force and to the reconstruction effort' (my emphasis). It was, in effect, a licence to kill in some circumstances and to be paid well in the process. Furthermore, the limits imposed by Order 17 on paper often remained just that: words that were not implemented.

In its preamble, the 29-page order recognised the need for all private security companies to be registered with Iraqi ministries. The companies also had to be registered in their home states, identify all employees, details and serial numbers of weapons carried and to accept vetting to exclude criminals or private armies. The freelance soldier had to be older than 20, mentally and physically fit, 'be willing to respect the law and all human rights and freedoms of all citizens of the country [Iraq]'.

On paper, each company had to put up a refundable bond of at least $25,000 – depending on the number of employees in Iraq – before receiving an operating licence. The bond would be forfeit if the company failed to give regular information to the Iraqi Interior Ministry. This reassurance was undermined, according to some of the players, by the fact that none of the companies operating in Iraq did in fact put up a bond.

Companies were also required to have 'sufficient public liability insurance to cover possible claims against them'. As the civilian body count rose, this was to be a particularly significant condition in a society where prompt cash settlement for loss of an innocent life was the local custom.

An entire section of the Order was devoted to weapon control. Each company soldier should have been issued with a weapons card, licensing him to possess and use company firearms identified by the Ministry. Many dispensed with that formality also. In theory, no privately owned weapons could be used for company duties. This provision was also ignored by operators, who were able to buy almost any type of weapon on Iraq's black market.

One freelance soldier, asked how he test-fired his Kalashnikov, told me, 'I went onto the roof of our accommodation block in Baghdad after dark when a wedding celebration was happening nearby. The party, as usual, included shots fired into the air. I joined in.' In practice, he could and should have used a dedicated firing range.

The use of force was further controlled by Bremer's insistence that 'the primary role of PSCs is deterrence'. Reflecting the British Army's Yellow Card rules for the 30-year war in Northern Ireland, Order 17 – drafted by a British veteran – accepted that

> nothing in these rules limits your inherent right to take action necessary to defend yourself . . . You may use NECESSARY FORCE [*sic*] up to and including deadly force . . . in the following circumstances: (a) in self-defense[;] (b) in defense of persons as specified in your contract[;] (c) to prevent life-threatening offenses against civilians.

Force had to be 'graduated', escalating from shouted warnings, to physical restraint, to showing the weapon before shooting 'to remove the threat only where necessary'. When firing, the licensed gunman was expected 'to fire only aimed shots with due regard for the safety of innocent bystanders'. Civilians were to be treated with dignity and respect and, if detained, humanely. 'You may stop, detain, search and disarm civilian persons if required for your safety or if specified in your contract.'

All these rules were reinforced by a formal 'Private Security Company Code of Conduct for Operations in Iraq', emphasising the need for ethical behaviour. While the code carried with it the odour of a Boy Scout Promise, given the anarchic circumstances of a country plagued by suicide bombers disguised as non-combatants, it provided a model for PSCs and PMCs in future, if they wished to avoid the attention of the International Criminal Court.

The most utopian of these rules, reflecting the long-forgotten idealism of Colonel Mike Hoare in the Congo, half a century earlier, required a pledge 'to support to the best of ability the professionalism of Private Security Companies operating in Iraq; to contribute to better community relations; through work and deed to elevate the status of the Private Security Company profession'.

But the requirement to work within the laws of the host nation was undermined by a key revision to Order 17 specifying that foreigners, including international consultants, 'shall be subject to the exclusive jurisdiction of their Sending States. They shall be immune from any form of arrest or detention other than by persons acting on behalf of their Sending States.' So it remained, in practice, even after the emergence of a new Iraqi government in 2006, following an election safeguarded by PSC operators that opened up political and religious faultlines that had been part of the state ever since the British mandate of the 1920s. The election was followed by general mayhem and anarchy virtually indistinguishable, at times, from civil war.

Immunity from local law, while typical of visiting forces' agreements between, for example, postwar Germany and non-German NATO troops on German soil, also reflected the fear that American citizens could fall under non-American jurisdiction (such as that of the International Criminal Court) to be accused of war crimes, frivolously or not, while on operations overseas. But under Bremer's Rules, any freelance soldier who posed a risk of injury to himself or others could be detained temporarily by regular soldiers of the multinational force, before being handed over to his state of origin. In practice, in spite of an unknown number of civilian deaths in Iraq at the hands of freelance soldiers, there were no prosecutions.

Fundamentally, the status of the modern freelance soldier in Iraq was ambiguous. He was not within the jurisdiction of a military court in his own country or overseas, since he was a civilian. He was not answerable to

Iraqi law. The international legal definition of a mercenary did not fit the case. It was equally unclear how far his own country's jurisdiction would apply to his professional activities in Iraq. Finally, he would probably not qualify for prisoner-of-war status as laid down by the Geneva Conventions.

As the writer David Isenberg put it,

There is no clarity about the exact relationship between governments and PMCs. In their own interests, governments (and military institutions such as the Pentagon) often publicly distance themselves from PMCs ... If they stray over borders they are combatants under the Geneva Convention, as they bear arms and are clearly working on behalf of one side in a conflict; yet they could also be treated as non-combatants, as they do not wear recognizable uniforms nor are they (generally) under military command. Those working for their own government are clearly not mercenaries in the field.

Even with the new regulations from the CPA it is likely that questions will still remain over the combat status of PMC employees ... Currently [September 2004], the lack of a proper legal framework in Iraq gives PMCs more or less carte blanche to conduct their activities as they see fit.[14]

Contractors were also granted immunity from Iraqi legal process 'with respect to acts performed by them pursuant to the terms and conditions of a Contract'. Otherwise, companies were expected, under the Code of Conduct, to respect 'relevant Iraqi laws'.

Bremer's Law did nothing to satisfy the disquiet of a leading international human rights judge, Richard Goldstone, who said that the situation in Iraq in May 2004 (after the first Fallujah siege) was such that private firms should not do jobs that should be done by the army because of a lack of control and accountability. The situation in Iraq, he said, was 'crying out' for international regulation. 'People are going to have to look at the ultimate responsibility of where the buck stops when these private companies get involved in criminal activity,' he said in a BBC radio interview.[15] In 2007, that aspiration remained an aspiration, as the British government sat on its hands even though the leading 'Best-of-British' security companies, members of the British Association of Private Security Companies, themselves begged for a regulatory system within which they could run, as they saw it, legitimate business.

Britain's ambassadors, meanwhile, were obliged to live in a world of realpolitik. They needed protection. As a result, much of the £82 million they spent on security (the heaviest item on the FCO budget during the financial year 2004/5) went to private companies engaged to prevent the abduction or assassination of Our Man in Kabul, and elsewhere, a function once performed by SAS or Royal Military Police bodyguards. In Kabul, a formidable team from ArmorGroup, rumoured to number around 30, was in place to protect, among others, a diplomatic 'eradication' team headed by an MI6 officer, charged with the task of eliminating the poppy fields of Helmand, pursuing a policy that was a triumph of naïveté and political correctness over reality.

Since a Bill to regulate the international security industry had not appeared before Parliament, there was no debate about the dual role of the FCO, as customer *and* potential regulator. However, it goes some way towards explaining Monbiot's assertion that the 2002 (Jack Straw) Green Paper, read 'like a PR brochure for the dogs of war'. In practice, as we shall see, the discussion document carefully presented the dangers and difficulties of licensing, as well as the practical advantages.

The Green Paper did not demonise all freelance military activities. Indeed, in its reply to MPs it conceded that the Ministry of Defence held 'contracts with private companies where appropriate to support a wide variety of deployed commitments, including peacekeeping and humanitarian operations. These contracts are primarily for logistical support.'[16] It also agreed, as noted above, that PMCs 'have the potential in some circumstances to play a positive role' in unstable countries, where weak governments needed to protect border points and highways.

In a further effort at balance, not to the satisfaction of the industry, the shorthand used within the ministry was 'PMC/PSCs' – *private military* and *private security companies* – as a collective noun, overriding the wish by many of them to be described, more neutrally, as 'consultants' or certainly anything other than 'private *military* companies'.

After so much effort, the Foreign Office team could be forgiven for disappointment that its carefully crafted proposals were left lying on the Cabinet table for five years or more after 2002. The team's proposals increasingly creaked like a stable door closing on empty space. Its members might have consoled themselves with the thought that the government's impotence and immobility in regulating the private military sector was all of a piece with the British experience of the preceding couple of centuries.

Beyond British shores there were other brave and utopian efforts to address the plague of uncontrolled mercenaries. In 1977, sponsored by the International Red Cross, the First Additional Protocol to the Geneva Conventions produced a definition of 'mercenary' that the British government regards as unworkable since it depended upon proving motivation.[17] The Organisation of African Unity (OAU) Convention for the Elimination of Mercenarism in Africa,[18] according to the Foreign Office, 'defines mercenaries narrowly according to their purpose' (as does the Diplock Report). For that reason, says Whitehall, 'it would not have included employees of Executive Outcomes in Sierra Leone or Angola, nor anyone else working for a recognised government, probably including the so-called "White Legion" employed by President Mobutu (Zaïre) during his last days in power'.

The United Nations, while sometimes relying on freelance soldiers to protect its people in the field, has been particularly active in its attempts to invent definitions and concepts that would finally pin down the freelance warrior in a secure, containable legal framework. The organisation's involvement began in 1980, with the appointment of an ad hoc committee to draft an international convention on the subject. It was a utopian enterprise, aimed at legislation to cover the spawning culture of freelance military activity anywhere, any time, in any jurisdiction, provided enough states could be found to sign up to it. From 1988 to 2004, the champion of control was Enrique Bernales Ballesteros, a Peruvian diplomat. The concepts he imprinted on the UN Human Rights Commission included linkage between mercenary activity and self-determination and the criminalisation of the mercenary as such, regardless of what the freelance soldier actually did.

His final report argued, 'Mercenary activity must be considered a crime in and of itself and be internationally prosecutable.'[19] His new definition included private military companies and even governments employing deniable mercenaries in a third country, which was 'a covert crime'. The effect of that might have been to disable much of the world's intelligence-gathering based upon 'ground truth' rather than electronic eavesdropping.

Mr Ballesteros was also quick to criticise the British government for its measured approach to the issue, following the false dawn of Robin Cook's 'ethical foreign policy' in 1997. Ballesteros suggested in April 2001 that the failure of the Foreign Office to publish its consultation Green Paper in advance of a general election due in June, was 'a serious and deplorable backward step by the British government . . . It sends a very negative signal to other European countries with interests in Africa who have been waiting for the British to introduce regulations before making any similar move themselves.'

When the FCO did finally produce the Green Paper ten months later, it rebutted some of Ballesteros's comments. His view that the state itself did not have the right to employ mercenaries, in any situation, was dismissed as 'an extreme point of view which ignored the UN's own Charter 'including the right of self-defence in Article 51'. As the FCO put it,

> Behind the sometimes inchoate concerns expressed by Mr Ballesteros and others lies the perception that the monopoly of violence remains essential to our notion of a state . . . The fact that a force is private or foreign does not prevent it from being under the control of the state and although such arrangements may not be ideal they may be far less damaging to sovereignty than an unchecked rebel movement.[20]

The Green Paper also challenged Ballesteros's view that in Sierra Leone, where order was restored following the intervention of Executive Outcomes, 'the presence of the private company . . . created an illusion of governability, but left untouched some substantive problems which could never be solved by a service company'. As the Foreign Office noted,

> EO was hired for a military task: it is not a criticism of a military body that it has failed to address underlying socio-economic problems. The function of military and other security organisations is to create an environment in which it becomes possible to tackle those problems.

The UNHCR adopted its ambitious International Convention against the Recruitment, Use, Financing and Training of Mercenaries in 1989.[21] This did not see the world through Tim Spicer's eyes. However, for the convention to have reality, it needed clear support from member states to sign up to it and then ratify its adoption into domestic law. But progress was slow. Over the next four years just 22 countries with a combined GDP that was probably less than that of the Colombian mafia signed up, enabling the convention to become effective. The signatories included such shrines of democracy as Uzbekistan, notorious for its repression and torture of political opponents. Belgium was the only European power to join. By 2005, only nine other states, including Germany, had signed the convention but had not ratified it.

An authoritative UN report described the low level of ratification as 'disappointing', possibly because of the problem of defining 'mercenary' in a world where 'self-determination' and the role of private security companies were mutating into something new. As the British Green Paper observed,

> In the 1960s and 1970s mercenaries were a real threat to legitimacy and self-determination. They were often associated with attempts to preserve quasi-colonial structures; and they took part in a number of attempted coups. Neither of these has been the case with PMCs in the 1990s.

Had it been written a year or so later it might have added that regime change was a policy now adopted officially in Washington and London, as well as by NATO, in the Balkans, Afghanistan and Iraq.

The UN was reluctant to move with the times. As Kofi Annan memorably put it in a lecture, 'When we had need of skilled soldiers to separate fighters from refugee fighters in the Rwandan refugee camps in Goma, I even considered the possibility of engaging a private firm. But the world may not be ready to privatise peace.'[22] In 2004, as he ended 16 years as Special Rapporteur on mercenary activity, Ballesteros lamented, 'A mercenary may become a social outcast, but the law can take no action against him.'[23]

His successor, Shaista Shameen, a civil rights campaigner from Fiji, turned many of his ideas on their head and proposed a policy that was closer to the acceptance by the UK and the US that international mercenary activity, however defined, was a fact of life and that control of private military companies, for the time being, was best left to self-regulation combined with discreet, indirect government pressure. She proposed a new definition of 'mercenary', one that would include reference to a written contract, and distinguish between 'traditional' mercenaries, willing to fight in any armed conflict, and those dedicated to the demolition of a political, constitutional order. Like Lady Thatcher, she suggested in 2005 that the new definition must distinguish 'between mercenaries and terrorists, stressing the distinction between material and ideological motives'. What was needed, she said, was 'a fundamental reconsideration of issues concerning mercenaries'.[24]

What of the existing UN Convention? 'It does not enjoy the support or attract the particular interest of the international community, as demonstrated by the remarkably small number of signatures and ratifications.' Very few replies have been received to requests for feedback on the proposed new definition of a mercenary. A possible explanation for the lethargy 'is that Member States and the United Nations itself employ entities that may be identified as mercenaries under the current definition'.

Challenging the Ballesteros view, and that of others, about the need for state monopoly in the use of force, Shameen suggested that, in the modern world,

> States are increasingly faced with the challenge of having to decide to what extent they are willing to cede their traditional prerogative and monopoly of the use of force to non-state actors, and whether they should rethink the responsibilities of the modern nation-state with respect to security and the use of force ... The legal definition of a mercenary can be decided only after a policy decision has been reached [by the UN] on the fundamental question of whether states wish to continue to be solely responsible for the use of force, for declaring war and for sanctioning the use of force within certain internationally acceptable rules of engagement.

While those major problems were being untangled by the UN, she advised, the best pragmatic approach would be to encourage companies in self-regulation. 'Private military companies may maintain the current status accorded them under international humanitarian law ... There is inadequate justification for their criminalization under the Convention.'

The UN response to Shameen's landmark report was to abolish the office of Special Rapporteur on mercenaries and appoint a whole new working group of five independent experts to start again. The thrust of its new resolution in 2005, however, did not follow the logic of the Shameen report. It expressed extreme alarm about 'recent mercenary activities in Africa and the threat they pose . . .' and remained convinced that mercenaries 'are a threat to peace, security and the self-determination of peoples'.[25] It called upon all states that have not yet signed the convention to do so.

Critically, it called on the working group to take into account the cumbersome Ballesteros definition of the mercenary in his 2004 farewell report. The new working group's remit was to elaborate, seek opinions, monitor, study and identify a range of issues that had been chewed over during the preceding 25 years. The UN's approach began to resemble the historian A. J. P. Taylor's (fictitious) Royal Commission on Kissing, which sat for generations and never reported. Worse was to come.

By May 2006, the UN Human Rights Commission itself had become discredited because too many of its members themselves had poor human rights records. Kofi Annan, the UN Secretary General, admitted that the Commission's decline was caused by 'the presence of serial abusers'.[26] In 203, Libya chaired the organisation and, in 2004, Sudan – notable for its activities in Darfur – was re-elected to membership. So the Commission was replaced by a Human Rights Council. Sixty-eight states submitted candidates for 47 places.

UN Watch, a respected NGO, feared that 43 per cent of the new council's membership would comprise countries with a poor human rights record. It commented,

> If egregious and systematic human rights violators like China, Cuba, Iran, Russia or Saudi Arabia win election . . . it will be an ominous sign that the Council is – as some of us had worried – nothing more than the Commission by another name.[27]

In fact, the new council included six countries accused of human rights abuses. They were Russia, China, Cuba, Pakistan, Saudi Arabia and Azerbaijan. Iran and Venezuela failed to get enough votes and rights violators such as Libya, Nepal, Sudan, Syria and Zimbabwe – which had served on the earlier Commission – did not even stand for election. Nor did the USA.[28]

Britain won a two-year term with 148 votes after last-minute lobbying at the UN by Margaret Becket, Straw's successor as Foreign Secretary, in May 2006.

If neither nation-states nor the UN could legislate effectively for the excesses of the worst kind of mercenary – and plenty of those were still at work – then there was a final, forlorn hope. That was the International Criminal Court (ICC), a worthy body invented by the UN in 1998 after a mere 50 years of gestation. As the UN itself explained,

> An international criminal court has been called the missing link in the international legal system. The International Court of Justice at The

Hague handles only cases between States, not individuals. Without an international criminal court for dealing with individual responsibility as an enforcement mechanism, acts of genocide and egregious violations of human rights often go unpunished.[29]

The ICC was able to start work in 2002 when 60 countries ratified the relevant treaty. Again, progress was slow. In October 2005 Mexico became the 100th state to ratify. It was another five months before the ICC was able to announce that it had arrested its first suspect, an obscure Congolese politician.

One of the reasons for this limping progress was the decision of President George Bush not to ratify the ICC treaty since he feared that American soldiers serving as peacekeepers in such places as Bosnia might be the victims of show trials characterising them as terrorists. In fact, the US did get its way in arranging with the UN that its peacekeepers were exempt from trial or arrest by the ICC for one year. The UN caved in after the US threatened to veto UN peacekeeping missions one by one.

Washington went further. It offered a number of hard-up governments trade-and-aid deals, so long as the recipients did not sign up to the ICC. The *Guardian* reported in June 2003

America is said to have been threatening some Balkan countries with a withdrawal of aid if they do not sign bilateral deals. Last month Albania became the third European country, after Romania and Georgia, to sign a deal [with the US]. Now Macedonia, Bosnia, Croatia and Serbia and Montenegro have been told to follow suit, or lose US aid and support.[30]

By then, a total of 37 countries worldwide, some in Africa, had agreed to join Washington's ICC-boycott club. Philippe Sands, an international lawyer and author of *Lawless World: America and the Making and Breaking of Global Rules*, recalled in 2005 a typical shoot-from-the-hip Bushism: 'I don't care what the international lawyers say.'[31]

Some observers noted the extent to which private security companies based in the US were on the ground in large numbers in some of the key areas affected by Washington's attitude towards the ICC. In such a climate the prospect of bringing the security companies (however they identified themselves) under the rule of law seemed very unlikely. It was not only

Paul Bremer's Order 17 that provided the better-connected freelance soldiers with a licence to kill in Iraq. Bush's opposition to the ICC potentially extended the process to many other parts of the world.

His approach had deep roots. One might almost say that to impose US law outside its proper jurisdiction was almost part of the American tradition by the time Bush expressed his distaste for any alternative. A policy known as 'the Presidential snatch option' – the arrest anywhere of terrorist suspects as an alternative to assassination – was invented by the Reagan administration in 1985.[32] The new doctrine was set out in a secret legal opinion entitled 'Authority of the FBI to Override Customary or Other International Law in the Use of Extraterritorial Law Enforcement Activities'. [33] In June of that year Fawaz Younis, a Lebanese citizen, was alleged to have taken part in the hijack of a royal Jordanian airliner in Beirut. Because US citizens were on board, the FBI started a manhunt for Younis.

The FBI's assistant director of investigations, Oliver Revell, revealed,

> In September 1987 Younis was arrested by the FBI in international waters in the Mediterranean Sea . . . He was convicted . . . in the Federal District Court in Washington DC. The fact that Younis was captured in international waters serves notice that the US government is willing to go to substantial lengths to apprehend those responsible for acts of terrorism against US nationals.

In the post-9/11 world, US jurisdiction was extended even beyond reach of US jurisdiction, at Guantánamo Bay and countless secret CIA prisons around the world. In such a world, the prospects for any viable international law to control freelance soldiers were less than good. The British Foreign Secretary, Jack Straw, appeared to bow to the inevitable when he wrote the introduction to his department's Green Paper in 2002. He said, 'One of the reasons for considering the option of a licensing regime is that it may be desirable to distinguish between reputable and disreputable private sector operators, to encourage and support the former while, as far as possible, eliminating the latter.'

Selective self-regulation, commercially controlled in a world of privatised warfare and corporate peacekeeping, was now seen as an alternative to the vision of the Nuremberg War Crimes Tribunal, the Atlantic Charter and the United Nations in defending the rule of law and fundamental human rights.

One problem facing the UN and its agencies is that, while it attempts to impose ethical policies on its own peacekeepers as well as freelance soldiers, it has no power to prosecute criminals in blue helmets. A new UN code issued by Secretary-General Kofi Annan in 1999, marking the 50th anniversary of the Geneva Conventions, conceded, 'In case of violations of international humanitarian law, members of the military personnel [*sic*] of a United Nations force are subject to prosecution in their national courts.'[34] This policy is similar to that subsequently adopted by the US towards the International Criminal Court, and by the Iraqi government in addressing lawlessness among occupation forces, including foreign freelance soldiers. All prefer to live with a legal vacuum.

The UN's lack of jurisdiction even over its own forces has led to repeated scandals, often involving sexual exploitation of vulnerable people in Africa. Alleged crimes recalling some of the worst excesses of King Leopold's Belgian Congo, exposed by Roger Casement in 1904, were reported by the pressure group Refugees International a century later:

Investigation into allegations of child pornography rings, sex shows and the rape of babies by Moroccan peacekeepers serving in MONUC [the UN mission in the Democratic Republic of the Congo] was terminated due to a reported lack of evidence and minimal support from the military contingent commanders . . .

The UN has no authority to follow through on any investigations currently under way. At most, after a lengthy process, the UN can repatriate an individual, but cannot see those cases followed through in the country of origin. There appears to be near-total impunity for MONUC soldiers.[35]

Two years later in 2006, a report by Save the Children UK on the activities of international aid workers in Liberia ('From Camp to Community: Liberia study on exploitation of children') asserted, 'Sexual exploitation of children by peacekeeping soldiers was described in every location where a contingent was stationed.' It quoted one witness as saying, 'If you go out with [have sex with] men you can get money to buy the things you need. My friend had no money before. Now she is selling because she is loving to UNMIL [United Nations Mission in Liberia].'[36]

The UN's record in providing clear rules of engagement for its soldiers is not much better than its protection of human rights in Africa. The

Canadian Lieutenant General Romeo Dallaire, pitched into the darkness of Rwanda as genocide was being prepared in 1994, drafted his guidance about using force and sent it to the troop-contributing nations as well as UN headquarters, asking them to agree his plan:

> Not only did I not get formal written approval of my rules from the UN, I never received any comment, positive or negative, from any nation, with the exception of Belgium, which had some concerns about its troops being used in crowd control and Canada, which protested as too broad the sanctioning of deadly force in defence of all UN property. We eventually amended the rules to address these concerns and considered the silence on all fronts as tacit approval.

When the moment to act came, the international organisation declined to give him the operational freedom he needed to stop the killing. He left Rwanda 'a broken man, disillusioned, suicidal'.

Dallaire also concluded, in his bitter account, *Shake Hands with the Devil*,

> For most countries, serving the UN's objectives has never seemed worth even the smallest of risks. Member nations do not want a large, reputable, strong and independent United Nations, no matter their hypocritical pronouncements otherwise. What they want is a weak, beholden, indebted scapegoat of an organisation, which they can blame for their failures or steal victories from.[37]

Regrettably, the UN's performance in managing conflict does not make it a credible critic, or controller, of other military forces in a world where the old verities, including the nation-state's monopoly over lethal force, are increasingly challenged. This inevitably raises the ancient question, '*Quis custodiet ipsos custodies*?' Who watches the watchers? Who guards the guardians? Who polices the police?

The only realistic movement to fill this vacuum, arising from one high-profile case in Iraq, was civil litigation. On 31 March 2004, four freelance soldiers working for the US company Blackwater were lynched and murdered by a mob at Fallujah. Their next of kin brought actions against the company, alleging negligence. In the spring of 2007, the litigation was still striding bravely on, up to the US Supreme Court and back down to the

North Carolina state court. The company's defence has made many Congressmen and women angry. One of its counsel explained, 'You can't separate the contractors from the troops any more.' If that is correct, the four freelances were part of America's 'total force' in Iraq and subject to a law passed during World War Two, covering construction workers building bases in case of death or injury, whether they became casualties on or off the base. Under the terms of the Defense Base Act, says Blackwater, it is the US government that is liable for compensation, not the company.

At a pretrial hearing in North Carolina, Judge Donald Stephens warned the company, 'Blackwater has wrapped itself in the American flag . . . Blackwater Security Consulting LLC is not the United States government.'[38]

In Washington, members of Congress noted that the Pentagon could not even say how many freelance operators there were, or how many had committed crimes outside the US. Two members of Congress – Henry Waxman and Jan Schakowsky – now began the long trek along the yellow brick road towards that mythical place where might be discovered a law that would bring the industry under control, once and for all. Their progress was watched with interest from Whitehall.

18

THE GREAT REAPPRAISAL, 2006:

Dogs of War or Pussycats of Peace?

In the autumn of 2006, leading British security companies gathered in Whitehall to consider their future at a time when the Iraq bubble was deflating. An estimated 20,000 freelance operators in that country had declined to around 10,000. The figures might be suspect. The US official watchdog, the General Accountability Office, estimated in June 2006 that there were more than 48,000 freelance soldiers working for 181 different companies in the country. Almost 200 had been killed.

What was clear to the British companies was that the time was coming when an Iraqi government would want to take control of the sector, if the country did not melt down into total civil war, with all the haggling and nepotism that might imply. Something had to be done.

The companies took a deep breath, put aside their rivalries, and promised to reinvent themselves. As one of their spokesmen put it, they would no longer be dogs of war, but pussycats of peace.

No one pretended that this was an exercise in virtue for its own sake. But it was the future if private, armed security companies were to survive. A leading participant ('speaking for myself'), said, 'Here's a revelation. We are not saints. We are not in this industry necessarily to do good. We are not "NGOs" [non-governmental organisations]. We are companies. Nor, mostly, are we sinners ... We want to be left alone. We are motivated by profit. We exist to make money, but breaking rules is bad for our business.

Business growth depends on reputation . . . as professional security providers.'[1]

Sceptical outsiders had a problem with this collective conversion. Some of the new men had once been deniables, running offensive combat and sabotage operations in Latin America and elsewhere. But one of them told me, 'Just because I ran an Austin car twenty-five years ago, it does not follow that my current Mercedes is the same vehicle.' The essential difference, as Tim Spicer had been saying for some time, was that a modern PSC is answerable to shareholders, directors, company law and ultimately the public. It is not a motley collection of irresponsible Walter Mittys.

The security industry's tribal elders had good reason to fear the impact of the wrong sort of event and the bad smell that lingers in the nostrils of politicians. Following the spectacular failure of the African 'Wonga' plot, Andrew Bearpark, director general of the British Association of Private Security Companies, hosting the two-day conference in Whitehall, said they were in business 'to drive standards up and keep the cowboys out. Neither [Simon] Mann nor Thatcher will ever be members of BAPSC.'

The elders, representing 20 companies, were keenly aware that the failed attempt in 2004 to seize Equatorial Guinea still resonated around Africa and back in London. It had prompted draconian legislation in Pretoria that had hobbled thousands of South African freelance soldiers, forcing them into exile and onto an illicit market in Sudan and the Congo. It even threatened the status of South African citizens serving in the British armed forces. Worst of all, it was a further incentive for the British government to continue to sit on its hands, years after its own Green Paper had suggested routes to regulation, and, thereby, recognition that the security industry had come of age.

Its reluctance no doubt had something to do with the fact that the association represents 'companies that provide *armed* security services [my italics] in countries outside the UK' in a global market for bodyguards, convoy escorts and much else. The UK government's reluctance, as a senior civil servant privately confided to me, also had much to do with the need to cover one's back. The potato was still too hot for politicians and their advisers. This was a curious outcome, given the infestation of most government departments by hundreds of external consultants (usually with lamentable results) to say nothing of the government's own extensive use of armed private security bodyguards in Iraq and Afghanistan. Indeed one speaker suggested that government departments using private security for surveillance and intelligence-gathering, as well as protection, included the Home Office; Work and Pensions; Environment, Food and Rural Affairs; and International Development, HM Revenue Customs, as well as Defence Ministry training teams and the Defence College. At Sunderland, the Department for Work and Pensions was allegedly using private security operators 'to carry out surveillance in benefit fraud cases'.

A senior member of Control Risks Group detected another reason for the government's unwillingness to recognise the industry. The Foreign and Commonwealth Office had made a mess of the Sandline/Arms-to-Africa affair. The wound still festered. So the whole industry had to be scapegoated for a series of failures on the part of the FCO.

If government was coy, one venerable institution was happy to recognise the reformed nature of the trade. This was the Royal United Institute for Defence Studies, which hosted the conference. Founded in 1831, with the Queen as its patron, it is more venerable than the Ministry of Defence, the FCO or modern Cabinet government. It is a bastion of elitist Britain. A distinguished list of participants also underscored the changing perceptions of the business.

They included Sir Jeremy Greenstock, former UK Special Representative to Iraq, 2003–4; General the Lord Ramsbotham; Lieutenant General Sir Cedric Delves, an SAS hero of the Falklands war; Lieutenant General Sir Michael Willcocks, Gentleman Usher of the Black Rod; Sir Malcolm Rifkind, a former Foreign Secretary; Bruce George MP; and Rear Admiral Richard Cobbold, director of RUSI, as well as academics among a carefully vetted guest list of around 150 including, the author.

Failing government recognition, the BAPSC proposed 'aggressive self-regulation', a process through which bounders who broke club rules would be blackballed in the UK. But how to deal with them where it mattered in some faraway conflict zone? In Iraq, as one speaker noted, an operator dismissed by one company could find work with another within a week. The association places its faith in a notional ombudsman, who would be independent of the industry, empowered to investigate complaints and having international authority. Sir Jeremy Greenstock, among others, doubted the existence of Santa Claus. 'I don't think you will get an ombudsman,' he said. 'The government will not do it.'

Some other mechanism for accountability had to be found, all the same. Some participants spotted an absence of any international law to cover many crimes in which armed freelance soldiers enjoyed effective immunity. War crimes are indictable worldwide, provided evidence can be presented, and suspects subject to arrest. Yet, as the case of the Serbian General Ratko Mladic demonstrates, making an arrest, even after years of pursuit, appears to be virtually impossible. British citizens committing murder abroad, theoretically, can be tried at home. In practice, in the war zones in which the traditional freelance soldier functions, the only functioning law is gun law.

The Pussycats of Peace offer an alternative, broader agenda. It suggests a politically holistic approach to the unstable world that has emerged from the remains of the Cold War. Around the world 'failed states' – countries ruined by conflict and debauched by corruption – require skilled nursing back to health. The process can take 10 to 15 years. The Pussycats perceive new roles for themselves in this process. They identify post-conflict reconstruction including such ideas as 'SSR' (security sector reform, the retraining of security forces) and 'DDR' (disarmament, demobilisation, reintegration) as just the first step. The work might be as simple and basic as ArmorGroup's experience in Mozambique. Between 1985 and 1991, by helping to restore the railway from Malawi to the Indian Ocean, 'We delivered an economic zone because it was secure,' said its spokesman. By contrast, efforts by British contractors to train Iraqi police forces could not be said to be an unqualified success, in view of the penetration of the police by religious militias.

Eric Westropp, a veteran member of the Control Risks team, has a dream as visionary as that of Martin Luther King. It is to spread good governance to cure the instability of countries that are falling apart. He envisages linking multinational corporations with NGOs to win hearts and minds while simultaneously kick-starting derelict economies. The process, he argues, should enable investors to work in partnerships with the international aid agencies 'to create an ecosystem' in which peace would triumph over warlordism. In his view, timing is everything. Initial intervention in such territories as Afghanistan should seize the opportunity provided by 'the goodwill window', a cousin of the political honeymoon enjoyed by freshly elected presidents and prime ministers.

In Afghanistan the hard truth, as Clare Lockhart – a specialist in the emerging science of state building – reminded the Pussycats at the BAPSC conference in London in October 2006, is that the opportunity was lost as a result of flawed policies adopted or endorsed by Western occupation. 'In 2001 a window of opportunity was open for the Afghanistan people. This is now closed.' To achieve victory over the Taliban, military action was insufficient. A new dynamic and a new hearts-and-minds strategy were needed to tackle three issues: grinding poverty, opium-poppy eradication (the destruction of the only cash crop in southern Afghanistan) and Taliban propaganda.

Westropp himself identified a failure to use another window of good-will. Soon after the invasion of Iraq he had approached Paul Bremer, head of the Provisional Authority, to propose investment in the newly liberated country. Bremer, he said, snapped back: 'Investing in Iraq is illegal.'

Sir Cedric Delves, a director of Olive, shared at that conference the vision of 'support of governments . . . in volatile countries and regions abroad'. He identified three specific opportunities. First, he thought of supporting agencies of Western governments, international organisations, NGOs and the media in providing logistics and security to create 'an enabling environment'. Second came 'policy development' through which PSCs could advise governments about programmes to achieve security sector reform. Finally, he identified direct support to governments emerging from conflict in retraining security forces.

He also saw opportunities for private companies to relieve the impact of natural disasters. 'Olive Group, for example, supported the US Federal Emergency Management Agency's operations on the Mississippi Gulf Coast in the immediate aftermath of Hurricanes Rita and Katrina in 2005 and the international response to the Asian tsunami in Banda Aceh the same year.'

The new wave of PSCs would 'be led and managed increasingly by business leaders as distinct from ex-military and security services people. I am an exception on the board of Olive. My colleagues bring a mix of business and legal backgrounds.' The new advanced security providers could provide policy development and delivery of security sector work in such places as Sudan and generally become 'a force for good'.

Such praiseworthy ideas rested on two assumptions. First was the belief that Western ideas of good governance would be welcomed everywhere else. Yet the experience of the first six years of the 21st century was that some cultures, notably Islam, felt threatened, not by Western technology as such, but by the materialist values that usually accompany American 'can-do', quick-fix operations.

Will either Western governments or the private security companies have the stamina for programmes that run for up to 15 years without any visible return other than containing warlordism? Without government funds to run such programmes as a prophylactic against terrorism, they seem distinctly utopian. Security companies, after all, exist to make a profit. The alternative is that protection is focused on mineral assets such as oil, bankrolled by BP and Shell, at which point, the *raison d'être* of the companies is back to square one.

The second assumption is that there is a need, a hole, large enough to accommodate the services the proliferating security companies can offer. Many volunteers in the aid community would challenge that. They would claim that this is their territory. They feel compromised by contact with any armed force. Geoffrey Dennis, chief executive of CARE International in the UK, argued at the BAPSC conference that 'PSCs are not always the solution. They are often a symptom ... CARE's safety and security and that of the genuine NGOs is based on trust ... support and good relationship with a local community based on impartiality ... not armed deterrence.' He may have had in mind the case of Afghanistan, where 22 aid workers were killed during the first two post-Taliban years. As the writer Isabel Hilton commented, 'Experienced NGOs such as Oxfam, Christian Aid and the Red Cross now complain that in Afghanistan it is difficult to distinguish combat troops from the peacekeepers who provide security for humanitarian projects. In Iraq it is worse.'[2]

Geoffrey Dennis, while paying tribute to a security company that had saved the lives of one team while NATO forces did nothing, echoed the fear of many in the aid community, baldly expressed by one company executive: 'Private security companies are out to raid the humanitarian space. We want part of your market.'

With that analysis in mind perhaps, Doug Brooks, president of an American coalition, the International Peace Operations Association, commented, 'We are going to have to work on the NGOs and human rights organisations. How do we reach out to them? I think you will have a tough time with them.'

The British response, voiced by Andrew Bearpark, director general of BAPSC and a former chief of staff to Prime Minister Margaret Thatcher, was, 'We want a full debate with the NGOs. We need to intensify the debate. Only when we sweep away the fallacies do we get down to real issues. One [fallacy] is the private military companies. I know there are PMCs in Russia ... Kosovo ... perhaps in the US. I cannot find any in the UK ... who want to engage in combat and offensive operations.'

The conference was a brave attempt to build bridges between responsible security companies and academics, journalists and aid workers. The elephant that was not in the room was the British government. Though there was a sprinkle of people from parts of the civil service, including the Foreign and Commonwealth Office and the Ministry of Defence, not a single government minister showed any interest in the event. Meanwhile, the FCO still referred to the sector as 'PSMCs' – private security/military companies – to the irritation of those seeking to rebrand the product.

It was a very different story in the US, where PSCs are a routine part of military logistics. Since the days of the strike-breaking Pinkerton agency – an organisation that had more agents than the regular army of the day had soldiers – private security companies of every sort have been as much part of patriotic, official America as the national anthem. In the UK, it seemed, privatisation had touched every part of public life except the potential use of lethal force in a just cause.

The evolution of high-tech armies has played a critical role in shaping recent American experience. As more complicated weapons systems were adopted by the superpower, dedicated civilian technicians were required to maintain and often to run them. This form of logistical backup grew rapidly during the 1990s to cover every sort of provision from hot meals to computers. As the author P. W. Singer has noted,

> Illustrated by major US military exercises . . . the 'Army of the Future' will require huge levels of battlefield support from private firms . . . Companies such as Hughes and TRW have to send hundreds of employees into the field to act as trainers, repairmen, troubleshooters, programmers and hand-holders to military personnel . . . Areas as diverse as weapons testing, aerial refuelling and the highly technical maintenance of F-117 and B-2 Stealth bombers are all private now.[3]

Britain has been obliged to go down the same road, sometimes with less than happy results. In 1997 Devonport naval shipyard in Plymouth – the only yard licensed to refit nuclear-powered submarines – was sold to a group dominated by the American firm KBR, a subsidiary of Halliburton. In November 2006, ignoring pleas from the UK Defence Ministry, Halliburton launched KBR shares on the New York stock exchange.[4] Whitehall was concerned that KBR would not have enough capital to support Devonport and its workforce of 4,500. Shares in the company rose by $4. KBR also had a key role in the building of two new aircraft carriers in Britain. The incident was a reminder of one of the disadvantages of privatisation, that the UK's strategic interests could take second place to the commercial self-interest of a foreign company.

Dominick Donald, a former *Times* leader writer who became a senior analyst for Aegis, argues that, in future, British PSCs will operate in four main areas.

> These are intelligence provision and analysis; support to stabilization and post-conflict reconstruction efforts; security sector reform; and humanitarian and development assistance. The first two areas of activity will be for both commercial and government clients; the last two will be for government clients alone.[5]

While it is true that Aegis in Iraq, acting as the interface between regular Coalition Forces and the private security companies, provides sanitised tactical field intelligence on a 'top-down' basis, the role of such companies in producing and analysing highly classified data of strategic value is one that any British government will need to approach with caution. As with the Halliburton episode, it will need to establish who is the client and who is the master.

PART V

.

MONEY

19

MR MICAWBER'S MISSING MILLIONS

The boom in private security that followed the invasion of Iraq hit regular Special Forces teams such as the SAS with the disabling force of an incoming missile. Gone were the pre-Thatcher days when soldiers would take a pay cut for the honour of dying for Queen and country. '*Dulce et decorum est pro patria mori*' – the ultimate sacrifice – was not a marketable commodity. At first, the impact of market forces on old-fashioned patriotism provoked bleats of reproach from some of the top brass, or at least, from those who had not already retreated to the board-room. But, after three years of attrition and loss to the private sector, the Ministry of Defence finally bit on the bullet and accepted that, if it could not beat an increasingly mercenary culture, it would have to join it.

Within the SAS family, some senior NCOs were given official permission, as one tribal elder put it, to leave the regular army 'to earn money on the security circuit and then, having "loaded up", they were allowed to return to regular service some eighteen months later, resuming pensionable service in 22 SAS without loss of rank'. He added, 'So those are the present terms on offer in our bankrupt army. No patriotism there. All very disillusioned with Blair and his lot.'

More publicly, even as the army discovered that much of its equipment was worn out and insufficient for the threats presented by well-machined roadside bombs made in Iran, the MoD admitted that it had increased Special Forces pay by 50 per cent. The *Times* and *Sunday Times* defence editor, Michael Smith, reported that the increases, recommended by the armed forces pay-review body, 'were seen as crucial when the special forces are stretched by operations in Iraq and Afghanistan'.[1]

Security firms operating in Iraq and elsewhere, he added, were prepared to pay up to £100,000 a year for qualified Special Forces veterans. (I know one former brigadier who required 'not less than £120,000' for his services. Given his experience, he was worth it.) The new increases elevated an SAS trooper's annual salary from £25,000 to £40,000 a year, with sergeants receiving £50,000 (an increase of £18,000). A major – normally a squadron commander in the regular regiment – would now receive £70,000, an increase of £20,000.

The MoD's counteroffensive was mistimed. Its largesse coincided with the bursting of the Baghdad bubble, about which some leaders of the private security industry had been warning for more than a year. As Richard Fenning, CEO of Control Risks Group, put it in July 2006, 'The laws of supply and demand have caught up.'[2] However, in another manoeuvre to make good the loss of qualified men, the MoD agreed that Special Forces soldiers who had completed 22 years' service could continue to serve with the regular army on short-term contracts In spite of all that, PMCs/PSCs (private military/security companies) could still trump Whitehall with the fiscal equivalent of a get-out-of-jail card, or, more accurately, a 'pay-no-tax' card. The deities presiding over the Circuit now included Special Forces accountants, wise in the ways of offshore banking as well as the SAS. The key to a nil tax liability was the mercenary's status as one who was non-resident in the UK.

One of those involved explained, 'To be accepted by the Revenue authorities as a non-resident, you must be out of the country for one whole year. Once your status is established, you may spend a total of ninety-one days in the UK. You may spend less or more than that number of days in Britain during a so-called "split year", but over a four-year period, you must average ninety-one days for every year of non-residence.

'You must also have a contract to work overseas as a "security consultant" – the favourite description – and an offshore bank account. I also advise the employer to have an offshore office. Several security companies draw up the employee's contract in the UK, which is dangerous. I suggest that they open up an office in Dubai. The great thing is that, if the guys put their pay into an offshore account, it is treated as capital – beyond the reach of income tax – once the contract is over. After his employment overseas, the freelance soldier can repatriate the capital, without a tax liability, to a bank account in Britain.'

As a result of such finessed accounting, the freelance earning between £45,000 and £60,000 was still financially better off than the SAS sergeant whose new, enhanced pay of £50,000 was subject to anything up to 40 per cent income tax, deducted at source.

Many, perhaps most, contracts between the company and its foot soldier are not binding upon either party. 'It is the only contract I've encountered which contains a "walk-out" clause,' one specialist said. 'It is in truth a Mickey Mouse contract, but without it you cannot be treated as a non-resident for British tax purposes.'

It was not clear how long the tax-exile mercenaries would be permitted to walk on water as HM Revenue and Customs planned what *The Times* described as 'a crackdown on British citizens with offshore bank accounts'. New powers sought by HMRC – in those rare cases where seriously criminal concealment of funds was suspected – included the right to arrest anyone suspected of fraud, to take fingerprints, bail suspects and search people and premises without police assistance. Mike Warburton, a tax partner at Grant Thornton, described the potential new powers as frightening. He told *The Times*, 'Customs have always had greater powers because their ethos was that they were trying to catch villains. Now that Revenue and Customs are under one banner, I fear that this is the direction that the taxman is headed as well.' Another accountant grumbled, 'They're trying to tighten up on everything and it's creating an "us and them" situation.'[3] In practice, legal offshore payments were not likely – initially – to be treated in this way.

On the ground, as Iraq became mired in civil war, deteriorating security forced embassies to close outlying stations while some construction companies, such as the Scottish engineering firm Weir, left Iraq in 2005 after working there for more than 50 years.[4] When diplomats proved to be elusive targets, civilian Iraqi translators working for the occupation forces were assassinated instead. In such a climate, the economic boom that was expected post-Saddam did not materialise. As Harry Legge-Bourke, a principal in Oriel Solutions, noted, 'The companies people thought would go in as investors simply haven't arrived.'[5] The principal reason was that a new home-grown industry in Iraq was preying upon most foreigners, including aid workers, journalists, Christian idealists and Western soldiers. The industry was kidnap and ransom. A cynic might conclude that, in Iraq, the answer to Western capitalism was more capitalism.

As a result, in July 2004, 15 months after Bush boasted 'Mission accomplished!', the International Monetary Fund slashed its forecast of Iraq's economic growth (GDP) from 17 per cent to 4 per cent.[6] Oil production nose-dived from 2.6 million barrels a day on the eve of the invasion to 1.8 million barrels in January 2006. At least $2.5 billion earmarked for Iraq's dilapidated schools was diverted to guards for Saddam's trial. Funds destined for the electricity grid, to sewage and sanitation, were spent instead to train bomb squad and hostage rescue teams. Undeterred, the Chamber of Commerce in Iraq sponsored a 'Rebuild Iraq' exhibition, which attracted 1,000 companies and 20,000 visitors, excited by potential deals offering full and immediate repatriation of profits. The downside was that, because of the toxic security situation in Iraq, the exhibition had to be staged in Jordan.[7]

Other market forces combined to depress the freelance soldier's pay. The US government, disillusioned by the failure of its efforts to plant a model democracy in the inhospitable desert sand of Iraq, started, at last, to rein in its vast aid budget, an increasing proportion of which had to be dedicated to security rather than reconstruction. Bureaucrats trapped between the rock of reconstruction and the hard place that was the reality of life in Iraq, resorted to subterfuge. USAID, the financial Santa Claus at the centre of a reconstruction, budget worth $1.4 billion in 2005–6 (down from $18 billion during the spree of 2004, of which $4 billion – the largest single element – was spent on security), was accused by an official auditor of hiding cost overruns by listing them as overhead or administrative costs.

A case in point was a new children's hospital in Basra, the British-run area of occupied Iraq. According to the *New York Times*, '... in March 2005, AID asked the Iraq Reconstruction and Management Office at the US Embassy in Baghdad for permission to downsize some projects to ease widespread financing problems.' The hospital budget was $50 million. By April 2006, AID knew – because the constructor Bechtel had told it – that, as a result of escalating security costs, the project would actually cost as much as $98 million. In a report to Congress, the agency was still reporting the cost as $50 million.[8]

The additional $48 million was reclassified as 'indirect costs': the sort of creative accounting Dickens's Mr Micawber had described as a recipe for unhappiness, in the nineteenth century. In a climate in which armed protection for reconstruction workers became ever more necessary, the proportion of funds allocated to security increased exponentially. Initially, the Provisional Authority hoped that only 10 per cent of its $18 billion reconstruction budget would be required for security. But, as one of its officials later admitted, 'It was expected that coalition forces would provide adequate internal security and thus obviate the need for contractors to hire their own security. But the current threat situation [during the joint uprising in the spring of 2004] requires that an unexpected, substantial percentage of contractor dollars be allocated to private security.'[9]

There could be no more clear admission that freelances were now needed to do a job beyond that of regular armies. One source guessed that the share of reconstruction money allocated to security rose, after April 2004, to 25 per cent. If that is correct, then the Coalition was enmeshed in a financial, as well as military, war of attrition beyond its control.

The usual consequences of an ill-considered military adventure included, as well as the deaths of innocent people, a growing failure of financial integrity. As the occupation approached its third year, a former employee of one company pleaded guilty before a US federal court to accepting more than $100,000 in bribes from an Iraqi subcontractor he chose to renovate buildings in Iraq for the US army.[10] This was a drop in the ocean. The Coalition Provisional Authority, running Iraq for the first year after the invasion, 'could not adequately account for almost $100 million', according to the Special Inspector General for Iraq Reconstruction.[11]

The funds were a small part of the multibillion-dollar Development Fund of Iraq (or DFI), entrusted to the CPA by the United Nations, which, in turn, obtained the money from Iraqi oil revenues. On the streets of Iraq, meanwhile, the rackets were common knowledge. The 'Girl Blog from Iraq' included in her Internet diary, for 28 August 2003, the following anecdote:

One of my cousins works in a prominent engineering company in Baghdad ... well-known for designing and building bridges all over Iraq. My cousin, a structural engineer, is a bridge freak. He spends hours talking about pillars and trusses and still structures to anyone who'll listen ... [H]is manager told him that someone from the CPA wanted the company to estimate the building costs of replacing the new Diyala Bridge on the south-east end of Baghdad. He got his team together. They went out and assessed the damage, decided it wasn't too extensive, but it would be costly. They did the necessary tests and analyses (mumblings about soil composition and water depth, expansion joints and girders) and came up with a number they tentatively put forward: $300,000 . . . Let's pretend my cousin is a dolt. Let's pretend he hasn't been working with bridges for over seventeen years.

Let's pretend he didn't work on replacing at least twenty of the 133 bridges damaged during the first Gulf war. Let's pretend he's wrong and the cost of rebuilding this bridge is four times the number they estimated. Let's pretend it will actually cost $1,200,000. Let's just use our imagination. A week later, the New Diyala Bridge contract was given to a US company. This particular company estimated the cost of rebuilding the bridge would be around – brace yourselves – $50,000,000!!! Something you should know about Iraq: we have over 130,000 engineers. More than half of them are structural engineers and architects.[12]

A similar story was told to BBC2's *Newsnight*. An American company won a contract to repair a cement factory. Its bid – $15 million – was accepted. For some reason it could not deliver on the deal. An Iraqi company did the work for $80,000.[13]

There were other embarrassments. The auditor (the Special Inspector General for Iraq Reconstruction) discovered that the bill for a power station that ostensibly cost $6.6 million was inflated with another $27.6 million, thanks to 'overheads'. The *New York Times* commented, 'The project's overhead, a figure that normally runs to a maximum of 30 per cent, was a stunning 418 per cent.'[14]

There was also an Iraqi dimension to corruption. In October 2006 Ali Allawi, the country's former finance minister, accused the defunct interim government of stealing £425 million, which was to have equipped the Iraqi army. Some of the money was spent on old, unusable equipment. The rest simply disappeared in 'one of the biggest thefts in history'.

It got worse after that. An Iraqi general suspected of embezzling soldiers' pay and selling weapons and fuel on the black market was still in post in January 2007 more than two weeks after a high-ranking US and Iraqi military committee recommended his removal. The accused general's alleged crimes included running a roster of 'ghost soldiers', paid for by the government. In February 2007 Hakim al-Zamili, Iraq's Deputy Health Minister, was arrested by Coalition forces and accused of 'aiding death squads and siphoning off millions of dollars to Moqtada al-Sadr's Mahdi Army militia.'[15]

Meanwhile, facing reduced funding, some of the companies trained Iraqis or imported Third World soldiers willing to work for a fraction of the sums paid to highly trained Westerners, particularly when the task was unskilled perimeter security. Even Gurkhas were priced out of the market by cheap military labour imported from South America. In 2005 they were replaced by Peruvians. The Gurkhas had been paid $3,000 per month. The Peruvians settled for a third of that, as they reflected on their lot: 'No women, no beer, no fiesta.'[16] At Baghdad airport, Ugandans replaced Iraqis and Georgians while, inside the Green Zone, one correspondent noted, '. . . the State Department no longer feels it needs to pay top dollar to the world's best mercenaries . . . Even the Iraqi Security Forces (ISF) appear to have been pushed out so they can fight, leaving guard duties to lesser soldiers.'[17]

Another influence was the burgeoning second tier of security companies such as Phoenix and AKE, training ex-soldiers in close protection and defensive driving. One veteran of the trade complained, 'The bubble has burst on the Circuit due to the Phoenix course and their like inundating the market.' That said, both Phoenix and AKE also continued to provide front line, exemplary services in Iraq.

The sudden reduction in pay scales led to classic labour disputes between proletarian freelance soldiers and their employers. In May 2006, according to *The Times*, hundreds of British security guards employed by Control Risks Group in Iraq (a Rolls-Royce among PSCs) were urged to resign *en masse* when the firm proposed cuts in the salaries of front-line staff by between 19 and 37 per cent.[18]

The newspaper said that industrial action by the firm's bodyguards and convoy escorts raised questions about their future use in such roles, since a walkout 'could cripple operations at diplomatic missions and put the safety of officials at risk'. Since the 2003 invasion, PSCs had made hundreds of millions of pounds from dangerous jobs. The Foreign and Commonwealth Office alone had spent £110 million on private security during the 30 months following the overthrow of Saddam Hussein. Control Risk Group's contract to protect British diplomats in Baghdad and Basra had been worth more than £40 million annually before the crash.

'But with less money being spent on reconstruction and more security firms competing for the work, the contracts have become more competitive.' Control Risks, said *The Times*, could obtain a renewed FCO contract only by cutting costs, including front line pay. As a result, a senior team leader, paid £340 per day, would receive £275. A second-in-command would suffer a loss of more than a third, to £172. The dispute was settled out of public view, but not before one disgruntled team member said, '"CRG" in Baghdad no longer means "Control Risks Group", but "Cheap Rate Guys".'

This, if true, was a stark sea change. As a former CRG operator in Baghdad observed, 'When I worked for them they were conscious of the competition for high-calibre operators from other firms and, although they paid a little under the rates offered by some, they made up for it in terms and conditions. The risks of working in Iraq were mitigated by the better conditions offered by CRG. One of the most important was that each job was assessed, and as the client is a risk-averse HMG' – the UK government – 'the exposure to the threat for the operators was minimised. In addition, the client has always shown a willingness to change tactics/operating style, as well as pay out for additional measures when consulted by the CRG management in Baghdad.

'CRG vehicles, for example, are among the best equipped and maintained in Iraq, backed up by a good communications infrastructure. In all cases, the vehicles have at least two "comms" systems. Most have three. On long trips this is often boosted to four/five (VHF, HF, SATCOM, SATPHONE and mobile phone) among the team. The backup support when things go wrong are also better, because of the connection with the Foreign Office and Department for International Development.

'Under the new terms, a senior team leader's pay would be reduced to the level of an ordinary team leader in 2003–2005. As for a second-in-command now being paid £172 per day, he would get more escorting rich Arabs around London. It is hardly a rate to attract high-quality personnel.'

An operator named Joe Dzioba vented his anger in a letter that surfaced among Foreign Legion veterans of the Circuit. His complaint was that 'a company with integrity and good ethics' had deteriorated due to staff cuts. He alleged that only two men were available to protect an ambassador to Iraq. They were 'run ragged for a month until the Embassy was finally persuaded to increase the numbers again'.

There was further labour trouble in August 2006, when Colombian security guards learned that their salaries amounted to a quarter of the sum (£2,126) they alleged they were offered by recruitment agents in Bogotá representing the US company Blackwater. According to the *Financial Times*,

. . . the Colombians allege that they were given their contracts barely hours before departing Bogotá or en route to Iraq and only then realised that they would be paid $34 per day.

'We were tricked by the company into believing we would make much more money,' one former Colombian captain . . . told the *Financial Times*. As a result, 35 Colombians stationed in the Green Zone wrote to Blackwater demanding a salary of $2,700 in line with their compatriots. The newspaper quoted a security consultant that the lower pay could provoke accusations of exploitation and discrimination.[19]

These assertions were rebutted by Chris Taylor, a spokesman for Blackwater. 'Every single Colombian signed a contract for $34 a day before they went over to Iraq,' he said. Only two had pushed their protest to a point of accepting repatriation. The pay disagreement had arisen, he said, because of 'an overlapping change in contractual terms . . . There was a change in contract, one contract expired, another task order was bid upon, and so the numbers were different.'

What is not in doubt is the popularity among Peruvians, many with military experience born of internal conflict, of higher pay in Afghanistan as well as Iraq. One assessment suggests that around 2,000 Peruvians worked in both countries during 2005–6 for ten times the pay they would earn at home. Defion Internacional, a Lima company recruiting guards for the American firm Triple Canopy, provided 1,200 men as guards for the US Embassy, US official homes and Iraqi government offices inside the Baghdad Green Zone. Reuters reported,

> Emanuel Salvador, aged 24, who guards an export business twelve hours a day, seven days a week in Lima – where rooftop snipers guard some gas stations – says he would consider a job in Iraq because he wants a better life for his family. 'The streets of Lima can be just as dangerous,' said Salvador, wearing a black uniform, a small gun in his belt. 'I will do whatever I can to have a better future.'[20]

Most companies, not surprisingly, challenge the idea that they are cutting corners to win new contracts, or salvage existing ones. The US firm International American Products Inc. (IAP), which maintains electrical systems at US army bases, picked up another $10 million contract to supply power to Camp Victory, the base near Baghdad Airport, in June

2005. IAP's president, Dave Swindle, was at pains to point out, 'We are committed in our concern for our workers.'

There were winners as well as losers during the roller-coaster, boom–bust ride along Route Irish, from Baghdad Airport to the Green Zone.

An investigation by the *Independent* in March 2006 claimed that British businesses of all kinds including PR consultancies, urban planning and energy advisers, as well as security firms, had profited by at least £1.1 billion since the invasion. The profiteers, it said, include 'some of the best-known names in Britain's boardrooms as well as many who would prefer to remain anonymous . . . A total of 61 British companies are identified as benefiting from at least £1.1bn of contracts . . . but that figure is just the tip of the iceberg.'[21]

The story of ArmorGroup contains elements of both gain and loss. The London-based company offers close protection, security training and mine clearance primarily to governments around the world. It operates in 26 countries and employs 9,000 people. It is a major player in Iraq (the source of 57 per cent of its income in 2004) and Afghanistan.

In December 2003, it successfully floated its shares on the stock market, the only British PSC to make this public gesture of confidence in its own future. The following year its earnings totalled £99 million, a 92 per cent increase. In November 2005 it completed a £4.25 million takeover of Phoenix, founded by a former regimental sergeant major of 22 SAS. Phoenix, as noted above, trains security operators most of whom already have Special Forces experience. It enjoys 'preferred supplier status with the Ministry of Defence for Armed Forces' resettlement training'. During the year ended 31 August 2005, the firm reported operating profits of £469,000 on revenues of £1.65 million.

Thanks to the ArmorGroup takeover, the directors of Phoenix – Michael Clifford, James Devenney and Suzanne Clifford – received a total of £3.5 million in cash and £750,000 as shares in ArmorGroup. Michael Clifford remained managing director of Phoenix. Sources in the industry suggest that the allure of his firm was in part due to a contract it already held in Afghanistan. The reason offered by ArmorGroup's chief executive, Jerry Hoffman, was that it would 'let his company tap the pool of ex-soldiers who retrain as armed protection specialists after leaving military duty'.

The directors of Phoenix timed the deal better than those responsible for the MoD handout to men still serving with the SAS. In the month that the ArmorGroup takeover was formalised, ArmorGroup admitted that its profits for 2005 would be substantially less than earlier expectations. The *Financial Times* reported, 'Armor . . . floated late last year and its shares more than doubled initially. They fell to 107p yesterday [6 November 2005], below the 125p float price.'

The drop was caused by a delay in a convoy-protection contract after the firm had invested in 100 armoured pickup trucks and 100 armoured SUVs (off-road sports utility vehicles). That was not all: it was obliged to postpone another contract as the result of a spectacular riot following the arrest of two British Special Forces operators in Basra, and the confrontation that followed with local militia.

Hoffman said that volatility and commercial risk were facts of life when working in the world's most dangerous regions. He added, 'Maybe people need to take a different perspective and not look at us the same way as somebody making automobiles.'[22] Similar thinking was expressed by Tim Spicer, formerly of Sandline and, in Iraq, owner of the influential Aegis Defence team. As a result of increasing competition, he believed, 'many of the smaller PMCs may bank the money and go and live in Bermuda'.

As things turned out there were better times ahead for ArmorGroup. In April 2007 ArmorGroup was awarded a $189 million (£96 million) contract to guard the US Embassy in Kabul, one of the largest of its kind awarded to a private security company. The firm promised to employ ex-Gurkha soldiers. The firm was also being paid $30 million a year for services to the British government in Afghanistan. During the preceding four years, to release more regular soldiers for combat, the governments of London and Washington had spent £165 million on private security in Iraq.

The alternative to expansion was to diversify, a course also followed by ArmorGroup – whose acquisition of Phoenix gave it a base in training, rather than operations – and Aegis, which took over Rubicon International Services Ltd in October 2005. Rubicon specialises in intelligence, crisis management, force protection, surveillance and close protection. It is reputed to have offered consultation services in 50 of the world's danger areas.

Its founder, Major John Davidson, is described by SourceWatch – an American organisation that boasts a 'directory of the people, organizations and issues shaping the public agenda' – as 'a fifteen-year veteran of the army with experience advising oil and mining companies in Africa'.

A non-executive director, Major General Bob Hodges, 'was the former Commander of British Land Forces in Northern Ireland'.

The economic frost in Iraq did not even leave the US logistics giant, Halliburton, and its subsidiary, Kellog Brown & Root (KBR), untouched. Halliburton, purveyor of every kind of backup service to the US army in many parts of the world, from sock washing to oil-well management, is the world's largest private military contractor. It is the top of the food chain upon which most of the 20,000 freelance foot soldiers in Iraq, and thousands elsewhere, ultimately depend. Halliburton did well out of the war, picking up $13.5 billion to provide troop support in Iraq, plus $2.4 billion to ensure that Iraqi oil continued to flow under a controversial contract known as 'Restore Iraqi Oil' (RIO), with another $1.2 billion for a follow-up oil-assurance programme known as RIO 2. Very little of this trickled down to local Iraqi companies.

A congressional inquiry on behalf of Representative Henry A. Waxman, a critic of Halliburton, found in March 2006 that 'the Bush administration started planning for the takeover of Iraq's oilfields nearly a year before the invasion of Iraq'. (The Blair government, in July 2002, was discussing military action against Iraq, alongside the USA, as the notorious Downing Street memorandum of 23 July confirmed.) 'During 2002 a special team within the Pentagon called the Energy Infrastructure Planning Group was established and charged with developing a plan to restore and operate Iraq's oil infrastructure in the event that the US became an occupying power.'[23] Halliburton, whose former chief executive was Bush's vice-president Dick Cheney, was involved in this contingency planning from the outset, though Cheney himself claims he was not. It would later transpire that action on the RIO contract was in fact co-ordinated within the vice-president's office.

In November 2002, the company received a $1.9 million 'task order' – and advance payment – to start preparations for what was perceived to be a self-financing scheme. As Deputy Defense Secretary Paul Wolfowitz told Congress later, 'We are dealing with a country that can really finance its own reconstruction and relatively soon.' The American part of the cost would be 'just $1.7 billion'.[24] The US official watchdog in such matters, the Government Accountability Office, found that the contingency contract was 'not in accordance with legal requirements' and that the work 'should have been awarded using competitive procedures'[25]

A link with the vice-president's office apparently emerged from

Pentagon emails between a high-ranking Pentagon official working for the Deputy Defense Secretary, Paul Wolfowitz, and a senior officer in the Army Corps of Engineers. On 5 March 2003, two weeks before the invasion, an ACE officer sent, a 'RIO Status Update'. The officer reported that he had accompanied 'ORHA leader' – heading the emerging Office of Reconstruction and Humanitarian Assistance for Iraq – to obtain Pentagon 'authority to execute RIO' as well as a declassified press release. The signal continued, 'DepsecDef [Wolfowitz] sent us to UnderSecPolicy [Douglas] Feith and gave him to authority to approve both . . . Expect Feith will sign immediately.' The email added, 'We anticipate no issue, since action has been co-ordinated w VP's [vice-president's] office. Expect PA press release and Congressional coordination tomorrow a.m. and declass action to us early p.m.'[26]

The recipient responded joyfully at 8.36 next morning: 'The ball is in our court now to get the contract in place and complete the timeline to get boots on the ground so we can manage expectations . . . Let me know your timetable for deployment. I will be deploying soon as well. Hooah!'

A singular aspect of the RIO contract was that it was exclusively offered to Halliburton, and in secret. Companies such as Bechtel, which had experience of restoring Iraqi oilfields after the first Gulf war in 1991, were kept out of the loop. As the contract got under way, congressional representatives and others, including a whistleblower within the system (who lost her job as a result), alleged that KBR was overcharging and inflating costs. Her mantra was 'integrity within government is not an option' in spite of which, official attempts outside the Pentagon to get at the facts were frustrated by 'lack of accurate data'.

In February 2006, however, the US army concluded that KBR had done as well as could be expected in the 'in the haste and peril of war'. As a result, James Glanz reported in the *New York Times*, KBR would be reimbursed 'for nearly all of its disputed costs on a $2.4 billion no-bid contract to deliver fuel and repair oil equipment in Iraq, even though the Pentagon's own auditors had identified more than $250 million in charges as potentially excessive or unjustified.'

By then, it was bleakly obvious that the invasion of Iraq and control of its oil fields for the benefit of a major US corporation would not be, as Bush's people asserted before the war, a self-financing operation. Iraq, in spite of claims by the Office of Reconstruction and Humanitarian Assistance that it would rebuild the country, was in chaos. Late in 2004, KBR announced that, due to losses of $1 billion in the preceding four years, it had to make annual savings of $80 to $100 million. Harsher working conditions that equated with a pay cut were imposed mainly on its UK offices, in Leatherhead and Aberdeen.

In the UK, KBR was more than a humble supplier of laundry services. The Defence Manufacturers Association lists it as 'one of the UK's largest defence contractors'. Its products and services cover everything from aircraft carriers to the movement of hazardous materials. Its functions include 'management of nuclear facilities ... Tank Transporter operations, ground support and aircraft engineering for Hawk and Garrison redevelopment through PFI' (private finance initiatives).[27]

Meanwhile, in spite of a major military offensive intended to regain control of Baghdad on the run-up to 2006 mid-term congressional elections in the United States, and after, Iraq remained in a state of bloody anarchy. But what was happening to the oil revenues that were supposed to bankroll reconstruction? The body that monitored the money was the UN's International Advisory and Monitoring Board (IAMB) on the Development Fund for Iraq (DFI). The DFI was 'the principal repository for Iraq's oil-export receipts'.

In August 2006, the UN auditors concluded that DFI control systems were 'ineffective'.[28] The UN urged the Iraqi government to 'take concrete steps to address the audit findings'.[29] There were problems also relating to two special audits. One concerned a settlement between KBR and the US government. A second was to have examined 'sole source contracts using DFI resources'. Progress, said the UN, 'continues to be slow in executing these special audits'.

Why? For years, Henry Waxman, a senior Democrat member of the House of Representatives and one of the most outspoken critics of Halliburton, had argued that 'foot dragging' by the US government led to delays in supplying information to the UN body, and even then, documents that were supplied had been censored at the request of Halliburton.[30] This included a reference to $62 million that US auditors felt were 'unreasonable costs' relating to Halliburton's oil imports from Kuwait.

In the original version, one document said, 'KBR did not always provide accurate information.' As supplied to the UN monitors, the document did not contain that statement.

As 2006 ended, however, it seemed likely that the US government's campaign of foot dragging would end in some sort of victory. As a UN monitoring board news release said, with deadpan insouciance, 'IAMB was informed by the Iraqi representative that steps are being taken to establish an Iraqi oversight body to succeed IAMB with formal handover responsibilities in December 2006.'

It seemed unlikely that an independent inquiry into the elusive oil revenues would be complete before a US withdrawal from Iraq and with it, perhaps, the end of the greatest gravy train in mercenary history. The process of indefinite postponement reflected the UN's failed attempts to introduce a system to regulate freelance soldiers in other respects. It seemed that in both cases, even if there was a will to clean the stable, there was no practicable way to do it.

It was left to Alan Greenspan, chairman of the US Federal Reserve under four presidents and 'the world's most powerful banker', to identify plainly the economic motive that drove the Iraqi conflict in the first place. In 2007, he wrote: 'I am saddened that it is politically inconvenient to acknowledge what everyone knows: the Iraq war is largely about oil.' His comments coincided with the findings of an expert survey (by the British polling agency ORB) suggesting that the number of people killed by the 2003 invasion and its aftermath – most of them civilians – might have been as high as 1.2 million. Many thousands more became refugees within Iraq and as part of a worldwide diaspora.

EPILOGUE
After RIO

As the Anglo-American intervention in Iraq limped towards its miserable end in 2007, private security and military companies took stock of their situation. They knew, of course, that, when it came to beating a retreat, their respective patrons did things differently. The British liked to do it with slow dignity and ceremonial: 'The Last Post', the lowered flag and the march off, even under fire, though this time at least one colonel spoke of 'tiptoeing away from Basra'. Historically, the US is remembered for its more dramatic exits, whether at Little Big Horn or, by helicopter, from rooftops in Saigon. But what then?

The reality the companies faced, after the gunslinging freedom of four years in the Wild East alongside the world's biggest casino, where Russian roulette was obligatory, was that the impending departure of the US and British forces meant that their vital life-support systems were about to disappear. The moneybox – or that part of it provided by government – was about to close. There would be no more medevac (medical evacuation) helicopters, no emergency medical aid in Germany, no discreet medals from a grateful government, no massive road convoys rolling 300 miles up the road from Kuwait to import into Western compounds 12,000 tons of goodies each day in a paradigm of the Cargo Cult's dream of plenty.

Even before the great shakeout, relations between the companies and the Coalition were becoming somewhat flaky. A key component of survival was the shared intelligence flowing to and from the contractors about the threat lurking round the next corner. The information exchange was the Reconstruction Operations Centre, the ROC, managed by Tim Spicer's firm Aegis.

In December 2006 it seemed that all was not well with this arrangement, as US forces became uneasy about possible leaks of classified data. A confidential signal to members of a body called the Private Security Company Association Iraq (PSCAI) on 13 December 2006 expressed concern about tighter security within Coalition intelligence and more limited access to information by the contractors. The Association wrote,

> ROC personnel from Aegis are trying to report every bit of information that they are permitted to, but increasing pressure from official coalition entities has constricted their ability to get the word out. We've all witnessed the increasingly very tight scrutiny applied to dissemination reports.

As an example of the new tighter policy, the association cited

> an on-going kidnappings situation (a PSC) which I doubt many of you are aware. This situation is deemed 'too sensitive' for transmission . . . PSCs have a limited tool-chest upon which to draw when conducting missions in Iraq. Typically they are lightly armed, have armoured vehicles and use information to guide their decision matrix on whether to go or no go.
>
> Take away their information and you take away one of the three legs of the stool on which they sit . . . Let's take the case of the men who were kidnapped yesterday . . . There are up to eleven men who have been kidnapped in a particular area. This is an area that needs to be highlighted. Another PSC may go by that and see someone waving frantically toward them. If they were to know that eleven had been kidnapped and to Be On Look Out (BOLO) for them, maybe they might inadvertently stumble upon them and assist in a rescue. It has happened before . . . We are talking about lives here. This is not some abstract concept of information and propriety. Information helps save lives . . .
>
> To sum up, I am profoundly disappointed that all SIRs [Significant Incident Reports] will be sucked up into the SIPR [Secret Classified Internet] never to reach the consumers for which the system, the information exchange known as the ROC, was originally set up.

Insiders whispered that some of the British companies based in the country were discussing a consortium linked to local interests in joint ventures so as to stay in business after a Western withdrawal, but that course would lead, inevitably, to supping with the devil of tribal and religious politics.

Another manoeuvre, far from the bloody streets of Baghdad, most vividly demonstrated that the party was over. Halliburton, the all-purpose logistical giant that benefited more than any other from the corporate feeding frenzy, announced that it was moving its head office out of Texas and into Dubai.[1] Halliburton's popularity in Washington had already been damaged by its links to US Vice-President Dick Cheney and allegations that its government contracting subsidiary, KBR, had wasted billions of taxpayer dollars in Iraq.

A Democratic senator, Byron Dorgan, proposed a congressional investigation into the affair.[2] He said, 'I want to know, is Halliburton trying to run away from bad publicity on their contracts? Or are they trying to run away from the obligation to pay US taxes? Or are they trying to set up a corporate presence in Dubai so that they can avoid the restrictions that currently exist on doing business with prohibited countries like Iran?'

Dorgan's colleague, Senator Patrick Leahy, snapped, 'This is an insult to the US soldiers and taxpayers who paid the tab for their no-bid contracts and endured their overcharges for all these years.'[3]

The company denied that it would benefit financially from the move. Nonetheless, such a step was seen as a 'a blow to the US oil and gas industry, in which the company has played a prominent role since it was founded in 1919'.

In Iraq itself, the mayhem continued. By March 2007 the number of regular US servicemen and women killed (about 3,200) had exceeded the number slaughtered in the Twin Towers attack of 9/11. Blackwater lost another helicopter and five more operators shot down over a Sunni neighbourhood of Baghdad. The company, guarding US diplomats, had lost five others two months earlier when their helicopter – a readily identified Little Bird, marked with a single stripe – was shot down. At that time the company had picked up an estimated $320 million from a $1 billion five-year State Department budget for its Worldwide Personal Protective Service.

The grief of next of kin was less visible. The families of the four-man Blackwater team murdered by a mob at Fallujah in 2004 were still awaiting closure, which could come only with a full disclosure of the facts, probably through litigation. As *Time* magazine put it,

> The families want to know what happened that day in Fallujah. But they also want to press their claims that Blackwater, in its zeal to exploit this unexpected market for private security men, showed a callous disregard for the safety of its employees ... The case has stirred a nest of questions about accountability, oversight and regulations governing for-profit gunslingers in war zones.[4]

Beneath the surface, there were other, more sinister, developments. These included contingency plans within the Pentagon to pursue 'the El Salvador Option', a strategy of targeted assassinations to remove insurgent leaders, adopted during a dirty war in El Salvador in the eighties. John Barry, a former *Sunday Times* 'Insight' reporter, now writing for *Newsweek*, suggested,

> Following that model, one Pentagon proposal would send Special Forces teams to advise, support and possibly train Iraqi squads, most likely hand-picked Kurdish Peshmerga fighters and Shiite militiamen, to target Sunni insurgents and their sympathizers, even across the border into Syria, according to military insiders.[5]

One of the Pentagon's advisers was Stuart Herrington, a former army intelligence officer who, during the Vietnam war, took part in an assassination campaign against Vietcong leaders as part of Operation Phoenix. After visiting Iraq for the Pentagon he told Jonathan D. Tepperman, an executive with *Foreign Affairs* in 2005, 'I favoured using Shiites and Kurds to go after the Sunnis.'[6]

In the anything-goes culture of Iraq, there was other evidence that elements within the US military had adopted their own version of the El Salvador Option. 'A former military sniper' complained to *Soldier of Fortune* magazine in February 2007,

> I waited in a hide-site three weeks to take down the head of a black market fuel ring who was funding the primary terror group in the region. I literally had him in my sights, but when I called for the go-ahead, I was told to remain in over-watch while two platoons moved into blocking

positions and captured him. This sort of thing has happened too many times to list them all and was quite disheartening.[7]

In other cases, civilian contractors were embedded with regular US army sniper teams. One was known as 'Rover'. Writing in *Soldier of Fortune* about disciplinary proceedings he faced, a sergeant in charge of one of the teams said, 'I even spoke to Rover, the "civilian contractor". Rover said he would talk to the Regimental SMG [senior management group]. Rover said we did an outstanding job . . . we should be proud. He would see what he could do.'

Terrorist spectaculars – bombings, beheadings, kidnappings – had obscured the sniper war in Iraq, apart from publicity given to the legendary 'Baghdad Sniper', an insurgent who learned his trade from US military manuals. In fact, sniping emerged as a potent weapon employed by all sides. Private military companies operating in Iraq employed snipers to fight off attacks, as did Blackwater at Najaf in April 2004. That is not necessarily the same as targeted assassination. But, given the nature of the conflict and the fact that it is the most privatised war for around two centuries, it would be no surprise if highly sensitive strikes, requiring plausible deniability, were handed over to the private sector.

At least one professional assassin *was* identified, after his death, as an employee of a private security/military company in Iraq. Gray Branfield died bravely in a firefight at Kut in April 2004. A former Rhodesian police officer, he was part of the South African Defence Force's clandestine Project Barnacle. He admitted being part of a death squad that gunned down two anti-apartheid leaders in Harare on 31 July 1981. When he died he was working for the Hart Group, established in 1999 by a respected SAS officer. The company may not have known about Branfield's past. Its website says it 'supports the Voluntary Principles on Security and Human Rights which provide standards for companies on maintaining the safety and security of their operations within a framework that ensures respect for human rights'.

There were other, similar, cases. Deon Gouws, aged 43, was a former Pretoria police sergeant who admitted to the Truth and Reconciliation Commission that he had killed at least 15 people, and had blown up more than 40 houses of anti-apartheid militants. He was granted amnesty. After only 20 days in Iraq he was blown up by an ambulance packed with explosives while working for a subsidiary of Erinys. He lost his right arm, left eye and toes.

It is worth emphasising that neither Branfield nor Gouws was engaged in a dirty war in Iraq, whatever their past in South Africa. But their presence in private security inevitably meant that the expertise they and many others had acquired during the war to defend apartheid was available, if called upon, by various entities elsewhere.

Conscientious contractors and journalists were not alone in being troubled by the moral ambiguities of the Iraqi conflict in the years after the Bush–Blair victory. In June 2005, Colonel Ted Westhusing, aged 44, a dedicated Christian, was found dead in a trailer at the US base near Baghdad Airport. He was at that time the most senior officer to die in Iraq. US authorities concluded that he had used his service pistol to kill himself.

A few months earlier he had volunteered to go to Iraq. He was given the task of overseeing the activities of a private security company training Iraqi police in special operations. In May 2005 he received an anonymous letter alleging that the company concerned was implicated in the killing of Iraqis. The letter linked the incident to the big offensive against Fallujah in November 2004, claiming, according to one report, 'A . . . contractor accompanied Iraqi police trainees during the assault . . . and later boasted about the number of insurgents he had killed.' In a second incident, 'an employee saw Iraqi police trainees kill two innocent Iraqi civilians, then covered it up'.[8] A manager of the firm 'did not want it reported because he thought it would put his contract at risk'.

US officials investigated and discovered 'no contractual violations'. Westhusing's suicide note included the following: 'I cannot support a mission that leads to corruption, human rights abuse and liars. I am sullied. I came to serve honourably and feel dishonoured. Death before being dishonoured any more.' He had less than a month to serve in Iraq before returning home. A psychologist who studied the case after his death concluded, 'Despite his intelligence, his ability to grasp the idea that profit is an important goal for people working in the private sector was surprisingly limited.'

The corroding effect of disillusionment in an amoral war also had its impact on an experienced, serving SAS soldier, Ben Griffin. In March 2005, after three months in Baghdad, he told his commander that he was no longer prepared to fight alongside American forces. He said he had witnessed 'dozens of illegal acts' by US troops, who, he believed, saw all Iraqis as *untermenschen*.[9] Griffin was a soldier for eight years, including active service with the Parachute Regiment in Northern Ireland, Macedonia and Afghanistan.

His SAS commanding officer described him as 'a balanced and honest soldier who possesses the strength and character to genuinely have the courage of his convictions'. The Ministry of Defence threatened to sue him for breaching the notorious confidentiality contract imposed on Special Forces soldiers, a device that uses civil law as a substitute for the Official Secrets Act. Griffin's lawyer, Simon McKay, commented, 'The suggestion that Mr Griffin's comments damaged the SAS does not stand up to scrutiny. The truth is that this is an attempt to gag Mr Griffin, not because he disclosed details about SAS operations but because he embarrassed the government.'

As things stand there are only unverifiable rumours of assassins forming part, if a small part, of the private security sector in Iraq. One man with long experience of the intelligence war there told me, 'Given previous US practice in this area, and the neocons' belief that El Salvador was a success, the use of hit squads trained by CIA/Contractors in Iraq is a rumour that cannot be ignored. Unfortunately, the wrong lessons were drawn from El Salvador over the cultural factors that come into play in Iraq, especially the role revenge has, and how "revenge" can be passed down the generations.

'I suspect that the militia hits in Baghdad by rogue members of the US-trained Interior Ministry special commandos is an El Salvador option that has run out of control.'

Another shadow still hanging over the activities of security contractors in Iraq is the use of interrogators drawn from the private sector. While researching this book I received, from a South African operator specialising in interrogation, photographs that appear to show a suspect standing, presumably bound, up to his neck inside a pillar of motor tyres. The effect of this, in scorching heat, can be imagined but it would not leave any marks on the victim. Coincidentally, a similar case involving a reputable British company known to employ South Africans was exposed by the *Observer* in November 2004.[10] According to that report the photographs, taken in May of that year, 'show two employees of Erinys restraining the 16-year-old with six car tyres around his body' in a Kirkuk garage.

The newspaper was told that the youth was 'left immobile and without food or water for 24 hours'. The company – Erinys – claimed that he was released without harm within minutes. He was suspected of stealing a cable. Like Hart, Erinys is a reputable firm headed by former SAS officers who were apparently unaware of what some of their men were doing.

What other legacies did the privatised conflict of Iraq leave for governments to address? Covert operations, from the autumn of 2006, were authorised by President Bush to kill or capture Iranian agents in Iraq as part of a campaign to halt Iranians' suspected assistance to Shia militias.[11] In Baghdad, Western-trained commandos belonging to the Iraqi Interior Ministry were implicated in a campaign of kidnap and torture. The victims were often Sunnis, former members of Saddam's sinister secret Mukhabarat police.

A senior British police officer, mentoring the new Iraqi Police Force (that is, leading it by example) told the *Observer* that he had entered the room of a deputy minister to discover 'a man with a bag over his head standing in the corner'.[12] What happened to the hooded man is not recorded. It was a moment of surrealism, a Magritte moment, but also a symptom of a wider sickness.

Black operations proliferated in the Kurdish north, where, according to Israeli sources, Israeli special forces veterans were training Kurds in their own very special methods of anti-terrorism.[13] A Defence Ministry spokesman in Jerusalem offered a less than convincing rebuttal of the story: 'We haven't allowed Israelis to work in Iraq and each activity, if performed, was a private initiative, without our authorisation and is under the responsibility of the employers and employees involved.'

Another part of the Iraq legacy after the West's D (for Departure) day is the propaganda war and its impact on the integrity of information. For a change, the CIA was not involved in the process. Soon after the World Trade Center attack on 11 September 2001, the Pentagon, under Donald Rumsfeld, the much-criticised former Secretary of Defense, set up an Orwellian organisation known as the Office of Strategic Influence. Its agenda, leaked to the *New York Times*, proposed 'a broad mission ranging from "black" campaigns that use disinformation and other covert activities to "white" public affairs that rely on truthful news releases . . . from the blackest of black programs to the whitest of white'.[14] Once this creation was exposed to the light of day it was closed on 26 February 2002, but Rumsfeld told reporters, 'Fine. I'll give you the corpse . . . But I'm gonna keep doing every single thing that needs to be done.'[15]

Subsequently a series of companies took over much of the white propaganda effort in Iraq, planting unattributed stories in newspapers that reflected credit on the American army. The respected Center for Media and Democracy quoted General George W. Casey (3 March, 2006): 'The US military plans to continue paying Iraqi newspapers to publish articles favourable to the United States.' There was nothing wrong with that, apparently, since an internal review had concluded 'that the US military was not violating US law or Pentagon guidelines with the information operations campaign, in which US troops and a private contractor write pro-American articles and pay to have them planted without attribution in Iraqi media'.[16]

One company engaged in this process was the Lincoln Group, whose executive vice-president, Christian Bailey, grew up in Surrey and graduated at Lincoln College, Oxford. The company's subsidiary, Iraqex, won a multimillion-dollar contract from the Pentagon in 2005, as its own literature put it, 'to alter Iraqis' perception of the coalition forces'. Lincoln's chief executive, Christian Bailey, adopted the Edith Piaf defence when he was approached by the *Sunday Times*: he had no regrets. 'We have handled ourselves very appropriately. The confidence and trust of our clients is much more important to us than the temporary press flap.'[17] In December that year Martha Raddatz, an ABC Television reporter, revealed a Lincoln Group proposal entitled *The Making of Heroes: Lincoln Group and the Fight for Fallujah*.[18] Fallujah, a Sunni town besieged and largely destroyed by Coalition forces with the loss of hundreds of civilian lives in 2004 after the murder of four private security operators from Blackwater, is a synonym for military mayhem. Martha Raddatz claimed that Lincoln's version of the battle would promote 'the strength, integrity and reliability of Iraqi Forces during the fight for Fallujah'. The role of the Iraqi forces, until then, had largely gone unnoticed, probably because they played little part.

The achievements to which the Coalition laid claim, as their legitimate legacy, were successful elections and the innovation of Western-style democracy into Iraq, even if one effect of the process was to reopen religious and ethnic faultlines that had existed since the state's invention by the British and French after World War One. The dilemma facing those remaining after the departure of Coalition forces was that the very democratic institutions that the West sought to nurture lacked credibility because of the methods required to make them come to life overnight. So how would they view the future?

According to Andrew Bearpark, director of the British Association of Private Security Companies, some will see the new situation as one of opportunity. 'As the US military draw down,' he told me, 'there is a greater area of tasks which could be performed by PSCs, including training the new Iraqi army. The other side of the story is that, if the violence increases or does not stabilise, others will say it is too dangerous, it is time for us to go as well. No one has yet convinced me to believe one option or the other.'[19]

Another, less likely, prospect was that the withdrawal of Western forces would reduce the tension, since the forces were – as one British general believes – the source of the trouble.

Given that the Iraq bubble is over, however, what will be the economic effect on the industry as a whole? Will it implode? Bearpark believes, 'There will be a shakeout as in any other business. It is not possible to know the extent of it since none of the companies is publicly listed, with the exception of ArmorGroup. But, although the Iraq bubble has burst, the industry will not go back to where it was before. If you were to draw a graph that suggests the industry was at Level One before Iraq, and then went up to Ten on the back of the bubble, then, afterwards, it will level off at about Five.'

There will be other areas of endeavour, of course. The West's commitment to Afghanistan appears, in 2007, to bind it to development in that country, alongside a protracted guerrilla war, for between 10 and 20 years.

Meanwhile, the froth of political reports, initiatives and rumours proposing action to reform the private security industry seemed unlikely to deter any British citizen who chose to work for a foreign company on some battlefield beyond British jurisdiction. South Africa had tried and failed to bring its freelance soldiers to heel regardless of where they served and whom. A Pontius Pilate law might save faces in political London. This would be an appropriate outcome, perhaps, in a world in which old loyalties, ethics and national boundaries were being melted down like gold sovereigns in the service of those coiners of the Corporation.

Back in Baghdad, however, democracy was working. Top of the Iraqi government's agenda was legislation 'to open the door to much-needed investment' in – what else? – oil.[20] The new law, the brainchild of Washington, might permit Western oil companies to collect up to 70 per cent of profits for years, as they recovered their costs under new 'production-sharing agreements'.[21] The case for such an arrangement was that it was the only way to get the industry back on its feet. Its opponents argued that production-sharing agreements were highly unusual in the Middle East.

The oil industry in the two biggest producers – Saudi Arabia and Iran – is state-controlled.

It was exactly this distinction between state and company control, and the nationalisation of the Anglo-Iranian Oil Company, that provoked the first Anglo-American intervention, combining the threat of military force with political destabilisation, in the Gulf in the 1950s. As we have seen, the dubious side of the Iraq war began with a programme known as Restore Iraqi Oil. A congressional inquiry reported in March 2006: 'The Bush Administration started planning for the takeover of Iraq's oil fields nearly a year before the invasion of Iraq' – in the summer of 2002. 'From nearly the beginning, Halliburton had a major role in the [Bush] Administration's oilfield planning.'[22]

This began a process through which Halliburton, the largest private contractor in Iraq, was secretly given favoured status by the Pentagon and a contract worth $1.9 million. After much controversy, in January 2004, Halliburton was granted a second fat contract, worth $1.2 billion, to restore the country's oil infrastructure in southern Iraq, where the most productive oil fields are situated. It is worth wondering why, in 2007, further investment was required to revive the industry.

The congressional inquiry report, compiled at the request of Representative Henry A. Waxman, concluded,

> Two years ago [in 2004] despite warnings from auditors not to enter into further contracts with Halliburton, the Defense Department awarded Halliburton a new oil infrastructure contract, RIO 2. Internal government documents show that Halliburton's performance under RIO 2 has been deeply flawed. Among the serious and persistent problems identified in the document are repeated examples of apparently intentional overcharging, exorbitant costs, poor cost reporting, slipping schedules, and a refusal to co-operate with the government. The impact on the reconstruction effort in Iraq and on taxpayers is significant, with Pentagon auditors challenging $45 million in RIO 2 costs.

So was the war more to do with oil than, say, weapons of mass destruction or humanitarian intervention? On 18 March 2003, with the invasion imminent, Tony Blair proposed the Commons motion to back the war. He said, 'Let the oil revenues, which people falsely claim that we want to seize, be put in a trust fund for the Iraqi people and administered through the

UN . . . The United Kingdom should seek a new Security Council Resolution that would affirm . . . the use of all oil revenues for the benefit of the Iraqi people.'

Nothing came of it. Instead, after the war, Britain co-sponsored a Security Council resolution giving the US and UK control over Iraq's oil revenues. Around 90 per cent of the money was siphoned off while the Coalition Provisional Authority was running the country. The CPA shipped oil through a pipeline system with non-functioning meters. The revenue that remained (known as the Development Fund for Iraq) was held in the Federal Reserve Bank of New York, which made significant earnings from controlling its millions of dollars. Five per cent, at least, was handed over to Kuwait as compensation for the 1990 invasion.[23]

For the private security industry, Iraq was more than the source of the bubble. It was the template for a new style of warfare, one in which freelance soldiers formed the second largest armed force after the United States. By 2007, the estimated number of private contractors had grown from 20,000 to 100,000. The figures are not necessarily reliable. However, it is reasonable to suppose that around 8,000 expatriate freelance soldiers (about 1,000 from South Africa) were players, increasingly caught in the crossfire of an emerging civil war. Even before Departure Day, police officers and Iraqi soldiers trained by the companies were signing up to join sectarian militias.

With the departure of the regular US armed forces, the safest prediction was that the foreigners' chief priority would be to focus on one priority: safeguarding the oil for the benefit of such companies as BP, Shell and Exxon. As one anonymous contributor to the Aegis dialogues reminded his comrades-in-tax-avoidance, 'The companies are here to make as much money in a short time as possible. Isn't that why we are all here? Grow up!'

The challenge for the new, squeaky-clean companies following that act must be to find a more respectable *raison d'être* while staying solvent. That could be achieved only through government subsidies and a readiness on the parts of humanitarian bodies – NGOs engaged in reconstruction, without seeking a profit – to allow freelance soldiers to join in their endeavours. There is no guarantee that either of these objectives will be accomplished. The alternative is a return by freelance operators to the bad old days of a mercenary culture in which they scrape the barrel of lost causes.

It would be a return to the world identified by A. E. Housman:

> *What God abandoned, these defended,*
> *And saved the sum of things for pay.*

The Wild Geese flew long ago. These days, some of them prefer an alternative mantra, devised by John Keegan, to the effect that 'mercenaries are those who sell military service for money – though also for such inducements as land, admission to citizenship or preferential treatment. Regulars are mercenaries who already enjoy citizenship or its equivalent but choose military service as a means of subsistence.'[24]

APPENDIX

'The Best of British' – A Cross-Section of UK Private Security and Private Military Companies

This list that follows is far from comprehensive. Rather, it offers a snapshot of an industry that has multiplied and mutated since the Twin Towers attack of 2001 and the subsequent invasions of Afghanistan the same year, and of Iraq in 2003. All the companies identified are members of the British Association of Private Security Companies, an organisation that represents enterprises 'that provide armed security services in countries outside the UK'.

Aegis Defence Services Ltd/Aegis Specialist Risk Management

Mission: To identify, analyse and mitigate risk to corporate and individual clients around the world.

Workforce: 1,200 in Iraq; unknown number elsewhere. Probable total: 2,000. Offices in Afghanistan, Bahrain, Iraq, Kenya, Nepal and the USA.

Functions: Online terrorism database; research and intelligence; security operations; technical services.

Aegis occupies a uniquely powerful position in Iraq. Thanks to a $293 million, three-year contract awarded by the Pentagon in June 2004, it acts as the interface and tactical headquarters linking US and UK regular military armies with at least 50 security companies licensed to operate in the country. The arrangement emerged from the Fallujah disaster in April 2004, when four American security guards were lynched, their desecrated bodies strung head down from a bridge. The company's charismatic CEO, Tim Spicer, suggested a series of computerised control centres linked to an American military satellite system to monitor the movements of every private security team throughout the country.

The ROC teams include American and British military intelligence analysts who enjoy a high security clearance with their own governments. They are cleared to receive sensitive security data that is then sanitised in a way that is useful to the PSC teams, but not potential enemies. Three of its British contractors and one American received the US Commander's Award for Civilian Service.

In October 2005 Aegis was contracted by the UN to support the electoral referendum and the December general election. The fact that these elections were not disrupted by terrorist activity was to a considerable extent thanks to the work of its security teams. Contractors working for Aegis describe the firm as 'a good, caring employer'. Pay scales remain high thanks to the US contract. There are four scales ranging from about $120,000 per annum to $170,000.

AKE Group

Andrew Kain Enterprise, founded by a former senior SAS NCO in 1991, has prospered by identifying niche security markets around the world. It is particularly well known for training journalists, aid workers and other civilians to survive in combat zones. Its medical team provide crisis management by radio and telephone thanks to a former RAMC and SAS field medic, Paul Brown. One of his coups was medical advice to a client who had been struck by an arrow soaked in crocodile bile. With a turnover of nearly £6 million and a staff of more than 30 working out of London, Sydney, Washington and Baghdad, the Hereford-based company was awarded the Queen's Award for Enterprise in International Trade in 2005.

ArmorGroup International

Mission: To provide 'protective security services, security training and weapons reduction and mine action services, primarily to governments, major international peace and security organisations and multinational corporations'.

Workforce: 9,000 in 38 countries.

Functions: Four key areas: protective security; security training; security consultancy; weapons reduction and clearance.

2005 turnover: $233 million

ArmorGroup was founded in London in 1981 as Defence Systems Ltd (DSL) by Alastair Morrison, a recently retired SAS hero famous for his part in the rescue of hostages at Mogadishu in 1977. During the next 10 years, DSL and its subsidiaries provided security management and training in Papua New Guinea (cash-in-transit services only), Mozambique and Colombia.

In 1997 DSL was taken over by Armor Holdings Inc., a company listed on the New York stock exchange. As ArmorGroup, it was listed on the London stock exchange in 2004. In 2005 it acquired Phoenix CP Ltd, a company run by former SAS Regimental Sergeant Major Mick Clifford and another veteran, James Devenney, to train other veterans as close-protection bodyguards, winning preferred-supplier status with the Ministry of Defence for resettlement training.

ArmorGroup benefited substantially from the so-called Iraq Bubble. With revenue up 93 per cent between 2003 and 2004, 57 per cent was the result of operations in Iraq.

The award of a contract to safeguard the British Embassy in Baghdad was described by the *Financial Times* as 'a significant milestone in the emergence of the security industry as part of the UK economy'. A similar contract to protect embassy staff in Afghanistan in November 2006 was worth over $30 million a year. Between 2003 and 2005 the firm picked up 12 'significant' similar contracts to guard our men in Africa and the Middle East.

In April 2005, the firm recruited Stephen Kappes, a CIA veteran, as its head of global strategy. Twelve months later the Agency reclaimed him and made him deputy director general in a move seen as restoring experience and professionalism to the CIA. Close links with US government continue. ArmorGroup North America, for example, is the prime contractor for a £265 million weapons-clearance programme funded by the State Department. This effort – to remove from the wrong hands small arms and

surface-to-air missiles as well as clearing mines – is part of a 'global integrated weapons removal and abatement programme'.

That, in turn, was an early example of future diversification being
studied by the security industry known as 'DDR' (for disarmament, demobilisation, reintegration). Another example identified by the company is a
series of UK-funded police mentoring contracts in Iraq/Afghanistan. In
Afghanistan, the company ran mine-action programmes for more than 10
years prior to 2006.

Meanwhile, with a former Foreign Secretary (Sir Malcolm Rifkind) as
its chairman and such influential advisers as Professor Andrew Fulton, a
former diplomat in sensitive postings, on its team, ArmorGroup was
regarded as one of the 'gold standard' companies in an industry worth £1.5
billion. The reduced growth in profits from Iraq was more than offset by
significant growth in new trouble spots such as Afghanistan, Nigeria and
Moscow. In the two years 2004–6, as the firm points out, it has 'supported
its clients in over 160 countries across the Middle East, Africa, North and
South America, the CIS (Russian Federation) and Central Asia', often in
hazardous environments.

Blue Hackle Group Ltd

Incorporated in 2004 this company has made its name running 'low-
profile' escort teams in Iraq and Afghanistan. That strategy seems to have
paid off. It has lost only one man, killed by a roadside bomb near Basra. It
has a London headquarters staffed by 20 people and around 450 in the
field. It also has 200 'third-country nationals' – TCNs – working as static
guards. It is following the example of other companies in providing a helicopter service within Iraq.

Britam Defence Ltd

Britam, with a former SAS general (Sir Michael Wilkes) as chairman,
operates from London, Dubai, Singapore and Baghdad. It offers training
in a wide range of defence disciplines, including air-marshal techniques,
counterterrorism, sniper work, surveillance, high-risk search, crisis
management and explosive methods of entry. Much of its training is
online.

Centurion Risk Assessment Services Ltd

Founded in 1995, the company was included in the *Sunday Times* top 100 fast-track private companies in its tenth year. Staffed by former Royal Marine commandos, the company runs a 'flagship training course, the Hostile Environments and Emergency First Aid course, helps participants to protect themselves' through risk assessment.

Control Risks

Mission: 'To enable our clients to succeed in complex and hostile business environments.'

Workforce: Salaried staff plus contract workers, stringers and contacts – approximately 3,000.

Functions: Risk assessment/management worldwide, 24/7; close protection, corporate investigation.

In 1974 David Walker, a former SAS officer, was commissioned to examine how an insurance company, Hogg Robinson, might exploit the security market. He collaborated with Julian Radcliffe, managing director of a political-risk insurance company in the same group. The emerging subsidiary – Control Risks – according to one pioneer, was a shelf company acquired by Tim Royle, a cavalryman turned businessman. Walker was the firm's managing director (and only employee) for a year. He 'deployed to Rome and Milan to advise on kidnap and ransom cases'; devised procedures for kidnap negotiation; and recruited a team, including two more SAS veterans, Simon Adams-Dale and Arish Turle. After the firm was activated in 1975, Walker left to join Jim Johnson at KMS, a company that would be known for its high-risk, deniable operations run on behalf of SIS.

By then, Radcliffe had approached Lloyd's underwriters, inviting them to provide cover for businessmen against risk of kidnap-and-ransom ('K&R') and a service to contain the risk. Lloyd's agreed. Hogg Robinson, according to one long-serving member, now had to find people 'to deliver a service that did not formally exist'. More former SAS officers joined the company, which has since handled hundreds of K&R incidents, assisting companies, advising next of kin and usually arranging for the release of kidnap victims on terms that are less than the initial, outrageous demands.

In 1977 Turle and Adams-Dale were arrested by uncomprehending Colombian police while they were negotiating the release of George Curtis, vice-president of Beatrice Foods of America. Curtis was freed from his prison, a tiny cellar, after a ransom of $400,000 in local currency was handed over in four suitcases. Turle and Adams-Dale were detained for 10 weeks, during which time they rewrote what would become the firm's bible for crisis response, its Standard Operational Procedures.

In its annual report for that year, Hogg Robinson stated, 'Control Risks continues to expand . . . Its kidnap and ransom service is now being used by Lloyd's underwriters as well as by many international companies both within the UK and around the world.' In 1979, Control Risks successfully negotiated, on behalf of Lloyds Bank International, the release of two of the bank's British officials after they had been imprisoned by guerrillas in El Salvador.

Since then it has pioneered life-saving risk-management techniques in more than 130 countries for more than 5,000 clients, 'including most of the Fortune 100'. The firm's sophisticated advice is based on information supplied by networks of local agents. (It employs people of at least 38 different nationalities.) Its risk-analysis service provides an online advice service to clients about proposed visits to foreign places. Its hotline services are manned 24 hours a day, 365 days a year, with experts on hand to help clients who are in difficulty. One of the team told me, 'We take calls from people whose colleagues have just been shot, or who are experiencing gunfire on the hotel room. Since we have consultants who have been in the thick of it, they can offer sound advice.'

Its crisis-response group has handled more than 1,400 cases involving abduction, product extortion and political detention. Its agents in the field trace missing people, secure premises and extract individuals at risk in war zones. They have included people caught up in the tsunami disaster on Boxing Day, 2004; the Hurricane Katrina emergency in New Orleans, 2005; the first Gulf crisis in 1990; the terrorist bomb attacks on London's Underground system on 7 July 2005; and Israel's Lebanon offensive in 2006, when 109 people employed by 13 companies were evacuated by road into Syria in 14 days – some of those rescued were journalists.

The firm also hires bodyguards, usually unarmed, for a variety of clients. In Iraq, where it has 300 close-protection officers, and Afghanistan, CR men carrying firearms are a praetorian guard for British government officials. One of the company's principals says, 'We train our people before they go. They must reach certain basic standards to be accepted. That is followed by in-country training in specific topics. If they don't match our standards, they are not employed.'

In Iraq in 2004, CR bodyguards did heroic work to safeguard Rory Stewart, a diplomat seconded to the Coalition Provisional Authority. Control Risks' front line also extends to the boardrooms and back offices of many of its client companies. Corporate investigations; action to halt sabotage by contamination of company products, either for blackmail or ideology; forensic accounting; status checks on business partners and employees; due-diligence enquiries – all have become part of a substantial, though invisible security empire. On 5 July 1991, the firm was the first to secure the premises of the Bank of Credit and Commerce International (BCCI) on behalf of the Bank of England when it was learned that BCCI was a conduit for terrorist funds. Looking ahead, the company is working on 'good governance' and reconstruction programmes to assist countries and societies emerging from prolonged conflict.

Edinburgh International

This employee-owned company informs potential clients that it 'runs as a lean organisation: we do not pass on the costs of unnecessary overheads to our clients'. In Iraq it offers a package including accommodation complete with Internet, catering, gym facilities, vehicle hire and security.

Erinys International

Erinys International, based in Dubai, was founded in 2001 by Jonathan Garratt, a retired British officer. It currently offers 'private security services for businesses operating in Africa'. In 2002 it acquired the business of Strategic Concepts Pty Ltd, a South African based risk management consultancy. Erinys (UK) Ltd was incorporated in 2004 as a private limited company. Erinys is best known for its close links to Iraqi politicians and an £80 million contract to protect the country's oil infrastructure, using local guards. It has links to former SAS officers including Major General John Holmes. In its public pronouncements, the company stresses its integrity: no rackets, no money laundering, nothing, in fact, that would damage its image as an honest organisation.

Genric

This Hereford-based team specialises in countersurveillance operations, including office, home and personal security. It makes a point of identifying intrusions into personal as well as business issues.

Global Strategies Group

Global, founded by a former Royal Marine and a retired Scots Guards officer, believes in innovation combined with what the *Guardian* has described as 'an entrepreneurial edge'. Since 1998 it has impressed the US government with its ability to synthesise methods of security, infrastructure protection and counterterrorism. The firm's experience of nation rebuilding in Afghanistan and Liberia resulted, in February 2007, in a partnership with SFA Inc., a leading American defence firm, to 'support the US-led effort against international terrorism'.

Henderson Risk Ltd

Alongside other talents, HRL claims that its intelligence and investigation division has 'privileged access to information and contacts that fall outside normal "open source" material. These contacts have been established over years of professional contacts by our management team and their associates. We have the ability to look behind the official position of businesses and individuals in several territories and to obtain the "unofficial" view.' It offers services in the delicate area of due diligence, among others.

Janusian Security Risk Management

This company combines the experience of Arish Turle (formerly SAS Regiment, Control Risks, Kroll) with David Claridge, whose PhD from St Andrews was for a thesis entitled 'The Dynamics of State Terrorism'. Many of its operators worked as undercover military agents in Northern Ireland with 'the Dets', the detachments of 14 Intelligence Company. The firm has been in Iraq since 17 April 2003, running a variety of contracts with 400 operators and one fatality. In assisting businesses to get established in dangerous areas, it practises a form of futurology to anticipate a threat. It cites one case: a bank in South Asia, under the shadow of an insurgent group, was able to make an appraisal through which it could 'continue its operations at a time when its competitors were being forced to reconsider their positions'. One of its functions was to run trade delegations safely into and out of Baghdad.

Minimal Risk Consultancy Ltd

Mission: 'Our aim is to get people into work. We are not chasing the big bucks.'

Workforce: Six permanent staff.

Functions: Recruits professional security guards for high-risk assignments; confirms professional qualifications of self-employed security operators seeking employment; provides an online 'jobs vacant' service for those on its books; supplies PSCs with personnel at short notice.

Minimal Risk is a good example of a small but effective niche company in the new security industry. It is run by Bob Cole, a former Special Forces regimental sergeant major (warrant officer Class I) and his wife Gillian, a former teacher. After regular military service he worked as a security manager in the UK. In 2002 the Coles borrowed £10,000 from their bank and 'began networking with friends'. In 2003 Cole, an Arabist, went to Iraq, leaving his wife to run the business from their son's bedroom. He provided security for a BBC war reporting team including Kate Adie and Frank Gardner, working between Kuwait and Basra. After six weeks he joined the Olive Group on a 'high-profile' close-protection assignment. In June 2003 he became a project manager with Control Risks, escorting British diplomats. A team of 16 grew within four months to one of 300 men. They were obliged to run their own infrastructure, including a nationwide communications network.

Simultaneously, as the security boom took off – and with it 'contract hopping', as a result of which 'guys offered £10 a day more would take it' – word spread that his firm could provide reliable men. A joke was born, that not only was Cole *on* the Circuit, he *was* the Circuit. The Coles' recruiting agency found staff for Janusian, Control Risks and Aegis, initially as bodyguards. From its Hereford office, Minimal Risk can now call upon almost 7,000 qualified operators, of whom 435 are in the US, 40 in South Africa, and seven in Italy. Once accepted by the Coles' agency, operators can access a confidential jobs vacant list. Employers seeking staff from the agency know that it can make contact with 2,000 men simultaneously.

The skills required reflect the increasing complexity of the industry. As well as the usual convoy-escort and close-protection jobs, specialists are now required in intelligence analysis; administration and even insurance. To fill four UK government posts, the agency produced a shortlist of 25 potential recruits from an initial application list of 200, 'all ex-officers with junior command experience'.

Olive Group

Olive is a major global player, employing 500 people in 30 countries, with annual revenues of almost $1 billion. As well as the usual range of protections it owns a 700-acre training centre in Mississippi, providing live fire training up to Special Forces standards and explosive methods of entry. It supported US authorities after Hurricanes Rita and Katrina in 2005 and the international aid effort after the Asian tsunami the same year. A director is Sir Cedric Delves, an SAS hero of the Falklands war. He points out that his colleagues on the Olive board 'bring a mix of business and legal backgrounds to the leadership of the country'. PSCs, he argues, will increasingly be run by business leaders rather than former soldiers or spooks.

Oriel Solutions

Oriel is notable for the ideas of Harry Legge-Bourke, who told a security conference in London in 2006, 'There are better-trained close-protection teams in private security companies than in royal protection.' The Legge-Bourkes know about such matters from both sides of the fence. Harry's sister, Tiggy, was nanny to the Princes William and Harry. The Oriel company also occupies its own special niche: security of stadiums during international sporting events.

Saladin Security Ltd

Saladin, run by the Special Forces and freelance operator David Walker, is the direct descendant of KMS, which Walker began with Jim Johnson, after leaving Control Risks in 1975. The firm became a pioneer in privatised close protection for British diplomats around the world as well as the Saudi royal family. Towards the end of the 1980s the company reorganised, extending its range of conventional security services. It now provides the full menu of such services. It has a subsidiary company, Saladin Security (Afghanistan), and now, as always, has influential contacts within the Conservative Party. In 1993, for instance, Sir Archie Hamilton, MP for Epsom and Ewell, became a non-executive director of Saladin Holdings, having resigned as Armed Forces Minister.

Notes

Introduction

1. Dominick Donald, *After the Bubble: British Private Security Companies After Iraq*, paper, RUSI/AEGIS (2006)
2. Richard Norton-Taylor, 'Army fears loss of top troops to private firms', *Guardian* (8 August 2005)
3. Anon., Foreign and Commonwealth Office release, Freedom of Information Office (15 June 2005)
4. Anon., obituary, Pascal Kabungulu Kibembi, *Guardian* (24 August 2005)
5. Anon., Pascal Kabungulu (Kibembi), 'Still no justice for his murder', Amnesty International (24 July 2006)
6. Ken Connor, 'RAF jets are no substitute for a squad of SAS troopers', *Sunday Telegraph* (20 December 1998)
7. Jennings, Andrew, et al., 'Uncle Sam's British Mercenary', *World in Action* (26 July 1988)
8. Peter Oborne, 'What made Jack Straw tell the truth about the botched coup in Equatorial Guinea?', *Spectator* (25 November 2004)
9. Agence France-Presse, 'Coup confession "was forced" ', *The Times* (21 April 2007)
10. John Simpson, 'The foreign legion', *Guardian* (6 September 2005)
11. Kofi Annan, valedictory speech about Darfur (8 December 2006)
12. Singer, P. W., *Corporate Warriors: The Rise of the Privatized Military Industry*, Cornell University Press (2003), p. 15
13. Bill Bonner and Addison Wiggin, *Empire of Debt: The Rise of an Epic Financial Crisis*, John Wiley & Sons (2005)
14. Tony Benn, 'Bush is the real threat', *Guardian* (31 August 2005)
15. Max Hastings, 'Britain's Armed Forces Under Threat: A Journalist's Lament', *RUSI Journal*, Vol. 150(5) (October 2005)
16. P. W. Singer, *Corporate Warriors – The Rise of the Privatized Military Industry*, Cornell University Press (2003)
17. Joschka Fischer, 'The nation-state is irreplaceable', speech, Humbolt University, Berlin (12 May 2000)
18. Peter Beinart, 'The Kosovo Conundrum: How the legacy of the war that Tony Blair and Bill Clinton fought may split the US Democratic Party', *Time* (30 April 2007)

19. Thomas Harding, 'Crisis as SAS men quit for lucrative Iraq jobs', *Daily Telegraph* (14 February 2005)

20. Richard Norton-Taylor, 'Army fears loss of top troops to private firms', *Guardian* (8 August 2005)

21. Ibid.

22. Ian Griggs, 'Wounded in action and "tossed aside" ', *Independent on Sunday* (8 October 2005)

23. Mary Kaldor, 'Iraq: the wrong war', Open Democracy website, http://www.opendemocracy.net/conflict-iraq/wrong_war_2591.jsp (accessed June 2005)

24. Doug Brooks, president, International Peace Operations Association, 'Protecting People: The PMC Potential', online as PDF, http://www.hoosier84.com/0725brookspmcregs.pdf (25 July 2002)

25 Kevin A. O'Brien, 'PMCs, Myths and Mercenaries: the debate on private militaries [*sic*] companies', *Royal United Services Institute Journal* (February 2000)

26. Lt Col. Tim Collins, *The Moral Maze*, BBC Radio 4 (2005)

27. Kofi Annan, press conference, UN HQ (12 June 1997)

28. Philip Ball, 'This Means War', *Guardian* (4 August 2005)

29. Anon., 'Special Inspector General for Iraq Reconstruction', report to US Senate, US Congress (July 2005)

30. Christopher Coker, 'The Unhappy Warrior', *RUSI Journal*, Vol. 150(6)

Origins: 'The Business of America is Business'

1. Geraghty, Tony, *The Irish War*, HarperCollins (1998)

2. Ibid.

3. Anon., 'Pinkerton National Detective Agency', *Wikipedia*, http://en.wikipedia.org/wiki/Pinkerton_National_Detective_Agency (accessed 2006)

4. Maurice Chittenden, 'VE Day – and at last our war debt is over', *Sunday Times* (8 May 2005)

5. Ken Silverstein, 'Ford & the Führer', *Nation* (24 January 2000)

6. P. W. Singer, *Corporate Warriors: The Rise of the Privatized Military Industry*, Cornell University Press (2003)

7. William D. Hartung, 'Bombings Bring US "Executive Mercenaries" into the Light', *Los Angeles Times* (16 May 2003)

8. Wilbur Crane Eveland, *Ropes of Sand: America's Failure in the Middle East*, W. W. Norton & Co. (1980)

9. Stephen Dorril, *MI6: Inside the Covert World of Her Majesty's Secret Intelligence Service*, Fourth Estate (2000)

10. Hartnung, op. cit.

11. Jason Vest, 'State Outsources Secret War', *Nation* (23 May 2001)

12. Leslie Wayne, 'America's For-Profit Secret Army', *New York Times* (13 October 2002)

13. Singer, op. cit.

14. Ralph O. White and Christine S. Melody, Office of General Counsel, GAO: 'US Government Accountability Office Decision in the Matter of DynCorp International LLC', GAO File B-294232; B-294232.2 (13 September 2004)

1. Africa: They do things differently there

1. Barnaby Phillips, 'South Africa's "mercenary" village', *BBC News* (12 May 2004)

2. Congo, 1960–1: The unquiet spirit of Patrice Lumumba

1. Belgian Parliamentary Committee of Enquiry, 'The Exact Circumstances of the Assassination of Patrice Lumumba and Possible Involvement of Belgian Politicians' (December 2001)
2. Stephen R. Weissman, 'Opening the Secret Files on Lumumba's Murder', *Washington Post* (21 July 2002)
3. John Stockwell, *In Search of Enemies*, Replica Books (1997)
4. Jean Van Lierde, quoted by David Ackerman in "Who Killed Lumumba?", *Correspondent* series, *BBC News* (21 October 2000)
5. David Akerman, 'Who Killed Lumumba?' *Correspondent* series, *BBC News* (21 October 2000)
6. Anon., 'Nous les "affreux" du Katanga', Historia (Canadian cable TV) special, 'Les Mercenaires 1960–1980' (1980)
7. Ibid.

3. Congo 1964–7: The myth of the white giant

1. M. Hoare, *Congo Mercenary*, Robert Hale (1967)
2. Anthony Mockler, *The New Mercenaries*, Corgi Books (1986)
3. Anon., 'Needed: A Divine Force', *Time* (18 December 1964)
4. Jean-Pax Mefret, 'Au Yemen, pour le roi', Historia (Canadian cable TV) special, 'Les Mercenaires 1960–1980', Librairie Jules Tallandier, Paris (1980)
5. Lieutenant Colonel W. H. Glasgow, 'Operations Dragon Rouge and Dragon Noir', Operations Division, Historical Section, HQ, US Army Europe, online, http://www.army.mil/cmh-pg/documents/glasgow/glas-fm.htm (1965, accessed 15 June 2007)
6. Anon., 'The Congo Massacre', *Time* (4 December 1964)

4. Angola 1974–2002: A war for slow readers

1. CNN, 'Good Guys, Bad Guys', *Cold War Special*, Episode 17 (1998)
2. Jane Standley, *Cold War in a Hot Continent*, BBC Radio 3 (4 August 2006)
3. Ibid.
4. CNN, op. cit.
5. Stockwell, op. cit.
6. Hall, Mrs Lesley, statement on husband's role in mercenaries' recruitment (24 May 1976)
7. Graham Maclean, '. . . sold our guns in Ulster', *News of the World* (2 April 1972); anon., 'Para sold guns to the Ulster Protestants', *Aldershot News* (7 April 1972)
8. From *Fire Power* by Chris Dempster and Dave Tomkins, published by Corgi Books (1978), reprinted by permission of The Random House Group.
9. Martin Meredith, Nicholas Hall statement for the *Sunday Times*, not published (26 May 1976)

10. Linda Melvern and Stephen Clackson, 'How to blood a mercenary in W1', *Evening Standard* (29 July 1976)

11. Anon., Document 13: 'Telcon with Frank Sinatra, 16 January 1976, 8:09 p.m.', National Security Archive (2006)

12. Dempster and Tomkins, op. cit.

13. John Banks, affidavit cited in case of *R. v John Joseph Higgins* under headline 'A Case of British Justice', *The News Line* (9 April 1977)

14. James McManus, 'Some corner of a foreign field that is forever a shambles', *Guardian* (20 February 1976)

15. Garry Acker, 'Angolan Reflections Part II: Seven Years in Prison', *Soldier of Fortune* (March 1986)

5. Yemen 1965–8: 'Do you fancy going into Yemen and burning the Migs?'

1. Anthony Nutting, *Nasser*, Constable (1972)

2. George Kennedy Young, 'The final testimony . . .', *Lobster* magazine (May 1990)

3. Tom Bower, *The Perfect English Spy*, Mandarin (1996)

4. Johnny Cooper, with Anthony Kemp, *One of the Originals: The Story of a Founder Member of the SAS*, Pan (1991)

5. Ibid.

6. Jean-Pax Mefret, 'Au Yemen, pour le roi', Historia (Canadian cable TV) special, 'Les Mercenaires 1960–1980', Librairie Jules Tallandier, Paris (1980)

7. Peter de la Billière, *Looking for Trouble*, HarperCollins (1994)

8. D. Smiley and P. Kemp, *Arabian Assignment*, Leo Cooper, London (1975)

9. Clive Jones, *Britain and the Yemen Civil War, 1962–1965*, Sussex Academic Press (2004)

10. Mefret, op. cit.

11. Robin Neillands, *A Fighting Retreat: The British Empire 1947–97*, Hodder & Stoughton (1996)

12. Peter McAleese with Mark Bles, *No Mean Soldier*, Orion Books (1993)

13. Smiley and Kemp, op. cit.

14. Tony Geraghty, *Who Dares Wins*, 1st edn, Arms & Armour Press (1980)

15. Nutting, op. cit.

16. Jones, op. cit.

17. Smiley and Kemp, op. cit.

18. Ken Connor, *Ghost Force: The Secret History of the SAS*, Cassell & Co. (1998)

6. Oman 1970–95: How the Sandhurst Brotherhood saved a nation

1. Geraghty, op. cit.

2. Anon., statement of Ruler Sultan Qaboos, Ministry of Information, Sultanate of Oman website, http://www.omanet.om (accessed 7 June 2007)

7. Afghanistan 1979–89: 'The British will probably be most forthcoming'

1. Anon., 'CIA's intervention in Afghanistan', interview with Zbigniew Brzezinski, *Le Nouvel Observateur* (15 January 1998)
2. Anon., 'Western European Reaction to US–Soviet Tension', CIA secret document submitted to President Carter, declassified 30 January 2005, White House (8 January 1980)
3. Michael T. Kaufman, 'Mrs Thatcher Visits Afghans on the Frontier', *New York Times* (9 October 1981)
4. Tom Carew, *Jihad! The Secret War in Afghanistan*, Mainstream Publishing (2000)
5. Anon., Author 'lied about SAS membership', *BBC News*, (14 November 2001)
6. Ken Connor, *Ghost Force: The Secret History of the SAS*, Cassell & Co. (1998)
7. Anon., 'US Plot to Spy on Soviets in Afghanistan is Reported', Reuters (9 October 1983)
8. Anon., 'Afghans Expel US Envoy: Americans Reject Spy Charge', Associated Press (11 April 1984)
9. Patrick E. Tyler, 'Possible Diversion of Stinger Missile to Terrorists Causes Concern', *Washington Post* (8 April 1986)
10. Geraghty, op. cit.
11. Olivier Roy, 'The Lessons of the Soviet/Afghan War', Adelphi Papers 259, International Institute for Strategic Studies/Brassey's (1991)
12. Michael Gillard and David Connell, 'Customs haunted by the mole it lost', *Sunday Times* (24 July 2005)
13. Radek Sikorski, 'Afghanistan Revisited: Civil war between mujaheddin factions', *National Review* (23 August 1993)

8. Nicaragua and elsewhere, 1984–2006: Spreading democracy – America's first War on Terror

1. Anon., 'Bets Off on Terror Futures Index', Associated Press (29 July 2003)
2. Ronald Reagan, address to Members of the British Parliament (8 June 1982)
3. Andrew Jennings, Vyv Simpson, et al., 'Uncle Sam's British Mercenary', *World in Action* (26 July 1988)
4. Jennings, Simpson, op. cit.
5. Lawrence E. Walsh, Final Report of the Independent Counsel for Iran/Contra Matters, US Court of Appeals for District of Columbia Circuit (4 August 1993)
6. John Tower, Edward Muskie and Brent Scowcroft, Tower Commission Report (1987)
7. Robert Parry, 'The Shadow Warrior: Memoirs of the Man the White House Said Didn't Exist', *Washington Monthly* (November 1989)
8. James Lemoyne, 'Hasenfus Refers to Secret Airstrip', *New York Times* (24 October 1986)
9. Jennings, Simpson, op. cit.
10. Lieutenant Colonel Oliver North, testimony before Select Committee of US Congress on Secret Assistance to Iran and the Nicaraguan Opposition, Federal News Service, US Government
11. Jennings, Simpson, op. cit.
12. Anon., 'Observers Warn of US Manipulation in Nicaragua', National Public Radio (US) (5 May 2007)
13. Tim Padgett, Tim Rogers and Elaine Shannon, 'Ortega's Encore', *Time* (20 November 2006)

14. President Ronald Reagan, welcome-home address to US hostages released from Iran (27 January 1981)

15. President Ronald Reagan, National Security Decision Directive 138 (April 1984)

16. George P. Schultz, Secretary of State, 'Terrorism and the modern world', address by Secretary of State George P. Shultz, US Department of State Bulletin (December 1984)

17. Victor Ostrovsky and Claire Hoy, *By Way of Deception – An Insider's Devastating Exposé of the Mossad*, Bloomsbury (1990)

18. Nora Boustany, 'Beirut Bomb's Legacy: Suspicion and Tears', *Washington Post* (6 March 1988)

19. Bob Woodward, *Veil – The Secret Wars of the CIA*, Headline (1987)

20. Jonathan Marshall, 'Saudi Arabia and the Reagan Doctrine' Middle East Report (November–December 1998)

21. Anon., 'Target America – Terrorist Attacks on Americans, 1979–1988', Public Service Broadcasting, USA (2001)

22. R. Gregory Nokes, 'CIA involvement in car-bomb explosion just one more Mideast pitfall', Associated Press (18 May 1985)

23. Ibid.

24. Robert Timberg, *The Nightingale's Song*, Touchstone, New York (1996)

9. Sierra Leone 1997–8: A less than ethical foreign policy

1. Jane Austen, *Pride and Prejudice*: 'It is a truth universally acknowledged, that a single man in possession of a good fortune must be in want of a wife.'

2. Jack Straw, 'Private Military Companies: Options for Regulation', House of Commons (12 February 2002)

3. Will Scully, *Once a Pilgrim*, Headline (1998)

4. Ibid.

5. Tony Geraghty, interview with Peter Penfold (20 July 2006)

6. Scully, op. cit.

7. Lieutenant Colonel Tim Spicer, *An Unorthodox Soldier: Peace and War and the Sandline Affair*, Mainstream (1999)

8. Sir Thomas Legg and Sir Robin Ibbs, *Report of the Sierra Leone Arms Investigation*, HMSO (27 July 1998)

9. Ibid.

10. Robin Cook, Commons Hansard, Column 34 (27 July 1998)

11. House of Commons Foreign Affairs Committee, 2nd Report, Session 1998–9, Sierra Leone, HC 116 (3 February 1999)

12. Legg, Ibbs, op. cit.

13. Lord Avebury, letter to Ann Grant, head of Africa Department (Equatorial) (5 February 1998)

14. Spicer, op. cit.

15. Susana Raby, 'Best of Times, Worst of Times', interview with Craig Murray, *Sunday Times* (28 May 2006)

16. Anon., 'Hero's Welcome for ex-Ambassador', *Newsnight*, BBC2 (8 August 2002)

17. Bobor Tucker (Witness TF2-190), public testimony to Sierra Leone Special Court in

CDF Trial, from Sara Kendall, senior researcher, UC Berkeley War Crimes Studies Center (11 February 2005)

18. Witness TF2-187, public testimony to Sierra Leone Special Court (2 June 2005)

19. Colonel Richard Iron, British Army, public testimony to Sierra Leone Special Court (14 June 2005)

20. Tim Butcher, 'Soldier's rifle failed in battle, says secret report', *Daily Telegraph* (31 July 2000)

21. Ben Macintyre (former SIS officer), 'Deadlier than the male', *The Times* (15 May 2007)

22. Commons Intelligence and Security Committee, Report on Sierra Leone, House of Commons (May 1999)

10. Croatia 1995: America's junkyard dogs

1. Prosecutor, International Criminal Tribunal for the Former Yugoslavia, *The Prosecutor v. Ante Gotovina*, Case No. IT-01-45, Amended Indictment

2. Professor Dr Simun Sito Coric, Notice of the existence of information concerning serious violations of international humanitarian law (Submission to ICTFY Prosecutor), Croatian World Congress (4 July 2002)

3. Richard Holbrooke, *To End a War*, Random House (1999)

4. Mark Danner, 'Operation Storm', *New York Review of Books* (22 October 1998)

5. Ivo Pukanic, 'Thrilled with Operation Flash, President Clinton Gave the Go-Ahead for Operation Storm', *Nacional* (Croatian weekly magazine) (24 May 2005)

6. Roy Gutman, 'What Did the CIA Know?', *Newsweek* (21 August 2001)

7. Robert Fox, 'Fresh war clouds threaten ceasefire', *Sunday Telegraph* (15 October 1995)

8. Dominic Hipkins, 'Fugitive General threatens to expose US involvement in the reconquest of the Krajina region six years ago', *IWPR Balkan Crisis Report* No. 288 (16 October 2001)

9. Anon, 'US Links to Croatian War Crime?', *Spiegel Online*, http://www.spiegel.de/international/0,1518,396828,00.html (23 January 2006, accessed 7 June 2007)

10. Danner, op. cit.

11. Anon., profile of Ante Gotovina, *BBC News* (9 December 2005)

12. Tom Walker, and Ivanovic Milorad, 'Vengeful Serbs betray top MI6 man', *Sunday Times* (15 August 2004)

13. Ian Traynor, 'The fugitive who stands in the way of Croatia's EU entry', *Guardian* (18 March 2005)

14. Gutman, op. cit.

15. Mate Granic, HRTV1 TV, Zagreb (20 August 2001)

16. Holbrooke, op. cit.

17. Dr Robin Harris, 'The railroading of a former US ally', *American Spectator* (March 2006)

18. Florence Hartmann, *Milosevic: la diagonale du fou*, Editions Denoel, Paris (1999)

19. Milan Martic, 'Evacuation Order', *Politika* 23 (August 1995)

20. Anon., Croatia, January 2004, Human Rights Watch online, http://www.hrw.org (2006)

11. Iraq 2003–Present: A licence to kill – in some circumstances

1. Joyce Battle and Thomas Blanton (eds), *Top Secret Polo Step: Iraq War Plan Assumed Only 5,000 US Troops Still There by December 2006*, National Security Archive Electronic Briefing Book No. 214 (14 February 2007)

2. Anon, 'I am the Iraqi government', *Daily Telegraph* (5 March 2006)

3. David Isenberg, 'A Fistful of Contractors: The Case for a Pragmatic Assessment of Private Military Companies in Iraq', International Peace Operations Association/British American Security Information Council, online, http://www.basicint.org/pubs/Research/2004PMC.htm (28 September 2004, accessed 11 June 2007)

4. Edison Lopez, 'Ecuador: American entrepreneur scrutinised for offering mercenaries work in Iraq', Associated Press (15 August 2005)

5. Anon., 'Iraq Coalition Casualties: Contractors, a Partial List', Iraq Coalition Casualty Count (independent monitor), online, http://casualties.org/oif/civ/aspx

6. Chris Hughes, 'Two Killed in New Iraq Demo Shooting', *Daily Mirror* (1 May 2003)

7. Brian Bennett, 'Outsourcing the War. Four families want to know how their men, all guns for hire, died in Iraq', *Time* (26 March 2007)

8. Jonathan Freedland, 'By Sharon's Standards . . .', *Guardian* (5 May 2004)

9. Mark Franchetti and Hamoudi Saffar, 'Truce trembles in siege of Falluja', *Sunday Times* (18 April 2004)

10. Sarah Lyall, 'Britain Wields Legal Bludgeon in Effort to Stop Leaks', *New York Times* (13 July 2006) (original source: Robert Winnett, 'Memo reveals Blair's clash with Bush', *Sunday Times* (27 November 2005), suppressed by HM Government)

11. Matthew Hickley, and Bill Lowther, 'British brigadier branded a snob for attack on US', *Daily Mail* (12 January 2006)

12. Mark Etherington, *Revolt on the Tigris: The Al-Sadr Uprising and the Governing of Iraq*, C. Hurst & Co. (2005)

13. Tony Gosling, 'Bombers away!', *Journalist* (2007)

14. Dan Murphy, 'In Iraq, a "perfect storm" ', *Christian Science Monitor* (9 April 2004)

15. Simon Jenkins, 'Twelve months of living hopelessly', review of *My Year in Iraq* by Paul Bremer, *Sunday Times* (2006)

16. Anon, 'Being American in T.O.', *Iraqi Archives*, online blog, http://debbyestratigacos.mu.nu/archives/cat_iraq.html (accessed 11 June 2007)

17. Ross Davies, 'The Tragedy of Kut', *Guardian* (20 November 2002)

18. Etherington, op. cit

19. Isenberg, op. cit.

20. Stephen Gray, 'Iraq's new leaders target private guards', *Sunday Times* (6 June 2004)

21. Dana Priest, 'Private Security Guards Repel Attack on US Headquarters', *Washington Post* (6 April 2004)

22. Sam Kiley, 'The hogs of war', *Spectator* (17 April 2004)

23. Hala Jaber, 'Iraqi police in mystery killing', *Sunday Times* (12 September 2004)

24. Stewart, Rory, *Occupational Hazards: My Time Governing in Iraq*, Picador (2006)

25. Ibid.

26. Isenberg, op. cit.

27. Nicola Woolcock, 'We're expecting to be overrun and may have to fight . . .', *The Times* (10 April 2004)

28. Anon., 'Italian hostage "defied killers" ', *BBC News* (15 April 2004)

29. Tina-Marie O'Neil, 'Bush's Iraq Point Man', *Sunday Business Post* (31 August 2003)

30. Rusana Philander and Ziegfried Ekron, 'They Want Money for His Body', *Die Burger* (7 September 2004)

31. Awadh Al-Taee and Steve Negus, 'Shoot first, pay later culture pervades Iraq', *Financial Times* (19 March 2005)

32. Richard Norton-Taylor, ' "Carry out God's will" video shows insurgents shooting survivor of helicopter crash in Iraq', *Guardian* (23 April 2005)

33. Hala Jaber, 'Gunmen told: take British hostages', *Sunday Times* (2 October 2005)

34. Jon Lee, *Middle East Watch*, online subscription service, 2005–2007

35. Nick Meo, 'Gunmen kidnap 50 guards from their own office', *The Times* (9 March 2006)

36. David Phinney, 'Marines Jail Contractors in Iraq', *Corpwatch* online news service, http://www.corpwatch.org/article.php?id=12349 (7 June 2005, accessed 8 June 2007)

37. Andrew Gilligan, 'The sound of rockets in the morning', *Spectator* (17 April 2004)

38. Laura Peterson, 'Privatizing Combat, The New World Order', Center for Public Integrity, http://www.publicintegrity.org/bow/report.aspx?aid=148 (28 October 2002, accessed 7 June 2007)

39. Jamie Wilson, 'Private security firms call for more firepower in combat zone', *Guardian* (17 April 2004)

40. Peter Singer, 'Above Law, Above Decency', *Thinking Peace*, http://www.thinkingpeace.com/pages/arts2/arts193.html (4 May 2004, accessed 7 June 2007)

41. Isenberg, op. cit.

42. David Phinney, ' "Contract Meals Disaster" for Iraqi Prisoners', *Corpwatch* online news service, http://www.corpwatch.org/article.php?id=11744 (9 December 2004, accessed 8 June 2007)

43. Seymour Hersh, 'The unknown unknowns of the Abu Ghraib scandal', *Guardian* (21 May 2005)

44. L. Paul Bremer, Coalition Provision Authority Order Number 17 (Revised), Coalition Provisional Authority/ORD/27 (June 2004/17)

12. Iraq 2005: The thirty-two-second ambush

1. Route Irish, the world's most dangerous road, is so-called because of its links since 2003 with an American infantry regiment – the Fighting 69th – historically manned by Irishmen.

2. Christopher Farina, 'After Action Review: Operation Apollo Contact BIAP Road 20 April 2005', Report by Edinburgh Risk & Security Management ('The only official Edinburgh Risk report')

3. James Yeager, 'The Ambush of Edinburgh Risk & Security Management's Operation Apollo', http://mountainrunner.us/files/biap/BIAP_4.doc (accessed 9 June 2007)

13. The online dialogues: Grunts, muppets and the civvy bodycount

1. Andrew Joscelyne, *Aegis Iraq PSD Teams*, formerly online (12 October 2005)
2. Richard Beeston and Catherine Philp, 'Security guards investigated over "Iraq shootings" ', *Times* (1 December 2005)
3. Anon., 'Aegis Investigates Iraq Video Clips', Aegis information release (28 November 2005)
4. Anon., 'Aegis sues Stoner over Iraq trophy video', *More4 News* (6 April 2006)
5. Nima Elbagir, 'Road wars', *More4 News* (6 April 2006)
6. Andrew Ackerman, 'Tim Spicer's World', *Nation* (29 December 2004)
7. Tony Geraghty, *The Irish War*, HarperCollins (1998)
8. Ibid.
9. Ebagir, op. cit.
10. Anon., ' "Trophy Video" Allegations', Aegis (28 June 2006)

14. Afghanistan 2001–Future indefinite

1. Antonio Giustozzi, 'The privatising of war and security in Afghanistan: future or dead end?', *Economics of Peace and Security Journal*, Vol. 2(1) (2007).
2. Steve Coll, *Ghost Wars: The Secret History of the CIA, Afghanistan and Bin Laden from the Soviet Invasion to September 10 2001*, Penguin Press (2004)
3. Kim Sengupta, 'Two Britons and their translator murdered by Taliban', *Independent* (6 May 2004)
4. Anon., 'Don't call us mercenaries, says British company with lucrative contracts and cheap labour', *Guardian* (17 May 2004)
5. Alastair Leithhead, 'UN "Broke Pledges" on Afghanistan Aid', *BBC News* (23 October 2006)
6. Jason Lewis, 'Britain gave £400m to keep Afghan famine victims like Dawoud out of the Taliban's clutches. So where did it go, Mr Benn?', *Mail on Sunday* (21 January 2007)
7. James Glanz, David Rohde and Carlotta Gall, 'The Reach of War: US Report Finds Dismal Training of Afghan Police' *New York Times* (4 December 2006)
8. Howard J. Krongard and Thomas F. Gimble, 'Interagency Assessment of Afghanistan Police Training and Readiness', Inspectors General, US Department of State and US Department of Defense (November 2006)
9. Tod Robberson, 'DynCorp workers gamble with their lives: Dozens have died in Iraq and Afghanistan, *Dallas Morning News* (25 December 2006)
10. Krongard and Gimble, op. cit.
11. Sayed Yaqub Ibrahimi, 'Afghan police part of the problem', *Institute of War & Peace Reporting* (6 June 2006)
12. Anon., 'Afghanistan: Country Reports on Human Rights Practices, 2005', Bureau of Democracy, Human Rights and Labor, US Department of State (8 March 2006)
13. Andrea Weigl, 'Passaro will serve eight years for beating', *News & Observer*, online (21 February 2007)
14. Declan Walsh, 'Court cuts torture sentences', *Guardian* (1 April 2005)

15. Dr Kim Howells, Minister of State, 'Kidnap of David Addison', Foreign and Commonwealth Office (3 September 2005)

16. Anon., 'Afghanistan: Getting Disarmament Back on Track', International Crisis Group Asia Briefing No. 35 – Kabul/Brussels (23 February 2005)

17. Anon., 'Afghanistan: Country Reports . . .', op. cit.

18. Des Browne, 'Afghanistan – A Comprehensive Approach to Current Challenges', *RUSI Journal* (October 2006)

19. Lieutenant General David Richards, 'NATO in Afghanistan – Transformation on the Front Line', *RUSI Journal* (August 2006)

20. Ibid.

21. Anon. 'US chides "hostile" Karzai guards', *BBC News* (14 October 2006)

22. Nick Higgins, 'Taleban hires with hard cash', *The Times* letters (12 September 2006)

23. Camilla Cavendish, 'The war on drugs is not the War on Terror: save the Afghan poppy fields', *Times* (8 June 2006)

24. Dr Vivienne Nathanson, interview with James Naughtie, *Today*, BBC Radio 4 (23 January 2007)

25. Michael Gossop et al., 'The Unique Role of Diamorphine in British Medical Practice: A Survey of General Practitioners and Hospital Doctors' (free abstract), *European Addiction Research*, Vol. 11(2), S. Karger AG, Basel (2005)

26. Habibullah Qaderi, Counter-Narcotics Minister, Government of Afghanistan, 'UK Announces Increased Funding for Afghanistan Counter Narcotics Work', Foreign and Commonwealth Office (5 September 2005)

27. Rachel Morarjee, 'Afghanistan set to have record opium crop', *Financial Times* (4 July 2006)

28. Isabel Hilton, 'Hearts and minds at any cost', *Guardian* (13 July 2004)

29. Michael Evans, 'Karzai defies US demands over attack on opium crop', *Times* (26 January 2007)

30. Kristin Collins, 'Afghanistan: Families Sue Private Contractor Over Soldiers' Deaths', *News & Observer*, online (14 June 2005)

31. Anthony Lloyd, 'Drivers who run gauntlet of Taliban on highway through hell', *Times* (17 October 2006)

32. Anthony Browne, 'Our job will last in Afghanistan for a generation', *Times* (21 November 2006)

15. Licensed to save: The unarmed warriors

1. Jon Torode, 'A Hero of Our Hearts', *Daily Mail* (24 July 1996)

2. Martin Revis, 'Modern "Knights" Wage War on Minefields', http://www.britannia.com/newsbits/knights.html (accessed 10 June 2007)

3. Ibid.

4. Olivia O'Leary, *Between Ourselves*, BBC Radio 4 (5 September 2006)

5. Ibid.

6. Philip C. Winslow, 'The case against landmines', http://www.redcross.int/en/mag/magazine1997_2/10-11.html (2003)

7. Anon., 'Citation, Award of Queen's Gallantry Medal', *London Gazette* (12 February 2001)

8. Nicholas Cecil, 'Farewell to a son and hero', *Western Daily Press* (27 July 1998)

9. Anon., 'Group tied to Saudis behind murder of British weapons expert in Iraq', Israel News Agency/IMRA, Jerusalem (24 September 2003)

10. Hala Jaber, 'Cluster bombs leave "toys" that kill children', *Sunday Times* (27 August 2006)

11. Tony Geraghty, *Who Dares Wins: The Special Air Service, 1950 to the Gulf War*, Warner Books (1993)

12. Mark Bles and Robert Low, *The Kidnap Business*, Pelham Books (1987)

13. Roger Boyes, 'Smiling hostage is let off paying the bill for her rescue', *The Times* (6 April 2006)

14. Anon., 'BG Tony Hunter-Choat', Proceedings of Iraq Conference, Office of Small and Disadvantaged Business Utilization, 106 Army Pentagon, Washington, DC (downloaded 14 February 2007)

15. Ibid.

16. Robert Young Pelton, *Licensed To Kill: Hired Guns in the War on Terror*, Crown Publishers, New York (2006)

17. Daniel Serwer, 'A Need for NATO', *Washington Post* (23 January 1999)

18. Anon., 'Walker: KVM is Making a Difference', OSCE *Newsletter*, Vol. 6(1) (January 1999)

19. John D. Deverell, *A Personal Experience with the Iraq Survey Group*, private publication (2006)

20. Andrew Alderson, 'Working on the internet from an anonymous city office, the shadowy figures exposing Islamic extremism', *Sunday Telegraph* (19 November 2006)

21. Ibid.

22. Tim Whewell, 'Litvinenko Dossier Uncovered', *Newsnight*, BBC2 (9 February 2007)

23. Dominic Walsh, 'Howard becomes new chairman of World Spooks Inc.', *The Times* (19 June 2006)

24. Peter Larsen, 'Due diligence . . . Investigating a company that may be ripe for takeover involves more than looking at its balance sheet', *Financial Times* (10 April 2001)

25. Ian Morris, 'County men lead families out of war-zone', *Hereford Times* (27 July 2006)

16. The foreign enlistment act 1870–Present: Lying in state at Westminster

1. Nicholas Kiersey, 'Diplomats and Diplomacy of the American Civil War, online as PDF, http://homepage.mac.com/thenervousfishdown/files/page1_blog_entry25_1.pdf (March 1997, accessed 15 June 2007)

2. Richard Cobden, 'Speeches on Questions of Public Policy Richard Cobden MP', T. Fisher Unwin, London, online at the Library of Economics and Liberty, http://www.econlib.org/library/YPDBooks/Cobden/cbdSPP0.html (accessed 10 June 2007)

3. Jack Straw, op. cit.

4. Mary Krout, H., *A Looker-On in London*, Dodd, Mead & Company, New York (1899)

5. Elizabeth Pakenham Longford, *Jameson's Raid*, Weidenfeld & Nicolson (1960)

6. Professor S. P. Mackenzie, 'The Foreign Enlistment Act and the Spanish Civil War, 1936–1939', in *Twentieth Century British History*, Vol. 10(1), Oxford University Press (1999)

7. Margaret Thatcher, Angola mercenaries debate, House of Commons Report 10 (February 1976)

8. Diplock et al., 'Report of the Committee of Privy Counsellors Appointed to Enquire into the Recruitment of Mercenaries', Cmd 6569, HMSO, London (1976)

9. Ibid.

10. Hazel Blears, Written Answers, House of Commons Questions (23 March 2006)

17. Legal remedies 1976–Present:

1. George Monbiot, 'Pedigree dogs of war', *Guardian* (25 January 2005)

2. Jack Straw, op. cit.

3. House of Commons Foreign Affairs Committee, 2nd Report, op. cit.

4. Nick Fielding, 'British secrets leaked on web', *Sunday Times* (24 November 2002)

5. House of Commons Foreign Affairs Committee, 9th Report, Private Military Companies, Session 2001–2002, House of Commons (2002)

6. Jack Straw, Foreign Minister, Foreign Affairs Committee, Private Military Companies, Session 2001–2002: Response of the Secretary of State for Foreign and Commonwealth Affairs, House of Commons (October 2002)

7. Anon., Prohibition of Mercenary Activities and Prohibition and Regulation of Certain Activities in Areas of Armed Conflict Bill, *South African Government Gazette*, No. 28163 (24 October 2005) (see also Taljaard, Raenette, 'Implementing South Africa's Regulation of Foreign Military Assistance Act', in Alan Bryden and Marina Caparini (eds), *Private Actors & Security Governance*, Verlag, Munster, Zürich (2006))

8. P. W. Singer, 'The Law Catches Up To Private Militaries, Embeds', online, http://www.defensetech.org/archives/003123.html (January 2007, accessed 15 June 2007)

9. Anon, 'Undermining Global Security: the European Union's arms exports', Amnesty International, http://web.amnesty.org/library/index/engact300032004 (2003, accessed 15 June 2007)

10. Anon., 'French-born mercenary convicted in South Africa over role in Ivory Coast', Agence France Presse (8 January 2003)

11. Anon., 'Swiss initiative on private military and security companies', Swiss Federal Department of Foreign Affairs (22 November 2006)

12. Bremer, op. cit

13. Ibid.

14. Isenberg, op. cit.

15. Anon., 'British Victim of Baghdad Bomb Blast Named', *Times Online* (25 May 2004)

16. Department of Foreign and Commonwealth Affairs, 'Private Military Companies: Options for Regulation 2001–2002' (Green Paper), with foreword by Secretary of State for Foreign and Commonwealth Affairs Jack Straw, House of Commons 577 (12 February 2002)

17. Anon., Protocol Additional to the Geneva Convention of 12 August 1949 . . . Adopted 8 June 1977, Office of the High Commissioner for Human Rights

18. Anon., Convention for the Elimination of Mercenarism in Africa, Organisation of African Unity (3 July 1977)

19. Enrique Bernales Ballesteros, 'Use of Mercenaries as a Means of Violating Human Rights and Impeding the Exercise of the Right of Peoples to Self-Determination', UN General Assembly (2 July 2003)

20. Department of Foreign and Commonwealth Affairs, op. cit.

21. Anon., 'International Convention against the Recruitment, Use, Financing and Training of Mercenaries', UNHCR (4 December 1989)

22. Kofi, Annan, Ditchley Foundation Lecture, UK (26 June 1998; *UN Chronicle*, Fall 1998)

23. Enrique Bernales Ballesteros, 'Rights of Peoples to Self-Determination . . .', UN Economic and Social Council (24 December 2003)

24. Shaista Shameen, 'Report on the Question of the Use of Mercenaries as a Means of Violating Human Rights . . .', UN General Assembly (17 August 2005)

25. Anon., 'The Use of Mercenaries as a Means of Violating Human Rights . . .', Office of High Commissioner for Human Rights, Resolution 2005/2

26. UN Watch, 'Democracies Must Bar Abusers from New UN Rights Council', UN Watch, online,
http://www.unwatch.org/site/apps/nl/content2.asp?c=bdKKISNqEmG&b=1314451&ct=2382693 (3 May 2006, accessed 15 June 2007)

27. Neuer, op. cit.

28. Warren Hoge, 'New UN Rights Group Includes Six Nations with Poor Records', *New York Times* (9 May 2006)

29. Anon., Rome Statute of the International Criminal Court: Overview, online,
http://www.un.org/law/icc/general/overview.htm

30. Gary Younge and Ian Black, 'War Crime Vote Fuels US Anger at Europe', *Guardian* (11 June 2003)

31. Philippe Sands, *Lawless World: America and the Making and Breaking of Global Rules* Allen Lane (2005)

32. Tony Geraghty, 'Uncle Sam und die "Snatch Option" des Präsidenten' ('Uncle Sam and the Presidential Snatch Option'), *Telepolis*, German online news-analysis service (3 December 2002, accessed 15 June 2007)

33. Anon., 'Authority of the Federal Bureau of Investigation to Override International Law in Extraterritorial Law Enforcement Activities', US Justice Department Office of Legal Counsel (21 June 1989)

34. Anon., 'Annan issues rules of conduct for UN peacekeepers', CNN (10 August 1999)

35. Anon., 'Addressing the Sexual Misconduct of Peacekeepers', Refugees International (23 September 2004)

36. Anon., 'From Camp to Community: Liberia study on exploitation of children', Save the Children, UK (8 May 2006)

37. Romeo Dallaire, *Shake Hands with the Devil*, Arrow (2004)

38. Brian Bennett,' Victims of an Outsourced War', *Time* (15 March 2007)

18. The great reappraisal, 2006: Dogs of War or Pussycats of Peace?

1. Notes and papers taken by the author at the RUSI-BAPSC First Annual Conference (30–1 October 2006)

2. Hilton op. cit.

3. P. W. Singer, *Corporate Warriors*, op cit.

4. James Boxwell, 'Halliburton ignores MoD appeal for KBR float', *Financial Times* (16 November 2006)

5. Donald op. cit.

19. Mr Micawber's missing millions

1. Michael Smith, 'SAS get 50% pay rise to halt quitters', *Sunday Times* (6 August 2006)

2. Stephen Fidler, 'Baghdad bubble over as work dries up', *Financial Times* (21 July 2006)

3. Christine Seib, 'Taxman to get police powers in Revenue's proposals', *Times* (15 August 2006)

4. Philip Stafford, 'Security fears force Weir to pull out of Iraq contracts', *Financial Times* (18 August 2006)

5. Fidler, op. cit.

6. Alan Beattie, 'IMF slashes growth forecast for Iraq', *Financial Times* (12 July 2004)

7. Sharmila Devi, 'Business oils wheels ready for Iraq rebuild', *Financial Times* (12 May 2006)

8. James Glanz, 'Audit Finds US Hid Actual Costs of Iraq Projects', *New York Times* (30 July 2006)

9. David Barstow et al., 'Security Companies: Shadow Soldiers in Iraq', *New York Times* (19 April 2004)

10. Griff Witte, 'Former KBR worker admits to fraud in Iraq', *Washington Post* (23 August 2005)

11. Aram Roston, 'US probes $100 million missing in Iraq', *NBC News* (5 May 2005)

12. 'Girl Blog from Iraq', *Baghdad Burning*, online blog, http://riverbendblog.blogspot.com/2003_08_01_riverbendblog_archive.html#106208201 838841818#106208201838841818 (28 August 2003, accessed 11 June 2007)

13. Peter Marshall, 'The 50-Billion-Dollar Robbery', *Newsnight*, BBC2 (15 March 2006)

14. Glanz, op. cit.

15. Stephen Farrell, 'Minister held over financing death squad', *The Times* (9 February 2007)

16. Anon., 'Iraq ain't no Peru, say South American mercenaries', Agence France Presse (15 August 2006)

17. Michael Fumento, 'Arrival in Iraq', online, http://www.fumento.com/weblog/archives/2006/04/arrival_in_iraq.html (8 April 2006, accessed 11 June 2007)

18. Liz Chong and Richard Beeston, 'Diplomatic guards may quit in Baghdad pay row', *The Times* (27 May 2006)

19. Andy Webb-Vidal, 'Colombian ex-soldiers in Iraq pay dispute', *Financial Times* (21 August 2006)

20. Isabel Ordonez, 'Iraq, Afghanistan lure poor Latin American guards', Reuters (21 August 2006)

21. Robert Verkaik, 'The War Dividend – the British companies making a fortune out of conflict-riven Iraq', *Independent* (13 March 2006)

22. James Boxwell, 'Armor warns of profits "substantially" below expectations', *Financial Times* (7 November 2005)

23. US House of Representatives Committee on Government Reform, Minority Staff Special Investigations Division: 'Halliburton's Performance Under Iraqi Oil 2 Contract', House of Representatives, prepared for Rep. Henry A. Waxman (28 March 2006)

24. Paul Blustein, 'Wolfowitz strives to quell criticism', *Washington Post* (21 March 2005)

25. US House of Representatives Committee on Government Reform, op. cit.

26. Anon., 'RIO Status Update . . . Importance, High', US Army Corps of Engineers email (5 March 2003)

27. Anon., KBR company profile, Defence Manufacturers' Association (UK) website, http://www.the-dma.org.uk/Members/Details.asp?Type=1&ID=1573 website (accessed 15 June 2007)

28. Ernst & Young, 'Management Letter for Development Fund for Iraq for the period from July 1, 2005, to December 31, 2005', Ernst & Young report to the government of Iraq (10 July 2006)

29. International Advisory and Monitoring Board on the Development Fund for Iraq, press release (10 August, 2006)

30. Katherine Griffiths, 'Iraq: Oh What a Lovely War on Terror It's Been for Halliburton', *Independent* (27 March 2005)

Epilogue: After RIO

1. David Wighton, and Simeon Kerr, 'Halliburton to move its head office to Dubai', *Financial Times* (11 March 2007)

2. Byron Dorgan, 'Dorgan Issues Statement on Halliburton's Plan to Relocate Principal Office to Dubai', Office of Senator Dorgan (13 March 2007)

3. Anon., 'Halliburton's Dubai Move Sparks Outcry', CBS (12 March 2007)

4. Bennet, op. cit.

5. Michael Hirsh and John Barry, 'The El Salvador Option', *Newsweek* (8 January 2005)

6. Jonathan D. Tepperman, 'Salvador in Iraq: Flash Back', *Foreign Affairs*, Council on Foreign Relations (5 April 2005)

7. ' "A former military sniper": Our Snipers Have Spoken . . . Now It's Your Turn!' (Part 2), *Soldier of Fortune* (February 2007)

8. T. Christian Miller, 'Death Before Dishonor: Army Ethics Inspector's Death in Iraq Ruled Suicide', *Los Angeles Times* (27 November 2005)

9. Richard Norton-Taylor, 'SAS Man Quits in Protest at "Illegal" War', *Guardian* (13 March 2006)

10. Antony Barnett, and Patrick Smith, 'British guard firm "abused scared Iraqi shepherd boy" ', *Observer* (14 November 2004)

11. Suzanne Goldenburg, 'US troops authorised to kill Iranian agents in Iraq', *Guardian* (27 January 2007)

12. Peter Beaumont, 'Frontline police of new Iraq are waging secret war of vengeance', *Observer* (20 November 2005)

13. Anat Tal-Shir, 'Israelis Trained Kurds in Iraq', *Ynetnews*, online, http://www.ynetnews.com/articles/0,7340,L-3177712,00.html (12 January 2005)

14. James Dao and Eric Schmitt, 'Pentagon Readies Efforts to Sway Sentiment Abroad', *New York Times* (19 February 2002)

15. Anon., 'Secretary Rumsfeld Media Availability En Route to Chile', US Department of Defense News Transcript (18 November 2002)

16. SourceWatch, 'Lincoln Group', online, http://www.sourcewatch.org/index.php?title=Lincoln_Group (1 September 2006, accessed 15 June 2007)

17. Sara Baxter, 'Oxford socialite linked to Iraq propaganda row', *Sunday Times* (11 December 2005)

18. Martha Raddatz, 'Inside the Public Relations Blitz to Sell Iraq War Overseas', *ABC News* (14 December 2005)

19. Andrew Bearpark, interview with author

20. Steve Negus, 'Iraq approves draft oil legislation', *Financial Times* (26 February 2007)

21. Danny Fortson et al., 'Blood and oil – How the West will profit from Iraq's most precious commodity', *Independent on Sunday* (7 January 2007)

22. US House of Representatives Committee on Government Reform, op. cit.

23. Fortson et al., op. cit.

24. John Keegan, *A History of Warfare*, Random House of Canada (1994)

Picture Credits

P. 1 *(top)* AP Photo/STR *(bottom)* © Estelle Shirbon/Reuters/Corbis; P. 2 *(top)* © Bettmann/Corbis *(bottom)* © Bettmann/Corbis; P. 3 *(top)* Time & Life Pictures/Getty Images *(bottom)* Time & Life Pictures/Getty Images; P. 4 *(top)* © Patrick Chauvel/Sygma/Corbis *(bottom)* © Patrick Chauvel/Sygma/Corbis; P. 5 *(top)* AFP/Getty Images *(bottom)* AP Photo/David Stewart Smith; P. 6 *(top)* © Reuters/Corbis *(bottom)* © Bettmann/Corbis; P. 7 *(top)* Getty Images *(bottom)* MH30626, used with the permission of *The Trustees of the Imperial War Museum, London*; P. 8 *(top)* AFP/Getty Images *(bottom)* © Patrick Robert/Sygma/Corbis; P. 9 *(top)* © RANKO CUKOVIC/Reuters/Corbis *(bottom)* © Spanish Interior Ministry/Handout/Reuters/Corbis; P. 10 *(top)* © CEERWAN AZIZ/Reuters/Corbis *(middle)* © Ali Haider/Pool/Reuters/Corbis *(bottom)* AFP/Getty Images; P. 11 *(top)* © Mortenhvaal/WPN *(middle)* © Mortenhvaal/WPN *(bottom)* © Mortenhvaal/WPN; P. 12 *(top)* © Reuters/Corbis *(bottom)* © Adrees Latif/Reuters/Corbis

Index

A CLASSIC CHRISTMAS
MYSTERY NOVEL

London. 22nd December. Chief Inspector Brett Nightingale and Sergeant Beddoes have been called to a gloomy flat off Islington High Street. An elderly woman lies dead on the bed, and her trunk has been looted. The woman is Princess Olga Karukhin – an emigrant of Civil War Russia – and her trunk is missing its glittering treasure...

Out in the dizzying neon and festive chaos of the capital a colourful cast of suspects abound: the downtrodden grandson, a plutocratic jeweller, Bolsheviks with unfinished business? Beddoes and Nightingale have their work cut out in this tightly-paced, quirky and highly enjoyable jewel of the mystery genre.

BRITISH LIBRARY CRIME CLASSICS

ALSO AVAILABLE

Many of our titles are also available in eBook, large print and audio editions